THE

QUR'AN

THE

QUR'AN

A MODERN ENGLISH VERSION

Translated by

Majid Fakhry

*G*arnet
PUBLISHING

The late Dr Mahmud Zayid
offered valuable assistance with the revision and
annotation of this translation of the work,
prior to his untimely death in 1994.

The Qur'an: A Modern English Version

Published by
Garnet Publishing Limited,
8 Southern Court, South Street,
Reading RG1 4QS, UK

Copyright © 1997 Majid Fakhry and Mahmud Zayid

First Edition 1997
Reprinted 1997, 1998 (twice), 2005

Paperback edition ISBN 1 85964 086 9

British Library Cataloguing-in-Publication Data
A catalogue record for this book is available from the British Library

Jacket design by David Rose
Book design by Fred Price
Typeset by Columns Design and Production Ltd

Printed in Lebanon

CONTENTS

CONTENTS

Introduction

THE QUR'AN is the sacred scripture of Islam. It consists of 114 suras or chapters traditionally arranged according to length. However, a more meaningful arrangement or classification into Meccan and Medinan suras is usually given, the former totalling 86, the latter 28.

The Meccan suras, which belong to the period of struggle against the Prophet's own tribe of Quraysh in Mecca, are written in an incisive and impassioned style and proclaim in a fiery tone the imminence of the Hour and the horrors of Hell-fire. They summon mankind to heed the divine call with which Muhammad, the Apostle of God, is charged and which centres on the profession of the unqualified oneness and sovereignty of God and the urgency of returning to the true (*hanif*) religion of Abraham, founder of the Sacred Shrine of the Ka'ba in Mecca. This *hanif* religion, having been corrupted over the years by idolatry and other pagan practices, was now being revived and cleansed by Muhammad, whose spiritual call in the Qur'an is described for that reason as reviving or "confirming" the original or pure monotheism of Abraham. Even Jews and Christians, referred to as the People of the Book since they were recipients of a true revelation they are said to have corrupted, are summoned in the Qur'an to adhere to the only true revelation "sent down" to Muhammad.

This revelation, according to the Qur'an, has existed since all time in the Preserve Tablet (Sura 85, 22) or the Mother of the Book (Sura 13, 39) and was communicated to Muhammad through the Angel Gabriel (Jibril) in pure Arabic, so as to instruct his own people and through them the rest of mankind. It is believed by Muslims to be the infallible Word of God (*Kalam Allah*).

The earliest revelation came to Muhammad at the age of forty, as he was absorbed in meditation in Cave Hira', just outside Mecca. Here, according to Muslim tradition, the angel Jibril spoke to him thus: "Read (*iqra'*) in the name of your Lord Who created ..."; hence the name of the Qur'an, reading or recitation. Thereafter the revelations came to the Prophet at different intervals and were written down on palm-leaves, tablets of stone or simply committed to memory by the scribes or "secretaries of revelation", the most famous of whom was Zayd Ibn Thabit.

Following the death of the Prophet in 632 AD, a copy of the Qur'an based on this written or oral material was compiled by Zayd and entrusted to the care of Hafsah, daughter of the Caliph 'Umar and widow of the Prophet. However, due to the divergent readings of the sacred text and the danger of faulty oral transmission, a definitive edition was compiled in 651 AD by order of Uthman, the Third Caliph, and this edition, known as Mushaf Uthman (or Uthman's Codex), has remained ever since the authorized version of the Qur'an, read, chanted and meditated upon by millions of Muslims throughout the world.

The Medinan suras, on the other hand, belong to the period of Hijrah (or emigration to Medina), which began in 622 AD, marking the start of the Muslim calender. For the most part they are written in a prosaic and discursive style, and embody the fundamental principles of Islamic legislation, known as the *shari'ah* or holy law. This legislation covers social, economic and political matters, such as marriage and divorce, inheritance and almsgiving, the relation of Muslim subjects to their rulers and so on. Those subjects are specifically commanded to obey "God, the Apostle and those who wield authority among you" (Sura 4, 62) and to submit their differences to God and the Apostle, who was succeeded as head of the Muslim community by the so-called Caliphs, or "successors of the Apostle".

In Medina, originally called Yathrib, Islam became for the first time both a religious and political movement, so that one could speak thereafter of the rise and consolidation of the Muslim community (*Ummah*), with the Prophet at its head. In that respect, the Prophet now wielded a political authority in addition to his spiritual authority as the "Apostle" or Messenger of God, and in this double capacity he was able to confront his erstwhile enemies at Mecca, his native town. After repeated skirmishes outside Medina and a variety of "expeditions" further afield, the Muslims, led by the Prophet, were able to capture Mecca in the eighth year of the Hijrah, or 630 AD. Thereupon, Muhammad's first move was to enter the Ka'ba, or Sacred Shrine, and destroy the pagan idols – said to number 350 – housed in it, and to institute the rite of pilgrimage to this Sacred Shrine, which Abraham was said to have founded centuries earlier.

The Qur'an has defined clearly the relation of Muslims to other religious communities of the Near East, notably the Sabians, Christians and Jews. The Sabians (Sabi'ah) were recognized as monotheists and, like Christians and Jews, were tolerated (Sura 5, 73). However, infidels (*kafirun*) were not, and the Qur'an calls upon Muslims to fight them to the death, unless they embrace Islam. However, it does qualify this stipulation in a variety of ways, one of which is not to initiate aggression against them, "since God does not like the aggressors" (Sura 2, 190); the other is toleration, since "there is no compulsion in religion" (Sura 2, 257), and the third is "gracious pardon or ransom", once they have been subdued (Sura 47, 4).

As People of the Book, Jews and Christians are accorded a special and privileged status in the Qur'an, because "they believe in God and the Last Day" (Sura 2, 62), and although accused of having corrupted their scriptures, the Qur'an abounds in references to the Old Testament figures, including Abraham, Isaac, Moses, Jacob, Job and Lot, as well as New Testament figures, including Mary, John (the Baptist), Jesus, son of Mary, and many others. The miracles of Christ are given in full, and, in fact, the Qur'an attributes to Christ a number of other miracles which are not mentioned in the canonical Gospels, but are referred to in the Apocrypha. In addition, a large number of biblical narratives are given in the Qur'an, not for their historical interest but rather for their spiritual or moral interest; they are often intended to illustrate the justice of God's ways and His sovereignty in the world, and to underscore the trials and tribulations to which His prophets or messengers have been subjected throughout history. Those prophets or messengers are said to have been continually shunned or rebuffed, but were never abandoned by God, the Merciful and Compassionate. Muhammad, the last or "seal" of the prophets, was not spared his own share of tribulation, and he is proclaimed as the carrier of the same message of warning or good tidings (*nadhir* or *bashir*), which all his predecessors have carried to their own peoples, and which Muhammad was now summoned by God to revive or confirm.

In addition to the text of the Qur'an itself, a vast exegetical literature grew around it over the years and formed part of an independent science, that of *tafsir*, which together with the science of *hadith*, or Prophetic Traditions, is regarded as the cornerstone of what are known as religious sciences in Islam. The greatest classical commentaries of the Qur'an are those of al-Tabari (d. 923), al-Zamakhshari (d. 1143) and al-Baydawi (d. 1286), to which countless commentaries by modern or contemporary scholars, such as Muhammad 'Abduh (d. 1905) and Sayyid Qutb (d. 1966), may be added.

One of the most widely read books in the world, the Qur'an has been translated into almost all the languages of mankind. A large number of English translations have appeared in modern times, the best known of which are those of J. M. Rodwell, Marmeduke Pickthall, N. J. Dawood, Richard Bell and A. J. Arberry. These translations vary in point of conformity to the Arabic text and are not entirely free from error or deliberate departure from the original, for purposes of literary fluency or elegance. In the present translation, we have attempted to give as faithful an English rendering of the Arabic text as possible and to correct the errors or lapses of the above-mentioned translations, while acknowledging that we have profited from some. We have also tried to express ourselves in a simple, readable English idiom. For purposes of accuracy, we have often had to rely on the most authoritative commentaries, especially where the meaning of the text was either obscure or controversial, as the notes will show. These notes are intended to be purely explanatory and have for that reason been kept to a minimum.

In closing, I wish to acknowledge the contribution of my friend and colleague, the late Dr Mahmud Zayid, with whom I worked very closely up to his untimely death. Throughout the early part of the work we constantly exchanged notes, and many of his suggestions or corrections were actually embodied in the final version of the translation. Regrettably, however, Providence decreed that our co-operation be cut short; but I would like this translation to be regarded, none the less, as a joint endeavour, because of the way in which the original project was launched and the mutual understanding we reached in the early stages of the work on questions of procedure, style and classical sources or commentaries to be consulted.

MAJID FAKHRY
5 April 1996
Washington, DC

SURA 1[1]

Al-Fatiha, The Opening Chapter

In the Name of Allah, the Compassionate, the Merciful[2]

1 Praise be to Allah, the Lord of the Worlds,[3]
   The Compassionate, the Merciful,
   Master of the Day of Judgement,
   Only You do we worship, and only You do we implore for help.
5 Lead us to the right path,
   The path of those You have favoured
   Not those who have incurred Your wrath or have gone astray.

1. That is, the opening section or chapter of the Qur'an. It has various other names including Umm al-Kitab or the Quintessence of the Book and the Chapter of Prayer, because it is repeated in every one of the five daily prayers. It is also recited on many important occasions.
2. This verse is one of the most recurrent verses in the Qur'an. Muslims recite it at the commencement of their daily activities.
3. That is, the whole of creation.

SURA 2

Al-Baqara, The Cow

In the Name of Allah, the Compassionate, the Merciful

Alif, Lam, Mim.[4]

1   This is the Book which cannot be doubted and is a guidance to the God-fearing,

Those who believe in the unseen, perform the prayer and give freely from what We provided for them,

And who believe in what was revealed to you and was revealed before you and firmly believe in the life to come.

Those are guided by their Lord, and those are the prosperous.

5   Those who have disbelieved, whether you warn them or not, they will not believe.

Allah has sealed their hearts and their hearing; their sight is dimmed and a terrible punishment awaits them.

There are some who say: "We believe in Allah and the Last Day;" but they are not real believers.

They seek to deceive Allah and the believers, but they deceive none other than themselves, though they are not aware of that.

In their hearts is a sickness; so Allah has increased their sickness. A painful punishment awaits them because of their lying.

10   And when they are told: "Do not sow mischief in the land", they say: "We are only doing good."

It is they who make mischief, but they are unaware of that.

And when they are told: "Believe as the others have believed", they say: "Shall we believe as the fools[5] have believed?" It is they who are the fools, though they do not know it.

And when they meet the believers, they say: "We believe", but when they are alone with their devils[6] they say: "We are with you;[7] we were only mocking."

---

4. Those 'abbreviated letters' which preface some, but not all the suras of the Qur'an are believed by some scholars to be the secret symbols or indices with which the Angel Gabriel (Jibril) opened the relevation of the suras in question. They often mark the beginning of one sura and the end of another.
5. The ignorant.
6. Their chiefs.
7. We are your co-religionists.

Allah mocks them and gives them the latitude to wander aimlessly in their intransigence.[8]

15 Those are the people who traded away guidance for error; but their trade made no gains and they have not found the right way.

They are like one who kindled a fire, but when it lit all around him, Allah took away their light and left them in total darkness unable to see;

Deaf, dumb, blind; they shall never return.[9]

Or like those who in the midst of a cloudburst from the sky accompanied by darkness, thunder and lightning put their fingers in their ears to guard against thunderbolts for fear of death. And Allah encompasses[10] the disbelievers.

The lightning almost takes away their sight; when it flashes they walk on, but when it darkens they stand still. If Allah had willed, He would have taken away their hearing and sight. Surely Allah has power over all things.

20 O people,[11] worship your Lord who has created you as well as those who came before you so that you may guard against evil;

Who[12] has made the earth a couch for you, and the heavens a canopy, and Who sent down water from the sky, bringing forth by it a variety of fruits as a provision for you. Therefore do not knowingly set up equals to Allah.[13]

If you are in doubt as to what We have revealed to Our Servant,[14] then produce a sura similar to it and call upon your witnesses other than Allah,[15] if you are truthful.

If you will not do, and surely you will not, then guard yourselves against the Fire whose fuel is men and stones, prepared for the unbelievers.

Proclaim the good news to those who have believed and have done the good works; they will have gardens under which rivers flow.[16] Every time they get some of the fruits with which they are provided, they will say: "This is what we were provided with before", because they are given each time something that looks like it. They will also have their pure spouses[17] there, and they shall live there forever.

25 Surely Allah does not disdain to give as a parable an insect or something bigger. Those who have believed know that it is the Truth from their Lord;

8. Disbelief.
9. Return to the right path.
10. Surpasses them in knowledge and power.
11. People of Mecca.
12. Your Lord.
13. That is, worship none besides Allah.
14. The Prophet Muhammad.
15. That is, the gods you associate with Allah.
16. That is, rivers flow under its trees and structures.
17. Spouses who are subject to no impurity.

but those who have disbelieved say: "What does Allah mean by this parable?" By it, He leaves many in error, and guides well many others. And by it, he leaves in error only the sinners.[18]

Those who break Allah's covenant after its confirmation and sever what Allah ordered to be joined and make mischief[19] in the land – those are the losers.

How can you[20] disbelieve in Allah? You were dead[21] and He brought you back to life;[22] then He will cause you to die and then bring you back to life again; then unto Him you will return.

It is He who created for you everything on earth, then ascended to the heavens fashioning them into seven, and He has knowledge of all things.

When your Lord said to the angels: "I am placing a deputy on earth", they said: "Will you place one who will make mischief in it and shed blood, while we sing Your praise and glorify Your sanctity?" He said: "I know what you do not know."

30　　And He taught Adam all the names. Then He laid them before the angels. He said: "Tell me the names of these if you are truthful."

They said: "Glory be to You; we have no knowledge other than what You taught us. You are the All-Knowing, the Wise."

He said: "O Adam, tell them their names." When Adam told them their names He[23] said: "Did I not tell you that I know the unseen in the heavens and the earth, and that I know what you reveal and what you conceal?"

And when We said to the angels: "Prostrate yourselves before Adam", they all prostrated themselves except Iblis,[24] who refused, out of pride and was one of the disbelievers.

Then We said: "O Adam, dwell in Paradise, you and your wife, and eat from it as much as you wish and wherever you wish, but do not approach this tree[25] or you will both be unjust."[26]

35　　But Satan caused them to fall down from it and be turned out of the bliss they had been in. And We said: "Go down,[27] being enemies one to the other. And you will have in the earth an abode and sustenance for a while."

---

18. Those who disobey Allah.
19. By committing sins and obstructing faith.
20. The Meccans.
21. Being a life-germ i.e. not living yet.
22. As a child.
23. Allah.
24. Satan.
25. Meaning do not eat from it.
26. By being disobedient.
27. From Paradise to earth.

Then Adam received words from his Lord, Who forgave him. He is indeed the All-Forgiving, the Merciful.

We said: "Go down from here[28] all of you. And when in time My guidance is vouchsafed to you, those who follow My guidance will have nothing to fear nor will they grieve."[29]

And [as to] those who have disbelieved and denied Our revelations, they are the people of Hell, wherein they will dwell forever.

O Children of Israel, remember the grace which I bestowed on you. Fulfil your covenant[30] and I shall fulfil My covenant.[31] And Me alone you should fear.

40 Believe in what I have revealed confirming that which is with you[32] and do not be the first to deny it. Do not trade My revelations for a small price; and Me alone you should fear.

And do not confuse truth with falsehood and do not conceal the truth while you know it.

Perform the prayer; give the alms-tax and bow down with those who bow down.

Do you command others to be righteous and forget yourselves while you recite the Book? Do you not understand?

Seek assistance through patience and prayer. It is hard, except for the truly devout;

45 Who believe that they shall meet their Lord, and unto Him they shall return.

O Children of Israel, remember the grace which I bestowed on you, and that I preferred you to all the nations.[33]

And guard yourselves against the day when no soul shall avail any other soul and no intercession will be accepted from it, nor will a ransom be taken from it; and they will not be supported.

And [remember] how We saved you from Pharaoh's people who tormented you cruelly, slaying your children but sparing your women. Therein was a great trial from your Lord.

And [remember] how for your sake, We split the sea, rescued you and drowned the people of Pharaoh while you were watching.

50 And [remember] how We promised Moses forty nights;[34] and you took the calf[35] after him, thus becoming evil-doers.

28. Paradise.
29. Because they will be admitted into Paradise.
30. By believing that Muhammad is the Apostle of Allah.
31. By rewarding them.
32. Confirming your Scriptures.
33. The nations which were contemporaneous with the Israelites in their days of triumph.
34. At the end of which Moses was to receive the Scriptures.
35. As god and worshipped it.

But We pardoned you after that, so that you might give thanks.

And when We gave Moses the Book and the Criterion[36] so that you might be well-guided.

When Moses said to his people: "My people, you have wronged yourselves by taking the calf [as god]. Repent to your Creator. Kill yourselves;"[37] that would be better for you in the sight of your Creator. Then He forgave you. He is the All-Forgiving, the Merciful.

And when you said: "O Moses, We will not believe in you until we see Allah with our own eyes", whereupon you were struck by a thunderbolt while you looked on.

55   Then We raised you up after you had died, so that you might give thanks.

And We caused the clouds to overshadow you and sent to you manna and quails [saying]: "Eat from the good things We have provided for you." They did not wrong Us; they only wronged themselves.

And when We said: "Enter this city[38] and eat wherever you wish from its abundant provision", and enter the gate while bowing and say: "Forgiveness." We will [then] forgive you your sins and increase the reward of the righteous.

The evil-doers changed what was said to them into something else; and We sent down upon the evil-doers a plague from heaven as a punishment for their transgression.

And when Moses prayed for water for his people, We said: "Strike the rock with your staff." Thereupon twelve springs gushed out from it, and each tribe recognized its water trough. [We said:] "Eat and drink from Allah's provision and do not make mischief in the land."

60   And when you said: "O Moses, We will not put up with one kind of food; so pray to your Lord to bring forth for us some of what the earth produces: green herbs, cucumbers, corn, lentils and onions." He said: "Would you exchange that which is better for that which is worse? Come down to Egypt where you will get what you asked for." Humiliation and abasement were inflicted on them and they incurred Allah's wrath. That was because they disbelieved in Allah's revelations and unjustly killed the prophets, thus committing disobedience and aggression.

The believers,[39] the Jews, the Christians and the Sabians – whoever believes in Allah and the Last Day and does what is good, shall receive their reward from their Lord. They shall have nothing to fear and they shall not grieve.

---

36. "*Al-Furqan*" which distinguishes right from wrong.
37. Let the innocent kill the evil-doer.
38. Jerusalem or Jericho.
39. The Muslims.

And when We made a covenant with you and raised the mountain above you [saying]: "Take what We have given you earnestly and keep in mind what is in it so that you might guard yourselves against evil."

But after that you turned away; and had it not been for Allah's grace and His mercy on you, you would surely have been among the losers.

And you surely know those of you who violated the Sabbath; We said to them: "Be [like] dejected apes."

65 Thus We made that an example to their contemporaries and to those after them, and an admonition to the righteous.

And when Moses said to his people: "Allah commands you to sacrifice a cow", they replied: "Do you make a mockery of us?" He said: "God forbid that I be one of the ignorant."[40]

They said: "Call on your Lord to explain to us what [cow] it is." He replied: "He says: 'Let it be neither too old nor too young, but in between.' Therefore, do what you are commanded to do."

They said: "Call on your Lord to tell us what its colour should be." He replied: "He[41] says: 'Let it be a yellow cow which has a striking colour and which pleases the beholders.' "

They said: "Call on your Lord to tell us what it[42] is; for to us all cows seem to be alike. Thus if Allah wills, we will be rightly guided."

70 He said: "He says:[43] 'It is a cow which is neither harnessed to plough the land nor to water the field, but rather sound with no blemish.'" Then they said: "Now you speak the truth." Thereupon they slaughtered it after they had been reluctant to do so.

And when you slew a man and fell out among yourselves regarding him, Allah brought forth to light what you had concealed.

We said: "Strike him with a part of it."[44] Thus Allah brings the dead to life, and shows you His signs so that you may understand.

Then your hearts became as hard as stone or harder; for there are stones from which rivers flow, and others which splinter and water comes out from them, and others which tumble down for fear of Allah. Allah is surely not unaware of what you do.

Do you then hope that they will believe in you when a group of them[45] did hear the Word of Allah, then after they understood it, they knowingly perverted it?

40. That is, one of the mocking people.
41. Allah.
42. The cow.
43. Allah.
44. The cow. This could be its tongue or the end of its tail.
45. The Jews.

75   And when they meet those who have believed they say: "We believe," but when they come together privately, they say: "Will you tell them what Allah has revealed to you[46] so that they might dispute with you concerning it before your Lord? Have you no sense?"

    Do they not know that Allah knows what they conceal and what they reveal?

    Among them are illiterate people who know nothing of the Book[47] except illusory desires. Indeed, they are only conjecturing.

    Woe unto those who write the Book with their hands, then say that it is from Allah in order to sell it for a small price. Woe unto them for what their hands have written, and woe unto them for what they have earned.

    And they say: "The Fire will only touch us for a few days." Say: "Have you received a pledge from Allah, and Allah does not revoke His pledge, or are you imputing to Allah what you do not know?"

80   Indeed, whoever commits a sin and his sin takes complete hold of him is one of the people of Hell, wherein they will dwell forever.

    Those who believe and do good works are the people of Paradise, where they will dwell forever.

    When You made a covenant with the Children of Israel: "You shall worship none other than Allah; show kindness to your parents, to the near of kin, to the orphans and to the poor; speak to people; perform the prayers, give the alms-tax." But, with the exception of a few, you did not abide by the covenant and you turned away.

    And when We made a covenant with you: "We shall not shed your own blood, nor drive your people away from their homes", you accepted and you bore witness [thereto].

    Yet there you are killing each other and turning some of your folk from their homes, making common cause against them with sin and aggression. But should they come to you as captives you would ransom them. Surely it was unlawful for you to drive them away. Do you, then, believe in one part[48] of the Book and disbelieve in another?[49] The reward of those among you who do that is nothing but disgrace in this world, and on the Day of Resurrection they shall be turned over to the most severe punishment. Allah is not unaware of what you do.

85   Those are the people who have traded the life of this world for the Hereafter. Their punishment shall not be lightened, nor shall they be helped.

---

46. Revealed to you about Muhammad.
47. The Scriptures.
48. Paying the ransom.
49. Killing and driving away their people from their homes.

We have indeed given Moses the Book, and after him We sent one apostle after another. We also gave Jesus, son of Mary, clear signs[50] and strengthened him with the Holy Spirit. Do you, then, whenever an apostle brings you what you do not desire, become puffed up with pride accusing some [of them] of lying and killing others?

They said: "Our hearts are sealed." Nay, Allah has cursed them on account of their unbelief; for they have very little faith.

And when a Book[51] came to them from Allah confirming that which they had,[52] and though they used hitherto to pray for assistance against those who disbelieved; yet when there came to them what they already knew,[53] they disbelieved in it. So may Allah's curse be on the unbelievers.

Evil is that for which they sold their souls when they disbelieved in what Allah sent down, out of envy that He should send down from His bounty[54] on whomsoever of His servants He pleases. Thus they incurred wrath upon wrath. And there is a demeaning punishment for the unbelievers.

90   And when it is said to them: "Believe in what Allah has revealed", they say: "We believe in what was revealed to us", denying thereby what has been revealed thereafter,[55] although it is the Truth which confirms what they have.[56] Say: "Why, then, did you kill Allah's prophets in the past if you are true believers?"

Surely Moses came to you with clear signs;[57] then, in his absence you made of the calf a god, and thus you became evil-doers.

And [remember] when We made a covenant with you and raised the mountain over you saying: "Take what we have given you with earnestness and obey." They said: "We have heard. We disobey." They were made to imbibe the love of the calf into their hearts because of their unbelief. Say: "Evil is what your faith bid you, if you are true believers."[58]

Say: "If the abode of the Hereafter with Allah is for you alone to the exclusion of all other people, then wish for death if you are truthful."

But they will never wish for it, because of what they did earlier. Allah knows well the evil-doers.[59]

95   Indeed you will find them of all people the most attached to life, even

50. Miracles.
51. The Qur'an.
52. The Torah.
53. That Muhammad would be sent as the Apostle of Allah.
54. Reveal to them.
55. The Qur'an.
56. Their Scriptures.
57. Miracles.
58. The implication here is that they are not believers.
59. Hence the unbelievers.

more attached than those who associated other gods with Allah. Every one of them wishes to live for one thousand years. This long life, however, will not spare them the punishment. And Allah sees what they do.

Say: "Whoever is an enemy of Gabriel – it is he[60] who has instilled it[61] in your heart by Allah's permission confirming what preceded it,[62] and as a guidance and good tidings to the believers.

Whoever is an enemy of Allah, His angels, His apostles, Gabriel and Michael, surely Allah is the enemy of the unbelievers.

Indeed, We have revealed to you clear signs[63] in which only the wicked will disbelieve.

Will it be that every time they make a covenant, a group of them will cast it aside? Indeed, most of them do not believe.

100   And when an apostle came to them from Allah confirming what they had, a group of those who were given the Book[64] cast the Book[65] of Allah behind their backs, as if they knew nothing;

And they believed what the devils said about Solomon's kingdom. Not that Solomon disbelieved; but the devils did, teaching the people witchcraft and that which was revealed in Babylon to the two angels, Harut and Marut. Yet those two angels did not teach anybody without saying [to him]: "We are a temptation. So do not disbelieve." Those [who wished] learned from them what would sow discord between man and wife, but could not harm anybody with it,[66] except with Allah's permission. They learn what harms them and does not profit them. They knew that he who bought it will have no share in the Hereafter. Evil is the price for which they sold themselves, if only they knew.

And had they[67] believed and feared [Allah], a reward from Allah would have been better for them, if only they knew.

O believers, do not say:[68] "Ra'ina [listen to us] but Unzurna [look at us] and listen."[69] And for the unbelievers a painful punishment is destined.

Neither the unbelievers among the People of the Book nor the polytheists wish to see any good[70] sent down to you from your Lord. Allah favours with His mercy whomever He wishes, and Allah's bounty is great.

---

60. Gabriel.
61. The revelation.
62. What had been revealed.
63. Revelations.
64. The Torah.
65. The Qur'an.
66. With what they learned.
67. The Jews.
68. To Our Apostle.
69. Muhammad, the Apostle of Allah, had an aversion to the Arabic word [ra'ina], because the Jews frequently used it as a term of reproach.
70. Revelation.

105 Whichever verse We abrogate or cause to be forgotten, We bring instead a better or similar one. Do you not know that Allah has the power over all things?

Do you not know that to Allah belongs the dominion of the heavens and the earth, and that apart from Allah you have no guardian or helper?

Or would you rather question your Apostle as Moses was questioned before? He who veers from belief to unbelief has strayed from the right path.

Many of the People of the Book[71] wish, out of envy, to turn you back into unbelievers after the truth had become manifest to them. But pardon and overlook, until Allah makes known His will. Surely Allah has the power over all things.

Perform the prayers and give the alms-tax. Whatever good you do for your own sake, you will find it with Allah,[72] surely Allah is cognizant of what you do.

110 They say: "None will enter Paradise except those who are Jews and Christians." Such are their vain wishes. Say: "Bring forth your proof if you are truthful."

Indeed, those who submit themselves to Allah, while doing good,[73] will have their reward with Allah.[74] They will have nothing to fear and will not grieve.

The Jews say: "The Christians follow nothing [substantial]" and the Christians say: "The Jews follow nothing [substantial]," while both recite the Book. Thus also say those who know not. Allah will judge between them on the Day of Resurrection regarding what they differ on.

And who is more unjust than those who prohibit mentioning the name of Allah in His mosques, and who even seek to destroy them. Those people should not have been allowed to enter them except in fear. For them there is disgrace in this world, and terrible punishment in the Hereafter.

To Allah belong the East and West. So whichever way you turn,[75] there is Allah's face. Indeed, Allah is Omnipresent and Omniscient.

115 And they say: "Allah has begotten a son." Glory be to Him. His is everything in the heavens and the earth; all are obedient to Him.

Creator of the heavens and the earth. When He decrees a thing, He only says to it: "Be," and there it is.

Those who do not know[76] say: "If only Allah would speak to us,[77] or a sign come to us." Thus said those who came before them.[78] Their hearts are

71. Jews and Christians.
72. You will be rewarded for it.
73. Believing in the unity of Allah.
74. His reward will be Paradise.
75. While praying.
76. Mecca's unbelievers.
77. Tells us that you are His Apostle.
78. To their prophets.

all alike. Indeed, we have made clear the signs for people who firmly believe.

We have sent you with the Truth[79] as a bearer of good tidings and as a warner. You are not to be questioned about the people of Hell.

Neither the Jews nor the Christians will be pleased with you until you follow their religion. Say: "Allah's guidance is the [only] guidance." And were you to follow their desires after the Knowledge that came down to you, you will have no guardian or helper [to save you] from Allah.

120   Those to whom We have given the Book recite it as it ought to be recited. Those [people] believe in it; but those who disbelieve are the losers.

O Children of Israel, remember the grace I bestowed on you, and remember that I preferred you to all other nations.[80]

And guard against a day when no soul shall avail any other soul, and no ransom will be accepted from it, nor any intercession will benefit it, and they will not have any support.

And when Abraham was tried by his Lord with certain commandments which he fulfilled, He said: "I am making you a spiritual exemplar to mankind." Abraham said: "And what about my posterity?" He replied: "My covenant does not apply to the evil-doers."

And [remember] when We made the House[81] a place of residence for mankind and a haven [saying]: "Make of Abraham's *maqam* [stand] a place for prayer." We enjoined Abraham and Isma'il [saying]: "Purify My House for those who circle it, for those who retreat there for meditation, and for those who kneel and prostrate themselves."[82]

125   And when Abraham said: "My Lord, make this a secure city and feed with fruits those of its inhabitants who believe in Allah and the Last Day." Allah[83] said: "As for those who disbelieve, I shall provide for them for a while,[84] and then subject them to the scourge of the Fire, and what an abominable fate!"

And while Abraham and Isma'il raised the foundations of the House, [they prayed]: "Our Lord, accept [this] from us. Surely You are the All-Hearing, the Omniscient."

"Our Lord, cause us to submit to You, and make of our posterity a nation that submits to you. Show us our sacred rites, and pardon us. You are, indeed, the Pardoner, the Merciful."

"Our Lord, send them an apostle from among themselves who will recite

79. The guidance.
80. See comment on verse 47.
81. The Ka'ba.
82. Those who perform the prayers.
83. Having accepted Abraham's prayer.
84. In this life.

to them Your revelations, to teach them the Book[85] and the wisdom, and to purify them. You are truly the Mighty, the Wise."

And who would forsake the religion of Abraham except one who makes a fool of himself? We have chosen him in this world and in the Hereafter; he shall be one of the righteous.

130 When his Lord told him: "Submit", he said: "I have submitted to the Lord of the Worlds."

And Abraham bequeathed that to his sons, and so did Jacob saying: "O my sons, Allah has chosen the religion for you; so do not die except as submitting people."

Or were you present when Jacob was in the throes of death and said to his sons: "What will you worship when I am gone?" They replied: "We will worship your God and the God of your forefathers, Abraham, Isma'il and Ishaq – the One God; and to Him we submit."

That was a nation which passed away, Hers is what she has earned and yours is what you have earned. And you shall not be questioned about what they did.

They say: "If you become Jews or Christians, you shall be well-guided." Say: "Rather, we follow the religion of Abraham, who was upright and no polytheist."

135 Say: "We believe in Allah, in what has been revealed to us, what was revealed to Abraham, Isma'il, Ishaq, Jacob and the Tribes, and in what was imparted to Moses, Jesus and the other prophets from their Lord, making no distinction between any of them, and to Him we submit."

If they believe in what you have believed, they will be well-guided: but if they turn away, they are indeed dissenting: and Allah will protect you against them; for He is All-Hearing, Omniscient.

[We take on] Allah's own colour;[86] and what colour is better than Allah's? And we do worship Him.

Say: "Do you dispute with us concerning Allah when He is our Lord and your Lord? We have our works[87] and you have your works.[88] To Him alone we are devoted.

Or do you say: 'Abraham, Isma'il, Ishaq, Jacob and the Tribes were Jews and Christians?" Say: "Who knows better, you or Allah?" And who is more unjust than he who conceals a testimony which he has received from Allah? Allah is not unaware of what you do."

140 That is a nation which passed away. It shall reap what it has earned, and

---

85. The Qur'an.
86. Religion.
87. By which we shall be judged.
88. By which you shall be judged.

you shall reap what you have earned. You shall not be questioned about what they were doing.

The ignorant among the people[89] will say: "What caused them[90] to turn away from their former *qibla* towards which they used to turn?"[91] Say: "To Allah belongs the East and the West. He guides whom He wills towards the right path."

And thus We have made you[92] a just nation, so that you may bear witness unto the rest of mankind, and that the Apostle may bear witness unto you. We did not ordain your former *qibla* except that We may distinguish those who follow the Apostle from those who turn on their heels.[93] It was indeed a hard test except for those whom Allah guided. Allah would not allow your faith to be in vain. He is clement and Merciful to mankind.

Surely, We see your face turned towards heaven.[94] We shall turn you towards a *qibla* that will please you. Turn your face then towards the Sacred Mosque;[95] and wherever you are turn your faces towards it. Those who were given the Book[96] certainly know this to be the Truth from their Lord. Allah is not unaware of what they do.

Were you even to come to the People of the Book with every proof, they will not follow your *qibla*, nor will you follow their *qibla*. Nor will some of them follow the *qibla* of the others. And were you to follow their desires after all the knowledge that came to you, surely you would be one of the evil-doers.

145 Those to whom We gave the Book know him[97] as they know their own sons; but a group of them will knowingly conceal the truth.

The truth is from your Lord. So do not be one of the doubters.

To everyone there is a direction towards which he turns. So hasten to do the good works. Wherever you are, Allah will bring you all together.[98] Surely Allah has power over all things.

From whatever place you come out, turn towards the Sacred Mosque. This is indeed the truth from your Lord. Allah is not unaware of what you do.

From whatever place you come out, turn your faces towards the Sacred Mosque. And wherever you all are, turn your faces towards it, lest people should have cause to argue with you, except for the evil-doers among them.

---

89. Among the Jews and polytheist Arabs.
90. The Prophet Muhammad and the believers.
91. *Qibla* is the direction to which Muslims turn while performing the prayers. The first *qibla* was the Aqsa mosque in Jerusalem. In 2 AH/624 AD it was replaced by the Ka'ba in Mecca.
92. The Muslim nation.
93. Return to disbelief.
94. Yearning for guidance through revelation.
95. The Sacred Mosque of Mecca.
96. The Jews and Christians.
97. Muhammad, the Apostle of Allah.
98. In the Hereafter.

Do not fear them, but fear Me so that I may complete My grace upon you, and that you may be rightly guided.

150   Just as We sent forth to you an apostle[99] from among you reciting Our revelations[100] to you, purifying you,[101] instructing you in the Book[102] and the wisdom, and teaching you what you did not know.

Remember Me[103] then and I will remember[104] you. Give thanks to Me[105] and do not be ungrateful.[106]

O you who believe, seek assistance through forbearance and prayer. Allah is with the steadfast.

And do not say of those who are killed for the cause of Allah that they are dead. They are alive, but you are unaware [of them].

We will certainly test you with some fear and hunger and with some loss of property, lives and crops. Announce the good news to those who endure patiently.

155   Those who upon being visited by adversity say: "We are Allah's[107] and to Him we shall return."

Upon such people are blessings and mercy from their Lord; and those are the well-guided.

Surely Safa and Marwa[108] are beacons of Allah.[109] He who performs the proper or the lesser pilgrimage commits no sin if He goes around them.[110] And those who volunteer to do a good work[111] will find Allah Rewarding, All-Knowing.

Those[112] who conceal the clear proofs and guidance We sent down, after making them clear to mankind in the Book,[113] shall be cursed by Allah and the cursers.

Except those who repent, mend their ways and reveal [the truth];[114] these I shall pardon. I am the Pardoner, the Merciful.

---

99. Muhammad, the Apostle of Allah.
100. The Qur'an.
101. From polytheism.
102. The Qur'an.
103. By glorifying Me.
104. By rewarding you.
105. By obeying Me.
106. By disobeying Me.
107. Allah's servants.
108. Safa and Marwa are the names of two mountains near Mecca. They were the scene of Hagar's running to and fro in quest of water when she was left alone with Isma'il in the wilderness.
109. They are beacons of Allah's religion.
110. The early Muslims felt at first averse to do that because the pre-Islamic Arabs visited them and touched the two idols which stood there.
111. Without being enjoined to do that.
112. The Jews.
113. The Torah.
114. Which they had concealed.

160   Upon those who disbelieve and die as unbelievers is the curse of Allah, the angels, and the whole of mankind.

They abide forever in it;[115] their punishment will not be reduced, nor will they be given any respite.

Your God is One God. There is no god but He, the Compassionate, the Merciful.

In the creation of the heavens and the earth; in the alternation of night and day; in the ships which sail in the sea with what profits mankind; in the water which Allah sends down from the sky in order to bring the earth back to life after its death and disperses over it every type of beast; in the continuous changing of winds; and in clouds which are driven between heaven and earth – surely in these are signs for people who understand.

Yet, there are people who set up equals to Allah, whom they love as they love Allah. Those who believe, however, have greater love for Allah. If only the evil-doers could understand, upon seeing the punishment, that all power is Allah's and that Allah is stern in punishment.

165   Those who were followed will disown those who followed them[116] when they will see the punishment and their relations with each other will be severed.

Those who followed will say: "If only we could go back[117] we would disown them as they disowned us." Thus Allah will show them their works as sources of deep regret. And they will never come out of the Fire.

O people eat from the earth lawful and pleasant produce, and do not follow in Satan's footsteps; for he is a manifest enemy of yours.

He[118] commands you to do evil and indecency and to impute to Allah what you do not know.

When it is said to them: "Follow what Allah has revealed", they say: "We would rather follow that which we found our fathers doing." What, even though their fathers understood nothing and were not rightly guided!

170   Those who disbelieve are like one who screams but is heard by one who hears only calling and shouting. They are deaf, dumb and blind, and so they do not understand.

O believers, eat of the good things which We have provided for you and give thanks to Allah, if He is the One whom you worship.

He has only forbidden you [to eat] carrion, blood, pork and that over which[119] any name other than that of Allah is invoked.[120] But he who is

---

115. The curse or, according to some classical commentaries on the Qur'an, Hell.
116. They will deny that they had misled them.
117. To life on earth.
118. Satan.
119. When slaughtered.
120. Because the pre-Islamic Arabs used to invoke the names of their gods.

constrained,[121] without intending to disobey or transgress, will commit no sin. Allah is Forgiving, Merciful.

Those who conceal anything from the Book which Allah has revealed and sell it for a small price will swallow nothing but fire in their bellies.[122] Allah will not speak to them on the Day of Resurrection, nor will He purify them,[123] and their punishment is very painful.

It is those who prefer to commit error rather than seek guidance, and incur punishment in place of forgiveness. How bold they are in the face of the Fire!

175   That is because Allah has revealed the Book with the truth; and those who disagree about the Book are in great dissent.

Righteousness is not to turn your faces towards the East and the West; the righteous is he who believes in Allah, the Last Day, the angels, the Book and the prophets; who gives of his money, in spite of loving it, to the near of kin, the orphans, the needy, the wayfarers and the beggars, and for the freeing of slaves; who performs the prayers and pays the alms-tax. Such are also those who keep their pledges once they have made them, and endure patiently privation,[124] affliction[125] and in times of fighting.[126] Those are the truthful and the God-fearing.

O believers, retaliation for the slain is prescribed for you: a free [man] for a free [man], a slave for a slave and a female for a female. But if he is pardoned by his brother,[127] usage[128] should be followed and he should pay[129] him liberally and kindly. This is remission and mercy from your Lord. He who transgresses after that will have a painful punishment.

In retaliation there is life for you, O people of understanding, that you may be God-fearing.

It is prescribed for you that when death is imminent for one of you and he leaves wealth, he should equitably make a testament in favour of the parents and the near of kin.[130] This is incumbent upon the righteous.

180   Whoever then changes it after he had heard it, the sin committed is that of those who change it. Allah is All-Hearing, All-Knowing.

Should anyone, however, fear any iniquity or offence from a testator and reconciles them,[131] he shall incur no sin. Allah is Forgiving, Merciful.

---

121. Constrained to eat those forbidden things.
122. Because they will end in the Fire.
123. From their sins.
124. Particularly with regard to money.
125. Particularly with regard to illness.
126. In the way of Allah.
127. The aggrieved.
128. According to usage, capital punishment would be replaced by blood-money.
129. The aggrieved.
130. According to some classical commentators this verse was later abrogated by the law of inheritance.
131. The testator and the beneficiary.

O you who believe, fasting is prescribed for you as it was prescribed for those before you, so that you may be God-fearing;

For a fixed number of days. If any of you is sick or on a journey, then [an equal] number of other days. And those who find it extremely difficult[132] should, as a penance, feed a poor man. He who spontaneously does more good,[133] it is for his own good. To fast is better for you, if only you knew.

The month of Ramadan is the month in which the Qur'an was revealed, providing guidance for mankind, with clear verses to guide and to distinguish right from wrong. He who witnesses that month should fast it. But if anyone is sick or on a journey, [he ought to fast] a number of other days. Allah desires ease and does not desire hardship for you, that you may complete the total number;[134] glorify Allah for His guidance, and that you may be thankful.

185 And when My servants ask you about Me, say: "I am near; I answer the prayer of the supplicant when he calls; so they should answer My call[135] and believe in Me, that they may be rightly guided."

It has been made lawful to you on the night of fasting to approach your wives; they are a raiment for you, and you are a raiment for them.[136] Allah knows that you used to betray yourselves, but He accepted your repentance and pardoned you. So now get to them[137] and seek what Allah has ordained for you. Eat and drink until you can discern the white thread from the black thread of dawn. Then complete the fast till nightfall. But do not approach them[138] while you are in devotion at the mosque. Those are the bounds of Allah; do not approach them. Thus Allah makes clear his revelations to mankind, that they may fear Him.

Do not devour each other's money unjustly or offer it to the judges in order to devour a part of other people's money sinfully and knowingly.

They ask you about the crescents,[139] say: "They are times fixed for mankind and for the pilgrimage." It is not righteousness to enter houses from the back; but the righteous is he who fears Allah. Enter then the houses by their front doors;[140] and fear Allah that you may prosper.

And fight for the cause of Allah those who fight you, but do not be aggressive. Surely Allah does not like the aggressors.

132. That is, extremely difficult to fast.
133. If he increases the penance.
134. The total number of fasting days.
135. By obeying Me.
136. That is, you need each other.
137. The wives.
138. The wives.
139. The new moons.
140. The reference here may be to a pre-Islamic practice by which the Arabs, upon beginning the rituals of pilgrimage, used to enter a house from the back door.

190   Kill them wherever you find them and drive them out from wherever they drove you out.[141] Sedition is worse than slaughter. Do not fight them at the Sacred Mosque until they fight you at it. If they fight you there, kill them. Such is the reward of the unbelievers.

But if they desist, Allah is truly All-forgiving, Merciful.

Fight them until there is no sedition and the religion becomes that of Allah. But if they desist, there will be no aggression except against the evil-doers.

A sacred month for a sacred month; and retaliation [is allowed] when sacred things [are violated]. Thus, whoever commits aggression against you, retaliate against him in the same way. Fear Allah and know that Allah is with those who fear Him.

Spend [money] for the cause of Allah and do not cast yourselves with your own hands into destruction,[142] and be charitable. Surely Allah loves the charitable.

195   Perform the proper pilgrimage and the lesser pilgrimage for the sake of Allah. But if you are prevented, then make whatever offering[143] is available; then do not shave your heads until the offering reaches its destination.[144] Whoever of you is sick or has an injury in the head can atone for it by fasting, giving alms or sacrificing. When you are secure, whoever combines the lesser pilgrimage and the proper pilgrimage, should make whatever offering is available. But if he cannot, then let him fast for three days during the pilgrimage and seven days when he returns. That is a total of ten full days. This is incumbent on him whose family is not present at the Sacred Mosque. Fear Allah and know that His retribution is severe.

Pilgrimage is [during] the appointed months.[145] He who determines to perform the pilgrimage during them, shall abstain from intercourse, debauchery and acrimonious quarrel. And whatever good you do, Allah knows it. Make provision.[146] The best provision, however, is the fear of Allah. So fear Me, O people of understanding.

It is no offence to seek a bounty from your Lord. So when you take off from 'Arafat, remember[147] Allah at the sacred monument.[148] Remember Him as He guided you, although you were, before that, among those in error.

---

141. From Mecca.
142. By withholding money or giving up fighting for the cause of Allah.
143. A sheep.
144. Where it can be slaughtered.
145. These are the months of Shawwal, Dhul-Qa'da and the first ten days of Dhul-Hijja.
146. For your journey.
147. Pray to Him.
148. A mountain near Muzdalafa, where pilgrims stop for the night on their journey back from 'Arafat.

Then take off from where people take off and ask Allah's forgiveness. Surely Allah is All-Forgiving, Merciful.

Once you have performed your rites, remember Allah as you remember your fathers, or even with greater glorification. Some people say: "Our Lord, give us [a share] in this world." And yet they have no share in the Hereafter.

200   Others say: "Our Lord, give us a bounty in this world and a bounty in the Hereafter, and protect us from the torment of the Fire."

Those have a share[149] of what they have earned.[150] Allah is quick in retribution.

And remember Allah during appointed days;[151] but he who hastens [making] them two[152] incurs no sin. And he who stays behind[153] incurs no sin, if he fears Allah. So fear Allah and know that you will surely be gathered together before Him.

[You will find] among the people a person whose discourse about life in this world pleases you, and who calls Allah to vouch for what is in his heart, although he is your worst enemy.[154]

And when he departs,[155] he roams the land sowing corruption therein and destroying crops and livestock; but Allah does not like corruption.

205   And if it is said to him: "Fear Allah", he is seized with pride in sin. Hell shall be sufficient for him and what a miserable resting-place!

And some people sell themselves for the sake of Allah's favour. Allah is kind to [His] servants.

O believers, enter into complete peace[156] and do not follow in the footsteps of Satan; for he is truly your manifest enemy.

If however you slip after the clear proofs have come to you, know that Allah is Mighty, Wise.

Do they wait until Allah comes to them[157] in canopies of clouds with the angels, and thus the matter is settled? Unto Allah all matters shall be referred.

210   Ask the Children of Israel how many clear signs did We bring them. He who changes Allah's grace[158] after it has come to him [will find] Allah to be severe in retribution.

Life in this world has been made alluring for those who disbelieve. They

---

149. Reward.
150. The good they did.
151. The three days following the day of sacrifice.
152. The reference is to him who departs on the second day.
153. After the three days.
154. This verse refers to al-Ahknas Ibn Shurayq.
155. This may mean, according to some commentaries: when he is in authority or assumes power.
156. The Arabic equivalent for "complete peace" can also be rendered as "complete submission" or "true religion".
157. The coming of Allah stands for "the execution of His decrees".
158. This refers to those who turn away from Allah's clear signs to disbelief.

mock those who believe; but those who fear Allah will be above them on the Day of Resurrection. Allah provides for those whom He will without measure.

Mankind was one nation.[159] Then Allah sent forth the prophets as bearers of good news and as warners. He sent with them the Book[160] in truth, to judge between people regarding what[161] they differed on. And none differed on it[162] except those to whom it[163] was given after clear proofs had reached them, out of envy for one another. Allah, by His will, guided those who believed to the truth on which they had differed. Allah guides whom He will to the right path.

Or do you suppose that you will enter Paradise before the example of those who came before you had reached you? They were stricken by privation and affliction and were so shaken that the Apostle and those who believed with him said: "When is Allah's support coming?" Surely Allah's support is close at hand.

They ask you[164] what they should spend. Say: "Whatever bounty you give is for the parents, the near of kin, the orphans, the needy and the wayfarer." And whatever good you do, Allah is fully cognizant of it.

215   You are enjoined to fight, though it is something you dislike. For it may well be that you dislike a thing, although it is good for you; or like something although it is bad for you. Allah knows and you do not.

They ask you about the sacred month: "Is there fighting in it?" Say: "Fighting in it is a great sin; but to debar people from Allah's way and to deny Him and the Sacred Mosque, and to drive its people out of it is a greater sin in Allah's sight. Sedition is worse than murder." Nor will they cease to fight you until, if they can, they make you renounce your religion. Those of you who renounce their religion and die, while they are unbelievers, are those whose works come to grief, [both] in this world and in the Hereafter. And they are the people of the Fire, abiding in it forever.

Those who believed and those who emigrated and strove for the cause of Allah are those who may surely hope for Allah's mercy. Allah is Forgiving, Merciful.

They ask you about wine and gambling, say: "In both there is great sin and some benefit for people. But the sin is greater than the benefit." And they ask you about what they should spend, say: "What you can spare." Thus Allah makes clear to you his revelations so that you may reflect,

---

159. "One nation" may stand for common disbelief.
160. The reference is to all Books or Scriptures.
161. This stands for religion.
162. Religion.
163. The Book.
164. This question was put to the Apostle by a wealthy old man.

Upon this world and the Hereafter. And they ask you about orphans, say: "To improve their condition is better for them. And if you associate with them, they are your brethren." Allah knows the dishonest and the honest. And if Allah wills, He would overburden you with restrictions. Allah is Mighty, Wise.

220   Do not marry unbelieving women [polytheists] until they believe. A believing slave-girl is certainly better than an unbelieving woman, even if the latter pleases you. And do not give your women[165] in marriage to polytheists until they believe. A believing slave is certainly better than a polytheist, even if the latter pleases you. Those[166] call to the Fire and Allah calls to Paradise and forgiveness by His leave; and He makes clear His revelations to mankind so that they may be mindful.

And they ask you about menstruation, say: "It is an impurity." So keep away from women during their menstruation and do not approach them[167] until they are clean. Once they get clean get to them as Allah commanded you.[168] Allah loves the repentant and loves those who purify themselves.

Your women are a tillage for you. So get to your tillage whenever you like. Do good for yourselves, fear Allah and know that you shall meet Him. And give good news to the believers.

Do not make Allah in your oaths[169] a hindrance to doing good, to fearing Allah and to making peace between people. Allah is All-Hearing, All-Knowing.

Allah will not take you to task for what is not meant [to be said] in your oaths; but He will take you to task for what you mean in your hearts. Allah is Forgiving, Clement.

225   Those who swear not to approach their wives should wait for four months; then if they change their minds, Allah is Forgiving, Merciful.

If they resolve on divorce, Allah is All-Hearing, All-Knowing.

Divorced women should keep away from men for three menstrual periods. And it is not lawful for them to conceal that which Allah has created in their wombs, if they truly believe in Allah and the Last Day. Their husbands have the right in the meantime to take them back, should they seek reconciliation; and women have rights equal to what is incumbent upon them according to what is just, although men are one degree above them.[170] Allah is Mighty, Wise.

Divorce may be pronounced twice. Then they [women] are to be retained

---

165. Believing women.
166. The polytheists.
167. That is, do not have sexual relations with them.
168. The believers are commanded to approach women in the proper way.
169. When you swear by Allah.
170. What is meant here is that men have a superior authority. But this does not prejudice their rights which are stated above.

in a rightful manner or released with kindness. And it is unlawful for you [men] to take back anything of what you have given them, unless both fear that they cannot comply with Allah's bounds.[171] If you both fear that they cannot do that, then it is no offence if the woman ransoms herself.[172] Those are the bounds set by Allah. Do not transgress them. Those who transgress the bounds set by Allah are the wrongdoers.

If he divorces her, she shall not be lawful to him again until she has married another husband. If the latter divorces her, then it is no offence if they go back to each other, if they both think that they shall keep within Allah's bounds. Those are Allah's bounds which He makes clear to men who have knowledge.

230   If you divorce [your] women and they reach the end of their [waiting] period, retain them in an honourable manner or release them in an honourable manner. Do not, however, retain them for the sake of causing them harm and in order to commit aggression.[173] Whoever does that shall do wrong to himself. Do not make a mockery of Allah's revelations; and remember the grace Allah has bestowed upon you, and the Book[174] and the wisdom He has revealed to you in order to admonish you. Fear Allah and know that He knows everything.

If you divorce your women and they reach the end of their [waiting] period, do not prevent them from marrying their [former] husbands if they agree among themselves in a rightful manner. With this are admonished those who believe in Allah and the Last Day; it is better and more decent for you. Allah knows and you do not.

Mothers shall suckle their children for two whole years; [that is] for those who wish to complete the suckling. Those to whom the children are born[175] shall maintain and clothe them kindly. No soul is charged beyond its capacity. No mother should suffer on account of her child and he to whom a child is born should not suffer on account of his child. The same [duties][176] devolve upon the [father's] heir.[177] But they commit no offence if by mutual agreement and following consultation they choose to wean the child. You also commit no offence if you engage wet-nurses, provided that you give them what you promised to give kindly. Fear Allah and know that Allah has knowledge of what you do.

As for those of you who die leaving wives behind, their wives should

---

171. By obeying his commands.
172. Pays money to be set free.
173. By forcing them to ransom themselves, or by retaining them for a longer period.
174. The Qur'an.
175. The fathers.
176. The maintenance and clothing of divorced women.
177. If the heir is a child and has a guardian the latter would be charged with those duties.

observe a waiting period[178] of four months and ten days. When they have completed that period you incur no offence on account of what they may do with themselves[179] in a lawful manner. Allah has knowledge of what you do.

You incur no offence by disclosing your marriage proposals to women or by concealing them; Allah knows that you will remember them. And do not arrange anything secretly with them unless you speak what is recognized as true; and do not resolve on contracting the marriage until the prescribed period[180] ends. And know that Allah knows what you have in mind, and that Allah is Forgiving, Clement.

235 You incur no offence if you divorce women before the consummation of marriage or fixing the dowry. And provide for them in the rightful way: the wealthy according to his means, and the less fortunate according to his means. This is incumbent on the righteous.

If, however, you divorce them before the consummation of marriage, but after fixing a dowry, then [give them] half of the fixed dowry, unless they forgo that, or the man in whose hand is the marriage tie[181] forgoes his half. To forgo it is more righteous. And do not forget to be bountiful to each other. Allah sees what you do.

Attend regularly to the prayers including the middle prayer,[182] standing up in devotion to Allah.

If you are in danger, then[183] on foot or on horseback, when you feel secure remember Allah, just as He has taught you what you did not know.

Those of you who die leaving wives behind should bequeath to them a year's provision without turning [them] out.[184] If, however, they leave [their homes], then you[185] incur no offence for what they do in a rightful way to themselves. Allah is Mighty, Wise.

240 Divorced women should be provided with an affordable provision. This is incumbent on the righteous.

Thus Allah makes clear to you His revelations, so that you may understand.

Have you not considered those[186] who fled their homes in thousands for fear of death? Allah said to them: "Die." Then He brought them back to

---

178. During this period, they should keep away from men.
179. Such as adorning themselves or looking out for suitors.
180. The waiting period.
181. The husband.
182. Probably the afternoon prayer.
183. Perform the prayers.
184. From their homes.
185. The relatives of the dead.
186. The Israelites.

life. Surely Allah is gracious to mankind, but most people do not give thanks.

Fight for the cause of Allah and know that Allah is All-Hearing, All-Knowing.

Who is it that will lend Allah a generous loan,[187] so that He might multiply it for him manifold? Allah provides sparingly and generously, and to Him you shall be returned.

245   Have you not considered the leaders of the Children of Israel who after Moses said to one of their prophets: "Set up a king for us and we will fight in the way of Allah."

He replied: "What if you refuse to fight when you are ordered to fight?"

They said: "How could we refuse to fight when we have been driven, along with our children, from our homes?"

But when they were ordered to fight, they turned away except for a few of them. And Allah knows the wrongdoers.

Then their prophet said to them: "Allah has set up Saul to be your King." They replied: "How can he be given the kingship over us when we have a better right to it, and when he is not rich enough?" He said to them: "Allah has chosen him [to rule] over you and caused him to have greater knowledge and better stature. Allah bestows His sovereignty on whom he will. He is Munificent and All-Knowing."

250   Their prophet also said to them: "The proof of his kingship is that there shall come to you the Ark in which there is tranquillity from your Lord and the relics of Moses and the family of Aaron borne by the angels. In this there is a proof for you if you are real believers."

And when Saul set out with [his] troops he said: "Allah will test you with a river. He who drinks from it is no part of me,[188] but he who does not drink from it is part of me, except for him[189] who scoops up with his hand a handful from it." They drank from it except for a few of them; but when he, along with those who believed, crossed it, they said: "Today we are unable to face Goliath and his troops." But those of them who believed that they would meet Allah said: "How many a small band has defeated a large one by Allah's leave." Allah is with the steadfast.

And when they confronted Goliath and his troops, they said: "Lord, fill us with forbearance, enable us to stand fast, and help us against the unbelievers."

And so they defeated them by Allah's leave. David killed Goliath and Allah bestowed on him the kingship and the wisdom, and taught him what

187. Spends money in His way.
188. Stands for: "Is not one of my followers".
189. Means that such a person is one of my followers.

He pleased. Had Allah not caused some people to repel others, the earth would have been corrupted. But Allah bestows his favours on all mankind.

These are Allah's revelations. We recite them to you in all truth, and surely you are one of the Messengers.

255 [Of] those Messengers, We have made some excel the others; to some of them Allah spoke[190] and He exalted some many degrees [above the others].[191] We gave Jesus, son of Mary, clear signs and strengthened him with the Holy Spirit. Had Allah so willed, those who succeeded them would not have fought one another after they had received the clear signs. But they disagreed [among themselves]; some of them believed and some did not. Had Allah pleased they would not have fought each other, but Allah does what He wills.

O believers, spend of what we have provided for you before a day comes[192] in which there is neither trading, nor friendship, nor intercession. The unbelievers are the wrongdoers.

Allah! There is no god but He, the Living, the Everlasting. Neither slumber nor sleep overtakes him. His is what is in the heavens and on the earth. Who shall intercede with him except with His leave? He knows what is before them[193] and what is behind them.[194] And they do not comprehend of His knowledge except what He wills. His throne encompasses the heavens and the earth, and their preservation does not burden Him. He is the Exalted, the Great.

There is no compulsion in religion; true guidance has become distinct from error. Thus he who disbelieves in the Devil and believes in Allah grasps the firmest handle that will never break. Allah is All-Hearing, All-Knowing.

Allah is the Supporter of the believers. He brings them out of darkness into light. As for those who disbelieve, their supporters are the devils who bring them out of light into darkness. Those are the people of the Fire in which they shall abide forever.

260 Have you not considered him who disputed with Abraham regarding his Lord, because He had given him the kingdom? When Abraham said: "My Lord is He who gives life and causes death", the other said: "I give life and cause death." Abraham [then] said: "Allah brings the sun from the East, bring it up from the West." Thereupon the unbeliever was confounded. Allah does not guide the wrongdoers.

Or [consider] him who, passing by a ruined city[195] said: "How will God

190. The reference here is to Moses, or to both Moses and Muhammad.
191. The reference here is to Muhammad.
192. The Day of Judgement.
193. In this world.
194. In the Hereafter.
195. Jerusalem.

bring this to life after its death?" Thereupon Allah caused him to die for a hundred years, then brought him back to life.

Allah asked him: "For how long have you tarried?" He said: "I tarried for a day or part of a day."

Allah said: "No, you have tarried for a hundred years. Look at your food and drink; the years have not changed them. Look at your ass. With this We make of you a sign for mankind. Look also at the bones [and see] how We have restored them, then clothed them with flesh."

When [all] this became clear to him, he said: "[Now] I know that Allah has power over all things."

265   And when Abraham said: "My Lord, show me how you raise the dead", He replied: "Have you not embraced the faith?" Abraham said: "Yes, but so that my heart be reassured." Allah then said: "Take four birds, draw them to you, then [cut them to pieces] and place a part thereof on each mountain. If you then call them, they will come rushing to you. And know that Allah is Mighty, Wise."

Those who spend their wealth in the way of Allah are like a grain [of wheat] which grows seven ears, each carrying one hundred grains. Allah multiplies [further] to whom He will. Allah is Munificent, All-Knowing.

Those who spend their wealth in the way of Allah, and then do not follow what they spend with taunts and injury, their reward is with their Lord. They shall have nothing to fear and shall not grieve.

A kind word and forgiveness are better than charity followed by injury. Allah is Self-Sufficient and Forbearing.

O believers, do not render vain your charities by taunts and injury, like him who spends his wealth for the sake of ostentation and does not believe in Allah and the Last Day. He is like a smooth rock covered by earth; when heavy rain falls on it, it leaves it completely bare. Such people get no reward for their works. Allah does not guide the unbelievers.

270   But those who spend their money in order to please Allah and to strengthen their souls[196] are like a garden on a hill which, when heavy rain falls on it, its produce is doubled; and if no heavy rain falls on it, then a shower [suffices]. Allah is aware of what you do.

Does any one of you wish to have a garden of palms and vines, under which rivers flow and from which he gets all kinds of fruits; and when he gets old and has weak offspring a whirlwind with fire hits the garden and burns it down? Thus Allah makes clear to you His revelations so that you may reflect.

O believers, spend[197] of the good things you have earned and from what

196. By having a stronger grasp of the faith.
197. Spend as charity.

We bring out of the earth for you. Do not turn to the vile and spend from it. For you, yourselves, would not accept it except indulgently. Know that Allah is Self-Sufficient, Praiseworthy.

Satan induces you to expect poverty and orders you to be niggardly, and Allah promises you His forgiveness and His bounty. Allah is Munificent, All-Knowing.

He gives wisdom to whom He wills. And he who receives wisdom has received an abundant good. But none takes heed except people of understanding.

275   And whatever expense you spend and whatever vow you vow are known to Allah. The evil-doers shall have no supporters.

To give alms publicly is commendable; but to keep it secret and give it to the poor is better for you, and will atone for some of your sins. Allah has knowledge of what you do.

You are not responsible for guiding them. Allah guides whom He wills. And whatever good you spend is for yourselves; for you do not spend except for Allah's sake. And whatever you spend will yield good returns.[198] And you shall not be wronged.

[Alms is] for the poor who are held up [fighting] in the way of Allah, and thus cannot travel in the land. The ignorant think they are rich because they are too proud [to beg]. But you can recognize them by their mark. They do not importune people for alms. Whatever good you spend is known to Allah.

Those who spend their wealth day and night, in private and in public, will be rewarded by their Lord. They have nothing to fear and they shall not grieve.

280   Those who take usury will not rise up[199] except like those maddened by Satan's touch. For they claim that trading is like usury, whereas Allah has made trading lawful and prohibited usury. Hence, he who has received an admonition from his Lord and desisted can keep what he has taken[200] and his fate is to be left to Allah. But those who revert [to it][201] – those are the people of the Fire in which they shall abide forever.

Allah prohibits usury and does not bless it; but He compounds alms. And Allah does not like a vicious unbeliever.

Verily, those who believe, do good works, perform the prayers and give the alms-tax, shall find their reward with their Lord. They have nothing to fear, and they shall not grieve.

---

198. That is, it will be fully rewarded.
199. On the Day of Resurrection.
200. As usury, prior to the prohibition.
201. Taking usury.

O believers, fear Allah and forgo what is still due from usury, if you are [true] believers.

But if you fail to do that, take note of a war [waged] by Allah and His Apostle. But if you repent you will have your capital, neither wronging nor being wronged.

285   If he [the debtor] is in straits, then allow days of grace until he is at ease. But to remit [the debt] as alms is better for you, if you only knew.

Fear a day when you will return to Allah; then each soul will be rewarded fully for what it has earned;[202] and none shall be wronged.

O believers, when you contract a debt for a fixed period, write it down. Let a scribe write it for you with fairness. No scribe should decline to write as Allah has taught him. So let him then write and let the debtor dictate. He should fear his Lord and not diminish the debt in the least. If the debtor is feeble-minded or weak or ignorant, then let his guardian dictate with fairness. And call to witness two witnesses of your men; if not two men, then one man and two women from such witnesses you approve of, so that if one of them[203] fails to remember, the other would remind her. The witnesses should not decline [to testify] when they are called upon [to do so]. So do not be averse to writing down the debt, be it small or large, as well as when it is due. This is more equitable in Allah's sight, more suitable for testimony and less likely to rouse your doubts. If it is an instant transaction among yourselves;[204] then it is no offence if you do not write it down.

And let there be witnesses when you sell one to another; but neither the scribe nor the witness should be harmed, because if you do that, it is an act of transgression. Fear Allah; Allah teaches you. He has knowledge of everything.

If you are travelling and cannot find a scribe, a security should be taken. But if you trust one another, then let him who is entrusted deliver the security and fear Allah his Lord. Do not withhold the testimony. He who withholds it has a sinful heart. Allah has knowledge of what you do.

290   To Allah belongs whatever is in the heavens and on the earth. And whether you reveal or conceal what is in your hearts, Allah will call you to account for it. He will then forgive whom He wills, and punish whom He wills. He is able to do everything.

The Apostle[205] believes in what has been revealed to him by his Lord, and so do the believers too. All believe in Allah, His angels, His Books and His

202. For the good works it has done.
203. The two women.
204. Involving no debt.
205. Muhammad.

Messengers. We make no distinction between any of His Messengers. And they[206] say: "We hear and obey. Grant us your forgiveness, our Lord. And to you is our return."

Allah does not charge any soul beyond its capacity. It gets [rewarded for] what [good] it has earned, and is called to account for what [evil] it has committed. Lord, forgive us if we have forgotten or erred. Lord, do not lay on us a burden like that you laid on those before us, and do not burden us with what we cannot bear. Pardon us, forgive us and have mercy on us. You are our Protector. Give us victory over the unbelieving people.

206. The believers.

Al-'Imran, The Family of 'Imran

In the Name of Allah, the Compassionate, the Merciful

Alif, Lam, Mim.

1   Allah, there is no god but He, the Living, the Everlasting.

He has revealed the Book[207] to you in truth, confirming what came before it; and He has revealed the Torah and the Gospel, as a guidance to mankind.

He has also revealed the Criterion.[208] Verily, those who have disbelieved in Allah's signs, a terrible punishment awaits them; Allah is Mighty and stern in retribution.

Indeed, nothing is hidden from Allah whether on earth or in the heavens.

5   It is He who forms you in the wombs as He pleases; there is no god but He, the Mighty, the Merciful.

It is He who has revealed to you the Book, with verses which are precise in meaning and which are the Mother of the Book, and others which are ambiguous. As to those in whose hearts there is vacillation, they follow what is ambiguous in it, seeking sedition and intending to interpret it. However, no one except Allah knows its interpretation. Those well-grounded in knowledge say: "We believe in it; all is from our Lord"; yet none remembers save those possessed of understanding!

Lord, do not cause out hearts to vacillate after You have guided us and grant us Your mercy. You are indeed the Munificent Giver.

Lord, you will surely gather mankind for a Day[209] which is undoubted. Allah will never fail to keep the appointed time!

As to the unbelievers, neither their riches nor their children will avail them anything against Allah; in fact, they shall be the fuel of the Fire.

10   Like Pharaoh's people and those before them who denounced our revelations. Allah smote them on account of their sins. Allah is stern in retribution!

Say to those who disbelieved:[210] "You shall be defeated and driven together into Hell; and what an awful resting-place."

There surely was a sign for you in the two armies that confronted each

207. The Qur'an.
208. Of right and wrong, Arabic: *Al-Furqan*; that is, the Qur'an itself.
209. Day of Resurrection.
210. The Jews.

other;[211] the one side fighting for the cause of Allah, and the other consisting of unbelievers. The believers saw them with their very eyes to be twice their actual number. God will strengthen with His might whomever He pleases. Surely, there is in this a lesson for those who are possessed of vision.

Attractive to mankind is made the love of the pleasures of women, children, heaps upon heaps of gold and silver, thoroughbred horses, cattle and cultivable land. Such is the pleasure of this worldly life, but unto Allah is the fairest return.

Say: "Shall I tell you about something better than all that?" For those who are God-fearing, from their Lord are gardens beneath which rivers flow, and in which they abide forever [along with] purified spouses and Allah's good pleasure. Allah sees His servants well!

15   Those who say: "Our Lord, we have believed, so forgive us our sins and guard us against the torments of Hell."

They are the patient, the truthful, the devout, the charitable and the seekers of forgiveness at daybreak.

Allah bears witness that there is no god but He, and so do the angels and men of learning. He upholds justice. There is no god but He, the Mighty and Wise One.

The [true] religion with Allah is Islam. Those who were given the Book[212] did not disagree among themselves, except after certain knowledge came to them, out of envy among themselves. Whoever disbelieves in Allah's revelations will find Allah quick in retribution!

So, if they dispute with you, say: "I have submitted myself to Allah and so have those who followed me"; and say also to those who have received the Book and to the unlearned:[213] "Have you submitted?" If they have submitted, then they are rightly guided; but if they have turned their backs, then your duty is simply to deliver the message. Allah perceives His servants well.

20   Those who disbelieve in Allah's revelations and kill the prophets unjustly, and kill those people who enjoin fair dealing, announce to them a painful punishment.

Those are the people whose works have come to naught in this world and the next, and they will have no supporters whatsoever!

Have you not considered those who have received a portion of the Book? Upon being called to let the Book of Allah decide between them, some of them turn their backs, refusing to pay attention.

211. In the Battle of Badr, 2 AH/624 AD.
212. The Jews and the Christians.
213. The Arab idolaters of Mecca.

That is because they say: "The Fire will only touch us for a few days." They have been deluded in their religion by their lies.

But how will they fare when We gather them together on a day which is undoubted, and each soul shall be paid in full for whatever it has earned, and they shall not be dealt with unjustly?

25   Say: "O Allah, Master of the Kingdom, You give the kingship to whom You please and take away the kingship from whom You please. You exalt whom You please and humble whom You please. In Your hand is all the good, and You have power over everything!

"You cause the night to pass into the day, and the day to pass into the night. You bring forth the living from the dead and You bring forth the dead from the living, and You provide for whomever You please without measure."

Let not the believers take the unbelievers for friends, rather than the believers. Whoever does that has nothing to do with Allah, unless you guard against them fully! Allah warns you to beware of Him;[214] and unto Him is the ultimate return!

Say: "Whether you conceal what is in your hearts or you reveal it, Allah knows it; and He knows what is in the heavens or on the earth, and He has power over everything!"

The day [will come] when every soul shall find every good it has done set before it; and whatever evil it did, it wishes that it was far away from it. Allah warns you to be wary of Him, and Allah is Compassionate towards His servants!

30   Say: "If you love Allah, follow me; then Allah will love you and forgive your sins." Allah is Forgiving, Merciful.

Say: "Obey Allah and the Apostle." Should they turn their backs, surely Allah does not love the unbelievers.

Allah chose Adam, Noah, the family of Abraham and the family of Imran above all mankind;

Descending one from another; and Allah is Hearing, All-Knowing!

[Remember] when the wife of Imran said: "Lord, I have vowed to you what is in my womb to be devoted [to Your service]. Accept it from me, for You are the Hearing, the All-Knowing."

35   And when she delivered her, she said: "Lord, I have given birth to a female", – and Allah knew best what she gave birth to; the male is not the same as the female – "I have named her Mary and I commend her and her descendants to You to protect her from the accursed Devil."

Then her Lord accepted her graciously and made her to grow into a fine

214. Warns you of His anger.

child, entrusting her to Zachariah. Whenever Zachariah went in to see her in the sanctuary, he found that she had some provision. "Mary," he asked, "where did you get this?" She replied: "It is from Allah, and Allah provides for whom He wishes without measure."

Thereupon, Zachariah prayed to his Lord saying: "Lord, grant me from your bounty fine descendants. Indeed You hear every prayer!"

Then the angels called him while he was at prayer in the sanctuary, saying: "Allah bids you rejoice in John, confirming a word[215] from Allah, a master, chaste and a prophet and one of the righteous."

He said: "Lord, how will I have a son, seeing I have been overtaken by old age and my wife is barren?" "This is how Allah does whatever He pleases," He replied.

40 He said: "Lord, give me a sign." Allah said: "Your sign is that you will not speak to anybody for three days, except by signs; and remember your Lord often and give praise evening and morning."

And when the angels said: "O Mary, Allah has chosen you and purified you, preferring you to all womankind."

"O Mary, be obedient to your Lord, prostrate yourself and bow down with those who bow down."

This is part of the tidings of the Unseen which We reveal to you. You were not in their midst when they cast their pens[216] to see who will take charge of Mary, and you were not in their midst when they were disputing.

When the angels said: "O Mary, Allah bids you rejoice in a word from Him, whose name is the Messiah, Jesus, son of Mary. He shall be prominent in this world[217] and the next[218] and shall be near to God."

45 "He shall speak to people from the cradle and while an old man and will be one of the righteous."

She said: "Lord, how can I have a child when I have not been touched by any man?" Allah said: "Thus Allah creates whatever He pleases. When He decrees a matter, He simply says to it: 'Be', and it comes to be."

And He will teach him the Book, the Wisdom, the Torah and the Gospel.

And [send him forth as a] messenger to the Children of Israel [saying]: "I bring you a sign from your Lord. I will create for you out of clay the likeness of a bird; then I will breathe into it and it will become a bird, by Allah's leave. And I will heal the blind and the leper and will raise the dead, by Allah's leave. And I will inform you concerning what you eat and what you hoard in your homes. In all this there is surely a sign for you, if you are believers!"

215. Jesus.
216. They were casting lots.
217. Through prophethood.
218. Through intercession.

"I have come to confirm what came before me of the Torah and make lawful to you some of the things that were forbidden to you. I have come to you with a sign from your Lord; so fear Allah and obey me."

50   "Allah is indeed your Lord and my Lord; so worship Him. This is the straight path!"

When Jesus sensed their disbelief, he said: "Who are my supporters in Allah's way?" The disciples said: "We are Allah's supporters; we believe in Allah, so bear witness that we submit."

"Lord, we believe in what You have revealed, and we have followed the Messenger; write us down with those who bear witness."

And they[219] contrived and Allah contrived; Allah is the best of the contrivers.

When Allah said: "O Jesus, I will cause you to die, will lift you up to Me, purify you from those who have disbelieved and place those who followed you above those who have disbelieved, till the Day of Resurrection. Then unto Me is your return, so that I may judge between you regarding what you were disputing."

55   "But as for those who disbelieved, I will sternly punish them in this world and the Hereafter, and they shall have no supporters."[220]

And as for those who have believed and done the good deeds, He will pay them their rewards in full. Allah does not love the evildoers.

This is what We recite[221] to you[222] of the revelations and wise reminder.[223]

Jesus in Allah's sight is like Adam; He created him from dust, then He said to him: "Be", and there he was.

[This is] the truth from your Lord; so do not be one of the doubters.

60   To those who dispute with it[224] after the knowledge which has come to you, say [to them]: "Come now; let us call our sons and your sons, our wives and your wives, ourselves and yourselves. Then let us pray to Allah and so call down Allah's curse upon the liars."

This indeed is the true story, and there is no god but Allah, and Allah is truly the Mighty and Wise!

And if they turn their backs, then Allah certainly knows the mischief-makers.

Say: "O People of the Book, come to an equitable word between you and us, that we worship none but Allah, do not associate anything with Him

219. The Jews.
220. No protectors.
221. Reveal.
222. Muhammad.
223. The Qur'an.
224. The truth regarding Jesus.

and do not set up each other as lords besides Allah." If they turn their backs, say: "Bear witness that we are Muslims."

O People of the Book, why do you dispute concerning Abraham, when the Torah and the Gospel were only revealed after him. Do you have no sense?

65   There, you have disputed concerning what you know; so why do you dispute concerning what you do not know? Allah knows and you do not know.

Abraham was neither a Jew nor a Christian, but a *hanif*[225] and a Muslim.[226] And he was not one of the polytheists.

Surely, the people who are worthiest of Abraham are those who followed him, together with this Prophet[227] and the believers. Allah is the Guardian of the believers!

A party of the People of the Book[228] wished that they would lead you astray; they only lead themselves astray without perceiving it.

O People of the Book, why do you disbelieve in Allah's revelations while you yourselves know that they are true?

70   People of the Book, why do you confound truth with error and knowingly conceal the truth?

Some of the People of the Book say: "Believe in what has been revealed to the believers at the beginning of the day, and disbelieve in it at its end; perchance they[229] will turn back!"

"And do not believe except in him who follows your religion." Say: "True guidance is Allah's guidance. [Do not believe] that anyone would be given what you have been given, or that they will dispute with you before your Lord." Say: "Bounty is in Allah's hands; He gives to whom He pleases, and Allah is All-Embracing, All-Knowing."

He favours with His mercy whomever He pleases. Allah's bounty is unlimited!

And among the People of the Book there are those who, if you entrust them with a heap of gold will return it to you; and there are those who, if you entrust them with one dinar, will not return it to you, unless you keep on demanding it. That is because they say: "We have no obligation towards the Gentiles";[230] and they knowingly speak falsehood against Allah.

75   Yea, whoever fulfils his pledge and is pious – truly Allah loves the pious!

---

225. This Arabic word means "one who turned away from paganism".
226. "Muslim" here stands for one who believes in the unity of Allah.
227. Muhammad.
228. The Jews.
229. The believers.
230. *Al-Ummiyun.*

Those who sell the covenant of Allah and their own oaths for a small price will have no share in the life to come; Allah will neither speak to them nor look at them nor purify them on the Day of Resurrection. A painful punishment is in store for them!

And there is a group of them who twist their tongues while reading the Book, so that you may suppose it is part of the Book; whereas it is not part of the Book. They also say: "It is from Allah", whereas it is not from Allah; they only speak falsehood against Allah knowingly.

It is not given to any mortal that Allah should give him the Book, the judgement and the prophethood and then he should say to the people: "Be servants to me, rather than to Allah"; but rather: "Be learned men, by virtue of what you used to teach of the Book and what you used to study."

Nor would He enjoin you to take the angels and the prophets as lords. Would He enjoin you to be unbelievers after you have become Muslims?

80 And when Allah made His covenant with the prophets, [He said]: "I gave you the Book and the Wisdom. Then an apostle[231] came to you confirming what you already possessed; so you must believe in him and give him support." He said: "Do you affirm this and accept My covenant in this matter?" They said: "We do affirm it." Then He said: "Bear witness and I will be with you one of the witnesses."

"Whoever turns his back thereafter; such are the true sinners."

Do they desire a religion other than Allah's, after everyone in the heavens and on earth has submitted to Him willingly or unwillingly; and unto Him they shall all be brought back!

Say: "We believe in Allah and in what has been revealed to us and has been revealed to Abraham, Isma'il, Isaac, Jacob and the Tribes; and in what Moses, Jesus and the prophets have received from their Lord. We do not discriminate between any of them, and to Him we submit."

Whoever seeks a religion other than Islam, it will never be accepted from him, and in the Hereafter he will be one of the losers.

85 How will Allah guide a people who disbelieved after they had believed and bore witness that the Apostle is true, and after the clear proofs had come to them? Allah will not guide the unjust people.

The reward of those people shall be that the curse of Allah, the angels and mankind as a whole shall be upon them.

They will abide therein forever; their punishment shall not be lightened and they shall have no respite.

Except for those who repent afterwards and mend their ways; for Allah is Forgiving and Merciful.

231. Muhammad.

Surely those who disbelieve after believing, and then grow in disbelief, their repentance shall not be accepted. Those are the ones who have gone astray!

90　As for those who disbelieve and die as unbelievers, the earth's fill of gold will not be accepted from any of them, even if it is offered as ransom. For those, a painful punishment is reserved and they will have no supporters!

You will not achieve piety until you spend part of what you cherish; and whatever you spend, Allah knows it very well.

All food was lawful to the Children of Israel, save what Israel forbade itself before the Torah was revealed. Say: "Bring then the Torah and recite it, if you are truthful."

Whoever, afterwards, fabricates falsehood against Allah, those are truly the evil-doers.

Say: "Allah has spoken the truth. Follow then the religion of Abraham, the upright; he was not one of the polytheists."

95　The first House founded for mankind is truly that at Bakka,[232] blessed and a guidance to all the nations.

Therein are clear signs and the sacred site of Abraham. Whoever enters it will be secure. It is the duty to Allah incumbent on those who can, to make the pilgrimage to the House. But with respect to those who disbelieve, Allah has no need of all mankind.

Say: "O People of the Book, why do you disbelieve in the revelations of Allah, when Allah witnesses whatever you do?"

Say: "O People of the Book, why do you debar those who have believed from the path[233] of Allah, seeking to make it crooked, while you are witnesses?[234] Allah is not unaware of what you do!"

O believers, if you obey a group of those who have received the Book, they will turn you, after you have believed, into unbelievers.

100　How could you disbelieve, while God's revelations are recited to you, and His Apostle is in your midst? He who holds fast to Allah has been guided to a straight path.

O believers, fear Allah as He should be feared, and do not die except as Muslims.

And hold fast to Allah's bond,[235] all of you, and do not fall apart. And remember Allah's grace upon you; how you were enemies, then He united your hearts[236] so that you have become, by His grace, brethren. You were on

232. Mecca.
233. The religion.
234. While you know it is the right religion.
235. His religion.
236. By becoming Muslims.

42

the brink of the pit of Fire, but He saved you from it. Thus Allah manifests to you His revelations so that perchance you might be rightly guided!

And let there be among you a nation calling to goodness, bidding the right and forbidding the wrong. Those are the prosperous.

And do not be like those who fell apart and quarrelled, after the clear proofs came to them. For those a terrible punishment is in store.

105   On the day when some faces will turn white and others will turn black. As to those whose faces turn black [it will be said]: "Did you disbelieve after you had believed? Then taste the punishment because you have disbelieved."

But as for those whose faces turned white, they will dwell in Allah's mercy[237] forever.

These are the revelations of Allah. We recite them to you in truth, and Allah does not desire any injustice for mankind.

And to Allah belongs what is in the heavens and on earth, and unto Him all matters shall be referred.

You were the best nation brought forth to mankind, bidding the right and forbidding the wrong, and believing in Allah. Had the People of the Book believed, it would have been far better for them; some of them are believers, but most of them are sinners.

110   They will only cause you a little harm; and if they fight you, they will turn their backs on you,[238] and will have no support.

Ignominy shall attend them wherever they are found, unless [they are bound] by a covenant from Allah and a covenant from the people. They will incur Allah's anger, and wretchedness shall be stamped on them, because they disbelieved in Allah's revelations and killed prophets unjustly. That is because they disobeyed and exceeded the limits.[239]

They are not all alike. For of the People of the Book, there is an upright nation[240] who recite Allah's revelations, throughout the night, while prostrating themselves.

They believe in Allah and the Last Day, bid the right and forbid the wrong and hasten to do the good deeds. Those are among the righteous people!

And whatever good they do, they will not be denied it. Allah knows well the God-fearing!

115   As for the unbelievers, neither their riches nor their children will avail them anything against Allah. Those are the people of Hell, abiding therein forever!

237. In Paradise.
238. In defeat.
239. By doing what is unlawful.
240. Group.

That which they spend in this present life is similar to a frosty wind which smote the harvest of a people who had wronged themselves, and so destroyed it. Allah did not wrong them, but they wronged themselves!

O believers, do not take as close friends other than your own people;[241] they will spare no effort to corrupt you and wish to see you suffer. Hatred has already been manifested in what they utter, but what their hearts conceal is greater still. We have made clear Our signs to you if only you understand.

There you are, you love them, but they do not love you, and you believe in the entire Book.[242] When they meet you, they say: "We believe", but when they are alone they bite their fingertips with rage. Say: "Die of your fury. Allah knows what is hidden in the hearts!"

If you are visited by some good fortune, it vexes them; and if you are visited by some misfortune, they rejoice at it; but if you forbear and fear Allah, their wiles will not hurt you at all. Allah knows fully what they do!

120 [And remember] when you[243] went at daybreak, away from your family, in order to lead the believers to their battle-stations;[244] Allah is All-Hearing, All-Knowing!

Two of your battalions[245] were about to lose heart, and Allah was their protector. In Allah let the believers put their trust!

Allah had already given you victory at Badr, at a time when you were still powerless; so fear Allah that perchance you might be thankful!

When you were telling the believers: "Is it not enough that your Lord should reinforce you with three thousand angels sent down?"

Yes, if you forbear and fear Allah and the enemy attack you at once, your Lord will reinforce you with five thousand marked angels.

125 Allah has not intended this except as good news to you and that your hearts might be reassured thereby. Victory comes only from Allah, the Mighty, the Wise!

That He may cut off a group of the unbelievers or humiliate them,[246] so that they may turn away completely baffled.

It is no business of yours whether Allah forgives them or punishes them; for they are indeed evil-doers!

And to Allah belongs what is in the heavens and on earth; He forgives

241. Other than your co-religionists.
242. In all Scriptures.
243. Muhammad.
244. The Prophet led them to the Battle of Uhud, 2 AH/625 AD to fight Abu Sufyan who had led his troops to attack Medina.
245. They belonged to Banu Salamah and Banu Harithah who formed the two wings of the Muslim army which was led by the Prophet.
246. Humiliate them by their defeat.

whom He pleases and punishes whom He pleases. Allah is All-Forgiving and Merciful!

O believers, do not devour usury, doubled and redoubled, and fear Allah that you may prosper!

130 And guard yourselves against the Fire which has been prepared for the unbelievers.

And obey Allah and the Apostle, that perchance you may find mercy.

And hasten to forgiveness from your Lord and a Paradise as wide as the heavens and the earth, prepared for the God-fearing;

Those who spend freely in prosperity and in adversity, those who curb their anger and those who pardon their fellow men. Allah loves the beneficent!

And those who, when they commit an indecency or wrong themselves, remember Allah and ask forgiveness for their sins. For who but Allah forgives sins? And they will not persist in what they do knowingly.

135 The reward of these is forgiveness from their Lord and gardens beneath which rivers flow, abiding therein forever. Blessed is the reward of the workers!

There have been examples[247] before you; so travel in the land and behold the fate of those who disbelieved.[248]

This is a declaration for mankind, a guidance and admonition for the God-fearing.

Do not be faint-hearted and do not grieve; you will have the upper hand, if you are true believers.

If you have been afflicted by a wound, a similar wound has afflicted the others.[249] Such are the times; We alternate them among the people, so that Allah may know who are the believers and choose martyrs from among you. Allah does not like the evildoers!

140 And that Allah might purify the believers and annihilate the unbelievers.

Or did you suppose that you will enter Paradise, before Allah has known who were those of you who have struggled, and those who are steadfast.

You were yearning for death before you actually met it. Now you have seen it and you are beholding it.

Muhammad is merely an apostle, before whom many apostles have come and gone. If then he dies or gets killed, you will turn on your heels? Should any man turn on his heels, he will not cause Allah any harm; and Allah will reward the thankful.

It is not given to any soul to die, except with Allah's leave, at a fixed time.

247. Examples of how Allah dealt with the unbelievers.
248. Who disbelieved the apostles.
249. The unbelievers.

He who desires the reward of this world, We will give him [part] of it, and he who desires the reward of the life to come, We will give him [part] of it; and We shall reward the thankful.

145 How many prophets with whom large multitudes have fought; they were not daunted on account of what befell them in the cause of Allah. They did not weaken or cringe; and Allah loves the steadfast!

Their only words were: "Lord, forgive us our sins and our excess in our affairs. Make firm our feet and grant us victory over the unbelieving people."

Therefore Allah granted them the reward of this life and the excellent reward[250] of the life to come, and Allah loves the beneficent!

O believers, if you obey the unbelievers, they will turn you upon your heels,[251] and thus you will become complete losers.

Rather, Allah is your Protector, and He is the best Supporter!

150 We will cast terror into the hearts of the unbelievers on account of their associating with Allah that for which He sent down no authority. Their abode is the Fire and wretched is the dwelling-place of the evildoers!

Allah fulfilled His promise to you when, by His leave, you went on killing them; until you lost heart and dissented about the affair and disobeyed,[252] after He had shown you what you cherished. Some of you desired this world,[253] others the Hereafter. Then, He turned you away from them[254] in order to test you, and He has forgiven you. Allah is Gracious to the believers!

[Remember] how you fled and paid heed to no one, while the Apostle was calling you from the rear. Thus He rewarded you with grief upon grief, lest you should not be sorry for what you missed or what befell you. Allah is aware of what you do!

Then He sent down upon you, after the grief, as a security, slumber overcoming a group of you, whereas another group were only concerned about themselves, entertaining untrue thoughts about Allah, like the thoughts of the pagans. They say: "Do we have any part in the affair?" Say: "The whole affair is Allah's." They conceal in their hearts what they do not reveal to you.

They say: "Had we had any part in the affair, we would not have been killed here." Say: "Had you been in your homes, those who were destined to be killed would have sallied forth to the places where they would be slain; so

250. Paradise.
251. Thus turning you back from your true religion.
252. This part refers to the Battle of Uhud. The Muslims were victorious until the archers disobeyed the Prophet's orders.
253. They left their position to get a share of the booty.
254. The Qurashite foes of the Muslims.

that Allah might purify what is in your hearts. Allah knows well what is hidden in the breasts."

155 Those of you, who fled on the day the two armies met, were made to slip by the Devil, on account of something they had done. However, Allah has forgiven them; Allah is indeed Forgiving and Merciful.

O believers, do not be like the unbelievers, who say about their brethren when they [die] while travelling abroad or fighting: "Had they stayed with us, they would not have died or been killed." Allah wished to make that a cause of anguish in their hearts. It is Allah who causes men to live and die, and Allah has knowledge of what you do!

And were you to be killed or to die in the way of Allah, forgiveness and mercy from Allah are far better than what they amass.

And were you to die or to be killed, it is unto Allah that you will be gathered.

It was by a mercy from Allah that you dealt leniently with them;[255] for had you been cruel and hard-hearted, they would have dispersed from around you. So, pardon them, ask Allah's forgiveness for them and consult them in the conduct of affairs. Then, when you are resolved, trust in Allah; Allah indeed loves those who trust [in Him].

160 If Allah supports you, no one will overcome you; but if He forsakes you, then who will be able to support you after Him? And in Allah let the believers put their trust!

It does not benefit any prophet to cheat;[256] for whoever cheats will bring the fruit of his dishonesty with him on the Day of Resurrection. Then, each soul shall be paid in full for what it earned;[257] and they will not be wronged.

What, is he who follows Allah's good pleasure like him who brings upon himself God's wrath? Hell is his refuge, and what a wretched destiny!

They[258] have different grades in Allah's sight; and Allah has knowledge of what they do!

Allah has been gracious to the believers, sending them an apostle from among themselves to recite to them His revelations, to purify them and to teach them the Book and the Wisdom, though they had been in manifest error before that.

165 And when a misfortune befell you[259] after you had inflicted twice as much,[260] you said: "Whence is this?"; say: "It is from yourselves." Surely Allah has power over everything!

255. Those Muslim fighters who flinched in the midst of the battle.
256. To cheat in handling the booty.
257. For its works.
258. The believers.
259. In the Battle of Uhud.
260. In the Battle of Badr.

And what befell you on the day the two armies met[261] was by Allah's leave, that He might know the true believers;

And that he might know the hypocrites. When it was said to them: "Come, fight in the way of Allah or defend yourselves", they replied: "If only we knew how to fight, we would have followed you." On that day, they were closer to disbelief than to belief. They say with their tongues what is not in their hearts; and Allah knows best what they conceal!

Those who said to their brethren, while they themselves stayed at home: "Had they obeyed us they would not have been killed?" Say: "Then ward off death from yourselves, if you are truthful."

And do not think those who have been killed in the way of Allah as dead; they are rather living with their Lord, well-provided for.

170 Rejoicing in what their Lord has given them of His bounty, and they rejoice for those who stayed behind and did not join them; knowing that they have nothing to fear and that they shall not grieve.

They rejoice in the grace of Allah and His favour, and that Allah will not withhold the reward of the faithful;

Those who responded to Allah's call and the Apostle's after they had incurred many wounds. To those of them who do what is right and fear Allah, a great reward is in store.

Those to whom the people said: "The people have been arrayed against you; so fear them." But this increased their faith and so they said: "Allah is sufficient for us. He is the best Guardian!"

Thus they came back with a grace and bounty from Allah. No harm touched them: and they complied with Allah's good pleasure. Allah's bounty is great!

175 That indeed is the Devil frightening his followers; but do not fear them and fear Me, if you are true believers!

And do not let those who hasten to disbelieve make you grieve. They will certainly not cause Allah any harm. Allah wishes not to give them any share in the Hereafter, and a terrible punishment awaits them!

Those who trade belief for disbelief will not cause Allah any harm, and a painful punishment awaits them!

Let the unbelievers not suppose that Our prolonging their days is better for them. We only prolong their days so that they may grow in sin, and a humbling punishment awaits them.

Allah will not leave the faithful in the state in which you are, until He separates the vile from the decent. Nor will Allah make known to you the unseen; but Allah chooses of His apostles whomever He pleases. Believe

---

261. In the Battle of Uhud.

then in Allah and His apostles; and if you believe and fear Allah, you will have a great reward.

180   And let not those who are niggardly in spending what God has given them of His bounty suppose that it is good for them. No, it is evil; they shall carry what they stinted around their necks on the Day of Resurrection. And to Allah belongs the inheritance of the heavens and the earth. Allah is aware of what you do!

Allah has heard the words of those who said: "Allah is poor, and we are rich." We shall write down what they said, together with their killing of the prophets unjustly, and We shall say: "Taste the torment of burning [in the Fire]!"

That is, on account of what your hands did earlier, and that Allah is not unjust to His servants;

Those who say: "Allah has actually commanded us not to trust a messenger until he brings us an offering consumed by the Fire." Say [to them]: "Messengers have already come to you with clear proofs[262] before me, together with what you asked for. Why then did you kill them, if you are truthful?"

If, however, they accuse you of lying, messengers who before you brought clear proofs,[263] the Scriptures and the illuminating Book were also accused of lying.

185   Every soul shall taste death; and you shall receive your rewards in full on the Day of Resurrection. Whoever is removed from Hell and is admitted to Paradise wins. Life in this world is nothing but an illusory pleasure.

You shall be tried in your possessions and yourselves, and shall hear from those who received the Book before you,[264] and from the idolaters, a lot of abuse; but if you forbear and guard against evil, that indeed is a mark of great determination.

And when Allah made a covenant with those who were given the Book: "You shall reveal it to mankind and not conceal it", they simply cast it behind their backs, and sold it for a small price. Evil then is their deal.

Do not think those who are pleased with what they have done and love to be praised for what they have not done, immune from punishment; a painful punishment is in store for them.

And to Allah belongs the kingdom of the heavens and the earth, and Allah has power over everything!

190   There are in the creation of the heavens and the earth and the alternation of night and day real signs for people of understanding.

---

262. Miracles.
263. Miracles.
264. The Jews and the Christians.

Those who remember Allah while standing, sitting or lying on their sides, reflecting upon the creation of the heavens and the earth [saying]: "Our Lord you did not create this in vain. Glory be to You! Save us from the torment of the Fire.

"Our Lord, he whom you throw into the Fire will be disgraced by You. The evildoers shall have no supporters.

"Our Lord, we have heard a caller summoning to belief, saying: 'Believe in your Lord'; and so we have believed. Lord, forgive us our sins and acquit us of our evil deeds and cause us to die with the pious.

"Lord, and give us what you promised us through your messengers, and do not disgrace us on the Day of Resurrection. Surely you will never break a promise."

195 And so their Lord answered them saying: "Indeed, I will not cause the loss of the work of any worker among you, whether male or female; you come one from the other." Those who have emigrated[265] and were driven out of their homes, were persecuted for My sake, fought and were killed, I will forgive their sins and will admit them into gardens, beneath which rivers flow, as a reward from Allah. With Allah is the best reward!

Do not be deceived by the wanderings[266] of those who disbelieved in the land;

A little enjoyment, and then their abode is Hell; and what a wretched resting-place!

However, those who fear their Lord will have gardens, beneath which rivers flow, abiding therein forever, as a bounty from Allah. What Allah has is far better for the righteous.

Of the People of the Book, there are some who indeed believe in Allah and in what has been revealed to you[267] or has been revealed to them, humbling themselves before Allah and not selling Allah's revelations for a small price. Those will have their reward with their Lord; indeed Allah's reckoning is swift.

200 O believers, forbear and vie in forbearance and steadfastness; and fear Allah so that you may prosper!

265. The Meccan Muslims who, because of persecution, emigrated to Medina.
266. For business purposes.
267. The Qur'an.

SURA 4

Al-Nisa', Women

In the Name of Allah, the Compassionate, the Merciful

1 O people, fear your Lord who created you from a single soul,[268] and from it He created its mate,[269] and from both He scattered abroad many men and women; and fear Allah in whose name you appeal to one another, and invoke family relationships. Surely Allah is a watcher over you.

Render unto the orphans their property and do not exchange worthless things for good ones, and do not devour their property together with your property. That indeed is a great sin!

If you fear that you cannot deal justly with the orphans, then marry such of the women as appeal to you, two, three or four; but if you fear that you cannot be equitable, then only one, or what your right hands own.[270] That is more likely to enable you to avoid unfairness.[271]

And give women their dowries as a free gift, but if they choose to give you anything of it, then consume it with enjoyment and pleasure.

5 But do not give the feeble-minded the property that Allah assigned to you as a means of livelihood. Provide for them therefrom, clothe them and speak kindly to them.

Test the orphans until they reach the age of marriage; then, if you discern in them sound judgement, deliver to them their property; and do not consume it extravagantly and hastily before they come of age. He who is rich should be abstinent, and he who is poor should consume fairly. And when you deliver to them their property, call in witnesses thereon. God suffices as a Reckoner!

Men should have a share of what parents and kinsmen leave behind; and women a share of what parents and kinsmen leave, whether small or large, as an obligatory portion.

And if the division is attended by kinsmen, orphans or poor men, then give them a share of it and speak to them kindly.

268. Adam.
269. Eve.
270. Captives of war or slave-girls.
271. It should be noted that this verse permits polygamy under special circumstances, but does not enjoin it. No less important is the fact that this verse was revealed following the Battle of Uhud in which seventy Muslim fighters were killed, leaving many widows and other dependants without a provider for them. Hence most commentators regard the permission as an exception and not a rule.

And let those who worry about the weak offspring they may leave behind them[272] be mindful [of the orphans]. Let them fear Allah and speak justly.

10 Those who devour the property of orphans unjustly, devour fire in their bellies, and they will burn in a blazing fire.

Allah commands you, with respect to your children, that the male shall inherit the equivalent of the share of two females. If there be more than two females, then they should receive two-thirds of what he[273] leaves; but if there is only one female, she is entitled to one-half. To each of his parents, one-sixth of what he leaves, if he has any children; but if he has no children, then his parents will inherit him, the mother receiving one-third. But if he has any brothers, then his mother receives one-sixth, after any will he had made or any debt he had incurred [is taken care of]. Your fathers and sons – you know not who of them is of greater advantage to you. This is a law from Allah; Allah surely is All-Knowing, Wise.

You are entitled to half of what your wives leave, if they have no children; but if they have any children, then you are entitled to one-quarter of what they leave, after any will they had made or any loan they had incurred [is taken care of]. And they are entitled to one-quarter of what you leave, if you have no children; but if you have any children, then they are entitled to one-eighth of what you leave, after any will you had made or loan you had incurred [is taken care of]. And if a man or a woman dies having no children or parents, but has a brother or a sister, then each shall have one-sixth; if they are more than that, then they shall share one-third, after any will made or debt incurred [is taken care of] without prejudice. This is a commandment from Allah, and Allah is All-Knowing, Wise.

These are the ordinances of Allah, and whoever obeys Allah and His Apostle, He will admit him into gardens beneath which rivers flow, abiding therein forever. That is the great victory!

But whoever disobeys Allah and His Apostle and transgresses His bounds, He will admit him into the Fire, wherein he shall abide forever, and his will be a demeaning punishment!

15 As for those of your women who commit adultery, call four witnesses from your own against them; and if they testify, then detain them in the houses till death overtakes them or Allah opens another way for them.[274]

If two [men] of you commit it, punish them both. If they repent and mend their ways, then leave them alone. Allah is truly All-Forgiving, Merciful.

---

272. That is, after their death.
273. The deceased father.
274. This verse was later abrogated and replaced by a hundred lashes for the unmarried and stoning for the married. See Sura 24, verse 2.

Allah has taken upon Himself to accept the repentance of those who commit evil in ignorance and then repent immediately after that. Those, He will forgive and Allah is All-Knowing, Wise.

But not the repentance of those who commit evil deeds, and when one of them is faced with death, he says: "Now I repent"; nor the repentance of those who die as unbelievers. For these, we have prepared a very painful punishment!

O believers, it is not lawful for you to inherit the women [of deceased kinsmen] against their will;[275] nor restrain them in order to take away part of what you had given them, unless they commit flagrant adultery. Associate with them kindly; and if you feel aversion towards them, it may well be that you will be averse to something, from which Allah brings out a lot of good.

20   If you wish to have one wife in the place of another and you have given either of them a heap of gold, do not take any of it back. Would you take it by recourse to injustice and manifest sin?

For how can you take it back, when you have been intimate one with the other, and they had taken from you a solemn pledge?

And do not marry women that your fathers had married, unless it has already happened. Surely it is indecent and hateful, and it is an evil course!

Unlawful to you are your mothers, your daughters, your sisters, your paternal and maternal aunts, your brother's daughters and sister's daughters, your foster-mothers who gave you suck, your foster-sisters, your wives' mothers, your step-daughters who are in your custody, born to your wives whom you have lain with. But if you have not lain with them, then you are not at fault. [It is also not lawful to marry] the wives of your sons who are of your own loins, or to take in two sisters together, unless this has already happened. Allah is truly All-Forgiving and Merciful!

Or married women, except those your right hands possess.[276] This is Allah's decree for you. Beyond these it is lawful for you to seek, by means of your wealth, any women, to marry and not to debauch. Those of them you have enjoyed, you should give them their dowries as a matter of obligation; but you are not liable to reproach for whatever you mutually agree upon, apart from the obligatory payment.[277] Allah is indeed All-Knowing, Wise!

25   Whoever of you cannot afford to marry a free, believing woman, let him choose from whatever your right hands possess[278] of believing girls. Allah

275. The women of deceased relatives. Among the pre-Islamic Arabs, it was the custom that when a man died, his elder son or other relatives had the right to "own" his widow or widows. Then they either married them, themselves, without giving a dowry, or married them to others, or prohibited them from marriage.
276. The captives of war or slave-girls.
277. The dowry.
278. The captives of war or slave-girls.

knows best your faith; you come one from the other. So marry them with their parents' leave and give them their dowry honourably, as chaste women, neither committing adultery nor taking lovers. If they are legally married and commit adultery, their punishment shall be half that of a free woman. Such is the law for those of you who fear committing sin; but to abstain is better for you. Allah is All-Forgiving and Merciful!

Allah wants to explain to you [His laws] and to guide you along the paths of those who preceded you, and to be Merciful to you. Allah is All-Knowing, Wise!

Allah also wants to be Merciful to you, but those who follow their lusts want you to deviate greatly from the right course.

Allah wishes to lighten your burden; for man was created weak.

O believers, do not consume your wealth illegally, unless there be trading by mutual agreement among you; and do not kill yourselves. Allah is indeed Merciful to you!

30   And whoever acts aggressively and wrongfully, We shall cast him in the Fire; this being an easy matter for Allah.

If you avoid the grave sins you are forbidden, We will remit your evil deeds and let you enter into an honourable place.[279]

Do not covet that with which Allah has favoured some of you over the others. Men have a share of what they earned, and women a share of what they earned. And ask Allah to give you of His bounty. Allah indeed has knowledge of everything!

To every one We have appointed heirs to inherit part of what the parents or the kinsmen bequeath. Those with whom you made a compact, give them their share. Surely Allah is witness to everything.

Men are in charge of women, because Allah has made some of them excel the others, and because they spend some of their wealth. Hence righteous women are obedient, guarding the unseen which Allah has guarded. And those of them that you fear might rebel, admonish them and abandon them in their beds and beat them. Should they obey you, do not seek a way of harming them; for Allah is Sublime and Great!

35   And if you fear a breach between the two,[280] then send forth an arbiter from his relatives and another arbiter from her relatives. If they both desire reconciliation, Allah will bring them together. Allah is indeed All-Knowing, Well-informed.

Worship Allah and do not associate with Him anything. Show kindness to the parents, to kinsmen, to orphans, the destitute, the close and distant

---

279. That is, into Paradise.
280. The husband and wife.

neighbour, the companion by your side, the wayfarer and those whom your right hands possess. Allah does not love the arrogant and boastful,

Those who are niggardly, and order people to be niggardly, and conceal what Allah has given them of His bounty, We have prepared for the unbelievers a demeaning punishment;

And for those who spend their wealth in order to show off, and do not believe in Allah and the Last Day. He who has the Devil as a companion, an evil companion has he!

And what would it cost them were they to believe in Allah and the Last Day and spend part of what Allah has provided for them? Allah knows them very well!

40   Surely Allah will not wrong anyone an atom's weight; and if it is a good deed, He will multiply it and give from Himself in addition a great reward.

How then will it be, when We bring forward from each nation a witness[281] and We bring you[282] forth as a witness against them?

On that day, those who disbelieved and disobeyed the Apostle will wish that the earth were levelled upon them, and they will conceal nothing from Allah.

O believers, do not approach prayer while you are drunk, until you know what you say; nor when you are unclean – unless you are on a journey – until you have washed yourselves. And if you are sick or on a journey, or if any one of you has relieved himself, or you have touched women and could not find water, you might rub yourselves with clean earth, wiping your faces and hands with it. Allah indeed is Pardoning, All-Forgiving!

Have you not considered those who have received a portion of the Book, procuring error and wanting you to go astray?

45   Allah knows best your enemies; Allah suffices as Protector, Allah suffices as Supporter!

Some of the Jews take words out of their context and say: "We have heard, but disobey; and hear as though you hear not." And [they] say: "*ra'ina*",[283] twisting their tongues and slandering religion. Had they said: "We have heard and we obey: hear and look at us", it would have been better for them and more upright; but Allah has cursed them on account of their disbelief, so they – except for a few – do not believe.

O People of the Book, believe in what We have revealed confirming what you already possess, before We obliterate faces, turning them on their backs, or curse them as We have cursed the Sabbath-breakers, and Allah's command was accomplished!

281. Its prophet.
282. Muhammad.
283. A word of abuse.

Allah will not forgive associating [other gods] with Him, but will forgive anything less than that to whom He pleases. And he who associates other gods with Allah has committed a very grave sin.

Have you considered those who regard themselves as pure? Rather, only Allah will purify those whom He pleases, and they will not be wronged a whit.

50 Behold, how they invent falsehood about Allah; and that in itself is a manifest sin!

Have you not considered those who received a portion of the Book? They believe in idols and demons, and they say to the unbelievers: "Those are more rightly guided than those who believe."

Those are the ones whom Allah has cursed; and whomever Allah curses will have no supporter.

Or do they have a share in the kingdom? If so, they will not give the people a speck on a date-stone.

Or do they envy the people[284] for what Allah has given them of His bounty? For We have given Abraham's family the Book and the Wisdom and bestowed on them a great kingdom.

55 Some of them believed in him, others rejected him. Sufficient is the scourge of Hell.

Those who have disbelieved Our signs, We shall surely cast them into the Fire; every time their skins are burnt, We will replace them by other skins, so that they might taste the punishment. Allah indeed is Mighty and Wise!

As to those who have believed and do the good works, We shall admit them into gardens, beneath which rivers flow, abiding therein forever. They have therein purified spouses, and We will admit them to a very shady place.

God commands you to deliver trusts to their owners and, if you judge between people, to judge justly. Splendid is Allah's exhortation to you. Allah is indeed All-Hearing, All-Seeing.

O believers, obey Allah and obey the Apostle and those in authority among you. Should you quarrel over any matter, then refer it to Allah and the Apostle, if you really believe in Allah and the Last Day. That is far better for you and fairer in interpretation.

60 Have you not seen those who pretend that they believe in what has been revealed to you and what was revealed before you? They wish to submit their disputes to the Devil,[285] although they have been commanded to denounce him; but the Devil wishes to lead them far astray!

And if it is said to them: "Turn now to what Allah has revealed and to the Apostle", you will find the hypocrites turning away from you with aversion.

---

284. The reference here, according to some commentaries, is to the Arabs.

285. The reference here is said to be to a Jew called Ka'b Ibn al-Ashraf, who was a bitter enemy of the Muslims.

How then if they are afflicted with a disaster on account of what their own hands perpetrated, they come to you swearing by Allah: "We only sought kindness and conciliation"?

Allah knows what is in the hearts of those ones; so leave them alone, admonish them and say to them effective words about themselves.

We have not sent forth an apostle, but that he may be obeyed by Allah's leave. And had they, having wronged themselves, come to you and asked for Allah's forgiveness and the Apostle had asked forgiveness for them, then they would have found Allah All-Forgiving, Merciful.

65 But no, by your Lord, they will not believe until they call you to arbitrate in their dispute; then they will not be embarrassed regarding your verdict and will submit fully.

And had We commanded them: "Slay yourselves or go forth from your homes", they would not have done it, except for a few of them; but had they done what they were exhorted to do,[286] it would have been far better for them and more reinforcing.

And then We would surely have bestowed on them a great reward from ourselves.

And We would have guided them to a straight path.

Those who obey Allah and the Apostle will be in the company of those whom God has favoured of the prophets, the saints, the martyrs and the righteous people. What excellent companions they are!

70 Such is the bounty of Allah; Allah suffices as Knower.

O believers, be on your guard; so march in detachments or march all together.

Indeed, among you is the one who will stay behind, so that if a disaster befalls you, he will say: "Allah has favoured me, since I have not been a martyr with them."

If, however, a bounty from God comes to you, he will say, as though there was no friendship between you and him: "Would that I had been with them; then I would have won a great victory."

So let those who sell the present life for the life to come fight in the way of Allah. Whoever fights in the way of Allah and is killed or conquers, We shall accord him a great reward.

75 And why don't you fight for the cause of God and for the down-trodden, men, women and children, who say: "Lord, bring us out of this city[287] whose inhabitants are unjust and grant us, from You, a protector, and grant us, from You, a supporter."

286. That is, to obey the Prophet.
287. Mecca.

Those who believe fight for the cause of Allah, and those who disbelieve fight on behalf of the Devil. Fight then the followers of the Devil. Surely the guile of the Devil is weak.

Have you not seen those to whom it was said: "Hold back your hands, perform the prayer and give the alms-tax"; but when they were ordered to fight, a group of them appeared to fear men just as they fear Allah, or even more. They said: "Lord, why have you ordered us to fight? If only you would grant us respite for a short period." Say: "The pleasure of this world is small and the Hereafter is far better for the God-fearing; and you will not be wronged a whit."

Wherever you may be, death will overtake you, even if you are in high towers. And if a good fortune befalls them[288] they say: "This is from Allah." But when misfortune befalls them, they say: "It is from you."[289] Say: "All is from Allah." What is the matter with those people who barely understand any discourse!

Whatever good visits you, it is from Allah; and whatever evil befalls you, it is from yourself; and We have sent you[290] forth to mankind as an apostle. Allah is the All-Sufficient Witness!

80 Whoever obeys the Apostle actually obeys Allah. As for those who turn away, We have not sent you to be their keeper.

They say: "Obedience"; but when they leave you, a group of them secretly plan something other than what you say. Allah writes down what they have in mind. So, shun them and put your trust in Allah; Allah is the All-Sufficient Guardian.

Do they not, then, ponder over the Qur'an? Had it been from someone other than Allah, they would have found in it many inconsistencies.

And when a matter of security or fear reaches them, they broadcast it; but had they referred it to the Apostle or the people in authority among them,[291] those of them who investigate it would comprehend it. Had it not been for Allah's bounty to you and His mercy, you would all surely have followed the Devil, except for a few.

So, fight for the cause of Allah; you are charged only of yourself. Urge the believers on that Allah may perchance restrain the unbelievers' might. Allah's might is greater, and greater is His retribution!

85 He who offers a good intercession[292] shall have a share[293] of it; and he who offers a bad intercession shall suffer from its consequences. Allah has power over everything!

288. The Jews.
289. That is, Muhammad.
290. Muhammad.
291. That is, to the Companions of the Prophet.
292. That is, he who intercedes for people in accordance with Muslim law.
293. That is, he shall have a part of the reward.

And when you are greeted with a certain greeting, greet back with a better one or return it; for Allah keeps count of everything!

Allah, there is no god but He. He will gather you all together on the Day of Resurrection; there is no doubt about it. And who is more truthful than Allah?

How is it that you are divided into two parties regarding the hypocrites, when Allah turned them back[294] on account of what they earned?[295] Do you wish to guide those whom Allah leads astray? He whom Allah leads astray, you will not find a way out for him.

They wish that you disbelieve, as they have disbelieved, so that you will all be alike. Do not, then, take any companions from them, until they emigrate in the way of Allah. Then should they turn back, seize them and kill them wherever you find them; and do not take from them any companion or supporter;

90   Except for those who seek refuge with a people with whom you are bound by a compact, or come to you because their hearts forbid them to fight you or fight their own people. Had Allah wished, He would have made them dominate you; and then they would have certainly fought you. If, however, they leave you alone and do not fight you and offer you peace, then Allah allows you no way against them.

You shall find others who wish to be secure from you and secure from their own people; yet, whenever they are called back to sedition[296] they plunge into it. If these do not keep away from you, nor offer you peace, nor hold their hands back, then seize them and kill them wherever you find them. Those, We have given you clear authority over them.

It is not given to a believer to kill another believer except by mistake; and he who kills a believer by mistake should free a slave who is a believer and pay blood-money to his relatives, unless they remit it as alms. If he happens to belong to a people who are your enemies, but he is a believer, then you should free a believing slave. If he belongs to a people bound with you by a compact, then blood-money should be paid to his relatives and a believing slave should be freed. As for him who has not the means, he should fast for two consecutive months, as a penance from Allah. Allah is All-Knowing, Wise!

And he who kills a believer intentionally will, as punishment, be thrown into Hell, dwelling in it forever; and Allah will be angry with him, curse him and prepare for him a dreadful punishment.

O believers, if you journey in the way of Allah, be discerning and do not

---

294. Turned them back to disbelief.
295. That is, on account of their sins and disbelief.
296. That is, to polytheism.

say to him who greets you: "You are not a believer", seeking the fleeting goods of the present life. For with Allah are abundant gains. This is how you were before and Allah has been gracious to you; so discern well. Allah is indeed fully aware of what you do!

95   Those of the believers who stay at home while suffering from no injury are not equal to those who fight for the cause of Allah with their possessions and persons. Allah has raised those who fight with their possessions and persons one degree over those who stay at home; and to each Allah has promised the fairest good. Yet Allah has granted a great reward to those who fight and not to those who stay behind.

Degrees of honour from Him, forgiveness and mercy. Allah is All-Forgiving, Merciful.

Those whom the angels cause to die while they are unjust to themselves[297] will be asked [by the angels]: "What were you doing?" They will say: "We were oppressed in the land." They [the angels] will add saying: "Was not Allah's land spacious enough for you to emigrate to some other part?" Those people – their refuge is Hell, and what a wretched destiny!"

Except the oppressed men, women and children who have no recourse and cannot find a way out.[298]

Those, Allah may pardon them; Allah is All-Pardoning, All-Forgiving.

100   He who emigrates for the cause of Allah will find on earth many a place of refuge and abundance; and he who leaves his home as an emigrant to Allah and His Apostle and is then overtaken by death, has already earned his reward from Allah. Allah is All-Forgiving, Merciful!

And when you journey in the land, you are not at fault if you shorten the prayer for fear that the unbelievers will harm you. The unbelievers are your manifest enemies.

When you[299] are among them,[300] conducting the prayer for them, let a group of them rise with you and let them take their weapons; but when they have prostrated themselves, let them withdraw to the rear; and let another party who had not prayed come forward and pray with you, taking their precaution and carrying their weapons. The unbelievers wish that you would neglect your arms and your equipment, so that they may swoop down on you in a united attack. You are not at fault, however, if you lay aside your weapons in case you are hampered by rain or are sick; but take heed. Allah has prepared for the unbelievers a demeaning punishment.

When you have completed the prayer, remember Allah standing, sitting

---

297. The reference is to those Meccas who could have accepted the faith and emigrated, but did not.
298. The reference here is to those Meccas who were weak and could not emigrate.
299. Muḥammad.
300. The faithful.

and reclining. Once you feel secure, then perform the prayer; for prayer is enjoined on the believers at fixed times.

Do not be weak-hearted in pursuing the enemy. If you are suffering, they are suffering too; but you hope from Allah what they cannot hope. Allah is All-Knowing, Wise.

105 We have revealed the Book to you in truth, so as to judge between people in accordance with what Allah has shown you. And do not be an advocate of the treacherous!

And ask Allah's forgiveness; Allah is indeed All-Forgiving, Merciful!

And do not plead on behalf of those who betray themselves; for Allah does not like the treacherous or sinful.

They seek to hide themselves from men, but they cannot hide themselves from Allah; for He is with them while they secretly contemplate words that do not please Him. And Allah is fully aware of what they do!

There you are, you have pleaded on their behalf in the present world; who then will plead with Allah on their behalf on the Day of Resurrection, or who will be their Guardian?

110 But he, who does evil or wrongs himself, then asks Allah's forgiveness, will find Allah All-Forgiving, Merciful.

And whoever commits a sin, will only commit it against himself. Allah is All-Knowing, Wise!

And whoever commits an offence or a sin then charges an innocent man with it bears the burden of a falsehood and a manifest sin.

And, but for Allah's bounty and mercy upon you,[301] a group of them would have tried to lead you astray; however, they only lead themselves astray. They do not cause you any harm. Allah has revealed to you the Book and the Wisdom and taught you what you did not know, and Allah's goodness to you has been great.

There is no good in much of their secret talk, except for him who enjoins charity, kindness or conciliation between people. Whoever does that seeking God's good pleasure, We will surely grant him a great reward.

115 But he who opposes the Apostle after the guidance has been manifested to him, and follows a path other than that of the believers, We will let him follow the way he has chosen for himself, and throw him into Hell; and what a wretched fate!

Allah will not forgive associating [any other god] with Him, but will forgive anything less than that, to whomever He wills. He who associates [any other god] with Allah, has really gone very far astray!

301. Muhammad.

Apart from Him, they only invoke[302] the goddesses of Quraysh; they only invoke a rebellious devil,[303]

Cursed by Allah. For he[304] said: "I shall take from your servants for myself a fixed number,

"And I will lead them astray, will raise their expectations and order them to cut off the cattle's ears. I will order them to alter Allah's creation." Whoever takes the Devil for a companion, instead of Allah, has incurred a grave loss!

120 He promises them and raises their expectations; but the Devil promises them nothing but illusion.

Those people, their shelter shall be Hell and they shall find no escape from it.

But those who have believed and done the good deeds, We shall admit them into gardens beneath which rivers flow, dwelling therein forever. This is Allah's true promise; and who is more truthful in speech than Allah?

It will not be in accordance with your wishes or the wishes of the People of the Book. Whoever does evil shall be requited for it and will not find, apart from Allah, a friend or supporter.

And whoever does some good deeds, whether male or female, and is a believer – those shall be admitted to Paradise and shall not be wronged a whit.

125 And who has a better religion than one who submits himself to Allah, does right and follows the true religion of Abraham the upright one? Allah has taken Abraham for a friend.

To Allah belongs what is in the heavens and on earth, and Allah encompasses everything!

They consult you concerning women. Say: "Allah has instructed you concerning them, and concerning what is recited to you in the Book regarding orphan women for whom you do not give what is prescribed for them, although you wish to marry them, and concerning the weak children, and your duty to deal justly with orphans.[305] For whatever good you do, Allah knows it very well."

And if a woman fears maltreatment or aversion from her husband, they[306] would not commit an offence if they are reconciled amicably; reconciliation is best. Souls are prone to avarice, and if you are charitable and if you ward off evil, He is surely well aware of what you do!

You will never be able to treat wives equitably, even if you are bent on

302. What is meant here is worship.
303. Satan.
304. The Devil.
305. When considering the dowry and inheritance.
306. She and her husband.

doing that. So do not turn away altogether [from any of them] leaving her, like one in suspense; and if you do justice [to her] and guard against evil, He[307] is surely All-Forgiving, Merciful!

130 And if they separate, Allah will give each one plenty of His abundance; and Allah is Munificent, Wise.

And to Allah belongs what is in the heavens and on earth. We have enjoined those who received the Book before you, as well as yourselves: "Fear Allah, and if you disbelieve, surely to Allah belongs what is in the heavens and on earth. Allah is All-Sufficient, Praiseworthy."

To Allah belongs what is in the heavens or on earth, and Allah suffices as Guardian!

If Allah wants, O people, He would annihilate you and replace you by others. Allah has the power to do that.

Whoever desires the reward of this world, [let him know that] with Allah is the reward of this world and the next. Allah is All-Hearing, All-Seeing!

135 O believers, be upholders of justice, witnesses for Allah, even if it be against yourselves, your parents or kinsmen. Whether rich or poor, Allah takes better care of both. Do not follow your desire to refrain from justice. If you twist [your testimony] or turn away, Allah is fully aware of what you do.

O believers, believe in Allah and His Apostle and in the Book which He revealed to His Apostle, and the Book which He revealed before. Whoever disbelieves in Allah, His angels, His Books, His prophets and the Last Day has gone far astray.

Those who believe, then disbelieve, then again believe, then disbelieve, then grow in disbelief, Allah shall not forgive them nor guide them to the right path.

Announce to the hypocrites that a very painful punishment is reserved for them.

Those who take the unbelievers as friends, instead of the believers – do they seek glory from them? For all glory belongs to Allah.

140 He has revealed to you in the Book that, should you hear the revelations of Allah being denied or mocked, you should not sit with them until they engage in some other discussion. Otherwise, you are like them. Allah shall assemble all the hypocrites and the unbelievers in Hell;

Those who wait for [misfortune to befall] you. And if a victory is accorded to you from Allah, they will say: "Were we not on your side?"; and if the unbelievers have a share [in victory], they will say: "Did we not subdue you, and thus protect you from the believers?" Allah shall judge

307. Allah.

between you on the Day of Resurrection; and Allah will not give the unbelievers the upper hand over the believers.

Surely, the hypocrites seek to deceive Allah, but Allah causes their deceit to backfire. And if they rise to perform the prayer, they rise lazily, trying to show off in public and they remember Allah but little.

Vacillating between the two,[308] inclining neither to these nor to those;[309] and whomever Allah leads astray, you will not find him a way out.

O believers, do not take the unbelievers for friends, instead of the believers. Do you wish to give Allah a clear proof against you?

145 Surely, the hypocrites will be in the lowest depths of the Fire, and you will not find any supporter for them.

Except for those who repent and mend their ways, hold fast to Allah and are sincere in their obedience to Allah – those will be among the believers; and Allah shall grant the believers a great reward.

Why should Allah punish you, if you are thankful and faithful? Allah Himself is Thankful, All-Knowing.

Allah does not like the public uttering of foul words, except by one who has been wronged. Allah is All-Hearing, All-Knowing.

Whether you do good openly or secretly, or pardon an evil deed, Allah is indeed All-Pardoning, All-Powerful.

150 Those who disbelieve in Allah and His apostles and want to make a distinction between Allah and His apostles, and say: "We believe in some and disbelieve in the others", wanting to take a middle course in between,

Those are the true unbelievers, and We have prepared for the unbelievers a demeaning punishment.

But those who believe in Allah and His apostles and do not discriminate between any of them – those He will grant them their rewards. Allah is All-Forgiving, Merciful!

The People of the Book ask you to bring down a book from heaven for them; indeed, they asked Moses for greater than that, saying: "Show us God face to face." Thereupon the thunderbolt struck them for their wickedness. Then, they worshipped the calf, after they had received the clear proofs. Yet We pardoned all that and We gave Moses clear authority.

And We raised the Mount [Sinai] over them, in view of their covenant, and We said to them: "Enter the door prostrate", and We also said: "Do not transgress on the Sabbath", taking from them a solemn pledge.

155 But because they broke their covenant, disbelieved in Allah's revelations, killed the prophets unjustly, and said: "Our hearts are sealed", Allah has

308. Belief and disbelief.

309. That is, neither to the believers nor to the unbelievers.

sealed them on account of their disbelief. So they do not believe, except for a few!

And for their disbelief and their imputing to Mary a great falsehood;

And their saying: "We have killed the Messiah, Jesus, son of Mary and the apostle of Allah." They neither killed nor crucified him; but it was made to appear so unto them. Indeed, those who differ about him are in doubt about it. Their knowledge does not go beyond conjecture, and they did not kill him for certain;

Rather Allah raised him unto Him. Allah is Mighty, and Wise.

None of the People of the Book will believe in him[310] before his death, and on the Day of Resurrection he[311] will be a witness against them.

160   And it was on account of the wrongdoing of the Jews that We forbade them certain good things which had been lawful to them; as well as on account of their frequent debarring [of people] from Allah's path;

Their taking usury, although they had been forbidden from doing it and their devouring other people's wealth unjustly. We have prepared for the unbelievers among them a very painful punishment!

But those firmly rooted in knowledge among them and the believers do believe in what was revealed to you and what was revealed before you. Those who perform the prayers, give the alms and believe in Allah and the Last Day – to these We shall grant a great reward!

We have revealed to you, as We revealed to Noah and the prophets after him. And We revealed to Abraham, Isma'il, Isaac, Jacob and the Tribes; and to Jesus, Job, Jonah, Aaron and Solomon; and We gave David a Book.[312]

And [We sent forth] some apostles We have already told you about, and some We have not told you about. And Allah spoke to Moses directly.

165   Apostles, who were bearers of good news and warners,[313] so that mankind will have no plea against Allah, after the apostles' coming. Allah is Mighty and Wise!

But Allah bears witness[314] by what He has revealed to you, that He revealed it with His knowledge. The angels bear witness too, and Allah suffices as a witness!

Indeed, those who disbelieve and debar others from the path of Allah have gone far astray!

Those who disbelieve and act unjustly, Allah will never forgive them nor lead them to any path,

---

310. Jesus.
311. Jesus.
312. Zaburan, i.e. the psalms.
313. Bearers of good news to the believers and warners to the unbelievers.
314. Bears witness to your [Muhammad's] prophethood.

Other than the path of Hell, abiding therein forever. That for Allah is an easy matter!

170   O mankind, the Apostle has come to you with the truth from your Lord. If you believe, it would be better for you; but if you disbelieve then surely to Allah belongs what is in the heavens and on the earth. Allah is All-Knowing, Wise.

O People of the Book, do not exceed the bounds of your religion, nor say about Allah except the truth. The Messiah, Jesus, son of Mary, is only Allah's apostle and His word which He imparted to Mary, and is a spirit from Him! So believe in Allah and His apostles and do not say "three" [gods]. Refrain; it is better for you. Allah is truly one God. How – glory be to Him – could he have a son? To Him belongs what is in the heavens and on earth. Allah suffices as a Guardian!

The Messiah does not disdain to be a servant of Allah, nor do the angels nearest to Him. And those who disdain to worship Him, and are arrogant, He shall gather all unto Himself!

But as for those who believe and do good deeds, He will give them their rewards in full and will increase them from His bounty. And as for those who disdain and are arrogant, He will inflict on them a very painful punishment, and they will not find for themselves, apart from Allah, any friend or supporter.

O people, a proof from your Lord has come to you, and We sent down to you a clear light.[315]

175   As for those who believe in Allah and hold fast to Him, He will admit them into mercy and bounty from Him and guide them to Himself along a straight path.

[If] they consult you, say: "Allah enjoins you regarding him who dies leaving neither children nor parents. If he leaves a sister, she is entitled to half of what he leaves behind; and he inherits her if she has no children. If he leaves two sisters, they are entitled to two-thirds of what he leaves behind; but if they are brothers and sisters, the male will have the equivalent of the share of two females. Allah makes it clear to you lest you go astray. Allah has full knowledge of everything!"

---

315. The Qur'an.

SURA 5

Al-Ma'ida, The Table

In the Name of Allah, the Compassionate, the Merciful

1 O believers, fulfil your obligations. Lawful to you are the beasts of the flock, except what is being recited to you now: "Game is unlawful to you while you are on pilgrimage." Allah decrees whatever He pleases.

O believers, do not violate the rites of Allah, or the sacred month, or the sacrificial offerings, or the animals with garlands, or those who repair to the Sacred House, seeking the bounty and pleasure of their Lord. When you are through with the rites of pilgrimage, you can go hunting. And let not the hatred of those who debar you from the Sacred Mosque prompt you to transgress. Help one another in righteousness and piety, but not in sin and aggression. Fear Allah; Allah is severe in retribution.

You are forbidden the eating of carrion, blood, the flesh of swine as well as whatever is slaughtered in the name of any one other than Allah. [You are forbidden] also the animals strangled or beaten to death, those that fall and die, those killed by goring with the horn or mangled by wild beasts, except those which you slaughter and those sacrificed on stones set up [for idols]. [You are forbidden] to use divining arrows;[316] it is an evil practice. Today, those who disbelieve have despaired of your religion; so do not fear them, but fear Me. Today, I have perfected your religion for you, completed My grace on you and approved Islam as a religion for you. Yet, whoever is compelled by reason of hunger,[317] but not intending to sin, then surely Allah is All-Forgiving, Merciful.

They ask you: "What is lawful to them?" say: "The good things are lawful; and such hunting birds or hounds that you have taught, as Allah has taught you. You may eat whatever they catch for you, mentioning Allah's name over it. Fear Allah, for Allah is, indeed, quick in reckoning!"

5 This day the good things have been made lawful to you; the food of the People of the Book is lawful to you, and your food is lawful to them; and so are the believing women who are chaste, and the chaste women of those who were given the Book before you, provided you give them their dowries and take them in marriage, not in fornication or as mistresses. If any one

316. Arrows used by pre-Islamic Arabs to cast lots.
317. That is, compelled to eat what is forbidden.

denies the faith, his work shall be of no avail to him, and in the Hereafter he will rank with the losers.

O believers, if you rise to pray, wash your faces and your hands up to the elbows and wipe your heads and your feet up to the ankles. If you are unclean, then cleanse yourselves; and if you are sick or on a journey, and if one of you has come from the restroom, or if you have touched women and cannot find any water, then take some clean earth and wipe your faces and hands with it. Allah does not wish to burden you, but to purify you and complete His grace upon you, that you may be thankful.

And remember Allah's grace upon you and His covenant with which he bound you, when you said: "We hear and we obey." Fear Allah; Allah indeed knows well the thoughts in the hearts!

O believers, be dutiful to Allah and bearers of witness with justice; and do not let the hatred of a certain group drive you to be unequitable. Be equitable; that is nearer to piety, and fear Allah. Allah indeed is fully aware of what you do!

Allah has promised those who believe and do the good deeds – they shall have forgiveness and a great reward.

10 But those who disbelieve and deny our revelations – those are the people of Hell.

O believers, remember Allah's grace upon you, when certain people intended to reach out to you with their hands but Allah restrained them. Fear Allah, and in Allah let the believers put their trust.

Allah made a covenant with the Children of Israel, and We raised among them twelve chieftains. And Allah said: "I am with you. Surely, if you perform the prayer, give the alms, believe in My apostles and support them and lend Allah a fair loan,[318] I will forgive you your sins and admit you into gardens, beneath which rivers flow. But if any one of you disbelieves afterwards, he certainly strays from the right path.

And on account of their violating their covenant, We cursed them and caused their hearts to harden; they take the words[319] out of their context and forget part of what they were enjoined, and you do not cease to find them treacherous, except for a few of them. Yet, pardon them and forgive; God surely loves those who do good to others.

And with some of those who say: "We are Christians", we made a covenant; but they forgot part of what they were reminded of; so we stirred up enmity and hatred among them till the Day of Resurrection. Allah will let them know what they did.

---

318. That is, if you spend in the way ordered by Allah.
319. The words in the Torah.

15   O People of the Book,[320] Our Apostle came to you to show you much of what you used to conceal of the Book[321] and to pardon a great deal. Indeed, a light and a clear Book[322] has come to you from Allah.

Allah guides with it those who seek His good pleasure to the paths of peace, brings them out of the shadows of darkness into the light, by His leave, and guides them to a straight path.

Unbelievers are those who say: "Allah is the Messiah, son of Mary." Say: "Who could prevent Allah, if He wished, from destroying the Messiah, son of Mary, and his mother too, together with all those on the face of the earth?" To Allah belongs the kingdom of the heavens and the earth and what lies between them. He creates whatever He pleases, and Allah has power over everything!

The Jews and the Christians have said: "We are Allah's children and His beloved." Say: "Why then does He punish you for your sins? You are rather human beings, part of those whom He has created. He forgives whom He pleases and punishes whom He pleases." And to Allah belongs the kingdom of the heavens and the earth and what is in between, and unto Him is the final return!

O People of the Book, Our Apostle has come to you to make clear to you [the religious tenets] after a cessation of apostles, lest you should say: "No bearer of good news or a warner has come to us." So now a bearer of good news and a warner has come to you; and Allah has power over everything!

20   And when Moses said to his people: "O my people, remember Allah's grace upon you, how He raised up prophets among you, made you kings and gave you what He has not given any other nation.

"My people, enter the Holy Land which Allah ordained for you,[323] and do not turn back, lest you become the losers."

They said: "O Moses, there is in it a mighty people; we shall not enter it until they leave it. If they leave it, then we shall enter."

Two men of those who feared [Allah] and whom Allah favoured said: "Enter the gate and [fall] upon them; if you enter it, you will be victorious. In Allah put your trust, if you are true believers."

They said: "O Moses, we shall never enter it, so long as they are in it. So, go forth, you and your Lord, and fight; we are staying put here."

25   He said: "Lord, I have no power over anybody other than myself and my brother; so separate us from the ungodly people."

Allah said: "It shall be forbidden them for forty years, during which they shall wander aimlessly in the land; so do not grieve for the ungodly people!"

320. The Jews and the Christians.
321. The Scriptures.
322. The Qur'an.
323. That is, ordained that you should enter.

And recite to them in all truth the tale of Adam's two sons, when they offered a sacrifice, which was accepted from one, but not accepted from the other. The latter said: "I will surely kill you", the other replied: "Allah accepts only from the God-fearing.

"Should you stretch your hand out to kill me, I will not stretch my hand out to kill you; for I fear Allah, Lord of the Worlds.

"I only wish that you be charged with my sin and yours and thus be one of the companions of the Fire; and that is the reward of the evildoers."

30　　Then, his soul prompted him to kill his brother; and so he killed him and became one of the losers.

Then, Allah sent forth a raven digging the earth to show him how to bury his brother's corpse. He said: "Woe is me, am I unable to be like this raven and bury the corpse of my brother?" Thus he became one of the remorseful.

For that reason, we decreed for the Children of Israel that whoever kills a soul, not in retaliation for a soul or corruption in the land, is like one who has killed the whole of mankind; and whoever saves a life is like one who saves the lives of all mankind. Our apostles came to them with the clear proofs; but afterwards many of them continued to commit excesses in the land.

Indeed, the punishment of those who fight Allah and His Apostle and go around corrupting the land is to be killed, crucified, have their hands and feet cut off on opposite sides, or to be banished from the land. That is a disgrace for them in this life, and in the life to come theirs will be a terrible punishment.

Except for those who repent before you overpower them. Know, then, that Allah is All-Forgiving, Merciful.

35　　O believers, fear Allah and seek the means to win His favour. Fight in His way so that you may prosper.

As to the unbelievers, even if they had all there is on earth and the like of it too to redeem themselves from the punishment of the Day of Resurrection therewith, it will not be accepted from them, and a very painful punishment shall be in store for them.

They will then wish to come out of the Fire, but they will never come out, and theirs is an everlasting punishment!

As for the thieves, whether male or female, cut off their hands in punishment for what they did, as an exemplary punishment from Allah. Allah is Mighty and Wise.

But whoever repents after his wrongdoing and mends his ways, Allah will forgive him. Allah is indeed All-Forgiving, Merciful!

40　　Did you not know that to Allah belongs the kingdom of the heavens and the earth? He punishes whom He wills and forgives whom He wills; and Allah has power over everything!

O Apostle, do not grieve on account of those who hasten to unbelief, from among those who say with their mouths: "We believe", while their hearts do not believe; or those Jews who listen to falsehood or listen to other people who did not come to you, and who alter the words.[324] They say: "If you are given this,[325] then take it, and if you are not given it, then beware!" Whoever Allah wishes to leave in error, you can do nothing to save him from Allah. Those whose hearts Allah does not wish to purify will have nothing but disgrace in this world, and a terrible punishment in the world to come.

They are consistent listeners to falsehood, devourers of unlawful gain. Should they come to you, either judge between them or turn away from them. If you turn away from them, they will not harm you in the least; but if you judge, judge between them justly. Allah loves those who act justly!

But how will they ask you to judge, when they are in possession of the Torah, which contains Allah's judgement![326] Thus they soon turn away. Those people are not real believers!

We have indeed revealed the Torah, wherein is guidance and light. By it the prophets who submitted themselves [to Allah] did judge among the Jews, as did the rabbis and the masters, according to what they were made to guard of Allah's Book and were witnesses thereof. So fear not men, but fear Me and do not sell My revelations for a small price. Whoever does not judge according to what Allah has revealed – those are the unbelievers!

45 And We prescribed to them therein[327] that a life for a life, an eye for an eye, a nose for a nose, an ear for an ear, a tooth for a tooth, and for wounds retaliation; but whoever forgoes it charitably, it will be an atonement for him. Whoever does not judge according to what Allah has revealed, those are the evildoers!

After them[328] we sent Jesus, son of Mary, confirming what he had before him of the Torah, and We gave him the Gospel, wherein is guidance and light, confirming what he had before him of the Torah and a guidance and admonition to the God-fearing.

And let the People of the Gospel judge in accordance with what Allah has revealed in it. He who does not judge according to what Allah has revealed – those are the transgressors.

---

324. The words in the Torah.
325. That is, if you are given by Muhammad something similar to what we say.
326. What is meant here is that they are not serious.
327. In the Torah.
328. The prophets.

And We have revealed to you[329] the Book in truth, confirming the scriptures[330] that preceded it and supercede it. Judge between them, then, according to what Allah has revealed, and do not follow their illusory desires, diverging from what came to you of the Truth. To each of you, we have laid down an ordinance and a clear path; and had Allah pleased, He would have made you one nation, but [He wanted] to test you concerning what He gave to you. Be, then, forward in good deeds. To Allah is the ultimate return of all of you, that He may instruct you regarding that on which you differed.

And judge between them in accordance with what Allah has revealed, and do not follow their fancies. Beware of them lest they lure you away from part of what God has revealed to you. Should they turn away, know that Allah only wishes to afflict them for some of their sins, and that many people are indeed grave sinners!

50   Now, is it the judgement of the "period of Ignorance"[331] that they[332] desire? Yet who is a better judge than Allah for a people who believe with certainty?

O believers, do not take the Jews and the Christians as friends; some of them are friends of each other. Whoever of you takes them as friends is surely one of them. Allah indeed does not guide the wrongdoers.

Yet, you will see those in whose hearts is a sickness hastening to woo them, saying: "We fear that a misfortune will befall us." However, it may be that Allah will bring victory or some other matter from Him; whereupon they will regret what they concealed within themselves.

And the believers will then say: "Are those the ones who swore by Allah their most solemn oaths that they were indeed with you?" Their works will come to nothing and thus they will be losers.

O believers, whoever of you renounces his religion, Allah will certainly bring forth[333] a people whom He loves and they love Him, humble towards the faithful, but mighty towards the unbelievers. They fight in the way of Allah and do not fear anybody's reproach. That is a favour from Allah which He confers on whomever He pleases. Allah is Munificent, All-Knowing.

55   Your only friends are Allah, His Apostle and those who believe, performing the prayer and giving the alms, while they bow down.

Whoever takes Allah, His Apostle and those who believe as friends [must know] that Allah's party is indeed the triumphant.

O believers, do not take as friends those who take your religion as a

---

329. Muhammad.
330. That is, the Books preceding it.
331. This period is known in Arabic as "Jahiliyah", which began about 500 AD and lasted until the rise of Islam in 610 AD.
332. The Jews.
333. That is, Allah will replace them by a people.

mockery or a sport, be they from among those who received the Book before you, or the unbelievers. Fear Allah if you are true believers.

And when you call to prayer, they take it as a mockery and a sport; that is because they are a people who do not understand.

Say: "O People of the Book, do you resent anything we do other than that we believe in Allah and what has been revealed to us and what was revealed before, and that most of you are transgressors?"

60   Say: "Shall I tell you about those who will get a worse punishment from Allah? Those whom Allah cursed and on whom He poured forth His wrath, transformed them into monkeys and swine, and worshippers of the Devil. They are worse off and farther astray."

When they[334] come to you, they say: "We believe", although they come in as unbelievers and leave as unbelievers. Allah knows best what they conceal.

And you will see many of them hastening to perpetrate sin and aggression and the devouring of unlawful gain. Evil is what they have been doing!

Why do not the rabbis and masters forbid them from uttering sinful things and devouring unlawful gain? Evil indeed is what they used to do!

The Jews say: "Allah's hand is tied";[335] may their own hands be tied and may they be damned for what they say. His hands are rather outstretched; He grants freely as He pleases. And what has been sent down to you from your Lord will certainly increase many of them in arrogance and unbelief. And We have cast in their midst animosity and hatred till the Day of Resurrection. Whenever they kindle a fire for war, Allah extinguishes it; and they go about spreading mischief, but Allah does not like the mischief-makers.

65   Had the People of the Book believed and warded off evil, We would have remitted their sins and admitted them into the gardens of bliss.

And had they observed the Torah and the Gospel and what was revealed to them from their Lord, they would have eaten amply from above them and below their feet. Among them is a moderate group, but evil is what many of them are doing!

O Apostle, proclaim what has been revealed to you from your Lord; but if you do not, you would not have delivered His message. Allah will protect you from mankind. Allah surely does not guide the unbelieving people!

Say: "O People of the Book, you have nothing [that counts] until you observe the Torah and the Gospel and what has been revealed to you from your Lord." Surely that which has been revealed to you[336] from your Lord

---

334. The Jewish hypocrites.
335. That is, Allah is not generous in bestowing His bounties upon them.
336. The Prophet.

will only make many of them increase in arrogance and unbelief; so do not be sorry for the unbelieving people.

Surely, the believers, the Jews, the Sabians and the Christians – whoever believes in Allah and the Last Day and does good deeds – shall all have nothing to fear and they shall not grieve.

70 We made the covenant with the Children of Israel and sent forth apostles to them. Whenever an apostle brought them what they did not like, they accused some of lying and killed some.

They supposed that there will be no punishment, so they became blind and deaf. Then Allah forgave them; but again many of them became blind and deaf. Allah is fully aware of what they do!

Those who say that Allah is the Messiah, son of Mary, are unbelievers. The Messiah said: "O Children of Israel, worship Allah, my Lord and your Lord. Surely, He who associates other gods with Allah, Allah forbids him access to Paradise and his dwelling is Hell. The evildoers have no supporters!"

Unbelievers too are those who have said that Allah is the third of three. For there is no god except the one God; and if they will not refrain from what they say, those of them who have disbelieved will be severely punished.

Will they not repent to Allah and ask His forgiveness? For Allah is All-Forgiving, Merciful.

75 The Messiah, son of Mary, was only an apostle before whom other apostles had gone; and his mother was a godly woman. They both ate [earthly] food. Look how We make clear our revelations to them; then look how they are perverted!

Say: "Will you worship, instead of Allah, that which cannot hurt or profit you? Allah is All-Knowing, All-Hearing."

Say: "O People of the Book, do not exceed the bounds in your religion unjustly, and do not follow the fancies of a people[337] who went astray in the past and led others astray and strayed from the right path."

Those of the Children of Israel who disbelieved were cursed by David and Jesus, son of Mary; that, on account of their disobedience and their aggression.

They used not to forbid one another from committing any of the evils they were committing. Evil is what they did!

80 You[338] see many of them befriending the unbelievers. Evil is what their souls prompt them to do. They have incurred Allah's wrath and they will suffer torment forever.

337. The reference here is to their ancestors.
338. The Prophet.

Had they believed in Allah and the Prophet, and in what has been revealed to him, they would not have taken them as friends; but many of them are evildoers.

You shall find the most hostile people to the believers to be the Jews and the polytheists; and you shall find the closest in affection to the believers those who say: "We are Christians." For among them are priests and monks, and they are not arrogant.[339]

And when they hear what was revealed to the Apostle, you see their eyes overflow with tears on account of the truth they recognize. They say: "Our Lord, we believe, so write us down among the witnesses."

"And why should we not believe in Allah and in what has come to us of the truth, when we are eager that our Lord will let us enter along with the righteous people?"

85   Allah rewarded them for what they said with gardens beneath which rivers flow, dwelling therein forever. Such is the reward of the righteous.

But those who disbelieve and denounce Our revelations, such are the denizens of Hell.

O believers, do not forbid the good things that Allah has made lawful to you and do not transgress; for Allah does not like the transgressors.

Eat of the pleasant things which Allah has given you; and fear Allah in Whom you believe.

Allah will not take you to task for what is unintentional in your oaths, but will take you to task for the oaths you intentionally take. Expiation for it, is feeding ten poor people with such average food as you would feed your own families, clothing them or freeing one slave. But he who cannot find [the means] should fast three days. That is the expiation for your oaths when you have sworn.[340] Keep your oaths; that is how Allah makes clear His revelations to you, that you may be thankful.

90   O believers, wine, gambling, idols and divining arrows are an abomination of the Devil's doing; so avoid them that perchance you may prosper!

The Devil only wishes to stir up enmity and hatred among you, through wine and gambling, and keep you away from remembering Allah and from prayer. Will you not desist, then?

Obey Allah and obey the Apostle and beware; but if you turn back, then know that it is the duty of Our Apostle to deliver the clear message.

Those who believe and do the good deeds are not to blame for what they eat, if they are God-fearing, believe and do the good deeds, then fear God, and believe, then fear God and do good. Allah loves the charitable.

---

339. That is, their pride does not prevent them from following what is right.
340. The reference here is to those oaths which are not kept.

O believers, Allah will certainly test you with some game that your hands or lances may catch, so Allah may know who fears Him in secret. Whoever transgresses thereafter shall be painfully punished.

95   O believers, do not kill game while you are on pilgrimage. Whoever of you kills it wilfully will have to give the like of what he killed of cattle, as determined by two just men from yourselves, to reach the Ka'ba as an offering; or will have to feed as expiation a number of poor men, or the equivalent of that in fasting so that he may taste the evil consequences of his action. Allah will pardon what is past; but he who offends again, Allah will wreak vengeance upon him. Allah is Mighty, Capable of retribution.

Lawful to you is the catch of the sea and its food as an enjoyment for you and for travellers; but unlawful to you is the game of the land so long as you are on a pilgrimage. Fear Allah unto whom you shall be gathered.

Allah has made the Ka'ba, the Sacred House, a foundation of religion for all mankind, together with the Sacred Month and the sacrificial offerings and their garlands, so that you may know that Allah knows what is in the heavens and on the earth, and that Allah knows everything very well.

Know that God is severe in punishment and that Allah is All-Forgiving, Merciful.

The duty of the Apostle is only to deliver the message, and Allah knows what you reveal and what you conceal.

100   Say: "The evil and the good are not equal, even if the abundance of the evil should appeal to you." Fear then Allah, O people of understanding, that perchance you may prosper.

O believers, do not ask about things which, were they disclosed to you, would displease you; and which, should you ask about while the Qur'an is being revealed, will be disclosed to you. Allah has forgiven you for it; and Allah is All-Forgiving, Clement.

A people preceding you asked about them, then disbelieved in them.

Allah has not prescribed the designation of *Bahirah, Sa'ibah, Wasilah* or *Hami*;[341] but the unbelievers impute falsehood to Allah, and most of them do not understand.

And if they are told: "Come now to what Allah has revealed and to the Apostle", they reply: "Sufficient unto us what we found our forefathers doing", even if their forefathers knew nothing and were not rightly guided!

105   O believers, take care of yourselves; you will not be harmed by him who has gone astray, if you are well-guided. To Allah you all will return; then He will tell you what you were doing.

O believers, when death approaches any of you, let two just men from among you act as witnesses at the time of testament; or two others from

341. Cattle sacrificed to idols at the Ka'ba.

another folk, if you happen to be travelling abroad and are overtaken by the calamity of death. You will detain them[342] after the prayer and they will swear by Allah if you are in doubt: "We will not sell Him [Allah] for any price, even if a near kinsman is involved, and we will not keep secret the testimony of Allah;[343] for then we would surely be sinners."

If, however, it is discovered that they have committed a sin, then two others shall take their places from among those against whom the first two had sinned. Whereupon they shall swear by Allah: "Our testimony is more truthful than their testimony and we have not transgressed, or else we would surely be evildoers."

Thus, it is likelier that they will bear witness properly, or fear that other oaths will contradict their own oaths. Fear Allah and listen well; for Allah does not guide the wicked people.

The day when Allah shall assemble the apostles, then say: "What response were you given?" They shall say: "We have no knowledge; you are indeed the Knower of the Unseen."

110   When Allah will say: "O Jesus, son of Mary, remember My grace upon you and upon your mother, how I strengthened you with the Holy Spirit, so that you could speak to people in the cradle and as an old man; how I taught you the Book, the Wisdom, the Torah and the Gospel; and how, by My leave, you created out of clay the likeness of a bird, and breathed into it, and then, by My leave, it turned into a bird. And you could heal the blind and the leper by My leave and you could raise the dead by My leave. And [remember] how I restrained the Children of Israel from harming you, when you brought them the clear signs;[344] whereupon the unbelievers among them said: "That indeed is nothing but manifest sorcery."

And when I revealed to the disciples:[345] "Believe in Me and My Apostle", they replied: "We believe, and you bear witness that we submit."

When the disciples said: "Jesus, son of Mary, is your Lord able to bring down for us a table [spread with food] from heaven?"; he said: "Fear Allah, if you are true believers."

They said: "We would like to eat from it so that our hearts may be reassured and know that you have told us the truth and be witnesses thereof."

Jesus, son of Mary, then said: "O Allah, our Lord, send down to us a table spread with food from heaven that it may be a festival for the first and last of us and a sign from You; and provide for us, for You are the best Provider."

115   Allah said: "I will send it down to you, so that whoever of you disbelieves

342. The two others.
343. That is, the testimony which Allah enjoins.
344. That is, miracles.
345. That is, ordered them through Jesus.

thereafter I will inflict on him a punishment I do not inflict on any other being."

And when Allah said: "O Jesus, son of Mary, did you say to the people: 'Take me and my mother as gods, apart from Allah?' " He said: "Glory be to You. It is not given me to say what is untrue. If I said it, you would have known it; you know what is in my soul, but I do not know what is in Thine. You are indeed the Knower of the Unseen.

"I only told them what You commanded me: 'Worship Allah, your Lord and mine', and I was watcher over them while I was among them, but when You took me to Yourself, You became the Watcher over them; for You are the Witness of everything.

"Should you punish them, they are surely Your servants; but should You forgive them, You are truly the Mighty, the Wise."

Allah said: "This is a day in which their truthfulness shall profit the truthful; they will have gardens beneath which rivers flow, dwelling therein forever; Allah is pleased with them and they are pleased with Him. That is the great triumph."

120 To Allah belongs the dominion of the heavens and the earth and all there is in them, and He has power over everything.

SURA 6

Al-An'am, The Cattle

In the Name of Allah, the Compassionate, the Merciful

1 Praise be to Allah, Who created the heavens and the earth and made the darkness and the light; yet the unbelievers set up equals to their Lord.

It is He who created you from clay, then decreed a term [for you] and another set term with Him,[346] but still you doubt.

He is Allah in the heavens and on earth. He knows your secrets and public utterances, and He knows what you earn.[347]

And there comes not to them a revelation from Allah, but they turn away from it.

5 So, they denied the truth when it came to them; but surely the news of what they were mocking will come to them.

Do they not see how many generations before them We destroyed, after We had established them in the earth more firmly than We have established you, and how We let loose the sky upon them in torrents, and We made the rivers flow beneath them? Thus We destroyed them because of their sins. And after them We raised another generation.

Had We sent down upon you a Book on parchment so that they could touch it with their own hands, those who disbelieve would still have said: "This is nothing but manifest sorcery."

And they say: "Why has not an angel been sent down to *him* [the Prophet]?" But had We sent down an angel, their fate would have been sealed, and then they would not have been given any respite.

And had We made him an angel, We would have certainly made him [look like] a man and thus confounded them with what they are using to confound others.

10 Other apostles before you were mocked; but those who scoffed at them were stricken with that at which they scoffed.

Say: "Travel in the land and look what was the fate of those who disbelieved [the apostles]."

Say: "To whom does that which exists in the heavens and on earth belong?" Say: "To Allah. He has prescribed to Himself mercy. He will

---

346. Meaning a term in this world after which you die and another for resurrection.
347. Meaning the good and evil you do.

certainly gather you on the Day of Resurrection, which is undoubted. Those who lost their souls will not believe."

To Him belongs whatever comes to rest in the day and in the night; and He is the All-Hearing, the All-Knowing.

Say: "Shall I take as guardian any one other than Allah, Who created the heavens and the earth, and Who feeds and is not fed?" Say: "I have been commanded to be the first to submit and not to be one of the polytheists."

15 Say: "Indeed, if I disobey my Lord, I fear the punishment of a fateful day."[348]

Whoever is spared on that day has gained His mercy, and that indeed is the manifest triumph!

And if Allah lets you suffer an affliction, no one can lift it except He; and if He accords you any good, He surely has power over everything.

And He is Sovereign over His servants and He is Wise, All-Knowing.

Say: "What has the greatest testimony?" Say: "Allah is Witness between you and me, and He has revealed this Qur'an to me so that I may warn you and whomever it may reach. Do you indeed testify that there are gods beside Allah?" Say: "I do not testify." Say: "He is indeed one God and I am innocent of the association of idols [with Him]."

20 Those to whom We have given the Book know him,[349] as they know their own children; but those who have lost their souls will not believe.

And who is more unjust than he who imputes falsehood to Allah or denies His revelations? Indeed the unjust shall not prosper.

And on the day that We shall gather them all together, then say to those who associated other gods [with Allah]: "Where are those whom you allege to have been your associate-gods?"

Then their only excuse will be simply to say: "By Allah, our Lord, we have not been polytheists."

Look,[350] how they will lie to themselves and how that which they fabricated will fail them.

25 And some of them listen to you, but We have cast veils over their hearts, lest they should understand it,[351] and a deafness in their ears. And even were they to see every sign, they will not believe in it; so that when they come to dispute with you, the unbelievers will say: "This is nothing but fables of the ancients."

And they forbid others from [following] him[352] and they keep away from him, but they only destroy themselves, without perceiving it.

348. The Day of Resurrection.
349. The Prophet.
350. Look, O Muhammad.
351. The Qur'an.
352. The Prophet.

And if only you could see when they are stationed before the Fire and thus they say: "Would that we could be brought back so that we would not denounce the revelations of our Lord, but would be part of the believers."

Indeed, what they used to conceal before will become clear to them; and were they returned [to life], they would surely go back to that which they were forbidden from. They are indeed liars.

And they say: "There is only this life and we shall not be resurrected."

30 And if only you could see when they are made to stand before their Lord. He will say: "Is not this the truth?" They will say: "Yes, by our Lord." He will say: "Taste then the punishment, on account of your disbelief."

Those who deny the encounter with Allah are losers. And when the hour overtakes them suddenly, they will say: "Alas, We neglected much in it." For they carry their burdens on their backs. And evil is what they carry!

The earthly life is nothing but sport and amusement, and the world to come is surely better for those who are God-fearing. Do you not understand?

We know that what they say grieves you. For they do not deny what you say; but the wrongdoers [continue to] deny Allah's revelations.

Other apostles were denounced before you, but they put up with the denunciation, and they were injured until Our help came to them. None can change the words[353] of Allah. Tidings have already been imparted about those apostles.

35 And if you find their aversion unbearable, seek, if you can, a hole in the earth or a ladder to the sky in order to bring them a sign. Had Allah pleased, He would surely have led them all to guidance; so do not be one of the ignorant.

Only those who hear will respond, and the dead will be raised by Allah; and unto Him they shall be returned.

And they also say: "Why has no sign[354] come down to him from his Lord?" Say: "Allah is surely able to send down a sign, but most of them do not know."

There is no animal [crawling] on land or a bird flying with its wings, but are communities like yourselves. We have not left anything out in the Book. Then unto their Lord they shall be gathered.

And those who deny Our revelations are deaf and dumb in total darkness. Whoever Allah pleases, He will lead astray; and whoever He pleases, He will lead onto a straight path.

353. His promises to support His apostles.
354. That is, miracle.

40   Say: "Tell me, if Allah's punishment overtakes you,[355] or the Hour[356] strikes, would you call upon any other than Allah, if you are truthful?"

No, upon Him you will call and He will light that about which you call, if He pleases; and then you will forget what you used to associate [with Him].

We have indeed sent forth [apostles] to other nations before you and We afflicted them with misery and hardship that perchance they might humble themselves.

If only they humbled themselves when Our punishment overtook them; but their hearts were hardened and the Devil made what they were doing seem fair to them.

Then, when they forgot what they were reminded of, We opened wide for them the gates of everything [good]; so that as soon as they rejoiced at what they were given, We struck them down suddenly, and they were driven to despair.

45   Thus the remnant of the wrongdoing people were rooted out, Praise be to Allah, the Lord of the Worlds!

Say: "Tell me! If Allah were to take away your hearing and sight and seal your hearts, what god other than Allah would give them back to you?" Behold, how we make plain Our revelations, but they turn away.

Say: "Tell me! If Allah's punishment should seize you suddenly or openly, will any be destroyed other than the wrongdoing people?"

And We only send forth the apostles as bearers of good tidings or warners. Those who believe and mend their ways have nothing to fear and have no cause to grieve.

But those who deny our revelations will be punished for having been sinful.

50   Say: "I do not tell you that I have the treasures of Allah, and I do not know the Unseen; nor do I tell you that I am an angel. I only follow what is revealed to me." Say: "Are the blind man and the one who sees alike? Do you not reflect at all?"

And warn with it[357] those who fear that they will be gathered before their Lord, other than Whom they have neither a protector nor an intercessor, so that they may be God-fearing.

And do not drive away those who call upon their Lord morning and evening, seeking nothing but His face. You are not in the least accountable for them, nor are they in the least accountable for you, so as to drive them away and become one of the wrongdoers.

---

355. In this life.
356. Day of Resurrection.
357. The Qur'an.

Likewise, We test some of them through others so that they may say: "Are these the ones whom Allah has favoured among us?" Does not Allah know best the thankful?

And when those who believe in Our revelations come to you, say: "Peace be upon you. Your Lord has prescribed mercy upon Himself, that he who perpetrates evil in ignorance, repents afterwards and mends his ways [will find Him] All-Forgiving, Merciful.

55 And thus We expound the revelations so that the way of the criminals becomes clear.

Say: "I have been forbidden to worship those you call upon apart from Allah." Say: "I do not follow your fancies, or else I would have gone astray and would not be one of the well-guided."

Say: "I have clear proof from my Lord, and you deny Him. I do not possess that with which you seek to hasten [punishment]. Judgement is Allah's alone; He determines the right, and He is the best decision-maker."

Say: "If I possessed that which you seek to hasten, the matter between you and me would have been settled; and Allah knows best the wrongdoers."

With Him are the keys of the Unseen; only He knows them, and He knows what is on land or in the sea. Not a leaf falls but He knows it; and there is no grain in the dark bowels of the earth, nor anything green or dry, but is [recorded] in a clear Book.

60 And it is He who makes you die at night and knows what you do by day. He raises you up in it, until a fixed term is fulfilled; then unto Him is your ultimate return. He will declare to you what you used to do.

He is the supreme Ruler over His servants, and He sends guardians[358] to watch over you, so that when death overtakes any one of you, Our messengers[359] carry him off; and they do not fail [to perform their duty].

Then they are brought back to Allah, their true Master. Truly the judgement is His and He is the fastest reckoner.

Say: "Who will deliver you from the dark depths of the land and the sea? You call upon Him humbly and secretly saying: 'If He delivers us from this, we will certainly be thankful.' "

Say: "Allah delivers you from this and from every distress; yet you associate [other gods with Him]".

65 Say: "It is He Who has the power to inflict upon you punishment from above you or from under your feet; or to mix you up dividing you into factions, and make you taste the might of one another." See, how We make plain our revelations, that, perchance, they might understand.

358. Angels.
359. The angels.

And your people deny it,[360] whereas it is the truth. Say: "I am not your guardian."

For every event there is a fixed time, and you shall certainly know.

And when you see those who talk scornfully about our revelations, turn away from them, until they engage in another discourse. And should the devil cause you to forget, do not sit down after the reminder with the evil-doing people.

The righteous are in no way accountable for them; it is only a reminder so that they may fear [Allah].

70 And leave those who take their religion for sport and who are deluded by the life of this world, and remind by it,[361] lest any soul should perish on account of what it has earned.[362] Apart from Allah, it has no protector or intercessor; and if it offers any ransom, it will not be accepted from it. Such are those who are turned over [to be punished] on account of what they have earned. They will have a drink of boiling water and a very painful punishment, because they disbelieved.

Say: "Shall we call, besides Allah, on what neither profits nor harms us, and turn on our heels after Allah has guided us?" [We shall then be] like one who, being tempted by the devils in the land, is bewildered though he has friends who call him to guidance [saying]: "Come to us." Say: "Guidance from Allah is the true guidance. And we are commanded to submit to the Lord of the Worlds;

"And perform the prayers and fear Him; for He is the One unto Whom you shall be gathered."

It is He who created the heavens and the earth in truth, and the day He says: "Be", it will come to be. His word is the truth, and His is the sovereignty on the day the trumpet is blown. The Knower of the Unseen and the Seen, He is the Wise, the All-Knowing.

And when Abraham said to his father Azar, "Do you take idols for gods? I see you and your people are in manifest error."

75 Thus We show Abraham the kingdom of the heavens and the earth, that he might be one of those possessed of certainly.

And when night fell, he saw a star; so he said: "This is my Lord", but when it set, he said: "I do not like those that set."

Then, when he saw the moon rising, he said: "This is my Lord", but when it set, he said: "If my Lord does not guide me rightly, I will be one of the erring people."

Then, when he saw the sun rising, he said: "This is my Lord; this is

360. The Qur'an.
361. The Qur'an.
362. That is, on account of the person's deeds.

larger", but when it set, he said: "O, my people, I am innocent of what you associate [with God].

"I turn my face towards Him who fashioned the heavens and the earth, as an upright man, and I am not one of the polytheists."

80   His people disputed with him. He said: "Do you dispute with me regarding Allah Who has guided me? I do not fear what you associate with Him, unless my Lord wills anything. My Lord embraces everything in His knowledge; do you not remember [this]?

"And how should I fear what you associate [with Him], while you do not fear the fact that you have associated with Allah that for which He has sent down upon you no authority? Which of the two parties, then, is more deserving of safety? [Tell me] if you know."

Those who believe and do not mix their faith up with injustice – to these belongs the safety, and they are the well-guided.

That is Our argument which We imparted to Abraham against his people. We raise up in degrees whomever We please. Your Lord is indeed Wise, All-Knowing.

And We granted him Isaac and Jacob, and guided each of them; and Noah We guided before that, and of his progeny, [We guided] David, Solomon, Job, Joseph, Moses and Aaron. Thus We reward the beneficent.

85   And Zachariah, John, Jesus and Elias, each was one of the righteous.

And Isma'il, Elijah, Jonas and Lot; each We exalted above the whole world.

[We also exalted some] of their fathers, progeny and brethren. And We chose them and guided them to a straight path.

That is Allah's guidance by which He guides whom He pleases of His servants. Had they associated [other gods with Allah], all that they did would have been nullified.

Those are the ones to whom We gave the Book, wisdom, authority and prophethood. So if these[363] disbelieve in them,[364] We have entrusted them to a people who do not disbelieve in them.

90   Those are the ones whom Allah has guided; so follow their guidance. Say: "I ask you no reward for it; it is only a reminder to mankind."

They do not show proper regard for Allah's greatness when they say: "Allah has not revealed anything to a mortal." Say: "Who revealed the Book which was brought by Moses as a light and guidance to mankind? You put it in scrolls which you reveal, while you conceal much. And [now] you are taught[365] what neither you nor your fathers knew." Say: "Allah [revealed it]. Then leave them to revel in their nonsense."

363. The Meccan unbelievers.
364. The Book, wisdom and prophethood.
365. In the Qur'an.

And this is a Book which We revealed. [It is] blessed and confirms what preceded it, that you may warn therewith the Mother of Cities[366] and those around it. Those who believe in the Hereafter believe in it and observe their prayers.

And who is more unjust than he who imputes falsehood to Allah, or says: "It has been revealed to me", while nothing was revealed to him; or one who says: "I will reveal the like of what Allah has revealed?" If you could see the wrongdoers in the throes of death, and the angels, with arms outstretched, saying: "Give us your souls. This day you receive the punishment of humiliation for what you used to say untruly about Allah, while scorning His revelations."

You[367] have come to Us one by one, just as We created you initially, and you have left behind what We granted you. We do not see with you your intercessors whom you claimed were [Allah's] partners. Certainly what held you together is now cut off, and that which you claimed has failed you.

95 Allah is truly the Cleaver of the grain and the date-stone; He brings out the living from the dead and the dead from the living. That is Allah; how then were you perverted?

[He is] the Cleaver of the dawn; and He made the night a time of rest, and the sun and the moon a means of reckoning. Such is the ordering of Allah, the Mighty, the All-Knowing.

And it is He who created the stars for you so as to be guided by them in the dark depths of the land and the sea. We have made plain the signs for a people who know.

And it is He who created you from a single living soul; then [gave you] a resting-place and a repository. Indeed, We have made plain Our signs for a people who understand.

And it is He who sends down water from the sky. With it We bring forth all kinds of vegetation. From it We bring forth greenery, and clustered grain; and from the date-palm shoots come clusters of dates within reach. And [We bring forth] gardens of grapes, olives and pomegranates alike and unlike. Behold their fruits, when they bear fruit and their ripening, surely there are signs in that for a people who believe.

100 They set up the *jinn* as Allah's partners, although He created them; and they falsely ascribe to Him sons and daughters without any knowledge. Glory be to Him, and highly exalted is He above what they ascribe to Him!

[He is] the Creator of the heavens and the earth; how could He have a child when He has no consort, and has created everything and has knowledge of everything?

---

366. Mecca.
367. The following is said to them when they are resurrected.

That is Allah, your Lord; there is no god but He, Creator of all things. Worship Him then; He is the Guardian of all things.

Vision does not attain Him, but He attains the vision, and He is the Kind, the All-Knowing.

Clear proofs have come to you from your Lord. Thus, he who perceives, perceives for his own advantage, and he who is blind, that is to his loss; and I am not your Keeper.

105 And thus We make clear the revelations so that they may say:[368] "You have studied",[369] and that We may make it clear to a people who know.

Follow what has been revealed to you from your Lord; for there is no god but He; and turn away from the polytheists.

Had Allah pleased, they would not have associated [other gods]; and We have not made you their keeper, and you are not their guardian.

Do not curse those [deities] whom they call upon besides Allah, lest they wrongfully curse Allah without knowledge. Thus We have made the deeds of every nation seem fair to them; then unto their Lord is their return, and He will tell them what they were doing.

They swear by Allah most solemnly that, were a sign to come to them, they would surely believe in it. Say: "Signs are only with Allah"; but how do you know that, if those signs come, they will still not believe?

110 And We will divert their hearts and their sights [from the truth], as they failed at first to believe in it; and We shall leave them dumbfounded in their wrongdoing.

Even if We send the angels to them and the dead speak to them, and if We bring everything before them, they would not believe, unless Allah wills; but most of them are ignorant.

Likewise, We have assigned to every prophet an enemy, the devils of men and *jinn*, revealing one to the other tawdry speech in order to deceive; but had your Lord willed, they would not have done it. So leave them to what they invent;

So that the hearts of those who do not believe in the Hereafter may incline to it and accept it; as well as to perpetrate that which they themselves are perpetrating.

Shall I seek a judge other than Allah, when He is the One who sent down the Book to you fully expounded? Those to whom We have given the Book[370] know that it is revealed from your Lord in truth. Do not then be one of the doubters.

368. To Muhammad.
369. That is, discussed this with the People of the Book, or got it from the annals of the former peoples.
370. The Torah.

115 The word of your Lord has been completed in truth and justice; no one can change His words. He is the Hearing, the All-Knowing.

And were you to obey most people on earth, they will lead you away from the path of Allah. They follow nothing but conjecture, and they only lie.

Your Lord knows best who strays from His path, and He knows best who are the rightly guided.

Eat, then, of that upon which the name of Allah has been mentioned, if you really believe in His revelations.

And why is it that you do not eat from that upon which Allah's name is mentioned, when He has explained to you what is unlawful to you, except for what you are compelled to [eat]? Indeed many shall lead others astray by their fancies, without any knowledge. Surely, your Lord knows best the transgressors.

120 Avoid open and secret sins. Surely those who commit sin shall be punished for what they have perpetrated.

And do not eat from that over which the name of Allah has not been mentioned; it is indeed sinful. The devils shall insinuate to their followers to dispute with you; but if you obey them, then you will surely be polytheists.

Is one who was dead, then We brought him back to life and gave him light to walk among the people, like one who is in total darkness and cannot get out of it? Thus the unbelievers' evil deeds are made attractive to them.

And thus We have set up in every city its leading wicked sinners so as to plot therein. However, they only plot against themselves, although they do not realize it.

And if a sign comes to them, they say: "We will not believe, until we are given the like of what Allah's apostles have been given." Allah knows best where to place His message. Those who commit sins will suffer humiliation and severe punishment from Allah on account of their plotting.

125 Whomever Allah wants to guide, He opens his heart up to Islam, and whomever He wants to lead astray, He makes his heart extremely constricted, as though he were ascending to heaven. Thus Allah inflicts His punishment upon those who do not believe.

This is the path of your Lord, perfectly straight. We have expounded the revelations to people who take heed.

Theirs is the abode of peace with their Lord and He is their Protector, for what they used to do.

And on the day when He shall gather them all together [saying]: "O, company of *jinn*, you have misled a great many men." Their supporters among men will say: "Lord, we have profited much from each other and we have attained the term that you assigned for us." Then He will say: "The

Fire is your resting-place, abiding therein forever, except as Allah wills. Your Lord is truly Wise, All-Knowing."

And thus We cause some of the evil-doers to dominate the others, because of what they used to do.[371]

130   "O company of *jinn* and men, did there not come apostles from among yourselves to you, reciting to you My revelations and warning you of seeing this day?' They will say: "We bear witness against ourselves." They were deluded by the earthly life and will bear witness against themselves that they were unbelievers.

That is because your Lord would not destroy cities on account of their people's wrongdoing without warning them.[372]

And to all are assigned ranks according to what they have done; and your Lord is not unaware of what they do.

Your Lord is the All-Sufficient, the Merciful. If He wishes, He will destroy you and bring out after you, as successors, whomever He wishes, as He had produced you from the seed of another people.

Indeed, whatever you are promised will surely come to pass, and you are not able to escape [it].

135   Say: "O my people, do whatever you can; and I shall do what I can. You shall surely know whose is the happy outcome in the Hereafter. Indeed, the wrongdoers shall not prosper.

They assigned to Allah a share of the tilth and cattle He created, saying: "This is for Allah," – as they declare – "and this is for our associate-gods." And while that which is assigned to their associate-gods does not reach Allah, that which is set aside for Allah would reach their associate-gods. How evil is what they judge!

And likewise, their associate-gods have insinuated to them the killing of their children, so as to destroy them and confound them in their religion. Had Allah pleased, they would not have done it. So leave them to their fabrication.

And they say: "These cattle and tilth are taboo, and none shall eat them except those we wish," as they claim. And there are cattle whose backs are forbidden, and others over which they do not mention the name of Allah. Such is their fabrication about Him. [But] He will punish them for their lies.

And they say: "What is in the bellies of these cattle is lawful to our males, but forbidden to our wives. If it is still-born both can share it." [Allah] will punish them for what they attribute [to Him]. He is surely Wise, All-Knowing.

---

371. That is, because of the evil they commit.
372. By sending an apostle to them.

140   Those who kill their children foolishly without knowledge are real losers; and they forbid what Allah has provided for them, thus fabricating lies against Allah. They go astray and they are not well-guided.

It is He who created gardens, trellised and untrellised; palms and crops of diverse produce; and olives and pomegranates, both like and unlike. Eat of their fruits when they bear fruit, and pay their due on the day of harvesting them. And do not be prodigal; [for] He does not like the prodigal.

Of cattle there are some for burden and some for slaughter. Eat of what We provided for you and do not follow in the footsteps of the Devil. Surely he is a manifest enemy of yours.

[Take] eight in pairs: of sheep two and of goats two. Say: "Has He forbidden the two males, or the two females, or what the wombs of the two females contain? Tell me if you are truthful."

And [take] of camels two and of cows [and oxen] two. Say: "Has He forbidden the two males, the two females, or what the wombs of the females contain? Or have you been witnesses when Allah commanded you to do this?" Who then is more unjust than he who imputes falsehood to Allah, in order to lead people astray, without knowledge? Surely, Allah will not guide the wrongdoing people.

145   Say: "I do not find in what has been revealed to me anything forbidden to an eater to eat from, unless it is carrion, or running blood, or the flesh of swine – which are unclean. For it is profane and slaughtered to [gods] other than Allah. However he who is constrained, intending neither to commit a sin nor to exceed the bounds, then surely your Lord is All-Forgiving, Merciful.

We have forbidden the Jews every [animal] with claws; and the fat of oxen and sheep except what their backs or entrails carry, or what is mixed with bones. This was the punishment We inflicted on them on account of their aggression. We are surely Truthful.

If they accuse you of lying, say: "Your Lord has an all-encompassing mercy and His punishment cannot be prevented from afflicting the guilty people."

The polytheists will say: "If Allah pleased, we would not have associated [other gods with Him], nor would our fathers; nor would we have forbidden anything." Thus those before them denied the truth until they tasted Our punishment. Say: "Do you have any knowledge which you can produce for Us? You only follow conjecture and you only tell lies."

Say: "To Allah belongs the decisive argument. Had He pleased He would have guided you all."

150   Say: "Produce your witnesses to testify that Allah has forbidden this." Then, if they testify, do not bear witness with them, and do not follow the

fancies of those who deny Our revelations and those who do not believe in the Hereafter and set up equals with their Lord."

Say: "Come, I will recite what your Lord has forbidden you: that you associate nothing with Him; that you show kindness to your parents; that you do not kill your children for fear of poverty; We will provide for you and for them; that you do not approach indecencies, whether open or secret; and that you do not kill the living soul which Allah has forbidden you to kill except for a just cause. This is what Allah commands you to do, so you may understand."

Do not approach the property of the orphan, except in the fairest manner, until he comes of age; and give full measure and weight equitably. We do not charge any soul except with what is within its power. And if you speak, be just even if it is against a relative, and fulfil Allah's covenant. Thus He commands you, so that you may take heed.

This is indeed My path, the straight path; follow it and do not follow the [other] paths, lest they divert you from His path. Thus He commands you, that perchance you may fear God.

Then We gave Moses the Book, completing Our grace on him who would do good, making plain everything and serving as a guidance and mercy, so that they[373] may believe in the encounter with their Lord.

155 This Book[374] which We sent down is blessed; so follow it and fear God, so that you may receive mercy.

Lest you should say: "The Book was revealed only to two sects[375] before us, and we were unaware of their reading."

Or lest you should say: "Had the Book been revealed to us, we would have been better guided than they." A clear proof has come to you from your Lord, and a guidance and mercy, too. Who, then, is more unjust than he who denies Allah's revelations and turns away from them? We will surely inflict on those who turn away from Our signs grievous punishment, because they turned away.

What! Do they expect the angels, or your Lord or some of your Lord's signs to come to them? The day some of your Lord's signs come, faith will not avail any soul which did not already accept it, nor earned some good through its faith. Say: "Wait, we too are awaiting."

Surely, you are not in any way part of those who have differentiated between parts of their religion and split into sects. Their fate is in Allah's hands. He will inform them about what they have done.

160 He who comes up with a good deed shall have ten times its like; and he

---

373. The Children of Israel.
374. The Qur'an.
375. The Jews and Christians.

who comes up with an evil deed will only be requited for it once, and they shall not be wronged.

Say: "My Lord has guided me to a straight path, a right religion, the creed of Abraham, an upright man who was no polytheist."

Say: "My prayer and my sacrifice, my life and my death, are Allah's, the Lord of the Worlds.

"He has no associate, and thus I am commanded, and I am the first of those who submit."

Say: "Shall I seek a Lord other than Allah, who is the Lord of all things? Every soul is accountable for what [evil] it commits, and no soul shall bear the burden of another soul. Then, unto your Lord is your return; and He will inform you about that over which you used to differ."

165   And it is He who made you successors on earth, and raised some of you above the others in rank, so as to test you regarding what He has given you. Your Lord is indeed quick in retribution, and He is indeed All-Forgiving, Merciful.

SURA 7

Al-A'raf, The Ramparts

In the Name of Allah, the Compassionate, the Merciful

Alif, Lam, Mim, Sad.

1   [This is] a Book revealed to you;[376] let there be no gall in your heart because of it. [It is revealed] so that you may warn with it, and as a reminder to the believers.

Follow what has been revealed to you from your Lord and do not follow, apart from Him, other patrons. How little you heed the warning.

How many a town We have destroyed; Our might struck them at night or while they were napping.

Their only assertion when Our might struck them was to say: "We have indeed been wrongdoers."

5   So, We shall question those to whom apostles were sent, and We shall question the apostles.

Then, We shall recount to them in full knowledge; for We are never absent.

On that day the weighing of deeds will be just; those whose scales are heavy will prosper;

But those whose scales are light, are those who lost their souls on account of denying Our revelations.

And We have established you firmly in the earth and provided you therein with means of livelihood. But seldom do you give thanks.

10   And We created you, then fashioned you, then said to the angels: "Prostrate yourselves to Adam"; so they prostrated themselves, except for Satan who was not one of those who prostrated themselves.

He[377] said: "What prevented you from prostrating yourself when I commanded you?" He[378] said: "I am better than he; you created me from fire, and you created him from clay."

He said: "Get down from it,[379] then. It is not given you to be arrogant therein. Get out; you are indeed one of the lowly."

Satan said: "Give me a respite, until the day when they shall be resurrected."

He said: "You are one of those who are granted respite."

376. Muhammad.
377. That is, Allah.
378. Satan.
379. Paradise.

15   Satan said: "Because you have misled me, I will lie in wait for them on Your straight path.

"Then I will come upon them from before them and behind them, from their right and their left; and you will not find most of them thankful."

He said: "Get out of it despised and vanquished. I will fill Hell with all who follow you!"

And [We said]: "Adam, dwell you and your wife in Paradise, and eat from wherever you wish; but do not come close to this tree, lest you both become wrongdoers."

But Satan tempted them secretly in order to expose their nakedness to them saying: "Your Lord has forbidden you this tree, lest you become angels or become immortal."

20   And he swore to them: "I am indeed a sincere advisor to you both."

Then he brought about their downfall by deceit; so that when they tasted the tree, their private parts became visible to them, and they started to cover themselves with the leaves of Paradise. Then their Lord called out to them: "Have I not forbidden you that tree and said to you: 'Indeed Satan is your sworn enemy'?"

They said: "Our Lord, we have wronged ourselves and if you do not forgive us and have mercy on us, we will surely be among the losers."

He said: "Go down, some of you as enemies of the others. On earth you will have a dwelling-place and a means of enjoyment for a while."

He said: "Therein you shall live and therein you shall die, and from it you will be brought out.

25   "O Children of Adam, We have provided you with clothing and finery to cover your private parts. But the attire of piety is the best." Such are Allah's signs, that they may take heed.

"O Children of Adam, do not let Satan lead you astray as he drove your parents out of Paradise, stripping them of their clothes so as to show them their private parts. He and his host see you from a place where you cannot see them. We have made the devils the friends of those who do not believe."

When they commit an indecency, they say: "We have found our fathers doing it, and Allah commanded us to do it." Say: "Allah does not command indecencies. Do you impute to Allah what you do not know?"

Say: "My Lord commands justice. Set your faces straight at every place of prayer and call on Him in true devotion. As He originated you, you shall return.

"A group of you He has guided and another group were doomed to error; for they have taken the devils for patrons, apart from Allah, and they still think that they are rightly guided."

30   O Children of Adam, put on your finery at every place of prayer. Eat and drink, but do not be prodigal, He does not like the prodigal.

Say: "Who has forbidden Allah's finery which He fashioned for His servants, or the good things He provided?" Say: "These are meant, in this present world, for those who believe, and exclusively for them on the Day of Resurrection." Thus We make clear our revelations for a people who know.

Say: "My Lord has only forbidden open and secret indecencies, sin, unjust aggression, and your association with Allah that for which He sent down no authority, and your saying about Allah that which you do not know."

For every nation there is a [fixed] term, so that when its term comes, they will not be able to put it back or bring it forward a single hour.

"O Children of Adam, when apostles from your own people come to you reciting to you My revelations – then those who fear God and mend their ways have nothing to fear, and they will not grieve."

35 But those who deny Our revelations and reject them arrogantly – those are the people of the Fire; therein they shall abide forever.

For who is more unjust than he who fabricates lies about Allah or denies his revelations? Those will get their share of the punishment ordained for them. When our messengers[380] come to take their souls they will say: "Where are those upon whom you called besides Allah?" They will say: "They have left us", and they will bear witness against themselves that they were unbelievers.

Allah will say: "Enter together with nations who have gone before you, *jinn* and men, into the Fire. Every time a nation enters it, it curses its sister-nation; so that when they shall have followed each other into it, the last of them will say of the first: "Our Lord, these led us astray; inflict on them a double punishment in the Fire." He will say: "A double [punishment] to each, but you do not know."

And the first of them will say to the last: "In no way are you better than us; so taste the punishment for what you did."

Indeed, those who have denied Our revelations and rejected them arrogantly – the gates of heaven shall not be opened for them and they shall not enter Paradise until the camel passes through the eye of the needle. Thus We punish the wicked sinners.

40 Hell shall be their couch and over them shall be canopies [of fire]. Thus We punish the wrongdoers.

As to those who believe and do the good deeds, We do not charge any soul except with what is within its power. Those are the people of Paradise, abiding therein forever.

And We shall remove all rancour from their hearts; and under them rivers will flow. They will say: "Praise be to Allah who guided us to this; we would

380. The angels, messengers of death.

never have been guided, had not Allah guided us. The apostles of our Lord came with the truth." Then a voice will cry out to them: "This is indeed the Paradise which you have been made to inherit for what [good] you used to do."

And the people of Paradise will call out to the people of the Fire: "We have found what our Lord promised us to be true; so have you found what your Lord promised to be true?" They will say: "Yes". Thereupon a caller from their midst shall call out: "May Allah's curse be upon the wrongdoers;

"Who bar from [others] Allah's way and desire it to be crooked; and they disbelieve in the Hereafter."

45   Between them[381] is a veil, and on the Ramparts[382] are men who know everyone by his mark. And they will call out to the people of Paradise: "Peace be upon you." That is, before they[383] enter it, though they hope to do so.

And when their eyes are turned towards the people of the Fire, they will say: "Lord, do not place us among the wrongdoing people."

And the people of the Ramparts will cry out to some men whom they will recognize by their marks saying: "Your amassing [of wealth] and your arrogance are of no avail to you."

"Are those the people that you swore Allah will have no mercy on?" [To these people will be said]: "Enter Paradise, you have nothing to fear, and you shall not grieve."

Then the people of the Fire will call out to the people of Paradise: "Pour out upon us some water or part of what Allah has provided you with." They will say: "Allah forbids them both unto the unbelievers,

50   "Who take their religion as an amusement and sport, and the present life deludes them. Today, We forget them as they forgot the encounter of this day and used to deny Our revelations."

And We have brought them a Book, which we have expounded with knowledge, as a guidance and mercy for a people who believe.

Do they only wait for its fulfilment. The day its fulfilment comes, those who forgot it before will say: "The apostles of our Lord brought the truth. Have we then any intercessors to intercede for us, or shall we be taken back, so as to do something other than what we used to do?" They have indeed lost their souls, and what they fabricated has failed them.

Your Lord is truly Allah, who has created the heavens and the earth in six days, then He sat upon the Throne. He covers the day with the night, which pursues it relentlessly. The sun, the moon and the stars are made

---

381. The people of Paradise and the people of the Fire.
382. The walls separating Paradise from Hell.
383. Those on the Ramparts.

subservient by His command. To Him belongs the creation and the command. Blessed is Allah the Lord of the Worlds.

Call on your Lord humbly and secretly. He certainly does not like the aggressors.

55 And do not sow corruption in the land after it has been put in order. Call on Him with fear and hope. Allah's mercy is indeed close at hand for the beneficent.

It is He who sends forth the winds bearing good news of His mercy; so that when they bear heavy clouds, We drive them towards some dead land upon which We send down water. With it We bring forth every variety of fruit. Thus We bring out the dead, so that you may take heed.

Good land[384] produces vegetation by the will of its Lord; but that which has gone bad will not produce vegetation except with difficulty. Thus We make plain the revelations to a people who give thanks.

We sent Noah forth to his people, and he said: "O my people, worship Allah, you have no other god than He. I fear for you the punishment of an awful day."

The dignitaries among his people said: "We see you, indeed, in manifest error."

60 He said: "O my people, I am not in any error, but am a messenger from the Lord of the Worlds.

"I deliver to you the revelations of my Lord and give you good advice, and I know from Allah what you do not know.

"Do you wonder that a reminder from your Lord has come to you at the hands of a man from your own people to warn you, and to induce you to fear Allah so that mercy may be shown to you?"

However, they denounced him, and so We delivered him, together with those in the ark, and drowned those who denied Our revelations. For they were indeed a blind people.

And to 'Ad,[385] [We sent] their brother Hud. He said: "O my people, worship Allah; you have no other god than He. Will you not fear [Allah]?"

65 The dignitaries of his people, who were unbelievers, said: "We see that you are foolish and we believe that you are a liar."

He said: "O my people, I am not foolish but am a messenger from the Lord of the Worlds;

"Delivering to you the revelations of my Lord, and I am a sincere advisor of yours.

"Do you wonder that a reminder from your Lord has come to you through a man of your own people, in order to warn you? Remember how

384. That is, land with a good soil.
385. A pre-Islamic Arab tribe.

He made you successors[386] after the people of Noah and increased you in physical stature. Remember then Allah's bounties, that perchance you may prosper."

They said: "Have you come to us, so that we may worship Allah alone and forsake what our fathers used to worship? Bring us then what you promise us, if you are one of the truthful."

70 He said: "A scourge and wrath have descended on you from your Lord. Do you dispute with me over names[387] which you and your fathers have invented, and for which Allah has sent down no authority? Wait[388] then. Surely I shall be, along with you, among those who wait."

We delivered him thereupon, with those in his company, by a mercy from Us, and cut off the roots of those who denied Our revelations and were no believers.

And to Thamud[389] [We sent] their brother Salih. He said: "O my people, worship Allah; you have no other god than He. A clear proof from your Lord has now come to you. This is Allah's she-camel, to be a sign unto you; so let it graze in Allah's land and do not cause her any harm; for you will then be seized by a very painful punishment.

"And remember how He made you as successors after 'Ad, and established you in the land, wherein you built yourselves castles on its plains and hewed the mountains into houses. Remember then Allah's bounties and do not corrupt the earth with mischief."

The arrogant dignitaries among his people said to some of those who had believed and were deemed to be weak: "Do you *know* that Salih is sent forth from his Lord?" They said: "Indeed, we believe in what he has been sent with."

75 The arrogant dignitaries said: "In that which you have believed, we definitely disbelieve."

So they hamstrung the she-camel and defied their Lord's command and said: "O Salih, bring upon us what you are promising us, if you are one of the apostles."

Whereupon the earthquake overtook them, and so they lay prostrate in their own homes.

Then he turned his back on them and said: "O my people, I have delivered to you my Lord's message and given you advice, but you do not like the givers of advice."

And [remember] Lot when he said to his people: "Do you commit indecencies which no one in the whole world committed before you?"

386. That is, possessors of a vast kingdom.
387. Names of idols.
388. That is, wait for the punishment.
389. An Arab tribe.

80   "You approach men instead of women lustfully; you are rather a people given to excess."

His people's response was simply to say: "Expel them[390] from your city; for they are men who wish to remain chaste."

So We delivered him and his household, except for his wife who stayed behind.

And We rained a shower [of brimstone] upon them. See then what was the end of the sinners.

And [to the people of] Midian We sent their brother Shuʿayb, who said: "O my people, worship Allah, you have no other god but He. A clear proof has now come to you from your Lord; so fulfil the measure and the weight; and do not withhold anything of what is due to people; and do not make mischief in the land after it has been put in order. That is better for you if you are true believers.

85   "And do not sit down at every roadside, threatening and barring from Allah's path those who have believed, seeking to make it crooked. And remember when you were few in number and He multiplied you, and see what was the fate of those who sought to corrupt.

"And if one group of you believes in the message I have been sent with, and another group does not believe, wait then until Allah judges between us; for He is the best of judges."

The arrogant dignitaries of his people said: "O Shuʿayb, we will surely drive you, together with those who believe, out of our city, unless you return to our religion." He said: "Even if we were unwilling?

"We would actually be fabricating lies about Allah, if we were to return to your religion, after Allah has delivered us from it. It is not given to us to return to it, unless Allah our Lord wills it. Our Lord embraces all things in knowledge. In Allah we have put our trust. Our Lord, judge between us and our people in truth, for you are the best of judges."

The dignitaries of his people who disbelieved then said: "If you follow Shuʿayb, then you are the losers.'

90   Thereupon, the earthquake overtook them, and so they lay prostrate in their own homes.

Those who denounced Shuʿayb were as though they had never dwelt there; those who denounced Shuʿayb were the losers.

So he turned away from them and said: "O my people, I have delivered to you the revelations of my Lord and given you advice. How should I then grieve for an unbelieving people?"

We did not send forth a prophet to any city but afflicted its people with distress and suffering, that perchance they might humble themselves.

390. Lot and his followers.

Then We changed their adversity into well-being, till they multiplied. They said: "Hardship and prosperity did visit our fathers." Then, We seized them suddenly, while they were unaware.

95 Yet had the people of the cities believed and feared Allah, We would have opened upon them blessings from the sky and the earth;[391] but they denied [the prophets], and so We destroyed them on account of their misdeeds.

Did the people of the cities feel assured that Our punishment would not come upon them at night while they were sleeping?

Or did the people of the cities feel assured that Our punishment would not come upon them during the day while they were playing?

Or did they feel secure against Allah's scheming? For none feels secure from Allah's scheming save the losing people.

Is it not clear to those who inherit the earth after its people [are gone] that if We will, We can smite them for their sins and seal their hearts so that they cannot hear.

100 Those cities, We relate to you some of their tales; their messengers came to them with clear signs, but they would not believe in what they had denied earlier. Thus Allah seals the hearts of the unbelievers.

And We have not found among most of them any who honours a covenant; but We found most of them evil-doers.

Then after them, We sent Moses with revelations to Pharaoh and his people, but they repudiated them. See then what was the fate of the mischief-makers.

Moses said: "O Pharaoh, I am an apostle from the Lord of the Worlds.

"It is only proper that I should not say about Allah anything other than the truth. I have brought you a clear sign from your Lord; so send forth the Children of Israel with me."

105 He said: "If you have brought a sign, produce it if you are really truthful."

So he cast his staff and, behold, it was a manifest serpent.

And he drew his hand; and, behold, it appeared white to the onlookers.

The dignitaries among Pharaoh's people said: "This, indeed, is a shrewd magician.

"He wishes to drive you out of your land; so what do you advise?"

110 They said: "Leave him and his brother for a while, and send forth summoners to the cities;

"To bring you every shrewd magician."

The magicians then came to Pharaoh and said: "We shall surely have a reward, if we are the winners."

He said: "Yes, and you will be, indeed, among those I favour."

They said: "O Moses, either you cast or we will be the first to cast."

---

391. That is, rain from the sky and plants from the earth.

115 He said: "You cast"; but when they cast, they put a spell upon the eyes of the people and frightened them, producing a mighty feat of magic.

We revealed to Moses: "Cast your staff", and behold, it proceeded to devour what they faked.

So the truth was vindicated and what they were doing was nullified.

And they were vanquished there and then, and they turned away humiliated.

And the magicians fell down prostrate.

120 They said: "We believe now in the Lord of the Worlds;

"The Lord of Moses and Aaron."

Pharaoh then said: "Do you believe in Him before I give you leave? This is indeed a plot you contrived in the city, in order to drive its people out. Now you shall know.

"I will surely cut off your hands and your feet on opposite sides; then I will crucify you all together."

They said: "Unto our Lord we surely shall return."

125 "You only resent from us that we have believed in the signs of our Lord when they came to us. Lord, grant us patience and let us die as men who submit to you."

And the dignitaries among Pharaoh's people said: "Will you leave Moses and his people to make mischief in the land and to abandon you and your gods?" He said: "We will massacre their sons, but spare their women, and over them we shall surely triumph."

Moses said to his people: "Seek Allah's assistance and be patient; the earth is Allah's and He gives it to whomever of His servants He pleases; and for the righteous is the happy end."

They said: "We were persecuted before you came to us and after you came to us." He said: "Perchance your Lord will destroy your enemy and make you successors in the land and, then, observe what you will do."

And We made Pharaoh and his people suffer from drought and shortage of fruits, that perchance they may take heed.

130 So, when a good fortune came to them they said: "This is ours", but if a misfortune befell them, they ascribed the evil omen to Moses and his companions. In fact, their omen is with Allah; but most of them do not know.

And they said: "Whatever sign you may bring us in order to cast a spell upon us, we will not believe in you."

So, We let loose upon them the deluge, locusts, lice, frogs and blood, as explicit signs; but they grew arrogant and were a sinful people.

And when the scourge descended on them, they said: "O Moses, call upon your Lord for us in virtue of the covenant He made with you. If you lift the scourge from us, we will surely believe you and send forth the Children of Israel with you."

But when We lifted the scourge from them for a period We accorded them, behold, they broke their pledge.

135 Then We exacted retribution from them and drowned them in the sea, because they denounced Our signs and failed to pay heed to them.

And We bequeathed to the people who were held to be weak[392] the eastern and western parts of the land which we had blessed;[393] and the fairest word of your Lord in regard to the Children of Israel was fulfilled, because of their endurance; and We destroyed the houses and towers which Pharaoh and his people were building.

And We caused the Children of Israel to cross the sea, and they came upon a people devoted to idols of their own. They said: "O Moses, make us a god as they have gods of their own." He said: "You are indeed an ignorant people.

"Surely what those [people] are engaged in is doomed to destruction, and what they are doing is a vanity."

And he said: "Shall I seek for you a god other than Allah, who has preferred you to all mankind?"

140 And [remember] how We delivered you from Pharaoh's people who inflicted the worst punishment on you, killing your sons and sparing your women. In that was a grievous trial from your Lord.

And We appointed to Moses thirty nights to which We added ten, and thus the term appointed by his Lord was forty nights. And Moses said to his brother Aaron: "Succeed me at the head of my people, set matters right and do not follow the path of the mischief-makers."

And when Moses came on Our appointed time and his Lord spoke to him, he said: "Lord, show me [Yourself] so that I may look at you." He said: "You will not see Me; but look at the mountain. If it stays in its place, you shall see Me." But when his Lord revealed Himself to the mountain, He levelled it to the ground, and Moses fell down unconscious. When he woke up, he said: "Glory be to You, I repent unto You and I am the first of the believers."

Then He said: "O Moses, I have chosen you above all men for My message and My words; so take what I have given you and be one of the thankful."

And We wrote for him in the Tablets[394] about everything, providing exhortation and a clear exposition of everything: "So [We said] take it

392. The Children of Israel.
393. The Holy Land.
394. The Tablets of the Torah.

resolutely and bid your people to take the best part of it. I will show you the abode of the wicked.

145   "I will turn away from My signs whose who are unjustifiably arrogant on earth, and who, if they see each sign, will not believe in it; and if they see the path of rectitude will not follow it, but if they see the path of error, will follow it as their path. That is because they denied the truth of Our signs and failed to pay heed.

"Those who deny Our signs and the meeting of the Hereafter – their works are nullified. Will they be rewarded except according to what they do?"

And the people of Moses took, after he went away, a calf made of their jewellery – a mere body which lowed. Did they not see that it did not speak to them and could not guide them to any path? They took it [for worship] and were wrongdoers.

And when they felt deep regret, and saw that they had gone astray, they said: "If our Lord will not have mercy on us and will not forgive us, we will certainly be among the losers."

And when Moses returned to his people, angry and very sad, he said: "Evil is what you did following my departure. Were you in a hurry regarding your Lord's commandment?" He cast the Tablets down and took hold of his brother's head, dragging him towards him. He[395] said: "Son of my mother, the people deemed me weak and were about to kill me, so do not let the enemies rejoice at my plight, and do not reckon me one of the unjust people."

150   He[396] said: "Lord, forgive me and my brother and admit us into your mercy; for you are the most Merciful of all."

Surely, those who worshipped the calf will be visited by wrath from their Lord and humiliation in the present life; and thus we recompense those who invent lies.

And those who perpetrated the evil deeds and repented thereafter and believed – surely your Lord is thereafter All-Forgiving and Merciful.

And when the anger of Moses abated, he took up the Tablets, in the text of which are guidance and mercy for those who fear their Lord.

And Moses chose from his people seventy men for Our appointed time. When the earthquake overtook them, he said: "Lord, had you pleased, you would have destroyed them, together with me, before this time. Will you destroy us for what the fools among us have done? This is only Your trial, with which You lead astray whomever You will and guide whomever You will. You are our Protector; so forgive us and have mercy on us. You are the best Forgiver of all.

395. Aaron.
396. Moses.

155   "And ordain for us good in this world and in the Hereafter; we turn repentant to You." He said: "I smite with My punishment whomsoever I please, and My mercy encompasses all things; and I will ordain it to those who are pious and give the alms, and to those who believe in Our signs.

"And to those who follow the Apostle, the unlettered Prophet whom they find mentioned in their Torah and Gospel. He enjoins them to do good and to forbid evil, and makes lawful to them the good things and unlawful the impure things. And He relieves them of their heavy burden and the shackles that were upon them. Thus those who believe in him and who honour and support him and follow the light which has been sent down with him – those are the prosperous."

Say: "O people, I am Allah's Messenger to you all; He to whom belongs the dominion of the heavens and the earth. There is no god but He. He gives life and causes to die; so believe in Allah and His Apostle, the unlettered Prophet who believes in Allah and His words; and follow him, that perchance you may be well-guided."

And of the people of Moses, there is a group who guide by the truth, and by it act justly.

And We divided them into twelve nation-tribes; and We revealed to Moses, when his people asked him for water: "Strike the rock with your staff"; whereupon twelve springs gushed forth from it, with each tribe recognizing its drinking-place. And We spread the clouds over them to shade them and sent down upon them the manna and quails [saying to them]: "Eat from the good things We have provided for you." They did not wrong us, but they wronged themselves.

160   And it was said to them: "Dwell in this city and eat from it wherever you please. Seek forgiveness and enter the gate prostrate, so that We may forgive your sins. We shall give more to the beneficent."

But the evil-doers among them replaced what was said to them with other words; and so We sent upon them a punishment from heaven, on account of their wrongdoing.

And ask them about the city which stood close to the sea, when they violated the Sabbath. Their fish which used to come floating on the sea on the Sabbath did not appear when they violated the Sabbath. Thus We tried them because they transgressed.

And when one group of them said: "Why do you exhort a people whom Allah has doomed to destruction or to terrible punishment?", they replied: "As an excuse for your Lord, and that perchance they may fear God."

Then, when they neglected what they were reminded of, We saved those who were forbidding evil and inflicted upon the wrongdoers a terrible punishment, on account of their sinfulness.

165   Then, when they disdained arrogantly what they were forbidden, We said to them: "Be miserable monkeys."

Thereupon your Lord made it known that He would send against them one who would inflict on them the worst punishment until the Day of Resurrection. Your Lord is quick in retribution, and He is indeed All-Forgiving, Merciful.

And We split them up throughout the land into groups, some of them righteous and some otherwise. Then We tried them with prosperity and adversity, that perchance they might desist [from sinning].

Then there succeeded them [an evil] posterity who inherited the Book,[397] but chose the vanities of this world saying: "We shall be forgiven." And should similar vanities come their way, they would again seize them. Are they not bound by the covenant of the Book, that they should not say about Allah except the truth? They studied what is in it and the world to come is better for those who fear God. Do they not understand?

As for those who hold fast to the Book and perform the prayer – surely We do not dissipate the reward of the righteous.

170   And [remember] when We raised the mountain over them, as though it was a canopy; and they thought that it was about to fall down on them. Hold on firmly to what We have given you, and remember what is in it, that perchance you may be God-fearing.

And [remember] when your Lord brought forth from the loins of the Children of Adam their posterity and made them testify against themselves. [He said]: "Am I not your Lord?" They said: "Yes, we testify." [This] lest you should say on the Day of Resurrection: "We were in fact unaware of this."

Or you should say: "Our fathers associated [other gods with Allah] before [us] and we are their posterity. Will you destroy us for what the fabricators of falsehood did?"

And thus We expound the revelations so that they may return.[398]

And tell them [O Muhammad] about the man[399] to whom We gave Our revelations, but he renounced them and was followed by the Devil. Thus he became one of those condemned to perdition.

175   And had We pleased, We would have elevated him through them,[400] but he clung to earth and followed his fancy. His case is similar to that of a dog; if you attack it, it will pant, and if you leave it, it will pant too. Such are

397. The Torah.
398. Return to the Truth.
399. The person intended here may be a Jewish rabbi called Balaam.
400. The revelations.

those who deny Our revelations. So relate to them these narratives, that perchance they may reflect.

How evil is the example of the people who deny Our revelations. They only wrong themselves.

Whomever Allah guides is well-guided; and whomever He leads astray – those are the losers.

And We have created for Hell multitudes of *jinn* and men. They have hearts, but do not understand; and they have eyes, but do not see; and they have ears, but do not hear. Those are like cattle, or rather are even more misguided. Those are the heedless ones.

And to Allah belong the most beautiful names; so call Him by them and leave those who pervert his names. They shall be punished for what they used to do.

180 And among those We have created is a nation that guides by the truth, and by it the nation acts justly.

And those who deny Our revelations, We shall lure them step by step to destruction, whence they do not know.

And I will grant them respite. Surely My scheme is very effective.

Do they not consider that their companion[401] is not mad. He is only a plain warner.

Have they not considered the kingdom of the heavens and the earth and all the things Allah has created, and how perhaps their appointed term may have drawn near? In what other message after this[402] will they, then, believe?

185 Whomever Allah leads astray will have no guide; and He leaves them in their arrogance to wander aimlessly.

They ask you about the Hour, when it will strike. Say: "The knowledge thereof is with my Lord; none but He will disclose it at the right time. It will be fateful in the heavens and on earth, and will not come upon you except suddenly." They ask you, as though you know about it. Say: "The knowledge thereof is with Allah, but most people do not know."

Say: "I do not have the power to benefit or harm myself, except as Allah pleases. Had I the knowledge of the Unseen, I would have acquired much good, and misfortune would not have touched me. I am only a warner and a bearer of good news to a people who believe."

It is He who created you from a single soul from which He created her mate to live in comfort with her. Then when he approached her she bore a light burden; and so she carried on easily. When she became heavy, they called upon Allah, their Lord, saying: "If you grant us a righteous child, we shall be thankful."

---

401. Muhammad.
402. The Qur'an.

He then gave them a righteous child. But they considered it to be given not only by Him, but also by associates whom they set up with Him. But Allah is exalted above those associates.

190 Do they associate with Allah those who can create nothing, while they, themselves, are created?

And they can neither help them nor help themselves.

And if you call them to guidance, they do not follow you. It is the same, for you, whether you call them or you remain silent.

Indeed those you call, apart from Allah, are servants like you; so call them and let them answer you, if you are truthful.

Do they have feet to walk with; do they have hands to smite with; do they have eyes to see with; or do they have ears to hear with? Say:[403] "Call your associate-gods, then plot against me and give me no respite."

195 My protector is Allah who sent down the Book and He protects the righteous.

And those you call, apart from Him, are not able to help you or even to help themselves.

If you call them to the guidance they do not hear; and you see them look at you, but they do not see.

Hold to forgiveness, enjoin the good and turn away from the ignorant.

And if a temptation from the Devil troubles you, seek refuge in Allah; He is truly All-Hearing, All-Knowing.

200 Indeed, those who fear God, when a visitation from the Devil afflicts them, will remember [Allah's commands], and behold they will see clearly.

But their brethren will plunge them further into error, and [then] they will not desist.

And if you do not bring them a revelation, they say: "Why don't you yourself invent it?" Say: "I only follow what is revealed to me from my Lord. This[404] constitutes a clear proof from your Lord and a guidance and mercy to those people who believe."

When the Qur'an is recited, listen to it and pay attention, that perchance you may receive mercy.

And remember your Lord within yourself, in humility and awe and without raising your voice in the morning and evening; and do not be one of the heedless.

205 Indeed, those[405] who are with your Lord are not too proud to worship Him, and they glorify Him and prostrate themselves before Him.

---

403. Say, O Muhammad.
404. The Qur'an.
405. The angels.

SURA 8

Al-Anfal, The Spoils

In the Name of Allah, the Compassionate, the Merciful

1 They ask you about the spoils,[406] say: "The spoils belong to Allah and to the Apostle. So fear Allah and settle your differences." Obey Allah and His Apostle if you are true believers.

The true believers are those whose hearts, upon mention of Allah, quiver with fear; and when His revelations are recited to them, they strengthen their faith. They put their trust in their Lord.

Those who perform the prayer, and spend of what We provided for them.

Those are in truth the believers; they shall enjoy with their Lord a high station and receive forgiveness and a generous provision.

5 Just as when your[407] Lord brought you out in truth from your house, though a group of the believers disliked it.

They disputed with you concerning the Truth after it had become manifest, as though they were being led to their deaths while looking on.

And [remember] how Allah promised you that one of the two [enemy] groups[408] would be yours, and you wanted the unarmed one[409] to be yours. Allah, however, willed the Truth to triumph in accordance with his words and to cut off the remnants of the unbelievers.

So that He may cause the Truth to triumph and nullify falsehood, even though the wicked sinners dislike it.

And when you called upon your Lord for help, He answered you: "I will reinforce you with a thousand angels following one another."

10 Allah did this only as good tidings and that your hearts might be assured thereby. Victory comes only from Allah; Allah is indeed Mighty and Wise.

[Remember] when He allowed slumber to overcome you as an assurance from Him, and sent you water down from heaven so as to purify you, relieve you of the Devil's temptation, fortify your hearts and steady your feet therewith.

And when your Lord revealed to the angels: "I am with you; so support those who believe. I will cast terror into the hearts of those who disbelieve; so strike upon the necks and strike every fingertip of theirs."

---

406. The spoils taken by the Muslims following the Battle of Badr 2 AH/624 AD.
407. Meaning Muhammad.
408. The Meccan caravan of Quraysh and the army which was sent to defend it.
409. The caravan.

That is because they opposed Allah and His Apostle; and he who opposes Allah and His Apostle [will find] Allah's punishment very severe.

This is how it will be; so taste it; the torture of the Fire is awaiting the unbelievers.

15 O believers, if you meet the unbelievers on the march, do not turn your backs upon them.

Whoever turns his back on that day, unless preparing to resume fighting, or joining another group, incurs Allah's wrath and his refuge is Hell; and what an evil fate!

It was not you[410] who slew them, but Allah; and when you[411] threw[412] it was actually Allah who threw, so that He might generously reward the believers. Allah is Hearing, Knowing.

That was done, so that Allah might foil the machinations of the unbelievers.

If you seek victory, the victory has been granted you; and if you desist, it will be better for you; but if you come back, We will come back,[413] and your forces will avail you nothing, however numerous they are. Allah is on the side of the believers.

20 O you who believe, obey Allah and His Apostle, and do not turn away from Him while you hear.

And do not be like those who say: "We hear", while they hear not.

The worst beasts in Allah's sight are the deaf and dumb who do not understand.

If Allah knew of any good in them, He would have made them hear; and had He made them hear, they would still have turned away defiantly.

O believers, respond to Allah and to the Apostle if He calls you to that which will give you life; and know that Allah stands between a man and his heart, and that unto Him you shall be gathered.

25 And fear a calamity which will not only afflict the wrongdoers among you; and know that Allah is severe in retribution.

And remember when you were few and were deemed weak in the land, fearing that the people will snatch you away; but He gave you a shelter, strengthened you with His support and provided you with the good things, that perchance you may give thanks.

O you who believe, do not betray Allah and the Apostle, nor betray your trusts knowingly.

And know that your wealth and your children are a temptation, and with Allah is a great reward.

410. Those addressed are the Muslims.
411. Muhammad is addressed here.
412. Threw the pebbles or handful of dust at the enemy in retaliation.
413. That is, We will again support the believers.

O you who believe, if you fear Allah, He will provide you with a criteria [to distinguish right from wrong], and absolve you from your sins and forgive you. Allah's bounty is great.

30   And [remember] when the unbelievers plotted against you, so as to confine you, kill you or expel you. They schemed and Allah schemed, but Allah is the best of schemers.

And when Our revelations are recited to them, they say: "We have heard. Had we wished, we would have uttered the like of this; this is nothing but the fables of the ancients."

And when they said: "O Allah, if this is indeed the truth from You, then rain down upon us brickstones from heaven, or inflict upon us a very painful punishment."

And Allah did not wish to punish them while you[414] were in their midst, and Allah was not going to punish them while they were asking for forgiveness.

And what excuse do they have that Allah should not punish them, when they bar people from the Sacred Mosque, although they were not its guardians? Its guardians are only those who fear Allah; but most of them do not know.

35   Their prayer at the House is nothing but whistling and clapping; so taste the punishment for your disbelief.

Indeed, the unbelievers spend their wealth to bar [people] from Allah's path. They will continue to spend it, but it will become a source of anguish for them; then they will be vanquished. And those who disbelieve shall be gathered in Hell.

So that Allah might separate the foul from the fair and place the foul, one upon the other, piling them up all together and casting them into Hell. Those are truly the losers.

Say to those who disbelieve:[415] "If they desist, He will forgive them what is already done; but if they go back, then [they should remember] what befell those before them."

And fight them, so that sedition might end and the only religion will be that of Allah. Then if they desist, Allah is fully aware of what they do.

40   But if they turn away, then know that Allah is your Protector; and what an excellent Protector and Supporter He is!

And know that whatever booty you take, the fifth thereof is for Allah, the Apostle, the near of kin, the orphan, and the wayfarer, if you really believe in Allah and in what We revealed to Our servant on the day of decision,[416] the day when the two hosts met. Allah has power over everything.

414. The Prophet.
415. Those included Abu Sufyan, the Meccan leader, and his companions.
416. The reference here is to the Battle of Badr.

While you were on the nearer side [of the valley] and they were on the farther side, with the cavalcade beneath you. Had you made an appointment, you would surely have failed to keep the appointment. But [this happened] so that Allah might bring about a matter already decreed, and that those who were to perish would perish after a clear proof [had been given], and those who were to survive would survive after a clear proof [had been given]. And surely Allah is All-Hearing, All-Knowing.

[Remember] when Allah showed them to you [O Muhammad] in your sleep as few. Had He showed them as many, you would have lost heart and you would have differed over the matter. But Allah saved you. He knows what is hidden in the hearts.

And [remember] when He showed them to you, as you met, few in your eyes, and made you few in their eyes; so that Allah might bring about a matter already decreed. And unto Allah shall all matters return.

45 O believers, if you encounter an enemy host, stand fast and remember Allah frequently, that perchance you may prosper.

And obey Allah and His Apostle and do not quarrel among yourselves lest you lose heart and your strength dissipates. And stand fast, for Allah is on the side of those who stand fast.

And do not be like those who went out of their homes boastfully showing off in front of the people, while they barred others from the path of Allah. Allah is fully aware of what they do.

And the Devil made their [foul] deeds look fair to them saying: "No man shall overcome you today; and I am indeed by your side." But when the two hosts sighted each other, he turned on his heels saying: "I am quit of you; I see what you do not see; I fear Allah, and Allah is stern in retribution."

And the hypocrites and those in whose hearts is a sickness said: "Their religion has misled those people."[417] But he who trusts in Allah will find Allah is Mighty and Wise.

50 And if you could only see when the angels carry off the unbelievers, striking their faces and their rears [saying]: "Taste the punishment of the Fire."

That is on account of what you have done, and Allah is not unjust to His servants.

Just like the wont of Pharaoh's people and those who preceded them; they disbelieved their Lord's revelations; so Allah punished them for their sins. Allah is strong and stern in retribution.

That is because Allah never changes a favour He confers on a people unless they change what is in their hearts, and because Allah is All-Hearing, All-Knowing.

417. The Muslims.

Just like the wont of Pharaoh's people and those who preceded them; they denied Allah's revelations, so We destroyed them because of their sins and We drowned Pharaoh's people. They were all wrongdoers.

55 The worst beasts in the sight of Allah are those who disbelieve, because they will never believe.

Those, who each time you make a covenant with them, break it, and do not fear God.

So, if you should come upon them in the war, scatter[418] them with those behind them, that perchance they may pay heed.

And should you fear treachery from any people, throw back their treaty to them in like manner. Allah does not like the treacherous.

Let not the unbelievers think that they can escape [Us]. They will never be able to escape.

60 And make ready for them whatever you can of fighting men and horses, to terrify thereby the enemies of Allah and your enemy, as well as others besides them whom you do not know, but Allah knows well. Everything you spend in the path of Allah will be repaid in full, and you will never be wronged.

And if they incline to peace, incline to it too, and put your trust in Allah. He is truly the Hearer, the Knower.

And if they wish to deceive you, then Allah is sufficient for you and so are believers, it is He who has strengthened you with His support and with the believers;

He brought their hearts together. Had you spent all there is on earth, you could not have brought their hearts together, but Allah has brought them together. He is Mighty and Wise.

O Prophet, Allah is sufficient for you and so are the believers who follow you.

65 O Prophet, urge the believers to fight. If there are twenty steadfast men among you, they will defeat two hundred; and if there are a hundred, they will defeat a thousand of the unbelievers, because they are a people who do not understand.

Now Allah has lightened your burden; He knows that there is a weakness in you. So, if there are a hundred steadfast men among you, they will overcome two hundred; and if there are a thousand men among you, they will overcome two thousand, by Allah's leave. Allah is with the steadfast.

It is not up to any prophet to take captives except after too much blood is shed in the land.[419] You desire the fleeting goods of this world, but Allah desires the Hereafter, and Allah is Mighty, Wise.

---

418. That is, by punishing them severely.
419. What is meant here is that the Prophet should not allow the taking of captives for the sake of ransom. He may, however, allow taking captives after the enemy is hard hit and subdued.

But for a prior ordinance of Allah, you would have been afflicted on account of what you have taken[420] by a terrible punishment.

So eat of the lawful and good things you have taken as booty. Fear Allah; Allah is truly All-Forgiving, Merciful.

70 O Prophet, tell those captives in your keeping: "If Allah knows of any good in your hearts, He will give you in return better than what has been taken from you and forgive you." Allah is All-Forgiving, Merciful.

But if they wish to betray you, they have previously betrayed Allah, and so He subdued them. Allah is All-Knowing, Wise.

Those who have believed and emigrated and struggled with their wealth and their lives in the path of Allah, and those who gave refuge and support – those are friends of one another; but those who have believed, yet did not emigrate, you will not be responsible for their protection until they emigrate. Should they seek your support for religion's sake, you ought to support them, but not against a people with whom you have a compact. Allah is fully aware of what you do.

As to the unbelievers, they are friends of one another. If you do not do this,[421] there will be great sedition and corruption in the land.

And those who believed, emigrated and struggled in the path of Allah, and those who have given refuge and support – those are the true believers. They will have forgiveness and bountiful provision.

75 And those who believed afterwards, emigrated and struggled with you – those are part of you. And the blood relatives are closer to one another in Allah's Book. Allah is truly cognisant of everything.

---

420. An ordinance which made it lawful for the Muslims to take spoils and captives.
421. That is, if you do not support the Muslims and subdue the unbelievers.

SURA 9

Al-Tawba, Repentance

1   This is an immunity from Allah and His Apostle to those idolaters with whom you made compacts.

Travel, then, in the land freely for four months, and know that you will never be able to thwart Allah, and that Allah shall disgrace the unbelievers.

This is a proclamation from Allah and His Apostle to mankind on the day of the great pilgrimage,[422] that Allah is absolved of the idolaters, as is His Apostle. If you repent, it will be better for you; but if you turn away, know that you shall never thwart Allah. Proclaim to those who disbelieve a grievous punishment.

Except for those idolaters with whom you made a compact, then they did not fail you in anything and did not lend support to anybody against you. Honour your compact with them until the end of its term. Allah loves the righteous.

5   Then, when the sacred months[423] are over, kill the idolaters wherever you find them, take them [as captives], besiege them, and lie in wait for them at every point of observation. If they repent afterwards, perform the prayer and pay the alms, then release them. Allah is truly All-Forgiving, Merciful.

And if any one of the idolaters should seek refuge with you, give him refuge, so that he may hear the word of Allah; then convey him to his place of security. That is because they are a people who do not know.

How can the idolaters have a compact with Allah and His Apostle, except for those you made a compact with at the Sacred Mosque? So long as these honour their obligations to you, honour yours to them. Allah loves the righteous.

How [can that be]? If they overcome you, they will observe neither kinship nor compact with you. They only give you satisfaction with their mouths, while their hearts refuse, and most of them are sinners.

They have sold Allah's revelations for a small price, and have barred [others] from His path. Evil indeed is what they do!

10   They observe with the believers neither kinship nor compact. Those are the real transgressors.

Yet, if they repent, perform the prayer and pay the alms, they will be your brethren in religion. We expound the revelations to a people who know.

422. On the 10th of Dhul Hijja.
423. These are the four months during which war was prohibited in pre-Islamic times.

But if they break their oaths after their pledge [is made] and abuse your religion, then fight the leaders of unbelief; for they have no regard for oaths, and that perchance they may desist.

Will you not fight a people who broke their oaths and intended to drive the Apostle out, seeing that they attacked you first? Do you fear them? Surely, you ought to fear Allah more, if you are real believers.

Fight them, Allah will punish them at your hands, will disgrace them, give you victory over them, and heal the hearts of a believing people.

15 And He will remove the rage from their hearts. Allah shows mercy to whomever He pleases, and Allah is All-Knowing, Wise.

Do you imagine that Allah would leave you alone before knowing who of you fight [in the way of Allah] and do not seek supporters besides Allah and His Apostle? Allah is fully aware of what you do.

The unbelievers should not enter Allah's mosques bearing witness thereby against themselves that they are unbelievers. The works of those are vain and in the Fire they will abide forever.

Only he who believes in Allah and the Hereafter, performs the prayers, gives the alms and fears no one but Allah, shall visit Allah's mosques. Those shall be reckoned among the rightly guided.

Do you consider those, who give the pilgrims water to drink and maintain the Sacred Mosque like those who believe in Allah and the Hereafter and fight in Allah's way? They are not alike in Allah's sight, and Allah will not guide the wrongdoing people.

20 Those who have believed, emigrated and fought in the path of Allah with their lives are higher in rank in Allah's sight; and those are the winners.

Their Lord announces to them the good news of mercy from Him, good pleasure and gardens wherein they have everlasting bliss;

Abiding therein forever. With Allah is a great reward.

O believers, do not take your fathers and brothers as friends, if they prefer disbelief to belief. Those who take them as friends are the wrongdoers.

Say: "If you fathers, your sons, your brothers, your spouses, your relatives the wealth you have gained, a trade you fear might slacken, and dwellings you love are dearer to you than Allah and His Apostle or than fighting in his way, then wait until Allah fulfils His decree. Allah does not guide the sinful people.

25 Allah gave you victory in numerous places and on the day of Hunayn[424] when you were pleased with your large number; but if availed you nothing and the land became too strait for you, despite its breadth, whereupon you turned back and fled.

424. A valley between Mecca and Ta'if.

Then Allah sent down His tranquillity upon His Apostle and upon the believers, and He sent down soldiers you did not see, and punished the unbelievers. That is the reward of the unbelievers.

Then, Allah will pardon thereafter whom He pleases. Allah is All-Forgiving, Merciful.

O believers, the polytheists are truly unclean; so let them not come near the Sacred Mosque after this year of theirs; and if you fear poverty, Allah shall enrich you from His bounty, if He pleases. Allah is truly All-Knowing, Wise.

Fight those among the People of the Book who do not believe in Allah and the Last Day, do not forbid what Allah and His Apostle have forbidden and do not profess the true religion, till they pay the poll-tax out of hand and submissively.

30 The Jews say: "Ezra is the son of Allah", and the Christians say: "The Messiah is the son of Allah." That is their statement, by their mouths; they emulate the statement of the unbelievers of yore. May Allah damn them; how they are perverted!

They take their rabbis and monks as lords besides Allah, as well as the Messiah, son of Mary, although they are commanded to worship none but one god. There is no god but He; exalted He is above what they associate with Him.

They wish to put out Allah's light with their mouths, and Allah allows nothing less than perfecting His light, even if the unbelievers should resent it.

It is He who sent His Apostle with the guidance and the true religion, in order to make it triumph over every religion, even if the polytheists should resent it.

O believers, many of the rabbis and monks devour the property of the people unjustly and bar others from the path of Allah. Those who hoard gold and silver and do not spend them in Allah's path, announce to them a very painful punishment.

35 On the day when all that will be heated in the Fire of Hell, and their foreheads, sides and backs will be branded with it. This is what you hoarded for yourselves; taste now what you used to hoard.

The number of months, with Allah, is twelve months by Allah's ordinance from the day He created the heavens and the earth. Four of these are sacred. This is the right religion, so do not wrong yourselves during them; but fight the polytheists all together just as they fight you all together; and know that Allah is on the side of the righteous.

Postponing the [sacred month] is an added disbelief by which the unbelievers seek to mislead, allowing it one year and prohibiting it another year, so as to equal the number [of months] Allah has made sacred. Their evil deeds are made attractive to them; and Allah does not guide the unbelieving people.

O believers, what is the matter with you? If you are told: "March forth in the way of Allah", you simply cling heavily to the ground. Are you satisfied with the present life rather than the Hereafter? Yet the pleasures of the present life are very small compared with those of Hereafter.

If you do not march forth, He will inflict a very painful punishment on you and replace you by another people, and you will not harm Him[425] in the least; for Allah has power over everything.

40 If you will not support him, Allah will not support him, when the unbelievers drove him out – he being the second of two,[426] while they were both in the cave. He said to his Companion: "Do not grieve; Allah is with us." Whereupon, Allah sent down His tranquillity upon him and assisted him with soldiers you did not see, and made the word of the unbelievers the lowest. The word of Allah is indeed the highest and Allah is Mighty and Wise.

Charge forth, on foot or mounted, and struggle with your possessions and yourselves in the way of Allah. That is far better for you, if only you knew.

Had it been a gain near at hand and a short journey, they would surely have followed you. But the distance seemed too long to them. Still they will swear by Allah: "Had we been able, we would have marched forth with you." They damn themselves, and Allah knows that they are liars.

May Allah pardon you! Why did you allow them[427] before it became clear to you who were the truthful ones, and you knew who were the liars?

Those who believe in Allah and the Last Day do not ask you for [exemption from] fighting in the way of Allah with their wealth and lives. Allah knows well the righteous.

45 Only those who do not believe in Allah and the Last Day will ask you [for exemption] and their hearts are in doubt. Thus they vacillate in their state of doubt.

Had they wanted to go forth, they would have made preparation for that; but Allah was averse to their going forth, and so He held them back, and it was said to them: "Sit back with those who sit back."

Had they gone out with you, they would have only increased your confusion, and would have kept moving among you sowing sedition. And some of you would have listened to them. Allah knows well the wrongdoers.

425. Allah.
426. The Prophet and Abu Bakr.
427. The reference is to those whom the Prophet allowed to stay behind.

They have sought to sow sedition before and turned things around for you, until the truth came out and Allah's command was manifested, although they were averse [to it].

Some of them say: "Allow me and do not tempt me." Indeed they have already fallen into temptation and Hell shall encompass the unbelievers.

50 If a good fortune befalls you, they are displeased, and if a disaster befalls you they say: "We have taken our precaution before." Then, they turn away rejoicing.

Say: "Nothing will befall us except what Allah has decreed for us. He is our Lord, and in Allah let the believers put their trust."

Say: "Do you expect for us anything other than one of the two fairest outcomes;[428] while we await for you that Allah will smite you with a punishment, either from Him, or at our hands?" So wait and watch, we are waiting and watching with you.

Say: "Spend willingly or unwillingly; it shall not be accepted from you. You are truly a sinful people."

And nothing prevents what they spend from being accepted but that they disbelieve in Allah and His Apostle and that they do not perform the prayer except lazily, and do not spend [anything] except grudgingly.

55 So do not let their wealth and their children win your approval, Allah only wishes to torture them therewith in the present life, so that their souls might depart while they are still unbelievers.

They swear by Allah that they [are believers] like you, but they are not; they are a people who fear [you].

If they could find a shelter or dens or any place to crawl into, they would make for it in great haste.

And some of them disparage your handling of the alms. If they are given part of it they are satisfied, but if they are not given any, they turn away angrily.

And would that they were satisfied with what Allah and His Apostle gave them and said: "Allah suffices us; Allah will give us of His bounty, as will His Apostle. We turn humbly to Him."

60 The alms are for the poor, the needy, their collectors and those whose hearts are bound together, as well as for the freeing of slaves, [repaying] the debtors, spending in Allah's path, and for the wayfarer. Thus Allah commands. Allah is All-Knowing, Wise.

And some of them molest the Prophet saying: "He hears [all what is said and believes what he hears]." Say: "He hears what is good for you. He believes in Allah and believes what he hears from the believers; and he is a

---

428. Martyrdom and victory.

mercy for those who believe." Those who hurt the Apostle of Allah will have a very painful punishment.

They swear to you by Allah to please you; but Allah and His Apostle they should rather please first, if they are true believers.

Do they not know that whoever opposes Allah and His Apostle, the Fire of Hell is reserved for them, abiding in it forever. That indeed is the great disgrace.

The hypocrites fear that a sura will be revealed informing them of what is in their hearts. Say: "Go on mocking, Allah will surely bring into the open what you fear."

65 And should you ask them, they would surely say: "We were only talking idly and playing." Say: "Were you then mocking Allah, His revelations and His Apostle?"

Make no excuses; you have disbelieved after believing. If We pardon a group of you, We shall punish another group, because they are wicked sinners.

The hypocrites, males and females, are all alike. They enjoin evil and forbid what is good and close their fists.[429] They have forgotten Allah,[430] and so He has forgotten them.[431] The hypocrites are the wicked sinners.

Allah has promised the hypocrites, males and females, and the unbelievers the Fire of Hell, abiding in it forever. It is sufficient unto them. He has also cursed them, and a lasting punishment awaits them.

Like those who came before you;[432] they were mightier than you and had more wealth and children. So they enjoyed their share;[433] then you enjoyed your share as did those before you, and you engaged in idle talk as they did. Those, their works in this world are vain; they are the losers.

70 Have you not heard about those who came before them, the people of Noah, of 'Ad, of Thamud, the people of Abraham, the people of Madyan, and the overturned towns?[434] Their messengers came to them with clear proofs; Allah never wronged them, but they wronged themselves.

As to the believers, males and females, they are friends of one another. They enjoin what is good and forbid what is evil, perform the prayers, give the alms and obey Allah and His Apostle. It is those on whom Allah will have mercy. Allah is Mighty, Wise.

Allah has promised the believers, males and females, gardens beneath which rivers flow, abiding therein forever, and fair dwellings in the Gardens

429. That is, they do not spend in Allah's way.
430. That is, they have been disobedient.
431. That is, He has deprived them of His mercy.
432. The hypocrites.
433. Share of earthly life.
434. The towns of Lot's people.

of Eden. However, Allah's good pleasure is greater. That is the great triumph.

O Prophet, fight the unbelievers and the hypocrites and be stern with them. Their abode is Hell, and what a terrible fate!

They swear by Allah that they said nothing [evil], but they said the word of disbelief and disbelieved after professing Islam, and they aimed at[435] what they could not attain. They only resented that Allah and His Apostle have enriched them from His bounty. If they repent, it will be better for them; but if they turn away, Allah will inflict a very painful punishment on them in this world and the Hereafter, and they will have on earth no friend or supporter.

75 And some of them make a compact with Allah: "If He gives us of His bounty, we shall give in charity and be among the righteous."

But when He gave them of His bounty, they grew mean and turned away disobediently.

So he caused hypocrisy to cling to their hearts until the day they meet Him, on account of revoking what they promised Allah and on account of lying.

Do they not know that Allah knows their hidden thoughts and private talk, and that Allah knows fully the things unseen?

Those disparage the believers who give voluntary alms and those who find nothing to offer but their utmost endeavour, and they scoff at them. May Allah mock them. There is a painful punishment [in store] for them.

80 Ask forgiveness for them or do not ask forgiveness for them. If you ask forgiveness for them seventy times, Allah will not forgive them; because they disbelieve in Allah and His Apostle. Allah does not guide the sinful people.

Those who stayed behind[436] rejoiced at tarrying behind the Apostle of Allah and hated to struggle with their wealth and their lives in Allah's path, saying: "Do not march forth in the heat." Say: "The Fire of Hell is hotter, if only they could understand."

Let them laugh a little and cry a lot, as a reward for what they used to do.

Then, if Allah brings you back to a party of them and they ask your permission to go forth with you, say: "You will never go forth with me, and you will never fight with me against any enemy. You were content to sit back the first time; so sit back with those who stay behind."

And do not ever pray over any one of them who dies, or be present at his grave; indeed they disbelieve in Allah and His Apostle, and die while still ungodly.

435. According to some commentators they aimed at killing the Prophet, while he was returning from Tabuk.
436. Those who failed to join the Tabuk expedition.

85 And do not let their wealth or children win your admiration. Allah only wishes to punish them therewith in the present life, so that their souls may depart while they are still unbelievers.

And if a sura is revealed stating: "Believe in Allah and fight along with His Apostle", the affluent among them will ask your permission and say: "Let us be with those who stay behind."

They are content to be among the women who stay behind, and a seal is set upon their hearts, and thus they do not understand.

But the Apostle and those who believe with him struggle with their wealth and their lives. To those are the good things reserved, and those are the prosperous.

Allah has prepared for them gardens beneath which rivers flow, abiding therein forever. That is the great triumph!

90 Some of the desert Arabs who gave excuses came to seek permission, whereas those who lied to Allah and His Apostle stayed behind. Those of them who disbelieved shall be afflicted with a very painful punishment.

The weak, the sick, and those who have nothing to spend are not at fault, if they are true to Allah and His Apostle. There can be no blame on the beneficent; and Allah is All-Forgiving, Merciful.

Nor on those who, when they came to you asking you for mounts, you said: "I do not find that whereon I can mount you." Thereupon they went back, their eyes overflowing with tears, sorrowing for not finding the means to spend.[437]

The blame is on those who ask your permission, although they are rich. They are content to join those women who stay behind. Allah has placed a seal upon their hearts and so they do not know.

They present to you [false] excuses when you return to them. Say: "Do not offer excuses; we will not believe you. Allah has told us [all] about you. Allah shall see your work, and His Apostle too. Then you will be turned over to Him Who knows the unseen and the seen, and He will apprise you of what you used to do."

95 They will swear by Allah to you, when you return to them, that you may leave them alone. So leave them alone; they are an abomination and their abode is Hell, as a reward for what they used to do.

They swear to you that you may be well-pleased with them; but should you be well-pleased with them, Allah will not be well-pleased with the sinful people.

The desert Arabs are more steeped in unbelief and hypocrisy and are more likely not to know the bounds of what Allah has revealed to His Apostle. Allah is All-Knowing, Wise.

437. That is, to provide the expenses of war.

And some of the desert Arabs regard what they spend as a fine, and await the turns of fortune to go against you. May the evil turn go against them! Allah is All-Hearing, All-Knowing.

And some of the desert Arabs believe in Allah and the Last Day and regard what they spend [in the way of Allah] as means to get closer to Allah and to earn the prayers of the Apostle. Indeed, that will bring them closer [to Allah]. He will admit them into His mercy. Allah is truly All-Forgiving, Merciful.

100   The early Emigrants[438] and the Helpers[439] and those who followed them up in beneficence – Allah is well-pleased with them, and they are well-pleased with Him, and He has prepared for them gardens beneath which rivers flow, abiding therein forever. That is the great triumph!

And some of the desert Arabs around you are hypocrites, and some of the people of Medina persist in hypocrisy. You do not know them, but We know them. We shall punish them twice, then they will be afflicted with a terrible punishment.[440]

Others have confessed their sins; they mixed a good deed with a bad one.[441] Perhaps Allah will pardon them. Allah is truly All-Forgiving, Merciful.

Take of their wealth voluntary alms to purify and cleanse them therewith; and pray for them, for your prayers are a source of tranquillity for them. Allah is All-Hearing, All-Knowing.

Do they not know that Allah is He who accepts the repentance from His servants, and accepts voluntary alms, and that Allah is All-Forgiving, Merciful?

105   And say: "Work, for Allah shall see your work, and His Apostle and the believers too. And you shall be brought back[442] to Him Who knows the Unseen and the Seen, and He will apprise you of what you used to do."

And others are deferred to Allah's decree; He will either punish them or pardon them. And Allah is All-Knowing, Wise.

And those who built a mosque[443] or hurt [the Muslims], to spread unbelief, to disunite [the believers] and to await him[444] who had fought Allah and His Apostle – they will certainly swear that they meant nothing but good. Allah bears witness that they are liars.

438. The early Muslims who emigrated to Medina.
439. The early Muslims of Medina who supported the Emigrants.
440. That is, before they are thrown into the Fire.
441. The good deed is confessing sins and the bad one is that they stayed behind when the Muslims marched against the enemy.
442. On the Day of Resurrection.
443. The reference is to the mosque which the hypocrites built in the neighbourhood of the mosque of Quba', the first mosque to be built by the Muslims.
444. He is said to be Abu 'Amir surnamed al-Rahib [the Monk].

Do not stand up there [for prayer]; for a mosque founded on piety from the first day is worthier of your standing in it. Therein are men who love to be purified; and Allah loves those who purify themselves.

Is one who founds his edifice upon the fear and good pleasure of Allah better, or one who founds his edifice upon the brink of a crumbling precipice that will tumble down with him into the Fire of Hell? Allah does not guide the unjust people.

110 The edifice which they have built will continue to be a source of doubt in their hearts, unless their hearts are cut up into pieces. Allah is All-Knowing, Wise.

Allah has bought from the believers their lives and their wealth in return for Paradise; they fight in the way of Allah, kill and get killed. That is a true promise from Him in the Torah, the Gospel and the Qur'an; and who fulfils His promise better than Allah? Rejoice then at the bargain you have made with Him; for that is the great triumph.

Those who repent, worship, praise, fast, kneel down, prostrate themselves, enjoin what is good and forbid what is evil and observe the ordinances of Allah – to [such] believers give the good tidings.[445]

It is not for the Prophet and those who believe to ask forgiveness for the polytheists even if they are near relatives, after it becomes clear to [the believers] that they are the people of the Fire.

Abraham asked forgiveness for his father, only because of a promise he had made to him; but when it became clear to him that he was an enemy of Allah, he disowned him. Indeed Abraham was compassionate, forbearing.

115 Allah would not lead any people astray after He has guided them, until He makes clear to them what they should fear. Allah, indeed, has knowledge of everything.

To Allah belongs the dominion of the heavens and the earth; He gives life and causes death and, apart from Allah, you have no friend or supporter.

Allah has forgiven the Prophet, the Emigrants and the Helpers who followed him in the hour of distress, after the hearts of a group of them had almost deviated. Then He forgave them; for He is, indeed, Most Kind and Most Merciful towards them.

And [He also forgave] the three[446] who were left behind till the earth, for all its vastness, became too small for them,[447] and their souls were distressed, and they realized that there was no refuge from Allah except with Him. Allah then forgave them so that they might repent. Allah is the All-Forgiving, the Merciful.

445. That they shall be pardoned.
446. Three of the Helpers of Medina.
447. Meaning that they could not find refuge.

O you who believe, fear Allah and side with the truthful.

120   It is not given to the people of Medina and the desert Arabs around them to stay behind the Apostle of Allah, nor to prefer their own lives to his life for they are afflicted neither by thirst nor fatigue nor hunger in Allah's way, nor do they take a step that upsets the unbelievers, nor inflict a blow on the enemy but a good deed is recorded for them on account of it. Allah does not allow the beneficent to lose their reward.

Nor do they spend anything whether small or large, nor cross a valley but it is recorded for them, so that Allah may reward them for the best of their deeds.

The believers should not all go to war. Why doesn't a company from each group go forth to instruct themselves in religion and admonish their people[448] when they return, that perchance, they may beware.

O you who believe, fight those of the unbelievers who are near to you and let them see how harsh you can be. Know that Allah is with the righteous.

Whenever a sura is revealed, some of them would say: "Who of you has this one increased in faith?" It will increase the faith of those who believe, and they will rejoice.

125   But for those in whose hearts there is a sickness, it will add disbelief to their disbelief, and they will die while they are unbelievers.

Do they not see that they are tried once or twice every year? Yet they neither repent nor take heed.

And whenever a sura is revealed, they look at each other [saying]: "Does anyone see you?" Then they turn away. Allah has turned away their hearts, because they are a people who do not understand.

There has come to you an Apostle from among yourselves. It grieves him to see you suffer, he cares much for you, and is kind and merciful towards the believers.

But if they turn away, say: "Sufficient for me is Allah; there is no god but He; in Him I put my trust. He is the Lord of the Glorious Throne."

---

448. Those who go to war.

Yunus, Jonah

In the Name of Allah, the Compassionate, the Merciful

Alif, Lam, Ra.

1   Those are the verses of the sound Book.[449]

Is it a wonder to the people that We have revealed to one of them: "Warn the people and announce to the believers the good news that they have a sure footing with their Lord?" The unbelievers say: "This indeed is a manifest sorcerer."

Truly, your Lord is Allah who created the heavens and the earth in six days, then He sat on the throne controlling all things. There is no intercessor without His leave. That is Allah, your Lord; so worship Him. Do you not pay heed?

Unto Him you shall all return; it is Allah's promise in truth. He originates the creation, then He brings it back to reward equitably those who believe and do the good deeds. But those who disbelieve shall drink boiling water and shall be severely punished on account of their disbelief.

5   It is He who made the sun a bright radiance and the moon a light, and determined phases for it[450] so that you may know the number of years and the reckoning. Allah did not create that except in truth, expounding the signs to a people who know.

Indeed, in the alternation of night and day and in what Allah has created in the heavens and the earth are real signs for a people who are God-fearing.

Those who do not hope to meet Us and are content with the present life and are at ease in it, and those who pay no heed to Our signs;

Their refuge is the Fire, on account of [what] they used to do.

Surely, those who believe and do the good, their Lord shall guide them for their belief; beneath them rivers will flow in the gardens of bliss.

10   Their prayer therein shall be: "Glory be to You, O Allah"; and their greeting in it shall be: "Peace!" and they conclude their prayer by saying: "Praise belongs to Allah, the Lord of the Worlds."

And were Allah to hasten the evil for mankind[451] just as they would hasten the good for themselves,[452] their term would have been fulfilled.

---

449. The Qur'an.
450. The moon.
451. That is, hasten their punishment.
452. From God.

Then We would leave those who do not hope to meet Us in their arrogance wandering aimlessly.

And if hardship afflicts man, he calls Us lying down, sitting or standing; but when We lift his hardship, he passes on, as though he never called Us to [lift] a hardship that afflicted him. Thus what the transgressors do seems fair to them.

And We have destroyed generations before you, when they did wrong and their messengers brought them the clear proofs, but they would not believe. Thus We reward the wicked sinners.

Then We made you successors on earth, after them, to see how you would behave.

15 And if Our revelations are clearly recited to them, those who do not hope to meet Us say: "Bring a Qur'an other than this one or alter it." Say: "It is not for me to alter it of my own accord. I only follow what is revealed to me. Indeed, I fear, if I disobey my Lord, the punishment of a fateful day."[453]

Say: "If Allah had willed, I would not have recited it to you, and He would not have told you about it. I have dwelt in your midst a lifetime before it. Do you not understand?"

For, who is more wicked than one who forges lies about Allah or denies His revelations? Indeed, the wicked sinners shall never prosper.

They worship, apart from Allah, what neither harms nor benefits them, and say: "These are our intercessors with Allah." Say: "Do you inform Allah about what he does not know in the heavens or on earth?" Glory be to Him, and may He be exalted above what they associate [with Him]!

Mankind were a single nation; then they differed. Had it not been for a prior order of your Lord, the matter over which they had differed would have been settled.

20 And they say: "If only a sign is sent to him from his Lord." Say then: "The Unseen belongs to Allah; so wait, and I will be waiting with you."

And if We let people taste a mercy after an affliction touches them, they begin to scheme against Our revelations. Say: "Allah is quicker at scheming."[454] Surely Our apostles write down what you scheme.

It is He who makes your journey on land and on sea; so that when you are in the ships and they sail with them driven by a fair wind, and they rejoice in it, a stormy wind comes upon them and waves surge over them from every side, and they think that they are being overwhelmed. Then they call upon Allah, professing submission to Him sincerely: "If You save us from this, we shall be truly thankful."

But when He saves them, they resort to aggression in the land wrongfully.

453. That is, the Day of Resurrection.
454. What is meant is quick retribution.

O people, your aggression shall recoil upon yourselves. It is what you enjoy in the present life; then unto Us shall be your return; whereupon We will inform you about what you were doing.

The present life is like water We send down from the sky, causing the vegetation of the earth, from which people and cattle eat, to grow luxuriant. But when the earth puts on its ornamental garb and is adorned, and its people think they are able to get what they want from it, Our retribution comes upon it day or night, making its produce like a cropped harvest, as if it had never flourished before. Thus We expound Our revelations to people who reflect.

25   And Allah summons to the Abode of Peace and leads whomever He pleases to a straight path.

To those who do the good is the best reward[455] and more;[456] and their faces shall not be covered with blackness or misery. Those are the people of Paradise, wherein they will abide forever.

But for those who do the evil deeds, the reward for an evil deed shall be its like, and humiliation shall overtake them. Against Allah they will have no defender; it is as though their faces have been covered with dark patches of the night. Those are the people of the Fire, abiding therein forever.

On the day We will muster them all together; then We will say to those who set up associates with Allah: "Stay in your places, you and your associates." Then We shall separate them, and their associates will say: "You were not worshipping us.

"Allah is a sufficient witness between us and you; for we were unaware of your worshipping us."

30   There, each soul shall know what it had done in advance; and they will be turned over to Allah, their true Master; and what [falsehood] they invented will stray away from them.

Say: "Who provides for you from heaven and earth? Who controls the hearing and sight? Who brings forth the living from the dead and brings forth the dead from the living? And who is in control of all things?" They will surely say: "Allah." Then say: "Will you not fear God?

"That indeed is Allah, your true Lord. What is there, after truth, except error? How can you then be turned away [from the Truth]?"

Thus, your Lord's word against those who have sinned has been accomplished, that they shall not believe.

Say: "Is there among your associates one who originates creation, then brings it back?"[457] Say: "Allah originates creation, then brings it back. How then are you perverted?"

455. That is, Paradise.
456. "More" refers to their ability to look at Allah.
457. Brings it back to life after death.

35 Say: "Is there any of your associates who guides to the truth?" Say: "Allah guides to the truth. Who is, then, more worthy of being followed, he who guides to the truth or he who does not guide, unless he is guided? What is the matter with you? How do you judge?"

Most of them follow nothing but conjecture. Surely conjecture avails nothing against the truth. Allah knows well what they do.

This Qur'an could never have been produced except by Allah. It is a confirmation of that [which was revealed] before it and an exposition of the Book. There is no doubt about it. It is from the Lord of the Worlds.

Or do they say: "He[458] has forged it." Say: "Come up, then, with a single sura like it, and call upon whomever you can, apart from Allah, if you are truthful."

No, they deny that[459] whereof they have no knowledge, and whose interpretation has not yet come to them. That is how those who came before them denied [it]. Look, then, what was the fate of the wrongdoers.

40 Some of them believe in it, and some do not; but your Lord knows best the mischief-makers.

If they deny what you say, then say: "What I do is mine, and what you do is yours. You are quit of what I do, and I am quit of what you do."

And some of them listen to you; but can you make the deaf hear, even if they do not understand?

And some of them look at you; but can you guide the blind, even if they do not see?

Surely, Allah does not wrong people at all; but people wrong themselves.

45 And on the day He musters them, it is as though they have only tarried for one hour of the day, recognizing each other. Those who have disbelieved in meeting Allah are the real losers, and are not well-guided.

And whether We show you[460] part of what We promise them or cause you to die, surely unto Us is their return; and then Allah is a witness of what they do.

Every nation has its messenger; and when their messenger comes, they will be justly judged, and they will not be wronged.

And they say: "When is this promise, if you are truthful?"

Say: "I have no power to harm or to profit myself, except as Allah wills. To every nation is a term;[461] when its term comes, it will not put it back a single hour, nor will it put it forward."

458. The Prophet.
459. The Qur'an.
460. That is, during your lifetime.
461. A term of life.

50   Say: "Tell me, if His punishment overtakes you by night or day, what part of it will the wicked sinners seek to hasten?"[462]

Is it then, when it has overtaken you, that you will believe in Him? Now [you believe] while you were seeking to hasten it!

Then it will be said to the wrongdoers: "Taste the everlasting punishment. Will you be rewarded except for what you did?"

And they ask you to tell them: "Is it true?" Say: "Yes, by my Lord, it is the truth, and you cannot escape [punishment]."

Had every soul which did wrong possessed whatever is on earth, it would offer it as ransom, and they will feel remorseful when they see the punishment; but they will be justly judged, and they will not be wronged.

55   Indeed, to Allah belongs what is in the heavens and the earth. Indeed, Allah's promise is true, but most of them do not know.

He gives life and causes death, and unto Him you shall be returned.

O mankind, there has come to you from your Lord an admonition,[463] a healing for what is in the hearts, and a guidance and mercy for the believers.

Say: "In Allah's bounty and mercy – in those let them rejoice. It is better than that which they amass."

Say: "Have you considered the provision Allah has sent down for you, and how then you made some of it unlawful and some lawful?" Say: "Has Allah allowed you or are you lying about Allah?"

60   And what will those who impute lies to Allah think on the Day of Resurrection? Allah is bountiful to mankind, but most of them are not thankful.

You[464] do not go about any affair, nor do you recite any portion of the Qur'an, nor do you[465] do anything, but We are witnesses thereof, as you press on with it. And not a speck's weight in the earth or in the heavens escapes Allah; and nothing smaller or bigger than that, but is in a manifest Book.

Indeed, the friends of Allah have nothing to fear, nor will they grieve.

Those who believe and are righteous;

Theirs is the good news in the present life and the Hereafter. And there will be no alteration of the words of Allah. That is the great triumph.

65   And let not what they say grieve you. All power is Allah's; He is the All-Hearing, the All-Knowing.

Indeed, to Allah belongs whoever is in the heavens or the earth. Those

---

462. That is, will the wicked sinners after seeing how terrible the punishment is still be seeking to hasten it through mockery and disbelief?
463. The Qur'an.
464. The Prophet.
465. The Prophet and the Muslims.

who call upon others, apart from Allah, do not follow any associate. They only follow conjecture and they are only lying.

It is He who created the night for you to rest therein and the day to see. Surely, in this are signs for a people who listen.

They say: "Allah has taken a child." Glory be to Him! He is the Self-Sufficient; His is everything in the heavens and on earth. You have no authority for this. Do you attribute to Allah what you do not know?

Say: "Those who invent lies about Allah will not prosper."

70 [It is only] a little enjoyment in this life; then unto Us is their return; then We will make them taste the terrible punishment, on account of their disbelief.

And relate to them the story of Noah, when he said to his people: "O my people, if my dwelling [among you] and my reminding you of the revelations of Allah, is too much for you, then in Allah I have put my trust. Agree upon a course of action with your associates; then let not that course of action be a burden to you; then pass to me [your decision] and give me no respite.

"If you turn away, I have asked for no reward from you. My reward is only with Allah. I have been ordered to be one of those who submit."

But they denounced him; so We delivered him and those with him in the Ark and made them successors, while drowning those who denied Our signs. See then what was the fate of those who were warned!

Then We sent after him messengers to their people. They brought them clear proofs; but they would not believe in what they had denied earlier. Thus do We seal the hearts of the aggressors.

75 Then We sent forth after them Moses and Aaron to Pharaoh and his dignitaries, with Our signs; but they were arrogant; they were sinful people.

Then when the truth came to them from Us, they said: "This indeed is manifest sorcery."

Moses said: "Do you say to the truth, when it has come to you: 'Is this sorcery?' Sorcerers will never prosper."

They said: "Have you come to us to turn us away from that[466] in which we found our fathers so that sovereignty may be yours,[467] in the land? We shall not believe in you both."

Then Pharaoh said: "Bring me every skilful magician."

80 Then, when the magicians came, Moses said to them: "Cast down what you intend to cast down."

Then, when they cast down, Moses said: "What you brought forward is

466. That faith.
467. Moses and his brother.

real sorcery. Allah will bring it to naught. Allah indeed does not uphold the work of the mischief-makers."

"Allah vindicates the truth by His words, even if the wicked sinners dislike it."

And so only a handful of his people believed in Moses for fear that Pharaoh and his dignitaries would persecute them. Pharaoh was truly a tyrant in the land and one of the transgressors.

And Moses said: "O my people, if you believe in Allah, then in Him put your trust, if you submit [to Him]."

85   Whereupon they said: "In Allah we have put our trust. Our Lord, do not let us be tried by the wrongdoing people."

"And deliver us by Your mercy from the unbelieving people."

And We revealed to Moses and his brother: "Take for your people dwellings in Egypt and make your dwellings places of worship, perform the prayer and announce the good news to the believers."

Moses then said: "Lord, you have given Pharaoh and his dignitaries adornment and wealth in the present life, with which they lead people away from Your path. O Lord, obliterate their wealth and harden their hearts so that they will not believe, till they see the very painful punishment."

He said: "Your prayer is answered; carry on both with your call and go straight, and do not follow the path of those who do not know."

90   And We brought the Children of Israel across the sea. Pharaoh and his troops followed them insolently and aggressively; but when he was about to drown, he said: "I believe that there is no god but He in whom the Children of Israel believe, and I am one of those who submit [to Allah]."

[It was said to Him]: "Now [you believe]! But you disobeyed earlier and you were one of the mischief-makers.

"Today, then, We shall save you bodily, so that you may become a sign to those who come after you. Indeed, many people are heedless of Our signs."

And We have established the Children of Israel in a dignified domain and provided them with good things. Thus they did not differ among themselves until the certain knowledge came to them. Surely, your Lord shall judge between them on the Day of Resurrection regarding that about which they differed.

So, if you[468] are in doubt concerning what We have revealed to you, then ask those who have been reading the Book[469] before you. Indeed, the truth has come to you from your Lord; so do not be one of the doubters.

95   And do not be one of those who deny Allah's revelations and thus become one of the losers.

468. The person addressed here, according to some commentators, is Muhammad.
469. The Torah.

Surely, those against whom the word of your Lord will be fulfilled are not going to believe;

Even if every sign comes to them, till they see the very painful punishment.

How is it, then, that no town believed so that its belief would profit it, except the people of Jonah? When they believed, We removed from them the punishment of disgrace in the present life and allowed them to enjoy life for a while.

Had your Lord willed, everybody on earth would have believed. Will you then compel people to become believers?

100   It is not given to any soul to believe, except by Allah's leave. And He lays the scourge on those who do not understand.

Say: "Behold what is in the heavens and the earth." But neither the signs nor the warnings will avail a people who do not believe.

Do they, then, expect anything other than the like of the days of those who passed away before them? Say: "Wait on, I am with you one of those who wait."

Then, We shall deliver Our messengers and the believers; it is only right that We should deliver the believers.

Say: "O people, if you are in doubt regarding my religion, [know that] I worship not those you worship, apart from Allah; but I worship Allah who causes you to die, and I have been commanded to be one of the believers."

105   And [it was said to me]: "Set your face towards religion, in an upright way, and do not be one of the polytheists."

"And do not call, apart from Allah, on anything which neither profits nor harms you. If you do, you are then one of the wrongdoers."

"And if Allah afflicts you with adversity, none can lift it other than He; and if He wills any good for you, none can bar His bounty. He will accord it to whomever He pleases of His servants and He is the All-Forgiving, the Merciful."

Say: "O people, the truth has come to you from your Lord; whoever is well-guided is well-guided only to his own advantage, and whoever goes astray goes astray only to his disadvantage, and I am not a guardian over you."

And follow what is revealed to you and be patient and steadfast, until Allah judges; for He is the best of judges.

SURA 11

Hud, The Prophet Hud

In the Name of Allah, the Compassionate, the Merciful

Alif, Lam, Ra.

1   [This is] a Book with verses which are elaborately formulated and clearly expounded from the Wise, the All-Aware.

That you should worship none other than Allah; I am truly a warner and a bearer of good news to you from Him;

And ask forgiveness of your Lord; then turn to him in repentance, that He may allow you a fair enjoyment [in this life] for a fixed term, and may bestow His bounty on every worthy one; but if you turn away I fear for you the punishment of a great day.

Unto Allah is your return, and He has power over everything.

5   Behold, they turn their breasts sideways so as to hide [what they harbour] from Him. Indeed, when they wrap themselves in their clothes He knows what they conceal and what they reveal. He knows the secrets of the hearts.

There is no beast on earth but its sustenance is [provided] by Allah; and He knows its resting-place and its repository. All is in a manifest Book.

And it is He who created the heavens and the earth in six days, and His throne was upon the water, that He might try you [and see] which one of you does the best work. And if you[470] say: "You will surely be raised up after death", the unbelievers will say: "This is nothing but manifest sorcery."

And if We hold punishment back from them for a fixed period, they will say: "What holds it back?" Surely, the day it will overtake them will not be turned away from them, and they shall be afflicted by what they used to mock.

And if We let man have a taste of mercy from Us, then wrest it from him, he yields to despair and becomes ungrateful.

10   And if We let him taste prosperity after an adversity has afflicted him, he will say: "Misfortunes have gone away from me", and becomes joyful and proud.

Except for those who are patient and do the good deeds; for those are forgiveness and a great reward.

Perhaps you are passing over[471] a part of what is revealed to you, and your heart is distressed lest they should say: "If only a treasure was sent down

---

470. The Prophet.
471. That is, you are not reciting.

upon him or an angel accompanied him!" You are only a warner, and Allah is in charge of everything.

Or will they say: "He has forged it."[472] Say: "Come up then with ten forged suras like it, and call upon whomever you can, apart from Allah, if you are truthful."

But if they[473] do not answer you, then know that it[474] was revealed with Allah's knowledge and that there is no god but He. Will you then submit?

15   Whoever desires the life of this world and its finery, We will reward them [during it] for their [good] works, and they will not be given less than their due.

[Yet] those [are the people] who shall have nothing in the Hereafter except the Fire, and what they did [here] will go there to waste, and their works will be in vain.

Are those then [like these] who have a clear proof[475] from their Lord recited by a witness from Him, and preceded by the Book of Moses as a guide and mercy? Those believe in it; but those who disbelieve in it from among the parties[476] – their appointed place is the Fire. So do not be in doubt about it. It is indeed the truth from your Lord; but most people do not believe.

And who is more perverse than he who invents lies about Allah? Those shall be brought before their Lord and the witnesses[477] shall say: "These are the ones who lied about their Lord. May Allah's curse be upon the wrongdoers!"

Those who bar people from the path of Allah, and wish it to be crooked; they truly disbelieve in the Hereafter.

20   Those will not escape on earth and they have, apart from Allah, no protectors. Their punishment will be doubled; they were unable to hear, nor did they perceive.

Those are the ones who lost their souls and that which they invented[478] strayed away from them.

Without doubt, they will be, in the Hereafter, the greatest losers.

As to those who believe and do the good deeds and turn humbly to their Lord, they shall be the people of Paradise, dwelling therein forever.

The case of the two parties[479] is like the blind and the deaf compared

---

472. The Qur'an.
473. Those gods set up besides Allah.
474. The Qur'an.
475. The Qur'an.
476. The Meccans and neighbouring tribes who opposed the Prophet.
477. The angels.
478. The associates they assign to Allah.
479. The believers and the unbelievers.

with the man who sees and hears. Are they both alike? Do you not pay heed?

25 And We have sent Noah forth to his people; [he said]: "I am a plain warner to you;

"That you worship none but Allah. I fear for you the punishment of a very painful Day."

Thereupon the unbelieving dignitaries among his people said to him: "We do not see in you except a mortal like ourselves; nor do we see in those who hastily followed you except the scum of our people. We do not see that you[480] have any merit over us, but rather think that you are liars."

He said: "O my people, do you think that if I have a clear proof from my Lord and He has granted me a mercy from Him but it has been hidden from your sight, we would force it on you while you are averse to it?

"And O my people, I do not ask you money for it; my reward is with Allah; and I will not drive away those who believe, for they will surely meet their Lord, but I see that you are an ignorant people.

30 "O my people, who will save me from Allah if I drive [the believers] away? Will you pay heed?

"I do not say to you that I possess Allah's treasures; and I do not know the Unseen. I do not claim to be an angel; nor do I say to those at whom you look with disdain that Allah will not accord them any good; Allah knows best what is in their hearts. For I would be, then, one of the wrongdoers."

They said: "O Noah, you have disputed and disputed much with us. Bring us, then, what you promise us, if you are truthful."

He said: "It is Allah who will bring it to you, if He wills, and you will not be able to escape.

"My advice will not profit you, should I wish to give you advice, if Allah wills to lead you astray. He is your Lord and unto Him you shall be brought back."

35 Or will they say: "He has forged it."[480] Say: "If I have forged it, my guilt is upon me and I am innocent of the evil you commit."

And it was revealed to Noah: "None of your people will believe except those who have already believed, so do not grieve at what they do;

"And make the Ark under Our gaze and as We reveal, and do not plead with Me regarding the wrongdoers; they shall be drowned."

So he started making the Ark, and whenever a group of his people passed by him, they mocked him. [But] he would say: "If you mock us, we will mock you, as you are mocking.

"You shall surely learn who will be afflicted by a degrading chastisement, and will undergo a lasting punishment."

480. The addressed here are Noah and the believers.

40   And when Our command came, and the water gushed forth from the earth, We said: "Carry in it[481] two of every kind, together with your family, except for those who have been doomed, and [take] those who believe." However only a few believers besides him were there.

And he said: "Embark on it. In the name of Allah will be its sailing and anchor. My Lord is indeed All-Forgiving, Merciful."

And as it[482] sailed along with them amid waves like mountains, Noah called out to his son, who stood apart: "My son, embark with us, and do not remain with the unbelievers."

He[483] said: "I will seek refuge in a mountain that will protect me from water." He[484] said: "Today, there is no protector from Allah's decree, except for him on whom He has mercy." Then the waves came between them and so he was one of those who were drowned.

And it was said:[485] "O earth, swallow your waters, and O heaven, desist." The water then subsided and the decree [of Allah] was accomplished; and it[486] settled upon al-Judi mountain; and it was said: "Away with the wrongdoing people."

45   Noah then called out to his Lord saying: "My Lord, my son is of my family; and your promise is surely the truth and you are the best of judges."

He said: "O Noah, he is not of your family. It is an act which is not righteous, so do not ask Me about that of which you have no knowledge. I admonish you not to be one of the ignorant."

He said: "Lord, I seek refuge with you, lest I should ask you that of which I have no knowledge. For unless you forgive me and have mercy on me I will be one of the losers."

It was said to Noah: "Come down [from the Ark] in peace from Us and blessings on you and on [some] nations [descending] from those with you, and We shall provide for others [in this life]. Then they will be afflicted by severe punishment from us."

That is part of the tidings of the Unseen which We are revealing to you. Neither you, nor your people knew it before this. Forbear, then, the [good] outcome belongs to the righteous.

50   And [We sent] to 'Ad their brother Hud. He said: "O my people, worship Allah; you have no other god but He. You are only lying [about Allah].

"O my people, I ask you no reward for it; my reward is only with Him who created me. Do you not understand?

481. The Ark.
482. The Ark.
483. Noah's son.
484. Noah.
485. By Allah.
486. The Ark.

"O my people, ask forgiveness from your Lord, then repent unto Him, for He will send you torrents of rain from the sky and add strength to your strength. And do not turn away guilty."

They said: "O Hud, you have not brought us any clear proof, and we will not abandon our gods because of what you say, and we will not believe in you.

"We only say that some of our gods have smitten you with some evil." He said: "I call Allah to witness and call you to witness that I am innocent of what you associate.

55 "With Him. So try your guile on me, all of you; then do not give me any respite.

"I have put my trust in Allah, my Lord and your Lord. There is no creature which crawls, but He takes it by the forelock.[487] My Lord is truly on a straight path.

"Then, if you turn away, I have actually delivered to you what I was sent forth to you with, and my Lord will raise up as successors a people other than you, and you will not cause Him any harm. My Lord watches over all things."

And when Our decree came, We saved Hud and those who believed with him, by a mercy of Ours, and delivered them from a harsh punishment.

Such were the [people of] 'Ad; they denied the signs of their Lord and disobeyed His messengers and followed the command of every obstinate tyrant.

60 And they were pursued by a curse in this world and [shall be cursed] on the Day of Resurrection. Surely, 'Ad disbelieved their Lord. Away with 'Ad, the people of Hud.

And to Thamud [We sent] their brother Salih. He said: "O my people, worship Allah; you have no other god but Him. He brought you out from the earth and made you inhabit it; so ask His forgiveness and repent unto Him. My Lord is indeed close at hand and answers [the prayer]."

They said: "O Salih, we set our hopes on you before this. Do you forbid us to worship what our fathers worshipped? We are indeed in grave doubt regarding what you are calling us to."

He said: "O my people, what if I am in possession of a clear proof from my Lord, and He has accorded me a mercy of His own? Who then will protect me from Allah if I disobey Him? Surely, you will only compound my perdition.

"O my people, here is the she-camel of Allah, a sign unto you. Let her graze in Allah's land and do not do her any harm, lest a swift punishment should overtake you."

487. That is, He controls it.

137

65   However, they hamstrung her, and so he said: "[You can] stay in your houses [only] for three days. This is a promise which will not be belied."

Then, when Our command came, We saved Salih and those who believed with him, by a mercy of Our own, from the disgrace of that day. Your Lord is truly the Strong, and Mighty.

And the evil-doers were overtaken by the [thundering] cry and they lay prostrate in their own homes,

As if they never dwelt therein. Truly, Thamud disbelieved their Lord. Away with Thamud!

Our messengers[488] indeed came to Abraham bearing good news. They said: "Peace", he said: "Peace." Then he brought a roasted calf at once.

70   But when he saw that their hands did not reach out to it, he became suspicious of them and conceived a fear of them. They said: "Fear not, we have been sent to the people of Lot."

His wife was standing by, so she laughed. Thereupon We announced to her the good news of Isaac, and after Isaac, of Jacob.

She said: "Woe is me, shall I bear a child while I am an old woman, and this, my husband, is an old man too? This is truly a very strange thing."

They said: "Do you wonder at Allah's command? May the mercy and blessings of Allah be upon you, O people of the House.[489] Surely He is Praiseworthy and Glorious."

Then when fear left Abraham and the good news came to him, he started pleading with Us concerning the people of Lot.

75   Abraham is truly clement, contrite, penitent.

"O Abraham, desist from this; the command of your Lord has come and an irreversible punishment shall surely smite them."

And when Our messengers came to Lot, he was grieved by them and felt unable to protect them. He said: "This is a dreadful day."

And his people came rushing towards him; and before that time they used to perpetrate evil deeds.[490] He said: "O my people, these are my daughters; they are purer for you. So fear Allah and do not disgrace me by [wronging] my guests. Is there not one right-minded man among you?"

They said: "You know that we have no right to your daughters, and you know well what we want."

80   He said: "Would that I had the power to stand against you, or could seek refuge with a strong supporter."

They[491] said: "O Lot, we are your Lord's messengers to you; they will not

---

488. They are generally believed to be angels who looked like men.
489. The House of Abraham.
490. That is, practise sodomy.
491. The angels who were Lot's guests.

reach you. So set out with your family in watch of the night and let no one look back, except for your wife.[492] She will be afflicted with what they have been afflicted with. Their appointed time is the morning. Is not the morning close enough?"

And when Our decree came, We turned [the town][493] upside down and rained down upon it stones of clay in clusters;

Marked from your Lord; and they were never far off from the wrongdoers.

And to Midian [We sent] their brother Shu'ayb. He said: "O my people, worship Allah; you have no other god but Him. Do not skimp the measure and the weight. I see that you are prospering, but I fear for you the punishment of an encompassing day.

85 "And my people, be just and give full measure and full weight, and do not cheat people out of things due to them, and do not sow corruption in the land by committing evil.

"What remains for you from Allah's provision is better for you if you are true believers; and I am not a watcher over you."

They said: "O Shu'ayb, does your prayer[494] command you that we should abandon what our fathers worshipped and that we should not do with our wealth what we wish? You are indeed the clement and right-minded one."[495]

He said: "O my people, do you think that if I have a clear proof from my Lord and He has granted me a fair provision from Him [I would commit any of those evils]? I do not want to do what I forbid you to do. I only want to do what I can to set things right. My success comes only from Allah. In Him I have put my trust and to Him I turn.

"O my people, let not my disagreement with you bring upon you what the people of Noah, the people of Hud or the people of Salih brought upon themselves.[496] The people of Lot are not far away from you.

90 "And ask forgiveness from your Lord; then repent upon him. My Lord is truly Merciful, Kind."

They said: "O Shu'ayb, we do not understand much of what you say; and surely we see you weak in our midst. Were it not for your family, we would have stoned you; for you are not too dear [to be stoned]."

He said: "O my people, is my family dearer to you than Allah? You have turned your backs on Him. My Lord knows what you do.

492. She was disobedient to her husband.
493. The town of Sodom.
494. That is, religion.
495. They said this mockingly.
496. That is, destruction.

"O my people, continue to do what you can, and I shall continue too. You will surely learn who will be seized by a punishment disgracing him, and who is a liar. Wait and see, and I shall be waiting with you."

And when Our decree came, We delivered Shu'ayb and those who believed with him by a mercy of Ours, and the wrongdoers were overtaken by the [thundering] Cry, and they lay prostrate in their own homes,

95 As if they never dwelt therein. Away with Midian. [It perished] as did Thamud before.

And We have indeed sent Moses with Our signs and a manifest authority,

To Pharaoh and his dignitaries; but they followed Pharaoh's command, and Pharaoh's command was not sound.

He shall be at the head of his people on the Day of Resurrection; thus he shall lead them into the Fire. How wretched is the place to which they will be led!

And they are followed in this life with a curse and on the Day of Resurrection too. Wretched is the support they shall be given!

100 That is part of the tidings of the towns We recount to you; some of them are still standing and some have been reduced to rubble.

And We have not wronged them, but they have wronged themselves. Their deities, upon whom they called, apart from Allah, did not avail them anything when the decree of your Lord came; but they only added to their destruction.

And such is your Lord's punishment when He punishes the cities which are unjust. His punishment is indeed very painful, very hard.

There is surely in this a sign for him who fears the punishment of the Hereafter. That is a Day on which men will be gathered together, and that is a Day to be witnessed.

And we shall not delay it, but for an appointed term.

105 The day it comes, no soul shall speak without His leave. Some of them[497] shall be wretched, some happy.

As for the wretched, they shall be in the Fire; they shall have therein groaning and moaning;

Abiding therein forever, so long as the heavens and the earth shall endure, except as your Lord pleases. Your Lord does indeed what He wants.

But as for the blessed, they shall be in Paradise abiding therein as long as the heavens and the earth shall endure; except as your Lord pleases, a gift, uninterrupted.

So do not be in doubt as to what these [people] worship; they only

---

497. Those gathered.

worship as their fathers worshipped before them, and We shall accord them their share[498] undiminished.

110   And We have given Moses the Book, but discord broke out around it; and but for a word that preceded from your Lord, the matter would have been decided between them. They are indeed in disturbing doubt with respect to it.

And your Lord will surely pay them all in full for their works. He is truly Aware of what they do.

Be then upright as you have been commanded, together with those who repented with you, and do not be unjust; for He sees whatever you do.

And do not incline towards the wrongdoers, lest the Fire should touch you. You have no supporters apart from Allah, and you will not be helped.

And perform the prayer at the two ends of the day and [the first] watches of the night. Surely the good deeds will wipe out the evil deeds; that is a reminder for those who remember.

115   And be patient; for Allah does not waste the reward of the righteous.

If only there had been among the generations who preceded you men possessing understanding and forbidding corruption in the earth, except for a few of them whom We saved! The wrongdoers continued to indulge in what they used to enjoy and, in fact, were wicked sinners.

And your Lord would not have destroyed the cities unjustly, had their inhabitants been righteous.

And had your Lord willed, He would have made mankind a single nation; but they will continue to differ among themselves,

Except for those on whom your Lord has mercy. To that end He created them, and the word of your Lord has been accomplished: "I will surely fill up Hell with *jinn* and humans, all together."

120   And all We relate to you of the tidings of the messengers is to strengthen your heart; and you have received in these the truth, admonition and reminder for the believers.

And say to the unbelievers: "Continue with what you are doing, and we shall continue with ours.

"And wait; we too are waiting."

To Allah belongs the Unseen in the heavens and on earth, and to Him the whole affair shall be referred. So worship Him and put your trust in Him; your Lord is not unaware of the things you do.

---

498. Their share of the punishment.

SURA 12

Yusuf, Joseph

In the Name of Allah, the Compassionate, the Merciful

Alif, Lam, Ra.
1   These are the verses of the clear Book.

We have revealed it as an Arabic Qur'an, that perchance you may understand.

We narrate to you the fairest narratives in revealing to you this Qur'an, although you were, prior to it, one of the heedless.

When Joseph said to his father: "O my father, I saw [in my dream] eleven planets and the sun and the moon, I saw them prostrating themselves before me."

5   He said: "My son, do not relate your dream to your brothers, lest they plot evil against you. Surely, the Devil is the sworn enemy of man."

And thus your Lord will choose you and teach you the interpretation of dreams[499] and will perfect His grace upon you and upon the family of Jacob, as He has perfected it formerly upon your two fathers, Abraham and Isaac. Surely your Lord is All-Knowing, Wise.

There are indeed in Joseph and his brothers signs for the inquiring.

When they said: "Joseph and his brother are dearer to our father than the rest of us, although we are a large group. Our father is truly in manifest error."

"Kill Joseph or cast him away in some land that your father's love may be wholly yours, and you may become after him a righteous people."

10   One of them said: "Do not kill Joseph, but rather throw him in the bottom of the pit, so that some traveller may pick him up, if you must do anything."

They said: "Our father, why do you not trust us with Joseph? We certainly wish him well.

"Send him forth with us tomorrow that he may frolic and play, and we will surely take care of him."

He said: "It grieves me to let you take him away; and I fear that the wolf may devour him while you are not watching him."

They said: "If the wolf should devour him while we are a large group, we should then be the real losers."

15   But when they took him away and decided to cast him in the bottom of

499. Dreams or, according to some commentators, events and signs.

the pit, We revealed to him: "You should tell them about their intention while they are unaware."

And they came to their father in the evening weeping.

They said: "Our father, we went away racing and left Joseph by our baggage; and so the wolf devoured him. You will not believe us, even if we are truthful."

And they stained his shirt with false blood. He said: "Rather, your souls tempted you to do something. So come gentle patience! To Allah I turn for help against what you say."

And some travellers came, and they sent their water-drawer, who let down his bucket. He said: "Good news! Here is a boy." And they hid him as merchandise, Allah being fully aware of what they were doing.

20 And they sold him for a cheap price, a number of dirhams, since they were not interested in him.

And the Egyptian who bought him said to his wife: "Make his stay honourable; perhaps he will profit us or we may take him for a son." Thus We established Joseph in the land and taught him the interpretation of dreams. Allah has control over His affairs though most people do not know.

When he was fully grown, We gave him judgement and knowledge, and thus We reward the beneficent.

And the woman, in whose house he was, sought to seduce him. She closed the doors firmly and said: "Come." He said: "Allah forbid. It is my Lord who gave me a good abode. Surely, the wrongdoers do not prosper."

Certainly she made for him and he would have made for her if it were not for a sign from his Lord. And that was to divert him from evil and indecency. He was indeed one of our sincere servants.

25 They raced to the door, and she ripped his shirt from behind. When they met her husband at the door, she said: "What is the penalty of one who intended evil for your wife except imprisonment or severe punishment?"

He[500] said: "She sought to seduce me." And a member of her household bore witness: "If his shirt was torn from the front, then she is telling the truth and he is a liar.

"But if his shirt is torn from behind, then she lies and he is one of the truthful."

When he[501] saw that his shirt was torn from behind, he said: "This is part of your guile, you women. Your guile is indeed very great.

"Joseph, overlook this matter; and you, woman, ask forgiveness for your sin. You are indeed one of the sinners."

30 And some women in the city said: "The wife of the governor has been

500. Joseph.
501. The husband.

seeking to seduce her slave; he has infatuated her with his love. We see her in manifest error."

When she heard about their wiles, she sent after them and prepared for each of them a dining couch. Then she gave each one of them a knife and said to him:[502] "Come out unto them." But when they saw him, they admired him and cut their hands and said: "Allah forbid! This is no mortal, he is but a noble angel."

She said: "This is the one you reproached me for. I have in fact sought to seduce him, but he held back. If he will not do what I command him, he will surely be imprisoned and will be one of the humbled."

He said: "My Lord, prison is dearer to me than that which they call me to. If you do not rid me of their guile, I will be inclined towards them and will be one of the ignorant."

Thereupon his Lord answered his prayer and so rid him of their guile. He is indeed the Hearer, the Knower.

35 Then it occurred to them after they had seen the signs[503] to imprison him for some time.

And there entered the prison with him two youths. One of them said: "I saw in my dream that I am pressing grapes." And the other said: "I saw in my dream that I am carrying on my head bread from which the birds were eating. Tell us their interpretation; we see that you are one of the righteous."

He said: "No food with which you are provided will be given to you but I will tell you its interpretation before it arrives. This is part of what my Lord has taught me. I have forsaken the religion of a people who do not believe in Allah, and disbelieve in the Hereafter.

"And I have followed the religion of my fathers, Abraham, Isaac and Jacob. It was not for us to associate anything with Allah. That is part of Allah's favour upon us and upon mankind; but most men do not give thanks.

"O my two fellow-prisoners, are diverse lords better, or the One, the Omnipotent?

40 "You do not worship, besides Him, except names you have named, you and your fathers, for which Allah has not sent down any authority. Judgement belongs only to Allah; He has commanded that you worship none but Him. That is the right religion, but most men do not know.

"O my two fellow-prisoners, one of you shall give his Lord wine to drink; whereas the other will be crucified, then the birds shall eat from his head. Thus the matter you are inquiring about is settled."

And he said to the one of the two whom he thought would be saved:

---

502. That is, Joseph.
503. Signs of Joseph's innocence.

"Mention me to your Lord." However, the Devil caused him to forget to mention him to his Lord and so he[504] remained in prison a number of years.

And the King[505] said: "I saw in my dreams seven fat cows devoured by seven lean cows, and seven green ears of corn together with seven other withered ones. O my dignitaries, explain to me my dream, if you are able to interpret dreams."

They said: "Confused dreams, and we know nothing about the interpretation of dreams."

45   And the one of the two[506] who had been released remembered after a while and said: "I will tell you its interpretation, so let me go."

"Joseph, O truthful one, enlighten us concerning seven fat cows devoured by seven lean ones, and concerning seven green ears of corn and seven withered ones, so that I might go back to the people, that perchance they might learn."

He said: "You shall sow for seven consecutive years, but what you harvest, you should leave in its ears, except for the little whereof you need to eat.

"Then, afterwards seven hard years will consume what you laid up for them, except for a little of what you have stored.

"Then there will come after that a year in which the people will receive help and will be able to press grapes in it."

50   The King said: "Bring him[507] to me." Then when the messenger came to him, he said: "Go back to your lord and ask him about the women who cut their own hands. My Lord knows well their guile."

He[508] said: "What was the matter with you, women, when you sought to seduce Joseph?" They said: "Allah forbid! We learnt nothing evil about him." The governor's wife then said: "Now the truth has come out, I was the one who sought to seduce him, and he is indeed one of the truthful."

[Joseph said]: "That was said so that [my Lord] may know that I did not betray him in secret, and that Allah will not guide the guile of the treacherous."

"I do not exonerate myself from sin. Surely the [human] soul commands evil, except for those on whom my Lord has mercy. My Lord is truly All-Forgiving, Merciful."

The King said: "Bring him to me; I will attach him to my person alone." And when he spoke to him, he said: "Today you are firmly established and secure with us."

504. Joseph.
505. The King of Egypt.
506. Fellow-prisoners.
507. Joseph.
508. The King.

55   He[509] said: "Put me in charge of the treasures of the land; I am a keeper who knows."

And thus We established Joseph firmly in the land, dwelling wherever he wished. We bestow Our mercy on whom We will, and We do not waste the reward of the righteous.

And the reward of the Hereafter is surely better for those who believe and fear God.

Then Joseph's brothers came and went in to him. He recognized them while they did not know him.

When he provided them with their supplies, he said: "Bring me a brother of yours from your father. Do you not see that I fill up the measure and am the best of hosts?

60   "But, if you do not bring him to me, you shall have no measure from me and you will not come near me."

They said: "We will solicit him from his father. Surely we shall do that."

He said to his servants: "Put their merchandise in their saddlebags, that perchance they may recognize it when they return to their people, and perchance they will come back."

When they returned to their father, they said: "Our father, we have been denied the full measure; so send forth our brother with us that we may receive the measure; we will surely guard him."

He said: "Can I entrust him to you except as I had entrusted his brother to you before? Allah is the best Guardian, and He is the most Merciful of those who show mercy."

65   And when they opened their bags, they found that their merchandise was returned to them. They said: "Father, what more do we desire? This is our merchandise; it has been returned to us. We shall get food for our family, guard our brother and receive an added camel's load. That is an easy measure."

He said: "I will not send him with you until you swear in Allah's name that you will bring him back to me, unless you are constrained." So when they brought him their pledge he said: "Allah is witness of what we say."

And he said: "My sons, do not enter by one door, but enter by separate doors. I cannot avail you anything against Allah; the judgement is truly Allah's; in Him I put my trust, and in Him let all who trust put their trust."

And when they entered wherefrom their father commanded them, nothing could avail them against Allah. It was only a desire in Jacob's breast which he satisfied. He was indeed in possession of knowledge, because We taught him. But most people do not know.

---

509. Joseph.

And when they came into Joseph's presence, he took his brother into his arms saying: "I am your own brother; so do not grieve at what they were doing."

70 Then, when he provided them with their supplies, he put the drinking-vessel in his brother's bag. Then a crier shouted: "O men of the caravan, you are thieves."

They said, as they approached them: "What is it that you miss?"

They said: "We miss the King's drinking-cup; and to him who brings it a camel's load will be given, and I am the guarantor thereof."

They said: "By Allah, you know well that we have not come to spread corruption in the land, and we are no thieves."

They said: "What is the penalty thereof, if you are liars?"

75 They said: "The penalty thereof is that whoever it is found in his bag shall himself be the penalty.[510] This is how we punish the wrongdoers."

And so he[511] began with their bags before the bag of his brother. Then he took it out from his brother's bag. This is how We contrived for Joseph's sake; for he could not take his brother in accordance with the King's law, except if Allah pleased. We raise by degrees whom We will, and above every man of learning, there is one more learned.

They said: "If he has stolen, a brother of his has stolen before." Joseph kept that to himself and did not reveal it to them. He said: "You are in a worse position, and Allah knows best [the truth of] what you say."

They said: "O mighty one, he has a very old father; so take one of us in his place. We see that you are one of those who are beneficent."

He said: "Allah forbid that we take any one other than the one with whom we found our property. For then we will be wrongdoers."

80 Then when they despaired of him, they conferred privately. Their eldest said: "Did you not know that your father took a solemn pledge in the name of Allah from you, and before that you failed to perform your duty in the case of Joseph. I will not leave this land until my father permits me or Allah decides for me; for He is the best of judges."

"Go back to your father and say: 'Our father, your son has stolen. We bear witness only to what we know, and we could not keep watch over the Unseen.'

" 'Ask the town where we were and the caravan which we came along with. Surely we are truthful.' "

He[512] said: "Rather, your souls made some matter look fair to you. Come gentle patience! Maybe Allah will bring them all back to me. He is indeed the All-Knowing, the Wise."

510. That is, he shall be enslaved.
511. Joseph.
512. Jacob.

And he turned away from them and said: "Alas for Joseph!" and his eyes turned white, because of the grief which he repressed.

85   They said: "By Allah, you shall continue to remember Joseph until you are about to perish or even when you do perish."

He said: "I only complain of my sorrow and grief to Allah and I know, from Allah, what you know not.

"O my sons, go forth and inquire about Joseph and his brother and do not despair of Allah's mercy. Surely no one despairs of Allah's mercy, except the unbelieving people."

When they went to him, they said: "O mighty one, we and our people have been visited by affliction and we have brought scant merchandise. So fill up the measure for us and be charitable to us; Allah will surely reward the charitable."

He said: "Do you know what you did with Joseph and his brother, in your dire ignorance?"

90   They said: "Are you truly Joseph?" He said: "Yes, I am Joseph and this is my brother. Allah has been gracious to us. Surely, whoever fears God and forbears will find that Allah will never deprive those who do the good of their reward."

They said: "By Allah, Allah has exalted you above us, and we have only been sinful."

He said: "Let there be no reproach against you today. Allah will forgive you and He is the most Merciful of those who have mercy.

"Take this shirt of mine and lay it on my father's face, and he will regain his sight; then come to me with all your family."

And when the caravan set out, their father said: "I find Joseph's scent, though you may deny it."

95   They said: "By Allah, you persist in your old error."

Then when the bearer of good news came, he placed it[513] on his face and so he regained his sight. He said: "Did I not tell you that I know from Allah what you know not?"

They said: "Father, ask forgiveness for our sins; we have indeed been sinful."

He said: "I shall ask my Lord to forgive you. He is indeed the All-Forgiving, the Merciful."

Then, when they went in to Joseph, he lodged his parents with him and said: "Enter Egypt, Allah willing, in security."

100   And he raised both his parents to the high seat, and they fell prostrate before him. He said: "Father, this is the interpretation of my old dream; my Lord has made it come true. He was kind to me when He brought me out

513. The shirt.

of prison and brought you out of the desert, after the Devil had sown mischief between me and my brothers. My Lord is truly Subtle in bringing about what He wills. He is indeed the All-Knowing, the Wise.

"Lord, you have given me power and taught me the interpretation of dreams. O Creator of the heavens and the earth; you are my Protector in this world and in the Hereafter; receive my soul as a submissive one, and let me join the ranks of the righteous."

That is part of the news of the Unseen [which] We reveal to you; for you were not with them when they concurred in their affair, while they plotted.

And even if you desire it, most people[514] are not believers.

And you do not ask them for a reward for it;[515] it is nothing but a reminder for all mankind.

105   How many a sign in the heavens and on earth by which they pass while they turn their faces away from it!

And most of them do not believe in Allah, unless they continue to associate others [with Him].

Do they guard against a crushing strike of Allah's punishment or the sudden coming of the Hour while they are unaware?

Say: "This is my way; I call to Allah with knowledge, I and those who follow me. Glory be to Allah; and I am not one of the polytheists."

We did not send forth [as messengers] before you except men from the people of the cities who received Our revelations. Have they[516] not travelled in the land and seen what was the end of those who came before them? The abode of the Hereafter is surely better for those who fear God. Do you not understand?

110   And when the messengers despaired and thought they would be regarded as liars, Our help came to them and We delivered whom We pleased. The sinners could not escape Our punishment.

In these narratives about them, there is a lesson for people of understanding. It is not an invented tale, but a confirmation of what came before it, and a clear exposition of all things, and a guidance and mercy for people who believe.

514. The Meccans.
515. Qur'an.
516. The Meccans.

SURA 13

Al-Ra'd, Thunder

In the Name of Allah, the Compassionate, the Merciful

Alif, Lam, Mim, Ra.

1   Those are the signs of the Book; and that which has been revealed to you by your Lord is the truth, but most people do not believe.

Allah is He who raised the heavens without pillars that you can see; there He sat upright on the throne and made the sun and the moon subservient, each running for an appointed term. He manages the [whole] affair and makes clear the revelations so that you may be certain of meeting your Lord.

And it is He who spread out the earth and placed therein firm mountains and rivers; and of each kind of fruit He created two pairs.[517] He causes the night to cover the day. Surely in that are signs for people who reflect.

And in the earth are plots adjoining each other and gardens of vines, tillage and palm-trees, from one or different roots, which are irrigated by the same water; yet, We prefer some of them over the others in produce. Surely in that are signs for a people who understand.

5   Should you[518] wonder, the wonder is their saying: "What, if we turn into dust, will we be created anew?" Those are the ones who disbelieve in their Lord, and those are the ones round whose necks are chains, and those are the people of the Fire, abiding therein forever.

And they ask you to hasten the evil before the good; yet there were punishments before them. Your Lord forgives people notwithstanding their wrongdoing, but Your Lord is truly severe in retribution.

Those who disbelieve say: "Why has no sign been sent down to him from his Lord?" You are only a warner; and for each people there is a guide.

Allah knows what every female bears and what the wombs carry for a shorter or a longer term; and everything with Him is by measure.

[He is] the Knower of the Unseen and the Seen, the Great, the Most High.

10   It is the same whether any of you conceals his words or utters them, and whether he hides by night or goes forth by day.

There are guardian [angels] before him and behind him, guarding him by Allah's command. Allah does not change the condition of a people until they change what is in their hearts. And if Allah wills to afflict a people with

517. That is, males and females.
518. Muhammad.

a misfortune, it cannot be turned away, and they have, apart from Allah, no protector.

It is He Who shows you the lightning, inspiring fear and hope, and originates the laden clouds.

And the thunder sounds His praise and the angels, too, in awe of Him. And He sends forth the thunderbolts smiting with them whomever He pleases. Nevertheless, they dispute about Allah, but He is Mighty in prowess.

To Him is the call of truth; and those on whom they call besides Him will not answer any of their prayers. They are like one who stretches out his hand to the water so that it might reach his mouth, but it will not reach it. The call of the unbelievers is only wasted.

15 Those in the heavens and on earth prostrate themselves to Allah willingly or unwillingly, and so do their shadows mornings and evenings.

Say: "Who is the Lord of the heavens and the earth?" Say: "Allah." Say: "Have you then taken, besides Him, protectors who have no power to profit or harm even themselves?" Say: "Are the blind and the man who sees alike; or are the darkness and the light alike? Or have they set up with Allah associates who created the likeness of His creation, so that both creations seemed to them alike?" Say: "Allah is the Creator of everything and He is the One, the Almighty."

He sends water from the sky making riverbeds flow, each according to its measure. Then the torrent carries along swelling foam; similar to it is the scum that comes out from that which they smelt on the fire for making ornaments or tools. Thus Allah illustrates truth and falsehood. The scum is cast away, but what profits mankind remains in the earth. Thus Allah sets forth the parables.

To those who obey their Lord belongs the best [reward],[519] but those who disobey Him, were they to have all that is on earth plus its equal, would offer it as ransom. To those a bad reckoning is reserved, and their abode will be Hell, and what a miserable resting-place!

Is he who knows that what is revealed to you from your Lord is the truth, like he who is blind? Indeed, only the people of understanding take heed.

20 Those who fulfil their pledge to Allah and do not violate the covenant;

And those who join together what Allah has commanded to be joined, fear their Lord and dread the terror of reckoning;

And those who forbear, seeking the face of their Lord, perform the prayer, spend freely of what We have provided them with, secretly and in public, and counter evil with good – to those belongs the blissful end of the Hereafter.

519. That is, Paradise.

They shall enter the Gardens of Eden, together with the righteous among their fathers, their spouses and their posterity; and the angels shall enter upon them from every gate [saying]:

"Peace be upon you for your forbearance and blessed is the final Abode!"

25 As to those who break Allah's covenant once it is contracted, sever what Allah commanded to be joined and spread corruption in the land, upon them shall be the curse and theirs is the evil abode.[520]

Allah enlarges and restricts the provision to whom He pleases. They rejoice at this worldly life, but worldly life is nothing but a fleeting pleasure compared with the life to come.

And the unbelievers say: "If only a sign were sent down to him by his Lord!" Say: "Allah leads astray whomever He pleases and guides to Himself those who repent,

Those who believe and whose hearts find comfort in remembering Allah." Indeed, in remembering Allah the hearts find comfort.

May those who believe and do the good works be blessed and have a happy homecoming!

30 Thus We have sent you forth to a nation before which other nations had passed away, so as to recite to them what We revealed to you; and yet they deny the Compassionate. Say: "He is my Lord; there is no god but He. In Him I have put my trust and unto Him is my return."

Had there been a Qur'an by which the mountains are made to move, or the land cleft asunder, or the dead spoken to [they would not believe]. No, the whole affair is Allah's. Do not the believers know that had Allah pleased, He would have guided all mankind? As for those who disbelieve, disaster will not cease to afflict them because of what they did or will settle near their homes until Allah's promise is fulfilled. Surely Allah does not break His promise.

Many messengers before you were mocked; so I gave the unbelievers a respite; then I seized them. How then was My retribution!

Is he, then, who watches every soul, noting what it earns [like one who does not]? Yet they set up associates with Allah. Say: "Name them. Are you informing Him about what He does not know on earth, or is it an outward speech only." Rather, the cunning of the unbelievers is embellished to them and they are kept away from the path.[521] Those whom Allah leads astray will have no one to guide them.

Theirs is punishment in the present life, but the punishment of the Hereafter is much harder; and they will have no one to protect them from Allah.

520. Hell.
521. That is, guidance.

35   The likeness of Paradise, which the righteous have been promised is this: rivers flow beneath it, its produce and shade are permanent. That is the ultimate fate of those who guard against evil; but the fate of the unbelievers is the Fire.

And those to whom We have given the Book rejoice in what was revealed to you, but some of the factions deny a part of it. Say: "I have only been commanded to worship Allah and not to associate any one with Him; Him I call, and unto Him is my return."

And thus We revealed it [to be a Book of] judgement in Arabic; and were you to follow their desires after the knowledge which came to you, you would have neither a guardian nor a protector [to save you] from Allah.

And We have sent forth messengers before you and given them wives and progeny; but no messenger had the power to come up with a sign except with Allah's permission. Every age has its own Book.

Allah blots out and confirms what He pleases; and with Him is the Mother of the Book.[522]

40   And whether We show you a part of what We promise them or cause you to die, your duty is to deliver the message and it is for Us to do the reckoning.

Do they not see how We tackle the earth, causing it to shrink from its extremities? When Allah judges no one can reverse His judgement. And He is quick in calling to account.

Those who came before them did scheme, but Allah is Master of all scheming. He knows what each soul earns, and the unbelievers shall know to whom is the happy end in the Hereafter.

The unbelievers say: "You are not an apostle." Say: "Allah suffices as a witness between me and you, as well as those who have a knowledge of the Book."[523]

---

522. That is, the original codex of the Qur'an, i.e. heaven.
523. The Book here stands for previous revelations from Allah.

SURA 14

Ibrahim, Abraham

In the Name of Allah, the Compassionate, the Merciful

Alif, Lam, Mim, Ra.

1   A Book which We have revealed to you so that you may, with the will of their Lord, bring mankind from darkness to light, to the path of the Mighty, the Praiseworthy One.

Allah to whom belongs what is in the heavens and on earth. And woe betide the unbelievers, for a terrible punishment!

Those, who prefer the present life to the Hereafter and bar others from Allah's path and seek to make it crooked, are far astray.

And We have sent forth no messenger except in the tongue of his own people so that he may expound to them clearly. Then Allah leads astray whom He pleases and guides whom He pleases. He is the Mighty, the Wise.

5   We have, indeed, sent Moses with Our signs [saying]: "Bring your people out of the darkness into the light and remind them of Allah's Days."[524] Surely in those are signs for every steadfast and thankful person.

And when Moses said to his people: "Remember Allah's favour to you, when He delivered you from Pharaoh's people, who were inflicting upon you the worst punishment, slaughtering your sons and sparing your women. In that, there truly was a great trial from your Lord."

[Remember] when your Lord proclaimed: "If you give thanks, I will increase you; but if you disbelieve, My punishment is certainly severe."

And Moses said: "If you are thankless, together with everyone on earth, surely Allah is All-Sufficient, Praiseworthy.

"Have you not heard the story of those who preceded you – the people of Noah, of 'Ad, Thamud, and those who came after them, whom none but Allah knows? Their messengers came to them with the clear proofs, but they put their hands in their mouths saying: "We disbelieve in what you have been sent forth with, and we are certainly in disturbing doubt regarding what you are calling us to."

10   Their messengers said: "Is there any doubt about Allah, Maker of the heavens and the earth? He calls you that He may forgive you some of your sins and reprieve you until an appointed term." They said: "You are only humans like ourselves; you want to turn us away from what our fathers worshipped. Bring us then a manifest authority."

---

524. What is meant by "Days" is major events or calamities.

Their messengers said to them: "We are only humans like yourselves. However, Allah bestows His grace on whom He pleases of His servants. It is not in our power to bring you an authority, save by Allah's leave; and in Allah let the believers put their trust.

"And why should we not put our trust in Allah, when He has guided us on our ways? We will surely endure patiently the harm you cause us; and in Allah let those who trust put their trust."

The unbelievers said to their messengers: "We will certainly expel you from our land, unless you return to our religion." Then their Lord revealed to them: "We shall destroy the wrongdoers.

"And We will make you dwell in the land after them. That is for him who fears My presence and fears My threats."

15 And they called [on their Lord] for help, and every stubborn tyrant was disappointed.

Behind him is Hell, and He is given stinking water to drink.

He sips it but can hardly swallow it, and death surrounds him from every side, but he will not die; and beyond this is still a terrible punishment.

The likeness of those who disbelieve in their Lord is this: their works are like ashes scattered by the wind on a stormy day, and they have no power over anything they have earned. That is truly the great perdition.

Do you not see that Allah created the heavens and the earth in truth? If He pleases He will destroy you and bring forth a new creation.

20 And that is not a difficult matter for Allah.

And when they all appear before Allah, the weak will say to the overbearing: "We were indeed your followers; can you, then, do anything to save us from Allah's punishment?" They will say: "Had Allah guided us, we would have guided you. Whether we fear or forbear, we have no escape."

And the Devil said when the issue was settled: "Allah has surely given you a true promise; and I made you a promise but did not keep it. I had no authority over you, except that I called you and you answered me. Do not blame me then, but blame yourselves; I cannot help you and you cannot help me. I deny your associating me [with Allah] before. The wrongdoers will have a very painful punishment."

And those who believe and do good works shall be admitted to gardens beneath which rivers flow, abiding therein forever, by their Lord's leave; their greeting therein shall be: "Peace."

Do you not see how Allah sets forth as a parable that a good word is like a good tree, whose root is firm and its branches are in the sky.

25 It brings forth its fruit all the time, by its Lord's leave. Allah gives parables to mankind that perchance they may be mindful.

And a foul word is like a foul tree which has been uprooted from the surface of the earth, having no stable base.

Allah confirms those who believe with the firm word in the present life, and in the life to come; but He leads the wrongdoers astray. Allah does whatever He pleases.

Have you not seen those who turn Allah's grace into disbelief and lead their people to the abode of ruin?[525]

In Hell they will burn, and what a wretched abode!

30   And they set up equals to Allah in order to lead people away from His path. Say: "Take your pleasure; for your fate is the Fire."

Tell My servants who believe, to perform the prayer and give freely of what We have provided them with, secretly and in public, before a day comes wherein there is no trade or friendship.

[It is] Allah who created the heavens and the earth and sends down water from the sky, bringing forth fruits for your sustenance. He has made the ships subservient to you so as to sail in the sea at His behest and He has subjected to you the rivers.

And He has made subservient to you the sun and the moon pursuing their courses, and subjected also the night and the day.

He gives you of all you ask Him for. And were you to count Allah's favours you will never be able to exhaust them. Man is truly unjust and ungrateful.

35   And [remember] when Abraham said: "Lord, make this town secure, and keep me and my sons away from worshipping the idols.

"Lord, they have led many people astray; therefore he who follows me, shall belong to me, and he who disobeys me, surely You are All-Forgiving, Merciful.

"Our Lord, I have settled some of my offspring in a valley which has no tillage, by your Sacred House, so that, Lord, they may perform the prayer. Make, then, the hearts of some people incline towards them, and provide them with some fruits, that perchance they may give thanks.

"Our Lord, You know what we conceal and what we reveal, and nothing on earth or in heaven is concealed from Allah.

"Praise be to Allah, who has given me, in old age, Isma'il and Isaac. Surely my Lord is the Hearer of Prayer.

40   "Lord, make me and my posterity keep up the prayers; and, our Lord, accept my supplication.

"Our Lord, forgive me, my parents and the believers, on the day when the reckoning shall come to pass."

And do not think that Allah is unaware of what the wrongdoers do. He only gives them respite until the day in which eyes shall stare blankly;

---

525. That is, Hell.

Hastening forward, their heads upraised, their gaze not returning to them, and their hearts vacant.

And warn mankind of the day when the punishment shall overtake them. Whereupon the wrongdoers will say: "Our Lord, give us respite for a near period and we will answer Your call and follow the messengers." [It will be said to them]: "Did you not swear before, that you will never cease to exist?"

45   You lived in the dwellings of those who wronged themselves, and thus you saw clearly how We dealt with them, and we made [them] examples to you.

And they hatched their plots, and Allah knew their plotting although their plotting was such as to move the mountains.

Do not think, then, that Allah will break His promise to His messengers. Allah is truly Mighty and Capable of Retribution.

On the day the earth shall change into another earth, and the heavens too; and they shall appear before Allah, the One, the Conqueror.

And you will see the wicked sinners on that day bound together in chains.

50   Their garments made of pitch, and their faces covered with fire.

That Allah may reward every soul according to what it has earned. Surely Allah is Quick at reckoning.

This is a proclamation to mankind that they may be warned thereby, and know that He is One God, and that men of understanding may remember well.

SURA 15

Al-Hijr, The Rock[526]

In the Name of Allah, the Compassionate, the Merciful

Alif, Lam, Ra.

1   These are the verses of the Book and a manifest Qur'an.

Perhaps, those who disbelieve wish they were Muslims.

Leave them to eat, enjoy themselves and let [false] hopes beguile them; for they will soon know.

We have never destroyed a town but it had a fixed decree.

5   No nation can hasten its term, nor defer it.

They say: "O you, to whom the Reminder[527] is revealed, you are indeed a madman.

"Why do you not bring us the angels, if you are truthful?"

We do not send the angels down except with the Truth; and then they will have no respite.

It is truly We Who have revealed the Reminder, and We are truly its guardians.

10   And We have sent forth messengers before you to the sects of old.

And no messenger came to them but they mocked him.

That is how We instil it into the hearts of the sinners.

They do not believe in him despite the example of the ancients.

And if We open for them a gate of heaven, so that they could continue to ascend through it;

15   They would simply say: "Our eyes have been covered over, or rather we are a people bewitched."

We have indeed set up constellations in the heavens and made them attractive to the beholders;

And guarded them against every accursed devil;

Except for him who eavesdrops stealthily and was pursued by a visible flame.

As for the earth, We have spread it out, laid down upon it firm mountains and caused to grow therein all sorts of fare [plants].

20   And We have made in it provisions for you and for those whom you do not provide for.

There is nothing for which We do not have the store-houses and sources, and We send it down only in a well-known measure.

---

526. The land of Thamud, north of Medina.
527. The Qur'an.

And We send forth the winds as fertilizers; and then We send down water from the sky and give it to you to drink. But you do not store it up.

It is We who give life and cause to die, and We are the Inheritors.

And We know those of you who came before and those who will come later.

25   And surely your Lord shall gather them. He is truly Wise, All-Knowing.

And We have created man from potter's clay, moulded out of slime.

And the *jinn* We created before that from blazing fire.

When your Lord said to the angels: "Behold, I have created a man from potter's clay, out of moulded slime.

"When I have fashioned him and breathed into him of My spirit, fall down prostrating yourselves to him."

30   The angels prostrated themselves, all together;

Except Satan who refused to be one of those who prostrated themselves.

He said: "O Satan, what keeps you from being one of those who prostrate themselves?"

He said: "I refuse to prostrate myself before a mortal You created from potter's clay out of moulded slime."

He said: "Get out of here,[528] then, for you are surely accursed.

35   "And the curse shall be upon you till the Day of Judgement."

He said: "My Lord, reprieve me till the Day of Resurrection."

He said: "You are indeed one of those reprieved,

"Till the Appointed Day."

[Satan said]: "My Lord, since you misguided me, I will make what is foul on earth seem fair to them, and I shall mislead them all,

40   "Except for your sincere servants among them."

He[529] said: "This is my straight path.

"Over My servants you have no authority, except for those sinners who follow you.

"Hell shall be the appointed place for them all.

"Seven gates it has; and to each gate a part of them is assigned.

45   "The righteous will surely be amidst gardens and fountains.

[It will be said to them]: "Enter therein in peace and security."

We shall remove all hatred from their hearts, and as brethren they shall recline, facing each other, upon couches.

They shall not be touched by fatigue therein, nor will they be driven out.

Tell My servants that I am truly the All-Forgiving, the Merciful.

50   And that My punishment is truly the painful punishment.

And tell them about the guests of Abraham.

528. That is, Paradise or the Garden of Eden.
529. Allah.

When they entered unto him saying: "Peace"; he said: "We are afraid of you."

They said: "Do not be afraid; we bring you the good news of a boy possessing knowledge."

He said: "Do you bring me good news, when old age has overtaken me? What good news do you bring, then?"

55 They said: "We bring you good news in truth, so do not be one of those who despair."

He said: "Who despairs of his Lord's mercy, except those who have gone astray."

He said: "What is your errand, O messengers?"

They said: "We have been sent forth to [destroy] a sinful people.

"Except for the family of Lot; we shall deliver them all,

60 "Except for his wife; We have decreed that she will remain behind [to perish]."

And when the messengers came to the family of Lot;

He said: "You are surely a people unknown [to us]."

They said: "No; we bring you that whereof they are in doubt.

"And we bring you the truth, and we are truthful, indeed.

65 "Set out, then, with your family in a watch of the night, and follow in their rear; and let no one of you look back, and go forth wherever you are ordered."

And We conveyed to him this decree that these [sinners] will be rooted out in the morning.

And the people of the town came rejoicing.

He said: "These are my guests, so do not disgrace me.

"And fear Allah and do not shame me."

70 They said: "Did we not forbid you [to approach] strangers?"

He said: "These are my daughters, if you are intent on doing anything."

By your life [O Muhammad] they wandered blindly in their folly.

Thereupon, the dreadful Cry overtook them at sunrise.

And so We turned their towns upside down, and We rained upon them stones of baked clay.

75 In this, there are truly signs for those who ponder.

And they[530] lie along an existing road.

In that, there is indeed a sign for the believers.

Surely, the People of the Thicket[531] were also wrongdoers.

So We punished them. And they[532] lie along a plain road.

530. The towns.
531. Near Midian.
532. Lot's towns and the Thicket.

80   And the people of al-Hijr⁵³³ denounced the messengers.
      We brought them Our signs, but they turned away from them.
      They hewed their houses in the mountains in security.
      The Cry overtook them in the morning.
      Thus, what they did availed them nothing.
85   We have not created the heavens and the earth and what lies between
      them save in truth; and the Hour is surely coming. So forgive them
      magnanimously.
      Your Lord is indeed the Creator, the Knower.
      And We have given you seven oft-repeated⁵³⁴ [verses] and the great
      Qur'an.
      Do not strain your gaze towards what We gave certain groups of them to
      enjoy, and do not grieve for them, and lower your wing⁵³⁵ to the believers.
      And say: "I am truly the plain warner."
90   Just as We sent down [punishment] upon the dividers,⁵³⁶
      Who divided the Qur'an into parts.⁵³⁷
      By your Lord, We shall question them all,
      Regarding what they used to do.
      So proclaim what you are commanded and turn away from the
      polytheists.
95   Our support to you against the scoffers will be sufficient;
      Those who set up another god with Allah. They will surely come to
      know.
      And We know well that your heart is distressed at what they say.
      So, celebrate the praise of your Lord and be one of those who prostrate
      themselves.
      And worship your Lord, till the certain⁵³⁸ [Hour] overtake you!

---

533. The dwellers in Hijr, north of Medina, were Thamud.
534. The seven oft-repeated verses of the Opening Sura of the Qur'an.
535. That is, be modest.
536. The Jews and Christians.
537. That is, they accepted a part of it and rejected the rest.
538. That is, certain death.

SURA 16

Al-Nahl, The Bee

In the Name of Allah, the Compassionate, the Merciful

1 Allah's decree will be fulfilled; so do not hasten it. Glory be to Him and may He be exalted above what they associate [with Him]!

He sends down the angels with the Spirit by His command upon whom He pleases of His servants [saying]: "Warn that there is no god but I; so fear Me."

He created the heavens and the earth in truth; may He be exalted above what they associate [with Him].

He created man from a sperm-drop and, behold, he is a professed disputant.

5 And the cattle He created for you. Therein are warmth and other advantages, and from them you eat.

And in them you witness beauty, when you bring them back [home], and when you drive them out for pasture.

And they carry your burdens to a distant land which you could only reach with great hardship. Surely your Lord is Clement and Merciful.

And horses, mules and asses [He created] for you to mount, and as an adornment; and He creates what you do not know.

It belongs to Allah to show the straight path; some, however, deviate from it. Had Allah pleased he would have guided you all.

10 It is He who sends down water from the sky; from it you drink, and through it grow the plants on which you feed your cattle.

From it He brings forth for you vegetation, olives, palms, vines and all kinds of fruit. In that, surely, there is a sign for a people who reflect.

And He has subjected to you the night and the day, the sun and the moon; and the stars are subjected by His command. In that there are signs for a people who understand.

And what He created for you in the earth is of multifarious colours; in that there is, surely, a sign for a people who are mindful.

And it is He who subjected the sea, so that you may eat from it tender meat and bring out from it jewellery for you to wear; and you see the ships cruising therein. [He subjected it for you] so that you may also seek His bounty and give thanks.

15 And He laid up in the earth firm mountains, lest it shake under you; as well as rivers and pathways that, perchance, you may be guided.

And He [laid] landmarks; and by the stars they are guided.

Now, is he who creates like him who does not create? Do you not take heed?

Were you to count Allah's blessings, you will not exhaust them. Allah is truly All-Forgiving, Merciful.

And Allah knows what you conceal and what you reveal.

20   Those they call upon, apart from Allah, do not create anything, but are themselves created.

[They are] dead, not alive, and they do not know when they will be raised from the dead.

Your God is One God; those, then, who do not believe in the Hereafter, their hearts deny and they are arrogant.

Undoubtedly, Allah knows what they conceal and what they reveal. Indeed, He does not like the arrogant.

And if it is said to them: "What has your Lord revealed?" they say: "Fables of the ancients."

25   So let them on the Day of Resurrection bear in full their burdens and some of the burdens of the ignorant whom they lead astray. How evil is that which they shall bear!

Those who came before them schemed and Allah razed their building from the foundations and the roof fell upon them from above them, and punishment came upon them from whence they did not know.

Then, on the Day of Resurrection, He will disgrace them and will say: "Where are My associates about whom you used to argue?" Those who are given knowledge will say: "Disgrace and evil will this day be upon the unbelievers;

"Who are carried off by the angels while still wronging themselves." Then, they will offer submission saying: "We did not evil." No, Allah surely knows well what you were doing.

Enter, then, the gates of Hell, abiding therein forever. Wretched indeed is the abode of the arrogant!

30   And it is said to those who fear God: "What has your Lord revealed?" They say: "Something good." To those who do good in this world is the good reward; and the Hereafter is surely much better. Blessed indeed is the abode of the God-fearing!

Gardens of Eden they shall enter, beneath which rivers flow. They will have therein whatever they desire. Thus Allah rewards the God-fearing.

Those whom the angels will carry off while in a state of grace, saying: "Peace upon you; enter Paradise for what you did."

Do they only expect that the angels should come to them, or that your Lord's command should come? This is what those who came before them did. Allah did not wrong them, but they wronged themselves.

They were afflicted by the evil consequences of their actions, and were overtaken by what they mocked.

35   The idolaters say: "Had Allah pleased, neither we nor our fathers would have worshipped any [gods] besides Him; nor would we have forbidden anything against His will." [But] thus did those who come before them. What should the messengers do except to deliver the plain message?

We have sent forth to every nation a messenger saying: "Worship Allah and avoid the idols. Some of them Allah guided and others were justly left in error. Travel, then, in the land and see what was the end of the denyers."

If you[539] are eager to guide them, Allah surely will not guide those whom He leads astray, and they will have no supporters.

And they solemnly swear by Allah that Allah will not raise from the dead anyone who dies. No, His is a true promise, but most people do not know.

[They shall be raised up] so as to make clear to them that whereof they differ, and that the unbelievers may know that they were lying.

40   Indeed, when We want a thing to be, We just say to it: "Be", and it comes to be.

To those who emigrated for Allah's sake, after they had been oppressed, We shall provide a good life in this world; but the reward of the Hereafter is greater, if only they knew.

[They are] those who are patient, and in their Lord they put their trust.

We have sent forth, before you, none but men to whom We have revealed. So ask those who have knowledge[540] if you do not know.

[We sent them] with clear proofs and scriptures. And We revealed to you the Reminder, so that you may make clear to mankind what has been revealed to them, and that, perchance, they may reflect.

45   Do those who devise evil feel assured that Allah will not cause the earth to swallow them up, or that punishment will not overtake them from whence they do not expect?

Or that He will not seize them in the course of their journeys, when they will not be able to escape?

Or that He will not seize them while in dread? Surely your Lord is Clement, Merciful.

Have they not considered all the things Allah has created, casting their shades right and left, and prostrating themselves before Allah in all humility?

And before Allah all creatures on the earth and the angels prostrate themselves, and they are not proud.

50   They fear their Lord, high above them, and they do what they are commanded.

---

539. Muhammad.
540. The Christians and Jews, who have knowledge of their scriptures.

Allah has said: "Do not take two gods; He is only one God. So fear Me alone."

To Him belongs what is in the heavens and on earth, and to Him obedience is due always. Do you, then, fear anyone other than Allah?

Whatever blessing you have is from Allah. Then, if adversity touches you, unto Him you turn for help.

Then, once He lifts the adversity from you, behold, some of you associate [other gods] with their Lord;

55   So as to deny what We gave them. Enjoy yourselves then, for soon you shall know.

And they set apart, for what they know not,[541] a portion of what We have provided for them. By Allah, you will be questioned about what you fabricated.

And they ascribe to Allah daughters [glory be to Him!], but to themselves what they desire.[542]

And if the birth of a daughter is announced to any of them, his face turns black, and he is enraged.

He hides from the people on account of the evil news broken to him; should he keep it in humiliation or bury it in the ground? Evil is what they judge!

60   As for those who do not believe in the Hereafter, theirs is the evil exemplar; but Allah's is the sublime exemplar. He is the Almighty, the Wise.

Were Allah to take mankind to task for their wrongdoing, He would not leave upon it[543] a single creature; but He reprieves them until an appointed term. Then, when their term comes, they will not delay nor advance it a single hour.

And they ascribe to Allah what they themselves dislike.[544] Their tongues utter the lie that theirs will be the best reward. There is no doubt that the Fire awaits them, and that they will be left [there].

By Allah We sent forth [messengers] to nations before you. But the Devil made their foul deeds seem fair to them. He is their patron, and they shall have a very painful punishment.

We have not revealed to you the Book but that you may make clear to them that wherein they differ, and as a guidance and mercy to a people who believe.

65   It is Allah who sends down water from the sky reviving thereby the earth after its death. Surely, there is in that a sign to a people who listen.

---

541. Their idols.
542. That is, whereas they ascribe daughters to Allah, they ascribe sons to themselves.
543. The earth.
544. That is, they ascribe daughters to Him.

And there is, surely, a lesson for you in the cattle. We give you to drink of what is in their bellies, between the bowels and blood, pure milk which is palatable to the drinkers.

And from the fruits of palms and vines, you get wine and fair provision. Surely, there is in that a sign to a people who understand.

And your Lord revealed to the bees: "Build homes in the mountains, the trees and in what men construct for you.

"Then eat from all the fruits and follow your Lord's smoothed paths." From their bellies comes out a syrup of different hues, wherein is healing for mankind. Surely, in that there is a sign for a people who reflect.

70   Allah created you, then He will cause you to die. For some of you will be brought back to the worst age, so that they will no longer know anything, after having acquired knowledge. Surely, Allah is All-Knowing, All-Powerful.

Allah has favoured some of you over the others in provision; but those favoured will not give their provision to those [slaves] whom their right hands possess so as to be equal therein. Will they then deny Allah's blessings?

Allah has given you wives from among yourselves, and from your wives sons and grandsons, and has provided you with all good things. Will they believe in falsehood, then, and deny Allah's blessings?

And they worship, besides Allah, what cannot provide anything for them from the heavens or earth and can do nothing.

Do not set forth parables for Allah. Surely Allah knows and you do not know.

75   Allah sets forth this parable. Consider an owned slave who is unable to do anything; one for whom We have provided from Our bounty a fair provision, and he spends from it secretly and publicly. Are they, then, alike? Praise be to Allah; but most of them do not know.

And Allah sets forth the parable of two men. One of them is dumb, unable to do anything and is a burden on his master; wherever he directs him, he brings no good. Is he equal to him who enjoins justice and is upon a straight path?

To Allah belongs the unseen of the heavens and the earth. The coming of the Hour is only like the twinkling of the eye, or even nearer. Surely, Allah has power over everything.

And Allah brought you out of your mothers' bellies knowing nothing; and gave you hearing, sight and hearts, that perchance you may give thanks.

Do they not see the birds subservient in the vault of the sky, nothing holding them aloft but Allah? Surely, there is in that signs for a people who believe.

80   Allah has made of your homes places for you to dwell in, and has made
for you from the hides of cattle light houses to carry on the day of moving
and on the day of settling down. And from their wools and their furs and
their hair He [has made for you] furnishings and means of enjoyment for a
while.

Allah has made for you from what He created, sunshades, and from the
mountains, places of retreat, and has given you garments to protect you
from the heat and coats of mail to protect you while fighting. Thus He
perfects his blessing to you so that you may submit.

Then, if they turn away, your duty is only to deliver the clear message.

They know Allah's blessing, then they deny it; and most of them are
ungrateful.

And on the day when We raise from every nation a witness, the
unbelievers shall not be given leave or allowed to repent.

85   And when the wrongdoers behold the punishment, it shall not be
lightened for them and they shall not be reprieved.

And when those who associated other gods with Allah see their associate
they shall say: "Our Lord, these are our associates whom we used to call
upon besides you." But their associates will retort: "Surely you are liars."

And they shall offer Allah submission on that day; and what they used to
fabricate shall stray away from them.

[As for] those who disbelieve and debar people from the path of Allah,
We will add punishment to their punishment on account of the mischief
they used to make.

On the day when We shall raise up in each nation a witness against them
from among themselves, We will bring you[545] a witness against them. We
have revealed to you the Book[546] which explains everything, is a guide,
mercy and good news to those who submit.

90   Allah enjoins justice, charity and the giving to kindred; He forbids
indecency, evil and aggression. He admonishes you that you may take heed.

Fulfil the covenant of Allah when you make a covenant [with Him], and
do not break the oaths after you solemnly affirm them, taking Allah as
witness. Surely Allah knows what you do.

And do not be like her who unravels her yarn after she has spun it first;
taking your oaths as means of deception among you, because one party is
more numerous than another. Allah only tries you by this, and He will
certainly make clear to you on the Day of Resurrection that whereon you
differ.

Had Allah pleased, He would have made you a single nation, but He

545. Muhammad.
546. The Qur'an.

leads whom He pleases astray and guides whom He pleases. And you will surely be questioned about what you did.

And do not make your oaths as means of deception among you, lest a foot should slip[547] after being firm, and lest you should taste evil on account of debarring others from Allah's path. Grievous will be your punishment!

95 Do not sell Allah's covenant for a small price. Surely what is with Allah is better for you, if only you knew.

What you have will be exhausted, and what is with Allah remains [undiminished]. And We will give the steadfast a better reward than the best of their actions [deserved].

Whoever does a good deed, whether male or female, while a believer, We shall make him live a good life; and We will give them a better reward than what they have done.

When you recite the Qur'an, seek refuge with Allah from the accursed Devil.

He has no authority over those who believe and have put their trust in their Lord.

100 His authority is only over those who befriend him and who associate others with Him.[548]

And if We replace a verse by another – and Allah knows best what He reveals – they say: "You are only a forger." Surely, most of them do not know.

Say: "The Holy Spirit[549] has brought it down from your Lord in truth, in order to reassure the believers, and as a guidance and good news to those who submit.

And We surely know that they say: "Surely a mortal teaches him." The tongue of him to whom they allude is foreign, whereas this is clear Arabic tongue.

Those who do not believe in Allah's revelations shall not be guided by Allah, and a very painful punishment awaits them.

105 It is those who do not belive in Allah's revelations that fabricate falsehood. It is they who lie.

He who disbelieves in Allah after he has believed, except him who is compelled, but his heart remains firm in belief;[550] but those whose hearts rejoice in disbelief shall incur Allah's wrath and a grievous punishment awaits them.

That is because they love the present life more than the Hereafter, and because Allah does not guide the unbelievers.

547. That is, lest your faith be shaken.
548. Allah.
549. Gabriel.
550. Will be forgiven.

They are those whose hearts, ears and eyes Allah has sealed; and those are the heedless.

There is no doubt that in the Hereafter they shall be the losers.

110 As for those who emigrated after they had been persecuted, then fought in the way of Allah and stood fast, your Lord is Forgiving, Merciful.

The day every soul shall come pleading for itself, and every soul shall be paid in full for what it did, they shall not be dealt with unjustly.

Allah has given as a parable a town which was safe and secure, and its provision came in abundance from every side; then it denied Allah's blessing, and so Allah made it taste the engulfing hunger and fear on account of what they[551] used to do.

An apostle from among them came to them, but they denounced him, and so they were smitten by Our punishment for being wrongdoers.

Eat then from the lawful and good things which Allah provided for you, and give thanks for Allah's blessing, if you truly worship Him.

115 He has forbidden you carrion, blood, the flesh of swine and that over which any name other than that of Allah is invoked. But whoever is compelled while neither transgressing nor exceeding the bounds, Allah is All-Forgiving, Merciful.

And when you speak do not lie by saying: "This is lawful and this is unlawful", in order to impute lies to Allah. Surely those who impute lies to Allah will not prosper.

A little enjoyment and then a great punishment is in store for them.

We forbade the Jews what We have related to you earlier. And We did not wrong them, but they wronged themselves.

Surely, with respect to those who commit evil in ignorance, and later repent and make amends, your Lord thereafter is All-Forgiving, Merciful.

120 Indeed, Abraham was a model [of virtue], obedient to Allah and upright; and he was not one of the polytheists.

[He was] thankful for His blessings, and Allah guided him to a straight path.

We made him praiseworthy in this world, and in the Hereafter he will be one of the righteous.

Then We revealed to you:[552] "Follow the religion of Abraham, the upright; for he was not one of the polytheists."

The Sabbath was ordained only for those who differed with respect to it.[553] Your Lord shall decide between them on the Day of Resurrection, regarding that wherein they differed.

---

551. Its people.
552. Muhammad.
553. The Jews.

125   Call to the way of your Lord with wisdom and mild exhortation, and argue with them in the best manner. Your Lord surely knows best those who stray from His path, and He knows well those who are rightly guided.

If you punish, then let your punishment be proportionate to the wrong done to you. Yet should you forbear, that is truly better for those who forbear.

Be patient; yet your patience is only through Allah. Do not grieve for them,[554] and do not be distressed on account of what they devise.

Allah is with those who are God-fearing and those who are beneficent.

---

554. The evildoers or unbelievers.

SURA 17

Al-Isra', The Night Journey

In the Name of Allah, the Compassionate, the Merciful

1 Glory be to Him who caused His servant to travel by night from the Sacred Mosque to the Farthest Mosque, whose precincts We have blessed, in order to show him some of Our Signs. He is indeed the All-Hearing, the All-Seeing.

We gave Moses the Book and made it a guidance to the Children of Israel [saying]: "Do not take besides Me any other guardian."

O progeny of those whom We caused to be carried along with Noah; He was truly a very thankful servant.

And We decreed for the Children of Israel in the Book: "You shall make mischief in the land twice, and you shall become very haughty."

5 And when the punishment for the first [making of mischief] became due, We sent forth against you servants of Ours possessing great might who went after you in your country. Thus Our threat was accomplished.

Then, We gave you back your turn against them and aided you with wealth and children and increased you in number.

[And We said]: "If you do good, you do good for yourselves, and if you do evil, you do it for yourselves too. And when the punishment for the second [making of mischief] became due, [We sent Our men again] to afflict you, and to enter the Mosque as they entered it the first time and to utterly destroy what they conquered.

It may be that your Lord will have mercy on you; but if you go back [to mischief], We shall come back and make Hell a prison for the unbelievers.

Surely, this Qur'an guides to that which is most upright and announces to the believers who do good works the good news that they shall have a great reward.

10 And those who do not believe in the Hereafter, We have prepared for them a very painful punishment.

Man prays for evil, just as he prays for good; and man is very hasty.

We have made the night and the day two signs; then We blot out the sign of the night and make the sign of the day luminous, that you may seek bounty from your Lord, and learn the number of years and the reckoning, and everything We have expounded clearly.

And every man's omen We have fastened to his neck; and on the Day of

Resurrection, We shall bring out for him a book which he will find spread wide open, [saying to him]:

"Read your book; your own soul shall suffice today as a reckoner against you."

15 He who is well-guided is well-guided for himself, and he who goes astray, goes astray to his own loss. No soul shall bear the burden of another soul, and We do not punish until We have sent a messenger.

And when We want to destroy a city, We command those of its people who are given to luxury; but as they transgress therein Our sentence against it is pronounced and We utterly destroy it.

How many generations We have destroyed since Noah! It suffices that your Lord knows and sees the sins of His servants.

He who desires the transitory life, We hasten to him and to whomsoever We desire whatever We please. Later We consign him to Hell in which he will burn despised and rejected.

But as for those who desire the Hereafter and strive for it, as they should, while they are believers, their effort will be appreciated.

20 For them all – these and those – We shall provide from Allah's bounty; and the bounty of your Lord will not be denied to anyone.

Behold how We have made some of them surpass the others, although the Hereafter is far higher in rank and more preferable.

Do not set up another god with Allah, lest you be despised and forsaken.

Your Lord has decreed that you worship none but Him and to be kind to your parents. If either of them or both reach old age with you, do not say to them "Fie", nor tell them off, but say to them kind words.

And lower to them the wing of humility out of mercy and say: "Lord, have mercy on them, as they took care of me when I was a child."

25 Your Lord knows best what is in your hearts. If you are righteous, He is All-Forgiving to those who repent.

And give the kinsman his due, and to the destitute and the wayfarer, and do not squander your wealth wastefully.

Surely the spendthrifts are the brothers of the devils; and the Devil is ever ungrateful to his Lord.

But if you turn away from them,[555] seeking mercy[556] from your Lord, speak to them kindly.

Do not keep your hand chained to your neck, nor spread it out fully, lest you sit around condemned and reduced to poverty.

30 Surely your Lord gives generously to whom He pleases, and He gives sparingly [to whom He pleases]. He knows and observes His servants well.

555. The kinsman, the destitute and the wayfarer.
556. That is, because you have nothing to give and you seek the bounty of your Lord.

Do not kill your children for fear of poverty. We will provide for you and for them. To kill them is a great sin.

Do not draw near adultery; it is an abomination and an evil way.

Do not kill the soul which Allah has forbidden except for just cause. Whoever is killed unjustly, We have given his heir the power [to demand satisfaction]; but let him not exceed the limit in slaying, for he will be the victor.

Do not go near the orphan's property except in the fairest way until he comes of age; and honour your pledge, because the pledge involves responsibility.

35 And give full measure when you measure, and weigh with a just balance. That is fair and better in the end.

Do not pursue what you have no knowledge of. Hearing, sight and the heart – all these shall be questioned about it.

And do not walk in the land haughtily; for you certainly will not pierce the earth, nor equal the mountains in height.

The evil of all this is hateful in the sight of your Lord.

That is part of what your Lord has revealed to you of wisdom. Do not set up with Allah another god, or else you will be cast in Hell, despised and rejected.

40 Has your Lord, then, favoured you with sons and taken to Himself females from among the angels? Surely, you are uttering a monstrous thing.

We have expatiated in this Qur'an so that they may be mindful, but it only increases their aversion.

Say: "If there were other gods with Him, as they say, then surely they would have sought access to the Lord of the Throne."

Glory be to Him and may He be greatly exalted above what they say.

The seven heavens, the earth and what is in them praise Him, and there is nothing which does not celebrate His praise; but you do not understand their praise. He is indeed Clement, All-Forgiving.

45 When you recite the Qur'an, We will place between you and those who do not believe in the Hereafter a hidden curtain.

And We have placed veils upon their hearts and deafness in their ears lest they understand it. And if you mention your Lord alone in the Qur'an, they turn their backs in aversion.

We know best what they listen to when they listen to you, as they confer secretly, when the wrongdoers say: "You only follow a man bewitched."

See how they coin similes for you and so go astray and are unable to find their way.

And they say: "What, when we have become bones and mortal remains, shall we really be raised up as a new creation?"

50   Say: "[Even if you] be stones or iron;

"Or some creation magnified in your minds." They will say: "Who will bring us back?" Say: "He who created you the first time." Then they will shake their heads at you and say: "When will that be?" Say: "Perhaps, it will be soon.

"The day He will summon you and you will respond with His praise, and you will imagine that you have tarried but for a short while."

And tell My servants to say that which is best. Surely the Devil sows dissension among them; the Devil is surely a sworn enemy of man.

Your Lord knows you best. If He pleases, He will have mercy on you, and if He pleases He will torture you. We have not sent you to be their guardian.

55   And your Lord knows best what is in the heavens and on earth. We bestowed on some of the prophets more gifts than on the others, and We gave David the Psalms.

Say: "Call on those whom you claim to be His associates. They will not be able to lift adversity from you nor divert it."

Those they call upon are themselves seeking means of access to their Lord, to show who is closer to Him. They hope for His mercy and fear His punishment. Indeed, the punishment of your Lord should be feared.

There is no city but We will destroy before the Day of Resurrection, or will punish terribly. That is written in the Book.

Nothing prevents Us from sending the signs except that the ancients denied them. We gave to Thamud the she-camel as a manifest sign, but they maltreated her. We do not send the signs except to warn.

60   [Remember] when We said to you: "Your Lord encompasses mankind. We did not make the vision We showed you except as a trial to mankind, and likewise the tree cursed in the Qur'an. We warn them, but that only increases their tyranny."

And when We said to the angels: "Prostrate yourselves before Adam", they all prostrated themselves, except Satan, who said: "Shall I prostrate myself before one You have created from clay?"

He[557] said: "Do you see this one whom you honoured more than me? If you would reprieve me until the Day of Resurrection, I will certainly destroy his progeny except for a few."

He[558] said: "Begone! Whoever of them follows you, Hell is surely your reward, an ample reward."

[Satan said] "Stir up those of them you can with your voice, rally against

557. Satan.
558. Allah.

174

them your horsemen and your infantry, share with them their wealth and children and promise them." Satan makes them only deceitful promises.

65 Surely, over My servants you have no authority. Your Lord suffices as a guardian.

Your Lord who drives for you the ships at sea, that you may seek His bounty. He is indeed merciful to you.

And if you are touched by adversity at sea, those you call upon other than He will wander away; but when He delivers you to land safely, you turn away. Man is ever thankless.

Are you, then, assured that He will not cause the land to cave in under you, or release a sandstorm upon you, and then you will find no one to protect you?

Or are you assured that He will not return you to it a second time, releasing upon you a roaring wind and drowning you, on account of your disbelief. Then you will find no one to defend you against Us.

70 We have honoured the Children of Adam and carried them on land and sea, provided them with good things and preferred them greatly over many of those We have created.

The day [will come] when We will call every people with their leader. Then they who are given their book in their right hand – those will read their book and will not be wronged a whit.

And he who is blind in this world will be blind in the Hereafter and will stray even more from the right way.

They were about to lure you away from what We have revealed to you, so that you might replace it with false inventions against Us. Then they would have taken you for a friend.

Had We not enabled you to stand firm, you might have inclined towards them a little.

75 Then, We would have made you taste double [the punishment in life] and double the punishment after death, and then you would not have found any supporter against Us.

They were about to provoke you so as to expel you from the land. Then they would not stay after you except a little while.

This was Our way with those messengers We sent before you, and you will not find any change in Our way.

Perform the prayer at the declining of the sun till the darkness of the night and recite the Qur'an at dawn. Surely the recital of the Qur'an at dawn is memorable.

And during the latter part of the night, pray as an additional observance. For your Lord may raise you to a praiseworthy position.

80 Say: "My Lord, make my entry a truthful one and my going out a truthful one, and grant me from You a supporting power."

And say: "The truth has come and falsehood has perished. Falsehood is ever perishing."

And We reveal of the Qur'an that which is healing and merciful for the believers, and it yields nothing but perdition to the wrongdoers.

And when We are gracious to man, he turns away and withdraws haughtily; and if adversity touches him, he is in despair.[559]

Say: "Everyone acts according to his own manner, but your Lord knows well who is best guided on his way."

85 And they ask you about the spirit. Say: "The spirit is of my Lord's command, and you have not been given except a little knowledge."

If We please, We certainly can blot out that which We have revealed to you; then you would find no guardian to assist you against Us.

[But it was left] as a mercy from your Lord. His favours upon you have surely been great.

Say: "Were men and *jinn* to band together in order to come up with the like of this Qur'an, they will never come up with the like of it, even if they back up one another."

We have indeed given mankind in this Qur'an every kind of example, but most people insist on being ungrateful.

90 And they say: "We will not believe you until you cause a spring to gush out from the ground for us.

"Or have a garden of palms and vines; then cause the rivers therein to gush out abundantly;

"Or cause heaven to fall upon us in fragments, as you claim; or bring Allah and the angels down, so that we can see them face to face.

"Or possess a house of gold, or ascend to heaven. Yet, we will not believe in your ascension, until you send down to us a book we can read." Say: "Glory be to my Lord; am I anything other than a human messenger?"

Men are not prevented from believing, once the guidance has come to them, except that they say: "Has Allah sent forth a human messenger?"

95 Say: "Were there on earth angels strolling in peace, We would have sent down upon them from heaven an angel as a messenger."

Say: "Allah suffices as a witness between me and you. He is, indeed, fully apprised and observant of His servants."

Whoever Allah guides is certainly well-guided, and those whom He leaves in error you shall not find for them, besides Allah, any protectors. We shall gather them on the Day of Resurrection, falling on their faces, blind, dumb and deaf. Their dwelling shall be Hell, and whenever it abates, We shall rekindle its flames.

---

559. That is, he loses hope in Allah's mercy.

That is their punishment because they disbelieve in our signs and say: "Shall we, after we have become bones and dust, be raised up as a new creation?"

Have they not considered that Allah, Who created the heavens and the earth, is able to create the like of them? He has appointed for them a term which is undoubted; yet the wrongdoers insist on being ungrateful.

00 Say: "Even if you possess the treasures of my Lord's mercy, you would still withhold them for fear of spending." Man has ever been niggardly.

And We gave Moses nine clear signs. Ask the Children of Irsael, then, how, when he came to them and Pharaoh said to him: "I really think you are bewitched, O Moses,"

He said: "You know that these [signs] have not been sent down by any one other than the Lord of the heavens and the earth as clear proofs, and I think that you, Pharaoh, are doomed."

So, he wanted to scare them out of the land, but We drowned him, together with all those who were with him.

And after him, We said to the Children of Israel: "Dwell in the land, and when the promise of the Hereafter comes, We shall bring you all together."

05 We have revealed it in truth, and in truth it came down; and We have sent you only as a bearer of good news and a warner.

It is a Qur'an which We have divided into parts that you may recite it with deliberation, and We revealed it piecemeal.

Say: "Believe or do not believe in it. Surely when it is recited those, who were given the knowledge[560] before it, fall down prostrate on their faces."

And they say: "Glory be to our Lord. Certainly the promise of our Lord is fulfilled."

And they fall down upon their faces weeping, and it adds to their humility.

10 Say: "Call on Allah or the Compassionate. By whatever name you call [Him], His are the most beautiful names." And pray neither with a loud nor with a low voice, but follow a middle course.

And say: "Praise be to Allah who has not taken a son to Himself, and Who has no partner in sovereignty and no supporter to protect Him from humiliation. And proclaim His greatness."

560. The People of the Book.

SURA 18

Al-Kahf, The Cave

In the Name of Allah, the Compassionate, the Merciful

1 Praise be to Allah, who revealed the Book to His servant and did not leave in it any crookedness.

He has made it straight to warn of severe punishment from Himself and announce the good news to the believers, who do deeds, that they shall have a good reward.[561]

Abiding therein forever.

And to warn those who say: "Allah has taken a son."

5 They have no knowledge thereof, nor do their fathers. What a dreadful word, that comes out of their mouths! They only utter a lie.

You may destroy yourself with grief, sorrowing after them,[562] if they do not believe in this revelation.

We have made everything on earth an adornment, in order to test them [and see] who of them is best in work.

And we shall reduce what is on it to barren dry soil.

Or did you think that the people of the Cave and al-Raqim[563] were the wonders of Our signs?

10 When the youths took refuge in the Cave saying: "Our Lord, accord us from Yourself mercy, and guide us well in our affair."

Then We sealed their hearing in the cave for many years.

Then We roused them to learn who of the two parties[564] was able to calculate the time they had lingered.

We relate to you their story in truth. They were youths who believed in their Lord and We increased them in guidance.

And We strengthened their hearts when they arose saying: "Our Lord is the Lord of the heavens and the earth. We will not call on any god besides Him. For then we would be uttering an enormity.

15 "These, our people have taken other gods besides Him. Why do they not bring a clear authority for them? Who is, then, more unjust than he who invents lies about Allah?"

When you withdrew from them and what they worship, apart from

561. Paradise.
562. Literally following after them in their wake.
563. The name of the mountain where the Cave was.
564. The two parties of the Sleepers of Ephesus, who, according to tradition, were not aware of the time they had spent in the cave.

Allah, take refuge in the Cave, and your Lord will extend to you some of His mercy and prepare for you a suitable course in your affair.

And you might have seen the sun, when it rose, inclining from their Cave towards the right, and when it set, inclining to the left, while they were in an open space inside it.[565] That was one of Allah's signs. He whom Allah guides is well-guided; and he whom Allah leads astray, you will not find a friend to direct him.

You would think them awake, whereas they were sleeping. We turned them over to the right, then to the left, while their dog was stretching its paws in the yard. If you looked at them, you would have turned away from them in flight, and would have been filled with fear.

Thus We roused them, that they might question each other. One of them said: "How long have you lingered?" They said: "A day or part of a day." They said: "Your Lord knows best how long you have lingered. So send someone with this silver [coin] of yours to the city, and let him see what food is purest. Then let him bring you some provision thereof, and let him be gentle and let him apprise no one about you.

20 Surely, if they learn about you, they will stone you or force you back into their religion; and then you will never prosper."

That is how, We made them known [to people] so as to know that Allah's promise is true and that the Hour is undoubted. As they were arguing among themselves concerning their affair, they said: "Build over them an edifice; their Lord knows best their condition." Then those who prevailed over them said: "Let us build over them a mosque."

Some say: "[The sleepers were] three; their dog was the fourth of them", and [others] say: "Five; their dog was the sixth of them", interpreting the unseen. And they say: "Seven; their dog being the eighth of them." Say: "My Lord knows best their number; none knows them, save a few." Do not, then, dispute concerning them, except with reference to that which is clear to you, and do not question, concerning them, any of them."

And do not say of anything: "I will do that tomorrow," [unless you add]: "If Allah wills." Remember your Lord, if you forget, and say: "Perhaps, my Lord will guide me to something closer to this in rectitude?"

25 And they lingered in their Cave three hundred years, and [some] add nine.

Say: "Allah knows best how long they lingered. His is the Unseen of the heavens and the earth. How clear is His sight and His hearing! Apart from Him, they have no protector, and He has no associates in His sovereignty."

Recite what was revealed to you from your Lord's Book; no one can alter His words, and from Him, you will find no refuge.

565. The Cave.

And confine yourself to those who call upon their Lord, morning and evening, desiring His face. And let not your eyes wander away from them, desiring the finery of the present life. And do not obey him whose heart We have made heedless of Our remembrance, he has followed his own desires, and his case has become hopeless.

And say: "The Truth is from your Lord. Whoever wishes, let him believe; and whoever wishes, let him disbelieve." We have prepared for the wrongdoers a Fire whose canopy encompasses them all. If they call for relief, they will be relieved with water like molten brass which scars the faces. Wretched is that drink and wretched is the resting-place!

30   As for those who believe and do the good deed, surely, We will not waste the reward of him who does the good work.

Those shall have Gardens of Eden, beneath which rivers flow, bejewelled therein with bracelets of gold, and wearing green clothes of silk and brocade, reclining therein on couches. Blessed is their reward and fair is the resting-place!

And relate to them as a parable the case of two men. To one of them, We gave two gardens of vine, which We surrounded with palm trees and placed between them a cornfield.

Both gardens yielded their produce and did not waste any of it, and We caused a river to flow through them both.

And he had some fruit. So he said to his companion, while conversing with him: "I have greater wealth than you and a mightier following."

35   Then he entered his garden, wronging himself. He said: "I do not think this will ever perish.

"And I do not think the Hour is coming. If I am returned to my Lord, I will surely find a better place than this."

His companion said to him, while conversing with him: "Do you disbelieve in Him who created you from dust, then from a sperm, then fashioned you into a man?

"But as for me, Allah is my Lord and I do not associate anyone with my Lord."

If only you were to say, upon entering your garden: "What Allah pleases [shall come to be]; there is no power save in Allah. If you see me possessing less wealth and children than you;

40   "Perhaps, my Lord will give me a better garden than yours and will release upon yours a thunderbolt from the sky, so that it will turn into a barren wasteland.

"Or its water will sink into the ground, so that you will not be able to draw it."

Then, his fruit was destroyed, and so he began to wring his hands at what he had spent on it, while it had fallen down upon its trellises, and he was saying: "I wish I had not associated anyone with my Lord."

And he did not have a faction to help him besides Allah, nor was he able to defend himself.

There, protection is from Allah, the True God. He is Best in rewarding and Best in requiting.

45   And give them the simile of the present life; it is like the water We send down from the sky; then the vegetation of the earth is mixed with it, and so it becomes straw which the wind scatters. Allah has power over everything.

Wealth and children are the adornment of the present life, but the everlasting good works are better in your Lord's sight in reward and better in expectation.

And on the day We shall cause the mountains to move and you see the earth uncovered, and we gather them all, having left no one behind.

And they will be brought before your Lord in rows: "Now you come to Us as We created you the first time. No, you claimed that We would not fix for you an appointed time."

And the book will be set down, and you will see the wicked apprehensive at what is in it, and they will say: "Woe betide us. What book is this? It does not leave out anything, small or big, but enumerates it." And they will find what they did in front of them; and your Lord will not wrong any one.

50   And [remember] when We said to the angels: "Prostrate yourselves to Adam", and they all did except Satan; he was one of the *jinn*, then he disobeyed the command of his Lord. Will you, then, take him and his progeny as protectors, besides Me, while they are all your enemies? Evil is that exchange for the wrongdoers!"

I did not call them to witness the creation of the heavens and the earth, nor their own creation; and I did not take those who lead astray as supporters.

And on the day He will say: "Call on whom you claimed to be My associates." They will call on them, but they will not answer them, and We will set a valley of destruction between them.

The wicked will see the Fire and will think that they will fall in it, and will find no escape from it.

We have set out, in this Qur'an for the people, every manner of example; but man is the most contentious being.

55   Nothing prevents men from believing when the guidance comes to them, or from seeking forgiveness from their Lord; but they wait for the fate of the ancients to overtake them, or to be confronted with the punishment.

We do not send messengers except as bearers of good news or warners; yet the unbelievers dispute with falsehood, to refute the truth thereby; and they take My revelations and what they were warned about as an object of mockery.

And who is more unjust than one who, upon being reminded of his Lord's revelations, turns away from them, and forgets what His hands have done? We have placed coverings upon their hearts lest they understand it,[566] and put a deafness in their ears. If you call them to the guidance, they will never be guided.

And your Lord is All-Forgiving and Merciful. Were He to call them to account for what they have earned, He would have hastened their punishment. However, they have an appointment from which they will find no escape.

And those towns, We have destroyed them when they did wrong, and we set for their destruction an appointed time.

60   And [remember] when Moses said to his servant:[567] "I will not give up until I reach the confluence of the two seas,[568] or else walk on for years."

Then, when they reached their confluence, they forgot their fish, and thus it slipped away into the sea unhindered.

But when they had passed on, he said to his servant: "Bring us our food; we have been exposed in our travels to a lot of fatigue."

He[569] said: "Do you see; when we repaired to the rock, I forgot the fish. It was only the Devil who made me forget to mention it; and so it slipped away into the sea in a strange way."

He[570] said: "This is what we were seeking"; and so they turned back retracing their steps.

65   And so, they found one of Our servants whom We had accorded a mercy of Our own and had imparted to him knowledge from Ourselves.

Moses said to him: "Shall I follow you so that you may teach me of the good you have been taught."

He said: "You will not be able to bear with me.

"And how will you bear with what you have no knowledge of?"

He[571] said: "You will find me, Allah willing, patient and I will not disobey any order of yours."

70   He said: "If you follow me, do not ask me about anything, until I make mention of it."

So, they set out; but no sooner had they boarded the ship than he made a

566. The Qur'an.
567. He is believed to be Joshua.
568. The Gulf of Aqaba and Gulf of Suez in the Red Sea.
569. The servant.
570. Moses.
571. Moses' servant.

hole in it. He [Moses] said: "Have you made a hole in it so as to drown its passengers? You have indeed done a grievous thing."

He said: "Did I not tell you that you will not be able to bear with me?"

He[572] said: "Do not reproach me for what I have forgotten, and do not overburden me with hardship."

Then they departed; but when they met a boy, he killed him. Moses said: "Have you killed an innocent person who has not killed another? You have surely committed a horrible deed."

He said: "Did I not tell you that you will not be able to bear with me."

He [Moses] said: "If I ask you about anything after this, do not keep company with me. You have received an excuse from me."

So, they went on, until they reached the inhabitants of a city. Whereupon they asked its inhabitants for food, but they refused to offer them hospitality. Then, they found in it a wall about to fall down, and so he straightened it. He[573] said: "Had you wished, you could have been paid for that."

He said: "This is where we part company. [Now] I will tell you the interpretation of that which you could not bear patiently with.

"As for the ship, it belonged to some poor fellows who worked upon the sea. I wanted to damage it, because, on their trail, there was a king, who was seizing every ship by force.

"As for the boy, his parents were believers; so we feared that he might overwhelm them with oppression and unbelief.

"So We wanted that their Lord might replace him with someone better in purity and closer to mercy.

"And as for the wall, it belonged to two orphan boys in the town; and beneath it there was a treasure for both of them. Their father was a righteous man; so your Lord wanted them to come of age and dig up the treasure, as a mercy from your Lord. What I did was not of my own will. This is the interpretation of what you could not bear with patiently."

And they ask you about Dhu'l-Qarnayn.[574] Say: "I will give you this account of him."

We established him firmly in the land and We gave him access to everything.

And so he followed a course;

Then, when he reached the setting-place of the sun, he found that it sets in a spring of black mud and found, by it, a people. We said: "O Dhu'l-Qarnayn, either you punish them or show them kindness."

---

572. Moses.
573. Moses.
574. He is believed to be Alexander the Great.

He said: "As to the wrongdoer, we shall torture him; then he will be returned over to his Lord, who will punish him a terrible punishment.

"But he who believes and does good deeds, he will have the fairest reward,[575] and We will command him to do what is easy for him."

Then he[576] followed [another] course.

90   But when he reached the rising-place of the sun, he found it rising on a people whom We have not provided with any screen against it.

So it was. We had full knowledge of what he had.

Then he followed another course.

But when he reached the point separating the two barriers, he found beside them a people who could barely understand what is said.

They said: "O Dhu'l-Qarnayn, surely Gog and Magog[577] are making mischief in the land. Shall we pay you a tribute so that you may build a barrier between us and them?"

95   He said: "What my Lord has empowered me to do is better. So help me forcefully and I will build a barrier between you and them."

"Bring me large pieces of iron." So that when he had levelled up [the gap] between the two sides, he said: "Blow." And having turned it[578] into fire, he said: "Bring me molten brass to pour on it."

Then, they[579] could neither scale it nor make a hole through it.

He said: "This is a mercy from my Lord; but when my Lord's promise comes to pass, He will turn it into rubble, and the promise of my Lord is ever true."

And on that day, We shall make them surge upon one another, and the trumpet shall be blown, and We shall gather them together.

100   On that day We shall boldly set Hell before the unbelievers.

Those whose eyes were closed to My Reminder[580] and they could not hear [it].

Have the unbelievers, then, supposed that they can take My servants besides Me, as friends? We have indeed prepared Hell for the unbelievers as an abode.

Say: "Shall We inform you about the greatest losers of their works?"

Those whose endeavour in the present life has gone astray and they still believe that they are doing well.

105   Those who disbelieve in the revelations of their Lord and in meeting Him. Their works are vain and We will not take any account of them on the Day of Resurrection.

575. That is, Paradise.
576. Dhu'l-Qarnayn.
577. Gog and Magog are the names of two tribes.
578. The iron.
579. Gog and Magog.
580. The Qur'an.

That is their reward – Hell, on account of their disbelief and their taking My revelations and My messengers as objects of scorn.

Indeed, those who believe and do the good works, the gardens of Paradise shall be their dwelling.

Abiding therein forever and not desiring to be ever removed therefrom.

Say: "Were the sea to become ink for my Lord's words, the sea would be exhausted before the words of my Lord are exhausted, even if We were to bring its like to replenish it."

10   Say: "I am only a mortal like you. It has been revealed to me that your God is One God. Let him who hopes to meet his Lord, do what is good and associate none in the worship of his Lord."

SURA 19

Maryam, Mary

In the Name of Allah, the Compassionate, the Merciful

Kaf, Ha, Ya, Ain, Sad.

1   This is the story of your Lord's mercy unto His servant Zacharia;
When he called upon his Lord secretly.

He said: "Lord, my bones have weakened and my head is aflame with grey hair, and I have not, Lord, in vain called upon you."

"In truth, I fear my kinsmen, after I am gone, as my wife is barren. Grant me, then, from Your bounty, a successor.

5   "To inherit me and inherit the house of Jacob, and make him, Lord, well-pleasing to You."

[It was said to him]: "O Zacharia, We announce to you the good news of a boy whose name is John; We have not hitherto given the same name to anyone else."

He said: "Lord, how shall I have a boy, seeing that my wife is barren and I have reached an advanced old age?"

He said: "That is what your Lord says. It is easy for Me. Indeed I created you formerly, when you were nothing."

He said: "Lord, give me a sign." He said: "Your sign is that you will not talk to anybody for three nights, although you are sound of body."

10   He came out to his people from the sanctuary and told them by signs: "Pray and glorify morning and evening."

It was then said to John: "O John, hold fast to the Book." And We granted him wisdom when he was still a child;

And tenderness from Us and purity. He was devout;

And devoted to his parents; and he was not arrogant and disobedient.

Peace be upon him the day he was born, the day he dies and the day he is raised from the dead.

15   And remember [the account] of Mary in the Book when she withdrew from her people to an Eastern place.

She screened herself away from them, and We sent to her Our Spirit and it appeared to her in the form of a well-shaped human being.

She said: "I seek refuge with Allah from you, if you fear God."

He said: "I am only the messenger of your Lord to grant you a boy most pure."

She said: "Shall I have a boy, when no man has touched me and I have not been an unchaste woman?"

20 He[581] said: "Thus [it will be]," your Lord has said: 'This is an easy matter for Me; that We may make him[582] a sign unto mankind and a mercy from Us.'" And thus it was decreed.

So, she conceived him and she withdrew with him to a distant place.

Then labour pangs drove her towards the trunk of a palm tree. She said: "I wish I had died before this and had become completely forgotten."

Whereupon [a voice] called her from beneath her: "Do not grieve. Your Lord has created below you a stream."

"Shake the trunk of the palm tree towards you and it will drop upon you fresh ripe dates."

25 "Eat, drink and rejoice. Then if you see any human say: 'I have vowed to the Compassionate to fast, and so I shall not talk today to any human being.'"

Then she brought him[583] to her people, carrying him. They said: "O Mary, you have surely committed a strange thing."

"Sister of Aaron, your father was not an evil man and your mother was not unchaste."

Whereupon she pointed to him. They said: "How will we talk to one who is still an infant in the cradle?"

He said: "Indeed, I am the servant of Allah, who gave me the Book and made me a prophet.

30 "And He made me blessed wherever I am, and has commanded me to pray and to give the alms, so long as I live;

"And be devoted to my mother; and He did not make me arrogant and mischievous.

"Peace be upon me the day I was born, the day I die and the day I rise from the dead."

Such was Jesus, son of Mary; it is the truth which they[584] dispute.

It is not fitting for Allah to have a son. Glory be to Him; when He decrees a thing, He simply says: "Be", and it comes to be.

35 Allah is truly your Lord and my Lord; so worship Him. That is a straight path.

Yet, the sects among them differed. Woe to those who have disbelieved from the spectacle of a great day!

How well they will hear and how well they will see, on the day they will come unto Us; but the wrongdoers today are in manifest error.

581. The angel.
582. The boy, Jesus.
583. The child.
584. The Christians.

And warn them of the day of sorrow, when the issue is decided, while they are heedless and do not believe.

It is We who shall inherit the earth and whomever is on it, and to Us they shall be returned.

40 And remember in the Book Abraham. He was a truthful man, a prophet.

He said to his father: "Father, why do you worship that which neither sees nor hears, and can do nothing to help you?

"To me has come knowledge which has not come to you; so follow me and I will guide you to a straight path.

"Father, do not worship the Devil; for the Devil has been rebelling against the Compassionate.

"Father, I fear that a punishment from the Compassionate shall afflict you, and so you will become a friend of the Devil."

45 He said: "Are you forsaking my gods, O Abraham? If you will not desist, I will certainly stone you. So leave me alone for a while."

He said: "Peace be upon you. I will seek forgiveness for you from my Lord. He has, indeed, been gracious to me.

"And I will draw away from you and from those you call upon besides Allah, and I will pray to my Lord. Perhaps I may not be unfortunate in praying to my Lord."

Then, when he drew away from them and what they worshipped besides Allah, We granted him Isaac and Jacob and each we made a prophet.

And We gave them freely of Our mercy and We accorded them an honourable and true renown.

50 And [remember] in the Book Moses; he was sincere, a messenger and a prophet. We called him from the right side of the Mount, and brought him closer in communion.

And We granted him, out of Our mercy, his brother Aaron, a prophet.

And mention in the Book Isma'il; he was true to his promises and was a messenger and a prophet.

He enjoined on his people prayer and almsgiving and was well-pleasing to his Lord.

55 And mention in the Book Idris; he was truthful and a prophet.

And We raised him to a high place.

Those are the ones whom Allah favoured from among the prophets of the progeny of Adam, of those We carried with Noah, of the progeny of Abraham and Israel and of those We have guided and elected. When the revelations of the Compassionate are recited to them, they fall down prostrate and weeping.

Then there came after them a posterity who forgot all about prayer and followed their lusts. They shall face perdition.

Except for those who repent, believe and do what is right. Those shall enter Paradise and will not be wronged at all,

60   Gardens of Eden that the Compassionate has promised His servants in the unseen. His promise will certainly be accomplished.

They hear therein no idle talk, but only: "Peace"; and they receive their provision therein morning and evening.

Such is the Paradise which We shall give as inheritance to those of Our servants who are God-fearing.

We[585] do not come down except at the command of your Lord. His is what is before us, is behind us and is in between. Your Lord is never forgetful.

Lord of the heavens and the earth and what is between them. So worship Him and be steadfast in His worship; do you know anyone who is worthy of the same name?

65   Man says: "If I die, shall I be raised from the dead?"

Does not man remember that We created him before, when he was nothing?

By your Lord, then, We shall certainly gather them together with the devils, then We will lead them around Hell on their knees.

Then, We shall seize from each group the most rebellious against the Compassionate.

And, We certainly know best who among them deserves most to be burned therein.

70   There is no one of you but will go down to it.[586] That is for your Lord a decree which must be accomplished.

Then, We shall deliver the righteous and leave the wrongdoers therein on their knees.

And when Our revelations are clearly recited to them, the unbelievers will say to the believers: "Which of the two parties is better in position and fairer in company?"

How many generations before them We have destroyed, who had better furnishings and appearance?

Say: "Whoever is in error, let the Compassionate prolong his term; so that when they see what they are threatened with, whether it be the punishment or the Hour, they will know who is worse in position and weaker in supporters."

75   Allah increases in guidance those who are rightly guided; and the good works which last will receive a better reward from Allah and better returns.

585. That is, the angels.
586. That is, Hell.

Have you seen him who disbelieves in Our revelations and [yet] says: "I shall certainly be given wealth and children."

Does he have knowledge of the Unseen, or did he take a pledge from the Compassionate?

No, We shall write down what he says and shall add punishment to his punishment.

And We will inherit from him what he says and he will come to Us alone.

80 And they took, besides Allah, other gods, to be for them a source of strength.

No, they shall repudiate their worship and turn against them.

Have you not seen how We sent the devils against the unbelievers to keep inciting them [to sin].

So do not hasten [their punishment]. We are indeed counting for them the days.

The day We shall gather the God-fearing before the Compassionate as one party.

85 And drive the wicked into Hell as one thirsty herd.

They have no power of intercession, except for him who has taken a pledge from the Compassionate.

And they say: "The Compassionate has taken to Himself a son."

You have, indeed, made a shocking assertion,

From which the heavens are almost rent asunder, the earth split and the mountains fallen to pieces.

90 For they ascribe a son to the Compassionate.

Whereas, it is not fitting that the Compassionate should have a son.

Everyone in the heavens and on earth will surely come to the Compassionate as a servant.

He keeps count of them and has numbered them.

And every one of them will come to Him on the Day of Resurrection alone.

95 Those who believe and do what is right, the Compassionate will favour with love.[587]

For We made it easy[588] [to understand] in your own tongue, so as to announce the good news to the God-fearing and warn through it.[589]

And how many a generation before them We have destroyed! Do you perceive any one of them or hear any sound of theirs?

---

587. His love and that of their fellow creatures.
588. The Qur'an.
589. The Meccan unbelievers.

SURA 20

Ta Ha, Symbols, or *Taha*

In the Name of Allah, the Compassionate, the Merciful

Ta Ha.[590]

1 We have not revealed the Qur'an to you so as to make you unhappy.
But only as a reminder to him who fears.
A revelation from Him who created the earth and the high heavens.
The Compassionate has sat upon the Throne.

5 To Him belongs what is in the heavens, and what is in earth, and what is in between them, as well as what is beneath the ground.
If you speak aloud, He surely knows the secret and what is even more hidden.
Allah, there is no god but He. His are the most beautiful names.
Has the story of Moses reached you?
When he saw a fire, he said to his people: "Stay. I see a fire. Perhaps I can bring you a lighted torch therefrom or find guidance by the fire."

10 Then, when he came to it, a voice called out: "O Moses,
"I am truly your Lord; so take off your shoes, you are in the holy valley, Tuwa.
"And I have chosen you; so listen to what is being revealed.
"I am truly Allah; there is no god but I; so worship Me and perform the prayer for my remembrance.
"Surely, the Hour is coming – but I keep it almost hidden – so that each soul may be rewarded for its work.

15 "Let no one, who does not believe and follows his own desires, bar you from it lest you perish.
"And what is that in your right hand, O Moses?"
He said: "It is my staff. I lean on it and I beat leaves for my sheep with it and I have other uses for it."
He said: "Cast it down, O Moses."
So he cast it down, and lo and behold, it was a serpent, sliding.

20 He said: "Pick it up and do not fear; We shall restore it to its original condition.
"And press your hand to your side; it will come out white, without blemish, as another sign,

---

590. These two Arabic letters mean, according to some commentators, "O man."

"That We may show you some of Our greatest signs.

"Go to Pharaoh; for he has transgressed."

He said: "Lord, open⁵⁹¹ my breast for me,

25   "And make my task easy for me.

"And unravel the knot of my tongue.

"That they may understand my words.

"And give me, from my own family, a supporter,⁵⁹²

"Aaron, my brother.

30   "And increase through him my strength.

"And associate him with me in my task.

"So that we may glorify you;

"And remember you often.

"You have surely been observant of us."

35   He⁵⁹³ said: "You have been granted your request, O Moses.

"And We have favoured you another time.

"When We revealed to your mother a revelation [saying]:

" 'Put him in a chest and cast him into the river. The river will then cast him off on the shore, and he will be taken by an enemy of Mine and an enemy of his. And I bestowed upon you a love from Me, so that you may be reared before My eyes.'

"When your sister went and said: 'Shall I tell you about one who will take charge of him?'⁵⁹⁴ so we turned you over to your mother, that she may rejoice and not grieve. Then you killed a living soul, but We delivered you from anguish; and We tried you repeatedly, so you stayed years among the people of Midian. Then you came, as decreed, O Moses.

40   "And I chose you for Myself.

"Go, then, you and your brother, with My signs, and do not tire of remembering Me.

"Go forth to Pharaoh; for he has surely transgressed.

"Speak to him gently, that perchance he may take heed or fear."

They said: "Our Lord, we fear that he may hasten to do us harm, or transgress."

45   He said: "Do not fear. Surely I am with you hearing and seeing.

"So go forth to him and say: 'We are your Lord's messengers; so send the Children of Israel along with us and do not torture them. We have brought you a sign from your Lord. Peace be upon him who follows the guidance.' "

It has been revealed to us [Moses and Aaron] that punishment shall afflict him who disbelieves and turns his back."

591. Literally, expand.
592. Literally, a minister.
593. Allah.
594. That is, will nurse him.

He[595] said: "Who, then, is your Lord, O Moses?"

He said: "Our Lord is He who gave everything its nature, then guided it."

50   He said: "What about the former generations?"

[Moses] said: "The knowledge thereof is with my Lord in a Book. My Lord neither errs nor forgets."

He who made the earth a bed for you, and opened routes for you in it, and sent down water from the sky; from it We bring forth diverse pairs of plants.

[Moses] said "Eat and pasture your cattle. In that there are signs for people of understanding.

"From it We have created you, and into it We shall return you, and from it We shall raise you a second time."

55   And We have shown him[596] all Our signs, but he denied them and refused [to believe].

He said: "Have you come, Moses, to drive us out of our land by means of your sorcery?

"We shall bring you similar sorcery; so make an appointment between us and you, which neither we nor you shall break, in a central place."

He said: "Your appointment is set for the day of the Feast, so let the people be gathered together before noon."

Pharaoh turned away and gathered [his men] of guile, then came along.

60   Moses said to them: "Woe to you. Do not lie about Allah lest He destroy you with punishment. Indeed, he who lies has failed."

So, they disagreed among themselves with respect to their affair and conferred secretly.

They said: "Those are two sorcerers who want to drive you out of your land with their sorcery and put an end to your ideal tradition.

"So gather your guile and then come forward in battle array; for today he who has the upper hand shall prosper."

They said: "O Moses, either you cast down, or we will be the first to cast down."

65   He said: "You had better cast down"; and behold, their ropes and staffs appeared to him, by reason of their sorcery, to glide.

So, Moses felt apprehensive within himself.

We said: "Do not be afraid, you certainly have the upper hand.

"Cast down what is in your right hand and it will swallow what they have faked. They have only faked the guile of a magician, and the magician will never prosper wherever he goes."

595. Pharaoh.
596. Pharaoh.

Then the magicians fell down prostrate. They said: "We believe [now] in the Lord of Aaron and Moses."

70   He[597] said: "Do you believe in him before I give you leave? It must be your chief who has taught you magic. I shall then cut your hands and feet on alternate sides, and I will crucify you upon the trunks of palm trees, and you will certainly know whose punishment is sterner and more lasting."

They said: "We cannot prefer you to what came to us of clear proofs and to Him who created us. So, decide what you will decide; you only decide regarding this present life.

"We have believed in our Lord, that He may forgive us our sins and what you forced us to practise of magic. Allah is best and most abiding."

For him who comes to his Lord, as a wicked sinner, is Hell, where he neither dies nor lives.

"But those who come to Him as believers, who have done good works will have the highest ranks;

75   "Gardens of Eden, beneath which rivers flow, dwelling therein forever. That is the reward of him who purifies himself."

And We revealed to Moses: "Set out at night with My servants and strike for them a dry path in the sea, not fearing to be overtaken nor dreading anything."

Then Pharaoh pursued them with his troops and so they[598] were overwhelmed by the water.

Pharaoh thus led his people astray and did not guide them rightly.

O Children of Israel, We have delivered you from your enemy and We made a covenant with you on the right side of the Mount, and sent down to you the manna and quails.

80   Eat of the good things We have provided you with, but do not be excessive therein, lest My wrath descend upon you. Those upon whom My wrath descends shall be ruined.

I am, indeed, All-Forgiving unto him who repents, does the righteous deed and is well-guided.

"What has led you to go ahead of your people, O Moses?"

He said: "Those people are on my tracks, so I have hastened towards You, O Lord, that You may be well-pleased."

He said: "We have tried your people after you left and the Samaritan[599] has led them astray."

85   So, Moses went back to his people furious and sorrowful. He said: "O my people, has not your Lord made a fair promise to you? Has the promise,

597. Pharaoh.
598. Pharaoh's troops.
599. A Samaritan Jew.

then, been protracted for you? Or did you want your Lord's anger to overtake you, and so you broke your promise to me?"

They said: "We have not broken the promise to you by our choice, but we have been forced to carry loads of the people's finery and so we threw them away, as the Samaritan also did."

Then he produced for them a calf – a mere body which lowed; and so they said: "This is your god and the god of Moses, but he has forgotten."

Do they not see that it does not return any reply to them and does not have the power to harm or profit them?

Aaron had said to them before: "O my people, you have been tried by it and your Lord is truly the Compassionate. Follow me, then, and obey my order."

90   They said: "We will not stop worshipping it, till Moses comes back to us." He[600] said: "O Aaron, what prevented you, when you saw them going astray,

"From following me. Have you, then, disobeyed my order?"

He said: "Son of my mother, do not seize me by the beard or the head, I feared that you would say: 'You have caused division among the Children of Israel and did not observe my words.'"

He[601] said: "What is the matter with you, O Samaritan?"

He said: "I perceived what they did not perceive, and so I grasped a handful of dust from the messenger's[602] trail and threw it down. That is what my soul prompted me to do."

95   He said: "Begone; it shall be given you in your lifetime to say: 'Do not touch' and you shall be given a promise which you will not break. Look then at your god, whom you continued to worship. We shall burn him; then We shall scatter his ashes in the sea."

Surely, your god is only Allah; there is no god but He. He has knowledge of all things.

That is how We relate to you some of the stories of things past; and We have imparted to you a reminder from Us.

Whoever turns away from it will bear a heavy burden on the Day of Resurrection;

Abiding therein[603] forever. And what a wretched burden they will bear on the Day of Resurrection!

100   On the day when the trumpet shall be blown and We will gather the wicked sinners blue-eyed [with terror];

600. Moses.
601. Moses.
602. Gabriel.
603. In this state.

Whispering to each other: "You have only lingered for ten [days]."

We know better what they say; for the straightest of them in direction will say: "You have only lingered a single day."

And they will ask you about the mountains, say: "My Lord will reduce them to dust,

"And leave them as bare flatland,

105   "In which you see no ups and downs."

On that day, they will have to follow the caller who is not crooked, and the voices shall be hushed unto the Compassionate, so that you will hear nothing but whispering.

On that day, intercession will not avail, except him to whom the Compassionate gives leave and He is pleased with his words.

He knows what is before them and what is behind them; but they have no knowledge of that.

And they shall submit to the Living and Self-Subsisting One, and he who carries [a burden of] wrongdoing shall lose hope.

110   And he who does the righteous deeds, while a believer, will fear neither injustice nor inequity.

Thus We have revealed it as an Arabic Qur'an and expounded therein in detail some of our warnings, so that they may fear God, and so that it may be a reminder for them.

Exalted be Allah, the True King. Do not hasten [to discuss] the Qur'an before its revelation to you is complete, and say: "Lord, increase me in knowledge."

And We commanded Adam before, but he forgot, and We found in him no firm resolve.

And when We said to the angels: "Prostrate yourselves to Adam", they prostrated themselves, except for Satan who refused.

115   So we said: "O Adam, this is surely an enemy of you and your wife; so do not let him drive you out of Paradise; for then, you will be miserable.

"You will certainly not be hungry therein, nor be naked.

"And you will not thirst therein, nor be exposed to the heat of the sun."

But the Devil whispered to him, saying: "O Adam, shall I show you the Tree of Immortality and a kingdom which will never perish?"

And so they both[604] ate from it; whereupon their shameful parts were revealed to them and they started fastening upon themselves leaves of Paradise. Adam thus disobeyed his Lord and so went astray.

120   Then, his Lord favoured him, and so We relented towards him, and guided him.

---

604. Adam and Eve.

He said: "Go down from it both of you, as enemies of one another; but should guidance from Me come to you, he who follows My guidance will not go astray or suffer.

"But he who shuns My remembrance will have a life of hardship, and We shall raise him up a blind man, on the Day of Resurrection."

He will say: "Lord, why did you raise me up a blind man, while I was originally capable of seeing?"

He will say: "That is how Our revelations came to you, but you forgot them; and that is how, today, you shall be forgotten."

25 And that is how We reward the extravagant who would not believe in the revelations of his Lord. The punishment of the Hereafter is surely more terrible and more lasting.

Did He not reveal to them, as a guidance, how many generations before them We destroyed as they were walking inside their dwellings? Surely, in that are signs for people of understanding.

And but for a word which preceded from your Lord and an appointed term, it[605] would have been inexorable.

So bear[606] patiently what they say, and celebrate the praise of your Lord before the rising of the sun and before its setting; and glorify Him during the hours of the night and at the two ends[607] of the day, that you may be well-pleased.

And do not allow your eyes to reach out to what We allowed some to enjoy of the flowers of the present life, so as to try them thereby. Your Lord's provision is better and more lasting.

30 And enjoin your family to pray and be constant therein. We do not ask you for any provision; We rather provide for you. The happy ending is reserved for righteousness.

They say: "If only he would bring us a sign from his Lord." Has not a clear proof come to them in the previous scriptures?

And had We destroyed them with a punishment before him,[608] they would have said: "Lord, if only you had sent us a messenger, we would have followed your revelation before we were humiliated and disgraced."

Say: "Everybody is waiting, so wait; and then you will know who are the people of the straight path and who are the well-guided."

---

605. The punishment.
606. This is addressed to Muhammad.
607. According to some commentators, the prayers at the two ends of the day are the evening and morning prayers.
608. The Prophet Muhammad.

SURA 21

Al-Anbiya', The Prophet

In the Name of Allah, the Compassionate, the Merciful

1 Mankind's reckoning is drawing near, but they are turning away heedlessly.

No new reminder comes to them from their Lord but they listen to it while they are at play.

Their hearts are distracted. The wrongdoers say in secret: "Is this not a mortal like you? Will you then take to sorcery, with your eyes wide open?"

He said: "My Lord knows what is said in the heavens and the earth, and He is the All-Hearing, the All-Knowing."

5 "No", they say: "It is just a load of dreams. He has rather forged it; he is rather a poet. Let him bring us a sign, just as the former [prophets] were sent [with]."

No city We destroyed, before them, actually believed. Will they, then, believe?

And we did not send before you but men to whom We revealed. So ask those acquainted [with the scripture] if you do not know.

And We did not make them as mere bodies that did not eat food; nor were they immortal.

Then We fulfilled the promise, and so We delivered them together with whomever We pleased, and We destroyed the extravagant.

10 We have indeed sent down to you a Book in which there is admonition for you. Do you not understand, then?

How many an unjust town We have levelled down and created in its wake another people.

Then, when they sensed Our might, behold, they started running away from it.

"Do not run. Return to what you enjoyed of luxury, and to your dwellings, that perchance you may be questioned."

They said: "Woe to us! We have indeed been wrongdoers."

15 This continued to be their lament, until We [cut them down] to stubble, senseless.

We did not create the heaven and the earth and what is in between them in sport.

Had We wished to take to Ourselves a means of sport, We would have found it within Us, if We wanted to do it.

No, We hurl the truth against falsehood and it overcomes it; and, behold, it has vanished. Woe unto you,[609] for what you describe.[610]

To Him belongs what is in the heavens and on earth; and those with Him[611] are not too proud to worship Him, nor do they tire;

20   Glorifying Him night and day without growing weary.

Or have they taken to themselves gods out of the earth, able to raise the dead?

Were there in them both[612] other gods than Allah, they would surely have been ruined. Allah be exalted, the Lord of the Throne, above what they describe.

He is not questioned about what He does, but they are questioned.

Or, have they taken, besides Him, other gods? Say: "Bring your proof. This is the Reminder[613] of those with me and the Reminder of those before me." However, most of them do not know the truth, so they turn away.

25   We have not sent before you any messenger, but We revealed to him that there is no god but I; so worship Me.

They say: "The Compassionate has taken to Himself a son. Glory be to Him; they[614] are [merely] honoured servants."

They never speak until He has spoken; they only act on His command.

He knows what is before them and what is behind them, and they do not intercede except for him whom He approves; and they tremble for fear of Him.

And whoever of them says: "I am a god besides Him" – that one We shall reward with Hell. That is how We reward the wrongdoers.

30   Have the unbelievers not beheld that the heavens and the earth were a solid mass, then We separated them; and of water We produced every living thing. Will they not believe, then?

And We set up in the earth immovable mountains lest it should shake with them; and We created therein wide roads, that perchance they may be guided.

And We made the sky a well-guarded canopy; and they still turn away from its signs.

It is He Who created the night and the day, the sun and the moon, each floating in its orbit.

609. The Meccans.
610. The way you describe Allah.
611. The angels.
612. Heaven and earth.
613. The Qur'an.
614. The angels.

And We did not grant immortality to any human before you. If you die, are they then immortal?

35   Every living soul shall taste death, and We test you by evil and good as a temptation and unto Us you shall be returned.

And if the unbelievers see you, they only take you as an object of mockery [saying]: "Is this the one who talks about your gods?" And they disbelieve in the mention of the Compassionate.

Man is created in haste. I will bring you My signs; so do not hasten them.

And they say: "When will this threat come to pass if you are truthful?"

If only the unbelievers knew the time when they will not be able to ward off the Fire from their faces or their backs, and they will not be helped!

40   But it will come upon them suddenly confounding them, and so they will not be able to repel it, nor will they be respited.

Many messengers before you were mocked; then those who scoffed at them were afflicted by that which they used to mock.

Say: "Who guards you night and day against the Compassionate?" Yet they turn away from the mention of their Lord.

Or do they have gods who will defend them against Us? They cannot help themselves and they will not be protected from us.

No, We gave ease to those people and their fathers until they became advanced in age. Do they not see that We come upon the land [under their control] reducing it from its extremities? Are they then the victors?

45   Say: "I only warn you through the Revelation; but the deaf people do not hear the call, when they are warned."

And if the least hint of your Lord's punishment touches them, they will surely say: "Woe to us; we have been truly wrongdoers."

We set up the just scales for the Day of Resurrection, so that no soul shall be wronged a whit; and even if it be the weight of a mustard seed, We shall produce it. We suffice as reckoners.

And We gave Moses and Aaron the criterion[615] and a light, and a reminder for the righteous,

Who fear their Lord secretly and are apprehensive of the Hour.

50   This is a blessed Reminder[616] We have revealed. Are you, then, going to deny it?

And We gave Abraham his right judgement formerly; for We knew him well.

When he said to his father and his people: "What are these statues to which you are devoted?"

They said: "We found our fathers worshipping them."

615. The Torah.
616. The Qur'an.

He said: "Indeed, you and your fathers have been in manifest error."

55   They said: "Have you brought us the Truth, or are you one of those who jest?"

He said: "No, your Lord is the Lord of the heavens and the earth, Who created them both; and I bear witness to that.

"And by Allah, I will show your idols my guile, after you turn your backs."

Then he reduced them to pieces except for their chief, so that they might turn to him.

They said: "He who did this to our gods is certainly one of the wrong-doers."

60   They said: "We heard a youth called Abraham mentioning them."

They said: "Bring him along in full view of the people, so that they may bear witness."

They said: "Are you the one who did this to our gods, O Abraham?"

He said: "No, but their chief did this; so ask them if they can speak."

Then, they turned to themselves and said: "Surely, you are the wrong-doers."

65   And so they were utterly confounded and [they said]: "You know that these [idols] do not speak."

He said: "Do you, then, worship, besides Allah, what does not profit or harm you a whit?

"Fie on you and on what you worship besides Allah. Do you not understand?"

They said: "Burn him and support your gods, if you are going to do anything."

We said: "O fire, be coolness and peace upon Abraham."

70   They wanted to plot against him, but We made them the worst losers.

And We delivered him and Lot unto the land which We have blessed for all mankind.

And We granted him Isaac and Jacob, his son's son, as a bounty and each We made to be righteous.

And We made them leaders, guiding others at Our behest; and We revealed to them to do good, perform the prayer and give the alms, and they have worshipped Us.

And Lot, We gave him good judgement and knowledge, and We delivered him from the city which practised foul deeds.[617] They were indeed an evil and sinful people.

75   And We admitted him into Our mercy; for he was one of the righteous.

---

617. Sodom.

And Noah, when he called before, and so We answered him and delivered him and his people from the great calamity.

And supported him against the people who had denied Our signs. They were an evil people, and so We drowned them all.

And David and Solomon, when they gave judgement, regarding the tillage, when the people's sheep wandered therein by night; and We bore witness to their judgement.

And so We made Solomon understand it, and to each We gave judgement and knowledge. And with David, We subjected the mountains and the birds so as to glorify God; and that We accomplished.

80 And We taught him the craft of making coats of mail for you, so as to protect you from your own might. Are you, then, thankful?

And to Solomon We subjected the stormy wind blowing at his command towards the land which We have blessed, and We have knowledge of everything.

And some of the devils dived for him and did other work besides that and We were watching them.

And [remember] Job, when he called upon his Lord saying: "Affliction has touched me and you are the most Merciful of the Merciful."

And so, We answered him and lifted the affliction which he suffered; and We gave him his people and the like thereof along with them, as a mercy from Us and a reminder to the worshippers.

85 And Isma'il and Idris and Dhu'l-Kifl; each was one of the steadfast.

And We admitted them into Our mercy; they were all truly righteous.

And Dhu'l-Nun,[618] when he went out enraged, and he thought that We will have no power over him. So he called out in the darkness: "There is no god but You; glory be to You; I have certainly been one of the wrongdoers."

So, We answered him and delivered him from distress; and thus We deliver the believers.

And Zacharia, when he called upon his Lord [said]: "Lord, do not leave me alone; for you are the best of the inheritors."

90 So, We answered him and gave him John and set his wife right for him. Indeed, they vied with each other in good deeds, and they called upon Us out of affection and out of fear; and they were submissive to Us.

And she who guarded her chastity,[619] and so We breathed into her of Our spirit and made her and her son a sign unto the world.

This, your community is indeed a single community and I am your Lord; so worship Me.

They fell apart into factions; but they will all return unto Us.

618. Another name for Jonah, the Arabic equivalent of which is Yunus.
619. Mary.

Whoever does what is good, while a believer, his endeavour will not be denied, and We are indeed writing it down for him.

95 And it is forbidden that any city We have destroyed should come back.

Until Gog and Magog are let loose, and they slink away from every quarter.

Then the true promise will draw near; and, behold, the eyes of the unbelievers are staring [and they will say]: "Woe to Us! We were heedless of this; no, we were wrongdoers."

You and what you worship, besides Allah, are the fuel of Hell, and into it you shall all descend.

Had those been real gods, they would not have gone down into it; yet they will all dwell in it forever.

100 They groan with pain therein and they do not hear.

Those to whom We had given the fairest reward are kept away from it.

They do not hear its hissing, and they abide forever in what their hearts desire.

The greatest terror shall not cause them to grieve and the angels shall receive them saying: "This is your day that you were promised";

The day when We will fold heaven like a scroll of writing, just as We began Our first creation, We shall bring it back – a promise [binding] on Us that We shall fulfil.

105 We have written in the Psalms that, after the Reminder, My righteous servants shall inherit the earth.

Surely, there is in this a message to a worshipping people.

And We have only sent you,[620] as a mercy to the whole of mankind.

Say: "It is revealed to me that truly your God is One God; will you then submit?"

If they turn away, then say: "I have warned you all equally, but I do not know whether what you are promised is near or far."

110 He knows what you say openly, and He knows what you conceal.

I do not know whether it is perhaps a trial for you, and an enjoyment for a while.

Say: "Lord, judge rightly. Our Lord is the Compassionate whose help is sought to counter what you allege."

620. Muhammad.

SURA 22

Al-Hajj, The Pilgrimage

In the Name of Allah, the Compassionate, the Merciful

1 O people, fear your Lord. Surely the clamour of the Hour is a terrible thing. The day you will witness it, every suckling mother will be distracted from the child she is suckling, and every pregnant woman will deliver her burden, and you will see people drunk, whereas they are not drunk; but the punishment of Allah is terrible.

And there are some people who dispute regarding Allah without any knowledge, and follow every rebellious devil.

It has been written against him that whoever takes him for a friend, he will lead astray and guide him to the punishment of Hell.

5 O people, if you are in doubt regarding the Resurrection, We have indeed created you from dust, then from a sperm, then from a clot, then from a little lump of flesh, partly formed and partly unformed, in order to show you. We deposit in the wombs whatever We please, for an appointed term; then We bring you out as infants, till you attain full strength. Some of you are made to die, and some are returned to the vilest age, so that they may not know, after having acquired some knowledge, anything. And you see the earth barren, but when We send down water upon it, it stirs and swells and produces vegetation of every pleasing variety.

That is because Allah is the Truth, and He brings the dead to life and He has power over everything.

And that the Hour is coming, no doubt about it; and that Allah raises up those who are in their graves.

And of the people, there is one who disputes concerning Allah without any knowledge, or guidance, or an illuminating Book.

Bearing himself proudly so as to lead people away from Allah's path. His is disgrace in the present world and, on the Day of Resurrection, We shall make him taste the agony of burning:

10 "That is what your hands have advanced in deeds and Allah is never unjust to His servants."

And of the people, there are some who worship Allah tepidly.[621] When good fortune comes his way, he is pleased with it, but if an ordeal befalls

---

621. Literally, they worship on the brink of faith.

him, he turns around,[622] losing both this world and the world to come. That is the manifest loss.

He calls, besides Allah, on that which neither harms nor profits him. That is the worst[623] error.

He calls upon him whose harm is likelier than his profit. Wretched is the master and wretched is the ally!

Allah shall admit those who believe and do the righteous deeds into gardens underneath which rivers flow. Allah surely does whatever He pleases.

15   He who thinks that Allah will not give him support in this world or the next, let him stretch a rope to the sky then cut it up. Let him then see if his guile will remove what angers him.

That is how We revealed it as clear revelations, and Allah guides whomever He pleases.

Indeed, the believers, the Jews, the Sabians, the Christians, the Magians and the idolaters – Allah shall decide between them on the Day of Resurrection. Surely, Allah is a witness of everything.

Have you not seen that to Allah bows down whoever is in the heavens and whoever is on earth, as well as the sun, the moon, the stars, the mountains, the trees, the beasts and many of the people? And for many the punishment has been decreed. And he whom Allah humiliates, will have no one to honour him. Allah does whatever He pleases.

Here are two adversaries who dispute about their Lord. To the unbelievers, garments of fire shall be cut up and over their heads boiling water shall be poured;

20   Whereby whatever is in their bellies and in their skins shall be melted. And for them are iron rods.[624]

Every time they want, in their gloom, to get out of it,[625] they are brought back into it. [And it is said to them]: "Taste the agony of burning."

Allah shall admit those who believe and do the righteous deeds into gardens, beneath which rivers flow. Therein they shall be adorned with gold bracelets and pearls, and their raiment there shall be of silk.

They had been guided to the fair words and guided to the path of the Praiseworthy.

25   But those who disbelieve and bar others from the path of Allah and the Sacred Mosque, which We have made open to all people equally – both those who dwell in it and those who visit it. He who wishes to incline in it towards wrongdoing, We shall make him taste a very painful punishment.

622. That is, goes back to disbelief.
623. Literally, the farthest from the way.
624. To beat their heads with.
625. The Fire.

And [remember] when We appointed for Abraham the site of the House [saying]: "You shall not associate with Me anything and purify My House for those who circle round, those who stand up, those who kneel and those who prostrate themselves;

"And proclaim the pilgrimage to the people, and then they will come on foot or on every lean mount, coming from every deep ravine,

"To witness benefits of theirs, and mention Allah's name, during certain numbered days, over such beasts of the flocks as He has provided them with. Eat, then, from them and feed the wretched poor.

"Then, let them complete their self-cleansing and fulfil their vows and circle round the Ancient House."

30   All that; and whoever venerates the sacred things of Allah, it shall be well for him with his Lord. Cattle have been made lawful to you, except what is recited to you [to avoid]: so shun the abomination of idols, and shun false testimony.

Remain true to Allah, associating no gods with Him. He who associates anything with Allah is like one who has fallen from the sky and is snatched by the birds, or the wind hurls him down a very steep place.

All that; and he who venerates the sacred rites of Allah – it is the fruit of the piety of the hearts.

You have some benefits therefrom, for an appointed term; then their place of sacrifice is the Ancient House.

And to every nation, We have appointed a holy rite, so that they might mention Allah's name over whatever He has provided them with of the beasts of the flock. For your God is One God. Submit to Him and announce the good news to the humble;

35   Those who, when Allah is mentioned, their hearts tremble, and those who endure what befalls them, and those who perform the prayer and spend from what We have provided them with.

And the camels We have made for you as parts of the sacred rites of Allah. You have some good therein; so mention Allah's name over them as they stand in line. When their sides fall to the ground, eat of them and feed the contented and the beggar. That is how We subjected them to you, that perchance you may be thankful.

Their flesh and blood will not reach Allah, but your piety will reach Him. Thus He subjected them to you, so that you may glorify Allah for guiding you. And announce the good news to the beneficent.

Allah will defend the believers; Allah surely does not like any thankless traitor.

Permission is given to those who fight because they are wronged. Surely Allah is capable of giving them victory.

40   Those who were driven out of their homes unjustly, merely for their saying: "Our Lord is Allah." Had Allah not repelled some people by others, surely monasteries, churches, synagogues and mosques, wherein the name of Allah is mentioned frequently, would have been demolished. Indeed, Allah will support whoever supports Him. Allah is surely Strong and Mighty.

Those who, if We establish them firmly in the land, will perform the prayer, give the alms, command the good and prohibit evil. To Allah belongs the outcome of all affairs.

If they denounce you as a liar, then the people of Noah, 'Ad and Thamud have denounced before them;

And the people of Abraham and the people of Lot, too;

And the people of Midian. And Moses was denounced. Then I reprieved the unbelievers; then I struck them down. How, then, was my punishment?

45   How many a city We destroyed when it was doing wrong; and now it is fallen down upon its turrets; and how many a deserted well, and lofty palace?

Have they not travelled in the land, so as to acquire hearts to reason with, or ears to hear by? For it is not the eyes which are blind, but the hearts within the breasts.

They ask you to hasten the punishment. Allah will never break His promise; but a day for your Lord is like a thousand years of what you reckon.

And how many a city have I reprieved, although it was unjust? Then I struck it down, and unto Me is the ultimate return.

Say: "O people,[626] I am only a plain warner to you.

50   "Those who believe and do the righteous deeds will receive forgiveness and a bountiful provision,

"But those who strive against Our revelations defying Us – those are the people of Hell."

We have not sent a messenger or prophet before you but when he recited the Devil would intrude into his recitation. Yet Allah annuls what the Devil had cast. Then Allah establishes his revelations. Allah is All-Knowing, Wise.

So as to make what Satan casts a temptation to those in whose hearts there is a sickness, and to those whose hearts are hard. The wrongdoers are indeed in profound discord!

And so that those who have been given the knowledge might understand that it is the truth from your Lord and so believe in it. Then their hearts will submit to it. Allah will certainly guide the believers to a straight path.

55   The unbelievers will continue to be in doubt concerning it, until the Hour comes upon them suddenly, or the punishment of a disastrous day seizes them.

626. The Meccans.

Dominion on that day shall be Allah's and He will judge between them. Then, those who believe and do the righteous deeds shall be in the Gardens of Bliss.

But those who disbelieve and deny Our revelation, to those a demeaning punishment is in store.

And those who emigrated in the path of Allah, then were killed or died, Allah shall provide them with a fair provision. Allah is surely the best provider.

He will admit them into a place with which they will be well-pleased. Surely, Allah is All-Knowing, Clement.

60   All that; and he who chastises in the same way he was chastised, then he is wronged, Allah shall support him. Allah is surely a Pardoner, All-Forgiver.

That is because Allah causes the night to pass into the day and the day to pass into the night, and that Allah is All-Hearing, All-Seeing.

That is because Allah is the Truth and what they call upon besides Him is the falsehood; and that Allah is the Exalted, the Great One.

Do you not see that Allah sends down water from the sky, whereupon the earth turns green. Allah is Gracious, Well-Informed.

To Him belongs what is in the heavens and the earth and it is Allah who is the Self-Sufficient and the Praiseworthy.

65   Do you not see that Allah has subjected to you what is on earth and the ships which sail in the sea at His command? And He keeps the sky from falling to the ground, save by His leave. Allah is Gracious and Merciful to mankind.

And it is He who gives you life, then He causes you to die, then He will bring you back to life. Man, however, is truly thankless.

To every nation, We have given a sacred rite which they observe. So do not let them dispute with you in this matter. Call them to your Lord, for you are on a straight course.

And if they dispute with you, say: "Allah knows best what you are doing."

Allah will judge between you on the Day of Resurrection, regarding what you disagree about.

70   Do you not know that Allah knows what is in the heavens and on earth. All that is in a Book; and that is an easy matter for Allah.

And they worship, besides Allah, that concerning which He did not send down any authority, and of which they have no knowledge. The wrongdoers shall have no supporter.

And when Our clear revelations are recited to them, you will recognize in the faces of the unbelievers the denial. They will almost fall upon those who recite to them Our revelations. Say: "Shall I tell you about what is worse than that? It is the Fire which Allah has promised the unbelievers; and what a wretched fate!"

O people, an example has been given; so listen to it. Surely, those whom you call upon, besides Allah, will never create a fly, even if they band together. And if a fly should rob them of something, they cannot retrieve it from it. How weak is the invoker and the invoked!

They do not give Allah His true measure. Surely, Allah is Strong and Mighty.

75   Allah chooses from angels and men messengers; Allah is All-Hearing, All-Seeing.

He knows what is before them and what is behind them, and to Allah are all things returned.

O believers, kneel down, prostrate yourselves and worship your Lord and do good, that you may perchance prosper.

And strive for Allah as you ought to strive. He elected you, and did not impose on you any hardship in religion – the faith of your father Abraham. He called you Muslims before and in this,[627] that the Apostle may bear witness against you and you may be witnesses against mankind. So, perform the prayer, give the alms and hold fast to Allah. He is your Master; and what a blessed Master and a blessed Supporter!

627. The Qur'an.

SURA 23

Al-Mu'minun, The Believers

In the Name of Allah, the Compassionate, the Merciful

1   The believers have prospered;
    Those who are submissive in their prayers,
    And those who turn away from idle talk,
    And those who give the alms.
5   And those who guard their private parts.
    Except from their wives and what their right hands possess.[628] [For these]
they are not blameworthy.
    Whoever seeks anything beyond that – those are the transgressors.
    Those who honour their trusts and promises;
    And observe their prayers;
10   Those are the inheritors,
    Who will inherit Paradise wherein they will dwell forever.
    We have created man from an extract of clay;
    Then We placed him as a sperm in a secure place;
    Then We created out of the sperm a clot; then made from the clot a lump
of flesh, then made the lump of flesh into bones; and then covered the
bones with flesh; then fashioned him into another creation. So Blessed be
Allah, the Best of Creators.
15   Then after that you will surely die.
    Then on the Day of Resurrection you will surely be raised from the dead.
    We have created above you seven spheres, and We were not oblivious of
the creation.
    And We send down water from heaven in measure, then lodge it in the
ground, although We are able to allow it to drain away.
    Then through it We produce for you gardens of palm trees and vines,
from which you get many fruits whereof you eat.
20   And a tree[629] growing out of Mount Sinai that produces oil and
condiment for eaters.
    And surely in the cattle you have a lesson. We give you to drink from
what is in their bellies, and you have therein many uses, and from them you
eat.
    And on them and on the ships you are borne.

628. Slave-girls.
629. The olive tree.

And We sent Noah forth to his people, and he said: "O my people, worship Allah; you have no god other than He. Do you not fear [Allah]?"

Then, the dignitaries of his people who had disbelieved said: "This is only a mortal like you, who wishes to show you favours. Had Allah willed, He would have sent down angels. We never heard of this from our forefathers.

25 "He is a man possessed; so watch him for a while."

He said: "Lord, help me, for they deny me."

We revealed to him, then: "Make the Ark under Our very eyes and according to Our revelation. Then when Our command comes and the oven boils over, take into it a couple of every kind, together with your family, except for him against whom the Decree has already been pronounced. Do not speak to Me concerning those who are wrongdoers; for they will certainly be drowned."

Then, when you are seated, you and your company, upon the Ark, say: "Praise be to Allah who delivered us from the wrongdoing people."

And say: "Lord, let me land in a blessed way; for you are the best of those who make people land."

30 Surely in that are signs. Thus We put them to the test.

Then, We brought out after them another generation.

So, We sent to them a messenger of their own, saying: "Worship Allah, you have no other god than Him. Do you not fear [Allah]?"

Then the dignitaries of his people, who had disbelieved and denied the meeting of the Hereafter and whom We had accorded ease in the present life, said: "This is, indeed, merely a mortal like you; he eats from what you eat and drinks from what you drink.

"If you obey a mortal like yourselves, you are surely the losers.

35 "Does he promise you that once you die and turn into dust and bones, you will be brought back?

"Far, far away is what you are promised!

"There is only this our earthly life; we die and we live, but we shall not be raised from the dead.

"He is only a man who fabricates lies about Allah and we will not believe in him."

He said: "Lord, support me against their calling me a liar."

40 He said: "In a little while they will regret."

Then the Cry seized them justly, and so We turned them into scum. Away then with the wrongdoing people!

Then We raised up after them other generations.

No nation hastens its term; nor will they put it back.

Then We sent Our messengers one after the other. Every time a messenger came to his nation, they denied him. So We made them succeed

one another and reduced them to mere tales. Away with a people who do
not believe.

45   Then We sent Moses and his brother Aaron with Our signs and a decisive
authority;

To Pharaoh and his dignitaries, but they were an arrogant people.

And so they said: "Shall we believe in two mortals like ourselves, while
their own people are serving us?"

Then they denounced them both as liars, and so they were destroyed.

And We gave Moses the Book, that perchance they may be guided.

50   And We made Mary's son and his mother a sign, and We sheltered them
on a lofty ground which had [settled] meadows and a spring.

"O messengers, eat from the good things and do what is right. Surely, I
am aware of what you do.

"And this your nation is a single nation and I am your Lord; so fear Me."

But they broke up, regarding their affairs, into factions, each party
rejoicing in what they had.

So, leave them in their error for a while.

55   What? Do you think that in what We provide them with of money and
children,

We are hastening to them Our bounties? No, they do not understand.

Those who are awed by the fear of their Lord,

And those who believe in the revelations of their Lord,

And those who do not associate anything with their Lord,

60   And those who give what they give while their hearts tremble for fear that
they are returning to their Lord;

All those shall hasten to do the right deeds and they are the first to attain
them.

We do not charge any soul beyond its capacity; and We have a Book
which utters the truth, and they shall not be wronged.

But their hearts are in confusion with respect to this;[630] and they have
works, other than that, which they continue to do.

Until We seize those who live in luxury among them, and then they
groan.

65   "Do not groan today; you shall not be supported against Us."

"My revelations were recited to you, but you were turning upon your
heels in flight;

"In arrogance, talking nonsense about it by night."

Have they not pondered the Word;[631] or have they received what was not
given to their forefathers?

---

630. The Qur'an.
631. The Qur'an.

Or have they not recognized their messenger, and so they are denying him?

70 Or do they say: "He is possessed"? Rather, he brought them the Truth, but most of them hate the Truth.

If the Truth followed their whims, the heavens and the earth would be corrupted, together with everything therein; but We have brought them their reminder, yet from their reminder they turn away.

Or are you asking them for a reward? But, the reward of your Lord is better, and He is the best Provider.

And you are surely calling them to a straight path.

Those who do not believe in the Hereafter are deviating from the path.

75 If We show them mercy and lift their affliction, they would persist in their arrogance, wandering aimlessly.

We seized them with the punishment; but they would not submit to their Lord and they would not supplicate.

Until We opened up against them a gate of terrible punishment and, behold, they were in utter despair.

It is He who created for you ears, eyes and hearts; but how little you give thanks.

And it is He who created and multiplied you in the land, and unto Him you will be gathered.

80 And it is He who gives life and causes death, and His is the alternation of night and day. Do you understand?

No, they said just what the ancients said.

They said: "What, when we are dead and become dust and bones, will we be brought back to life?

"We have been promised this, we and our fathers before. This is merely legends of the ancients."

Say: "Whose is the earth and all those in it, if you really know?"

85 They will say: "Allah's"; say: "Do you not reflect, then?"

Say: "Who is the Lord of the seven heavens and the Lord of the mighty Throne?"

They will say: "They are Allah's." Say: "Do you not fear God, then",

Say: "In whose hand is the dominion of everything, protecting and is not protected, if you really know?"

They will say: "[In] Allah's." Say: "How, then, are you bewitched?"

90 No, We brought them the truth, but they are liars.

Allah did not take to Himself a child and there was never another god with Him; or else each god would have carried off what he has created, and some of them would have risen against the others. Exalted be Allah above what they describe!

Knower of the Unseen and the Seen; He is exalted above what they associate.

Say: "Lord, if you would show me what they are promised.

"Lord, do not reckon me among the wrongdoing people."

95 And We are surely able to show you what We promise them.

Ward off evil with that which is fairer. We know best what they describe.

And say: "Lord, I seek refuge with You from the goadings of the devils.

"And I seek refuge with you lest they join me."

Yet, when death visits one of them, he says: "Lord, bring me back;[632]

100 "That perchance I might act rightly with respect to what I have omitted." No, it is just a word he is uttering; and behind them is a barrier till the day they are raised from the dead.

And when the Trumpet is blown, they will have no kinship to bind them on that day, and they will not question one another.

Then, those whose scales are heavy – those are the prosperous.

But those whose scales are light – those are the ones who have lost their souls. In Hell, they will dwell forever.

The Fire lashes their faces, and therein they shrivel.

105 "Were not My signs recited to you, but you used to denounce them as lies."

They will say: "Lord, our misery overcame us and we were an erring people.

"Lord, bring us out of it;[633] then, if we revert we are indeed wrongdoers."

He said: "Rot in it and do not talk to Me.

"There was a group of My servants who used to say: 'Lord, we believe, so forgive us and have mercy on us; you are the best of the Merciful.'

110 "But you took them for a laughing-stock, till they made you forget My name, while you were mocking them.

"I have rewarded them today for their forbearance, making them the winners."

Say: "How long did you linger on earth, in terms of years?"

They will say: "We lingered a day or a part of a day; so ask those who count."

He will say: "You only lingered for a little while, if only you knew.

115 "Did you, then, think that We created you in vain and that unto Us you will not be returned?"

Glory be to Allah, the True King; there is no god but He. He is indeed the Lord of the noble Throne.

632. To the world.
633. Hell.

He who calls, along with Allah, upon another god of whom he has no proof, his reckoning is with his Lord. Surely, the unbelievers will never prosper.

Say: "Lord forgive and have mercy; for you are the best of the merciful."

SURA 24

Al-Nur, The Light

In the Name of Allah, the Compassionate, the Merciful

1 A sura that We have sent down and stipulated, and We have sent down in it clear revelations, that perchance you might remember.

The adulteress and the adulterer, whip each one of them a hundred lashes; and let no pity move you in Allah's religion, regarding them; if you believe in Allah and the Hereafter. And let a group of believers witness their punishment.

The adulterer shall marry none but an adulteress or an idolatress; and the adulteress none shall marry her but an adulterer or idolater. That has been forbidden the believers.

Those who accuse chaste women, then cannot bring four witnesses, whip them eighty lashes, and do not ever accept their testimony. For those are the wicked sinners.

5 Except for those who repent afterwards and mend their ways. For Allah is surely All-Forgiving, Merciful.

And those who accuse their wives and have no witnesses except themselves, the testimony of one of them shall be to swear by Allah four times that he is truthful.

The fifth time shall be Allah's curse on him, if he is a liar.

And her swearing four times by Allah that he is a liar will ward off punishment from her.

And the fifth time will be that Allah's wrath be upon her, if he is truthful.

10 And, but for Allah's bounty towards you and His mercy and that Allah is a remitter of sins and is All-Wise;

Those who spread the slander[634] are a band of you. Do not reckon it an evil for you; rather it is a good thing for you. Everyone of them will be credited with the sin he has earned, and he who bore the brunt of it shall have a terrible punishment.

Would that the believers, men and women, when you heard it,[635] had thought well of themselves saying: "This is a manifest slander!"

And would that they had brought forth four witnesses [to vouch for it]! But since they did not bring any witnesses, those are, in Allah's sight, the real liars.

634. Against 'Aisha, wife of the Prophet, according to the commentators.
635. The slander.

216

And but for Allah's bounty to you and His mercy, in this world and the next, you would have been visited, due to your chatter, by a terrible punishment.

15 Since you received it on your tongues and you uttered with your mouths what you had no knowledge of, deeming it a simple matter; whereas in Allah's sight it was very grave.

And would that, upon hearing it, you were to say: "It is not for us to speak about this. Glory be to You; this is truly a great calumny."

Allah admonishes you never to return to the like of this, if you are real believers.

And Allah expounds clearly for you the signs. Allah is All-Knowing, Wise.

Indeed, those who love to see indecency spread among the believers will have in this world and the next a very painful punishment. Allah knows, but you do not know.

20 And but for Allah's bounty to you and His mercy and that Allah is truly Clement and Merciful;

O believers, do not follow in the footsteps of Satan; for he who follows in the footsteps of Satan, simply bids to indecency and disrepute. But for Allah's bounty to you and His mercy, no one of you would have ever been pure; but Allah purifies whomever He pleases. Allah is All-Hearing, All-Knowing.

Let not the bounteous and wealthy among you swear off giving freely to kinsmen, the destitute and the Emigrants in the path of Allah. Let them pardon and forgive. Do you not wish that Allah should forgive you? Allah is All-Forgiving, Merciful.

Surely those who slander married women, who are heedless and believing, are accursed in this world and the next, and they shall have a terrible punishment;

On the day when their tongues, their hands and their feet shall bear witness against them, regarding what they used to do.

25 On that day Allah will pay them their just dues and they will know that Allah is the manifest Truth.

Foul women for foul men, and foul men for foul women; and good women for good men, and good men for good women. Those are acquitted of the burden of what they say; they will have forgiveness and a generous provision.

O believers, do not enter houses other than your own before you ask leave and greet their occupants. That is better for you, that perchance you may remember well.

If you find no one in them, do not enter until you are given permission;

and if it is said to you: "Go back", then go back. That is purer for you, and Allah knows well what you do.

It is no offence for you to enter uninhabited houses in which you have some means of enjoyment. Allah knows what you reveal and what you conceal.

30   Tell the believers to cast down their eyes and guard their private parts. That is purer for them. Allah is conversant with what they do.

And tell believing women to cast down their eyes and guard their private parts and not show their finery, except the outward part of it. And let them drape their bossoms with their veils and not show their finery except to their husbands, their fathers, their husbands' fathers, their sons, the sons of their husbands, their brothers, the sons of their brothers, the sons of their sisters, their women, their maid-servants, the men-followers who have no sexual desire, or infants who have no knowledge of women's sexual parts yet. Let them, also, not stamp their feet, so that what they have concealed of their finery might be known. Repent to Allah, all of you, O believers, that perchance you may prosper.

Encourage the unmarried among you and the righteous among your servants and maids to marry. If they are poor, Allah will enrich them from His bounty. Allah is All-Embracing, All-Knowing.

Let those who do not find the means to marry be abstinent, till Allah enriches them from His bounty. Those whom your right hands own and who wish to pay for their emancipation, conclude a contract with them, if you know that there is some good in them, and give them of Allah's wealth which He gave you. Do not force your slave-girls into prostitution, if they wish to be chaste, in order to seek the fleeting goods of this life. Whoever forces them, surely Allah, after their being forced, is Forgiving, Merciful.

And We have sent down to you signs making everything clear, and an example of those who have gone before you, and an exhortation to the God-fearing.

35   Allah is the light of the heavens and the earth. His light is like a niche in which there is a lamp, the lamp is in a glass, the glass is like a glittering star. It is kindled from a blessed olive tree, neither of the East nor the West. Its oil will almost shine, even if no fire has touched it. Light upon light, Allah guides to His light whomever He pleases and gives the examples to mankind. Allah has knowledge of everything.

In houses Allah allowed to be raised and His name to be mentioned therein, He is glorified therein, mornings and evenings,

By men who are not distracted, by trading or trafficking, from mentioning Allah's name, performing the prayer and giving the alms. They fear a day whereon the hearts and eyesights shall be turned around;

So that Allah may reward them for their fairest works and increase them from His bounty. Allah provides for whomever He pleases without reckoning.

As to the unbelievers, their works are like a mirage in level ground, which the thirsty supposes to be water; but when he comes close to it, he finds that it is nothing. Instead, he finds Allah there and so He pays him his account in full. Allah is quick in reckoning.

40 Or like dark shadows in a turbulent sea, covered by waves upon waves, above which are clouds. Dark shadows above which are dark shadows; if he brings his hand out, he will hardly see it. He to whom Allah has not granted a light will have no light.

Have you not seen that Allah is glorified by whatever is in the heavens or the earth, and by the birds in flight. He knows the prayer of each and its glorification. Allah knows well what they do.

To Allah belongs the dominion of the heavens and the earth and unto Allah is the ultimate return.

Have you not seen that Allah drives the clouds, then brings them together, then piles them into a heap, from which you can see rain coming. He brings mountains of hail from the sky, with which He smites whomever He pleases and diverts it from whomever He pleases. The gleam of its lightning almost blinds the eyes.

He alternates the night and day. In that there is a lesson for those who have eyes to see.

45 Allah created every beast from water. Some of them crawl on their bellies, some walk on two feet and others walk on four. Allah creates whatever He pleases. Allah, indeed, has power over everything.

We have sent down signs making everything clear, and Allah guides whomever He pleases to a straight path.

They say: "We believe in Allah and the Apostle and we obey." Then a group of them turn away, afterwards. Those are not real believers.

And if they are called unto Allah and His Apostle to judge between them, behold, a group of them turn away.

But if they have the right, they come to him[636] submissively.

50 Is there a sickness in their hearts, or are they in doubt, or do they fear that Allah and His Apostle might deal with them unjustly? No, those are the wrongdoers.

As to the believers, if they are called unto Allah and His Apostle to judge between them, they only say: "We hear and obey." Those are the prosperous.

636. The Prophet.

Those who obey Allah and His Apostle and fear Allah and beware Him; those are the real winners.

They swear their most solemn oaths that, should you order them, they will go forth. Say: "Do not swear; it is a well-known obedience. Allah is fully conversant with what you do."

Say: "Obey Allah and obey the Apostle; but if you turn away, then upon him rests what he was charged with, and upon you what you were charged with. However, if you obey him, you will be well-guided. It is only incumbent on the Messenger to deliver the manifest message."

55   Allah promised those of you who have believed and done the righteous deeds that He will surely make them successors in the land, and He made those who came before them successors, and that He will establish firmly for them their religion, which He chose for them, and that He will give them, as a substitute for their fear, security. "They worship Me and do not associate anything with Me. He who disbelieves afterwards – those are the real sinners."

Perform the prayer, give the alms and obey the Apostle, that perchance you might receive mercy.

Do not suppose that the unbelievers are able to thwart Allah on earth. Their refuge shall be the Fire, and what a wretched fate!

O believers, let those your right hands possess[637] and those who have not reached the age of puberty ask your leave three times:[638] before the dawn prayer, when you put off your clothes at noon and after the evening prayer. These are three occasions of nudity for you; after which you or they are not at fault, if you approach each other. That is how Allah makes clear His signs to you. Allah is All-Knowing, Wise.

And when your children reach puberty, let them ask leave, as those who came before them asked leave. That is how Allah makes clear His signs to you. Allah is All-Knowing, Wise.

60   Those women who are past child-bearing and have no hope of marriage are not at fault if they take off their outer garments, not exhibiting any finery; but to refrain is better for them. Allah is All-Hearing, All-Knowing.

The blind are not at fault, the lame are not at fault, the sick are not at fault, nor are you if you eat in your houses, the houses of your fathers, the houses of your mothers, the houses of your brothers, the houses of your sisters, the houses of your paternal uncles, the houses of your paternal aunts, the houses of your maternal uncles, the houses of your maternal aunts, those of which you are in possession of the keys or those of your friend. You are not at fault if you eat all together or separately, but if you enter any houses,

637. Slaves and maid-servants.
638. To attend to you or approach you.

greet each other with a blessed and good greeting from Allah. That is how Allah makes clear to you the signs, that perchance you may understand.

The true believers, who believe in Allah and His Apostle, if they are with him for some common affair, will not depart till they take their leave. Indeed, those who ask leave from you are those who believe in Allah and His Apostle. If they ask leave from you for some affair of theirs, give leave to whom you wish and ask Allah's forgiveness for them. Allah is surely All-Forgiving, Merciful.

Do not make calling the Apostle out among you like your calling one another out. Allah knows those of you who slip away stealthily. So, let those who disobey His command beware of an ordeal that might befall them, or a very painful punishment that might befall them.

Surely, to Allah belongs what is in the heavens and on earth. He knows what you are about and the day they will be returned to Him. Then He will tell them about what they did. Allah knows everything.

SURA 25

Al-Furqan, The Criterion

In the Name of Allah, the Compassionate, the Merciful

1 Blessed is He who sent down the Criterion[639] upon His servant,[640] so as to be a warner to all mankind.

To whom belongs the dominion of the heavens and the earth and He has not taken to Himself a child, and has no associate in this dominion, and He created everything, preordaining it fully.

Yet they have taken, apart from Him, other gods who do not create anything, but are themselves created. They do not have the power to harm or profit themselves, nor the power over death, life or resurrection.

The unbelievers say: "This is nothing but deceit, which he has invented and was assisted therein by other people."[641] They have simply come up with wrongdoing and falsehood.

5 And they say: "Legends of the ancients which he solicited their writing down. Hence they are dictated to him morning and evening."

Say: "He who knows the secret in the heavens and the earth has sent it down; He is indeed All-Forgiving, Merciful."

And they say: "What is the matter with the Apostle? He eats food and strolls in the markets. If only an angel had been sent to him to be a warner with him;

"Or a treasure had been cast upon him, or he was given a garden from which he could eat." And the wrongdoers say: "You only follow a man bewitched."

See how they invent the parables for you, and so they err, and then cannot find their way.

10 Blessed is He who, if He wishes, will accord you better than that – gardens underneath which rivers flow, and will build palaces for you.

No, they deny the Hour; yet We have prepared for those who deny the Hour a blazing Fire.

When it sights them from a distance, they hear its raging and exhalation.

And if they are hurled in a narrow space therein, tied up in fetters, they would call out there for ruination.

Call not out today for one ruination, but call out for many ruinations.

---

639. Arabic *al-Furqan*, or Criterion, distinguishing right from wrong.
640. Muhammad.
641. That is, the Jews.

15   Say: "Is that better or the Garden of Eternity which the God-fearing have been promised, as a reward and ultimate resort?"

They have therein what they desire, abiding forever, as a promise binding upon your Lord.

And the day He shall muster them and what they worship, apart from Allah, then He says: "Was it you, then, who misled these My servants, or did they stray from the path themselves?"

They will say: "Glory be to You; we should never have taken, apart from You, any protectors; but You accorded them and their fathers momentary enjoyment, until they forgot the Reminder and became a lost people."

They have denounced you as liars, regarding what you say; and so you are not able to divert punishment or give support. He who does wrong among you, We shall make him taste a grievous punishment.

20   We never sent any messengers before you but they ate food and strolled in the markets; and We made some of you tempters of each other. Will you stand fast? Your Lord is All-Seeing.

And those who do not hope for Our encounter, say: "If only the angels were sent down to us, or we were made to see our Lord." They have grown arrogant within themselves and became most overbearing.

The day they see the angels, there is no longer any cause for rejoicing for the criminals; and they[642] will say: "A firm prohibition [upon you]."

And We shall proceed to the work they did and turn it into scattered dust.

The companions of Paradise on that day shall be better lodged and more fairly accommodated.

25   The day heaven shall be parted by clouds and the angels are sent down in throngs.

The true dominion on that day shall be the Compassionate's, and it shall be a strenuous day for the unbelievers.

The day the wrongdoer shall bite his hands and say: "Would that I had taken with the Apostle a common path.

"Woe betide me, would that I had not taken so-and-so as a friend.

"He led me away from the Reminder after it had reached me. Satan has always been a betrayer of man."

30   The Apostle says: "Lord, my people have taken this Qur'an as a thing to be shunned."

And that is how We appointed to every prophet an enemy from the criminals. Your Lord suffices as a guide and a supporter.

The unbelievers say: "If only the Qur'an had been sent down on him all

642. The angels.

at once." That is how We wanted to strengthen your heart with it and We have revealed it in stages.

They never bring you any simile but We bring you the truth and a better exposition.

Those who are mustered on their faces in Hell; those are in a worse position and are more wayward.

35 We have indeed brought Moses the Book and appointed his brother Aaron with him as minister.

Then We said: "Go forth to the people who denounced Our signs as lies"; and so We destroyed them fully.

And the people of Noah, when they denounced the messengers, We drowned them and made them a sign unto mankind. We have prepared for the wrongdoers a very painful punishment.

And 'Ad, Thamud, the companions of al-Rass and many generations in between;

To each, We proposed similes and each We ruined utterly.

40 And they came upon the city which was drenched by an evil rain. Did they not see it? No, they did not hope to be raised from the dead.

And when they see you, they only take you for a laughing stock: "Is this the one Allah sent as a messenger?

"He almost led us away from our gods, had we not stood fast by them." They will certainly know, when they see the punishment, who is more wayward.

Do you see him who has taken his fancy as his god? Will you, then, have to be his guardian?

Or do you suppose that most of them hear or understand? Indeed, they are merely like cattle; no, even more wayward.

45 Have you not considered your Lord, how He has stretched out the shadow? Had He willed, He would have made it still, then made the sun a signal thereof.

Then, We would have drawn it towards Us slowly.

It is He who made the night a raiment for you, and sleep a period of rest, and made the day a rising up.

And it is He who sent the wind as good news before His mercy; and We have sent down from heaven pure water,

To bring to life thereby a dead town, and give it to drink to such numerous cattle and humans as We have created.

50 And We have alternated it among them, so that they may remember. However, most men have refused all but thanklessness.

Had We wished, We would have sent forth to every city a warner.

So, do not obey the unbelievers and strive against them with it[643] mightily.

And it is He who mixed the two seas, this one sweet and pure and that one salty and bitter; and He set up between them a barrier and a firm prohibition.

And it is He who created from water a human being; then He made him a kin by blood or marriage. Your Lord is All-Powerful.

55   They worship, apart from Allah, what neither profits nor harms them; and the unbeliever has always been a partisan[644] against his Lord.

We have only sent you forth as a bearer of good news and a warner.

Say: "I do not ask you for any wages for this, except for him who wishes to follow a path leading to his Lord."

Put your trust in the Living God who does not die and sing His praise. He suffices as the All-Informed knower of the sins of His servants,

Who created the heavens and the earth and what lies between them in six days. Then the Compassionate sat upon the Throne. So ask about Him, the Well-Informed.

60   And if it is said to them: "Prostrate yourselves before the Compassionate"; they reply: "But who is the Compassionate? Shall we prostrate ourselves to what you order us?" This only increases their aversion.

Blessed is He who placed in the heaven constellations and placed in it a lamp and an illuminating moon.

And it is He who made the night and the day to succeed each other, for him who wants to remember or wants to give thanks.

And the servants of the Compassionate who walk in the land gently and, if the ignorant address them, they say: "Peace."

And those who pass the night prostrating themselves to their Lord or standing up.

65   And those who say: "Lord, divert from us the agony of Hell"; but its agony is unavoidable punishment.

Wretched it is as a final resort and a resting-place!

And those who, when they spend, do not squander or stint, but choose a middle course between that.

And those who do not call upon any other god than Allah, and do not kill the soul which Allah forbade, except justly; and they do not commit adultery. He who does that shall meet with retribution.

Punishment shall be doubled for him on the Day of Resurrection and he will dwell forever in it down-trodden;

70   Except for him who repents, believes and does the righteous deed. Those

643. The Qur'an.
644. Of Satan.

Allah will change their evil deeds into good deeds. Allah is ever All-Forgiving, Merciful.

He who repents and does the righteous deed returns to Allah unhampered.

Those who do not bear false witness; and when they pass by idle talk, pass by with dignity;

And those who, when reminded of the signs of their Lord, do not fall down upon them deaf and blind;

And those who say: "Our Lord, grant us, through our wives and progeny, beloved offspring, and make us a model for the God-fearing."

75   Those shall be rewarded with a high chamber[645] for their steadfastness, and will be received therein with greeting and peace.

Dwelling therein forever. What a delightful resort and lodging!

Say: "My Lord will take no notice of your supplication. For you have disbelieved and that shall be your inevitable perdition."

---

645. In Paradise.

Al-Shu'ara', The Poets

In the Name of Allah, the Compassionate, the Merciful

Tah, Sin, Mim.[646]

1   Those are the signs of the Manifest Book.

Perhaps, you are exhausting yourself, because they will not believe.

If We will, We would send down on them from heaven a sign, so their necks will stay subjugated thereto.

No new reminder from the Compassionate ever comes to them but they will turn away from it.

5   They have indeed disbelieved; therefore, there will come to them the news of what they used to mock at.

Have they not considered the earth, how much We have caused to grow therein of every noble pair?

There is surely in that a sign; but most of them will not believe.

Your Lord, indeed, is the All-Mighty, the Merciful.

When Your Lord called Moses: "Go forth to the wrongdoing people;

10   "The people of Pharaoh; will they not fear God?"

He said: "Lord, I fear that they will denounce me as a liar;

"And my chest would be constricted and my tongue will not be loosed. So, send for Aaron.

"And they accuse me of a guilt;[647] so I fear they might kill me."

He said: "Never; so go both of you with Our signs; We are with you listening."

15   "So go both of you to Pharaoh and tell him; 'We are the messengers of the Lord of the Worlds';

"So send with us the Children of Israel."

He said: "Did we not raise you[648] among us as a child, and you lingered among us for many years of your life?

"And you committed the crime you committed, being one of the thankless?"

He said: "Indeed, I did it then while I was one of the perverse.

20   "So I fled from you when I feared you. Then my Lord granted me wisdom and made me one of the envoys.

---

646. The same letters occur at the beginning of Suras 27 and 28; the significance of this is not clear.
647. Slaying the Egyptian, whom Moses saw smite an Israelite.
648. Moses.

"And this is a grace you reproach me with, having enslaved the Children of Israel."

Pharaoh said: "And what is the Lord of the Worlds?"

He said: "The Lord of the heavens and the earth and what lies between them, if you have any kind of certainty."

He[649] said to those around him: "Do you not hear?"

25 He[650] said: "Your Lord and the Lord of your fathers."

He[651] said: "Surely your messenger who has been sent forth to you is truly mad."

He[652] said: "The Lord of the East and the West and what is between them, if only you understand."

He said: "If you take a god other than me,[653] I will certainly make you a prisoner."

He said: "Even if I should bring you something manifest?"

30 He said: "Bring it, then, if you are truthful."

Then he cast his staff down, and behold, it was a manifest serpent.

And he held out his hand, and, behold, it appeared white to the onlookers.

He[654] said to the dignitaries around him: "This man is, indeed, a cunning sorcerer.

"He wants to drive you out of your land by his sorcery; so what do you commend?"

35 They said: "Leave him and his brother alone for a while and send out to the cities summoning agents,"

"To bring you every cunning sorcerer."

And so the sorcerers were gathered together for an appointment on a fixed day.

And it was said to the people: "Will you come together?

"So that we might watch the sorcerers, if they should be the winners."

40 So when the sorcerers came they said to Pharaoh: "Will we have a wage, if we are the winners?"

He said: "Yes, and you shall be, then, among those favoured."

Moses said to them: "Cast down what you wish to cast down."

So, they cast their ropes and staffs and said: "By the might of Pharaoh, we shall be the winners."

649. Pharaoh.
650. Moses.
651. Pharaoh.
652. Moses.
653. Pharaoh.
654. Pharaoh.

Then, Moses cast down his staff, and, behold, it swallowed forthwith what they had simulated.

45   Then the sorcerers fell on their faces prostrate.

They said: "We believe now in the Lord of the Worlds;

"The Lord of Moses and Aaron."

He[655] said: "You have believed before I gave you leave. He[656] is indeed your chief, who taught you sorcery, and so you will learn. I shall cut off your hands and feet alternately and will crucify you all."

They said: "No harm; we are returning unto our Lord.

50   "We hope that our Lord will forgive our sins, as we are the first believers."

And We revealed to Moses: "Go forth with My servants at night; for you are being followed."

Then Pharaoh sent out summoning agents to all the cities:

"These, indeed, are a small band;

"And they are enraging us;

55   "And we are all on our guard."

Then, We drove them out of gardens and springs;

And treasures and a noble abode.

That is how We bequeathed them to the Children of Israel.

So they followed them at sunrise.

60   Then when the two hosts sighted each other, the companions of Moses said: "We shall be overtaken."

He said: "Never; my Lord is with me, He will guide me."

So, We revealed to Moses: "Strike the sea with your staff;" whereupon it split, so that each part was like a huge mountain.

And there We brought the others closer.

And We delivered Moses and those with him, all together.

65   Then, We drowned the others.

Surely, in that is a sign; yet most of them were not believers.

Your Lord is surely the All-Mighty, the Merciful.

And relate to them the tale of Abraham;

When he said to his father and his people: "What do you worship?"

70   They said: "We worship idols, to which we continue to be devoted."

He said: "Do they hear when you call upon them?

"Or profit or harm you?"

They said: "No, but we found our fathers doing that."

He said: "Have you considered what you have been worshipping,

75   "You and your forefathers?

"They are surely an enemy of mine, except for the Lord of the Worlds;

"Who created me, and He guides me;

655. Pharaoh.
656. Moses.

"And He is the One who feeds me and gives me to drink;

"And if I am sick, it is He who heals me;

80 "And He is the One who causes me to die, then brings me back to life.

"And He is the One whom I hope will forgive me my sins on the Day of Judgement.

"Lord, grant me sound judgement and make me join the righteous;

"And give a truthful tongue among the others;

"And make me one of the heirs of the Garden of Bliss.

85 "And forgive my father; for he was one of the wayward.

"And do not disgrace me on the day they will be raised from the dead,

"The day when neither wealth nor children will avail one;

"Except for him who comes to Allah with a pure heart.

"And Paradise shall be brought closer to the God-fearing.

90 "And Hell shall be exhibited to the perverse."

And it will be said to them: "Where are those you used to worship;

"Apart from Allah? Will they support you or support themselves?"

Then they will be cast down, together with the perverse ones;

And the hosts of Iblis, all together.

95 They will say, while they disputed there with each other:

"By Allah, we were indeed in manifest error,

"When we made you equal to the Lord of the Worlds.

"We were only misled by the criminals;

"So, we have no intercessors;

100 "Nor, an intimate friend.

"If only we could have another chance; then we will be among the believers."

Surely in that is a sign; but most of them are not believers.

Your Lord is surely the All-Mighty, the Merciful.

The people of Noah have denounced the messengers as liars;

105 When their brother Noah said to them: "Do you not fear God?

"I am to you a faithful messenger.

"So, fear Allah and obey me.

"I ask you no wage for this; my wage is with the Lord of the Worlds.

"So, fear Allah and obey me."

110 They said: "Shall we believe in you, when the lowliest crowd has followed you?"

He said: "How could I know what they used to do?

"They will only be called to account by my Lord; if only you had any sense.

"And it is not for me to drive away the believers.

"I am only a manifest warner."

15 They said: "If you will not desist, O Noah, you will surely be stoned."
He said: "Lord, my people have called me a liar.
"So, judge between me and them decisively and deliver me and the
believers who have joined me."
And so, We delivered him and those who joined him in the laden Ark.
Then We drowned all the rest.
20 There is in that a sign, but most of them would not believe.
And your Lord is the All-Mighty, the Merciful.
'Ad called the messengers liars,
When their brother Hud said to them: "Do you not fear God?
"I am truly a faithful messenger to you.
25 "So, fear Allah and obey me.
"I do not ask you for it any wage; my wage is with the Lord of the
Worlds.
"Do you build upon every elevation an edifice for amusement?
"And acquire castles, that perchance you may live forever?
"And when you attack, you attack like giants?
30 "So fear Allah and obey me;
"And fear Him, who imparted to you whatever knowledge you have.
"He granted you cattle and children;
"And gardens and springs.
"I certainly fear for you the punishment of a great day."
35 They said: "It is the same to us whether you exhort or are not one of
those who exhort.
"This is only the manner of the ancients.
"And we shall not be punished."
They denounced him as a liar, and so We destroyed them. There is in
that a sign, but most of them would not believe.
Your Lord is surely the All-Mighty, the Merciful.
40 Thamud denounced the messengers as liars.
When their brother Salih said to them: "Do you not fear God?
"I am a faithful messenger to you.
"So fear Allah and obey me.
"I do not ask you any wage for this; my wage is with the Lord of the
Worlds.
45 "Will you be left herebelow in peace?
"In gardens and springs;
"And plantations and palm trees, whose shoots are tender?
"And will you hew skilfully houses in the mountains?
"So fear Allah and obey me.
50 "And do not obey the orders of the extravagant;

"Who work corruption in the land and do not make amends."

They said: "You are certainly a man bewitched.

"You are only a mortal like us. Produce, then, a sign, if you are truthful."

He said: "This is a she-camel; this has a drinking day, and you have a fixed drinking day.

155 "Do not cause her any harm, or else the punishment of a great day will smite you."

However, they hamstrung her, and became full of remorse.

Then, punishment smote them. There is surely in that a sign; and most of them were not believers.

Your Lord is truly the All-Mighty, the Merciful.

The people of Lot denounced the messengers as liars.

160 When their brother Lot said to them: "Do you not fear God?

"I am a faithful messenger to you;

"So, fear Allah and obey me.

"I do not ask you any wage for this; my wage is with the Lord of the Worlds.

"Do you approach the males from all mankind;

165 "And leave the wives that your Lord created for you? No, you are a transgressing people."

They said: "If you will not desist, O Lot, you will certainly be one of those expelled."

He said: "I am a detester of your deed.

"Lord, save me and my family from what they do."

So, We delivered him and his family, all together.

170 Except for an old woman who was one of those who lingered behind.

Then, We destroyed the others.

And We loosed on them a rain. Wretched is the rain of those forewarned!

There is in that a sign, but most of them were not believers.

Truly, your Lord is the All-Mighty, the Merciful.

175 The companions of the Thicket denounced the messengers as liars.

When Shu'aib said to them: "Do you not fear God?

"I am a faithful messenger to you.

"So fear Allah and obey me.

"I do not ask you for any wage. My wage is with the Lord of the Worlds.

180 "Fill up the measure and do not be swindlers.

"And weigh with the just scales.

"Fear Him who created you and the generations of old."

They said: "Surely, you are one of those bewitched.

"And you are only a mortal like us, and we think you are simply a liar.

185 "Do, then, bring down upon us chips from heaven, if you are truthful."

He said: "My Lord knows best what you do."
They denounced him as a liar, and so the punishment of the Day of the
Parasol seized them. It was, indeed, the punishment of a great day.
In that, there is a sign, but most of them were not believers.
And your Lord is truly the All-Mighty, the Merciful.

90   And it is the revelation of the Lord of the Worlds;
Brought down by the Faithful Spirit,[657]
Upon your heart, so that you might be one of the warners;
In manifest Arabic tongue.
And it is, indeed, in the scriptures of the ancients.

95   Is it not a sign for them that the scholars of the Children of Israel
recognized it?
Had We sent it down on some foreigner;
And he had read it to them; they would still not have believed in it.
Thus We have insinuated it into the hearts of the criminals.
They will not believe in it until they witness the very painful
punishment.

200   It will come upon them suddenly, while they are unaware.
Then, they will say: "Are we given any respite?"
Do they, then, seek to hasten Our punishment?
Do you see, if we were to allow them some enjoyment for some years?
Then, they are visited by what they were promised.

205   What would that whereof they derived enjoyment avail them?
We have never destroyed a city, but it had prior warners,
As a reminder; and We have never been unjust.
It was not brought down by demons.
They should not and could not.

210   For, they are barred from hearing.
So do not call, with Allah, upon another god. For then you will be one of
those chastized.
And warn your closest clan members.
And lower your wing humbly to those of the believers who follow you.
Should they disobey you, then say: "I am quit of what you are doing."

215   And put your trust in the All-Mighty, the Merciful;
Who sees you when you stand up;
And when you go around those who prostrate themselves.
He is indeed the All-Seeing, the All-Knowing.
Shall I tell you upon whom do the demons descend?

220   They descend upon every vicious impostor.
They listen, but most of them are liars.

657. Gabriel.

And as to the poets, the perverse follow them.
Do you not see that they wander aimlessly in every glen?
And that they say what they do not do?

225   Except for those who believe and do the righteous deeds, mention Allah frequently, and are victorious after they were wronged. Surely, the wrongdoers shall know what outcome is ultimately theirs.

SURA 27

Al-Naml, The Ants

In the Name of Allah, the Compassionate, the Merciful

Tah, Sin, Mim.[658]

1   Those are the verses of the Qur'an and a Manifest Book,
A guidance and good tidings to the believers,
Who perform the prayer, give the alms and are certain of the Hereafter.
Those who do not believe in the Hereafter, We have embellished for
them their actions, and thus they wander aimlessly.

5   Those are the ones who will receive the grievous punishment and will be,
in the Hereafter, the greatest losers.
You certainly receive the Qur'an from an All-Wise, All-Knowing One.
When Moses said to his family: "I have sighted a fire and will bring you
news of it, or bring you a flaming spark that you might warm yourselves."
Then, when he approached it, he was told loudly: "Blessed is he who is in
the fire and those around it,[659] and glory be to the Lord of the Worlds.
"O Moses, I am truly Allah, the All-Mighty, Wise;

10 "Cast your staff"; but when he saw it shaking, as though it was a serpent,
he turned around not looking back. "O Moses, do not fear; the messengers
do not fear in My presence;
"Except for him who has done wrong, then changed, doing good after
evil. For I am indeed All-Forgiving, Merciful.
"Introduce your hand into your bosom and it will come out white,
without blemish, as one of nine signs to Pharaoh and his people. They are,
indeed, a wicked people."
Then, when Our signs came to them fully visible, they said: "This is
manifest sorcery."
And they repudiated them, although their souls acknowledged them as
certain, wrongfully and arrogantly. Behold, then what was the fate of the
workers of corruption.

15 And We gave David and Solomon knowledge. They said: "Praise be to
Allah who preferred us over many of His believing servants."
Solomon inherited David, and he said: "O people, we have been taught
the speech of birds and have been given part of everything. This is indeed
the manifest bounty."

---

658. The same letters occur at the beginning of Suras 26 and 28; the significance of this is not clear.
659. Moses and the other prophets.

And Solomon's troops, *jinn*, men and birds, were mustered and duly held in check.

Until they reached an ants' hill; when an ant said: "O ants, enter your dwellings, lest Solomon and his troops crush you, without noticing it."

Then he smiled, laughing at its words, and said: "Lord, inspire me to be thankful for Your blessing, with which You blessed me and my parents, and to do the right pleasing to you. Admit me, by Your mercy, into the company of Your righteous servants."

20 He inspected the birds, then said: "Why do I not see the hoopoe?[660] Or is it gone away with the absent ones?

"I will punish it grievously or slaughter it, unless it brings me a manifest authority."

He lingered not for long, and so it[661] said: "I have learnt what you have not learnt and have brought from Sheba news which is certain.

"I have found a woman ruling over them and she has been given a share of everything and she has a great throne.

"I found her and her people prostrating themselves to the sun, instead of Allah, and Satan has embellished their actions, barring them from the path. Therefore they are not well-guided;

25 "So that they may not prostrate themselves to Allah, who brings out what is hidden in the heavens and the earth and knows what you conceal and what you reveal."

Allah, there is no god but He, the Lord of the Great Throne.

He[662] said: "We will see if you are telling the truth or are a liar.

"Take this letter of mine and deliver it to them; then turn away from them and see what they will give back in response."

She said:[663] "O my dignitaries, a gracious letter has been delivered to me.

30 "It is from Solomon and it says: 'In the Name of Allah, the Compassionate, the Merciful,

"'Do not rise against me, and come to me submissively.'"[664]

She said: "O my dignitaries, give me your counsel in this, my affair. I will make no decision until you bear witness to me."

They said: "We are endowed with force and great might, but the command is yours; so see what you will command."

She said: "When kings enter a city, they ruin it and reduce its proud inhabitants to subjection. Thus they will always do.

660. The hoopoe served Solomon as a carrier-pigeon would.
661 The hoopoe.
662 Solomon.
663. The Queen of Sheba in South Arabia.
664. Arabic *Muslimin*, which became the attribute Muslims.

35 "I am sending them a gift and will see what the envoys will bring back."

When [the emissary] came to Solomon, he said: "Are you supplying me with money? What Allah has given me is better than what He gave you. You are rather rejoicing in your gift.

"Go back to them;⁶⁶⁵ for we shall array against them troops which they cannot resist and we shall drive them out of it degraded and abased."

He said: "O dignitaries, which one of you will bring me her throne, before they come forward submitting?"

An afreet of the *jinn* said: "I will bring it to you, before you rise from your seat, and I am indeed capable of it and faithful."

40 He who had knowledge of the Book said: "I will bring it to you, before your glance returns to you." So when he saw it ensconced before him, he said: "This is a bounty from my Lord, to test me, whether I am grateful or ungrateful. He who gives thanks, only gives thanks to his own credit, and he who is ungrateful will find my Lord All-Sufficient and Generous."

He said: "Disguise her throne for her, so that we might see whether she will be well-guided or will be one of those who are not well-guided."

When she arrived, it was said: "Is your throne like this one?" She said: "It looks like it." "We⁶⁶⁶ were given the knowledge before her and were submissive."

However, what she worshipped, apart from Allah, barred her; she was indeed one of the unbelieving people.

It was said to her: "Enter the mansion"; but when she saw it, she thought it was a deep pond, and she barred her legs. He⁶⁶⁷ said: "This is actually a mansion made of glass." She said: "Lord, I have wronged myself and have submitted, along with Solomon, to Allah the Lord of the Worlds."

45 And We have sent to Thamud their brother Salih, saying: "Worship Allah"; and lo and behold, they split into two groups fighting each other.

He said: "O my people, who do you hasten the evil course before the fair? If only you would seek Allah's forgiveness, that perchance you may receive mercy!"

They said: "We augured ill of you and your companions." He said: "Your bird of omen is with Allah, but you are a people who are being tested."

And there were in the city nine individuals, who worked corruption in the land and did not set things right.

They said: "Swear one to the other by Allah: 'We will attack him and his

665. The people of Sheba.
666. The reference is to Solomon.
667. Solomon.

family at night; then we will tell his guardian: "We did not witness the slaying of his family, and we are indeed truthful." '"

50 They schemed a scheme and We schemed a scheme, while they were unaware.

See, then, what was the outcome of their scheming; We destroyed them together with all their people.

Their houses are in ruin, on account of their wrongdoing. There is in that a sign for a people who know.

And We delivered those who believed and were God-fearing.

And Lot, when he said to his people: "Do you commit the foul act, while you perceive?

55 "What then, do you approach men lustfully, instead of women? No, you are an ignorant people."

The only response of his people was to say: "Drive the family of Lot out of your city. They are a people who keep themselves clean."

We delivered him and his family, except for his wife; We decreed that she should stay behind.

And We sent down upon them a torrent of rain. Wretched is the rain of those who have been forewarned!

Say: "Praise be to Allah and peace upon those of His servants whom He has chosen. Is Allah better or those they associate with Him?"

60 Is He not the One who created the heavens and the earth and sent down upon you water from the sky; and so We caused to grow thereby delightful gardens. It was not in your power to cause their trees to grow. Is there, then, another god with Allah? Yet, they are a people who assign to Him an equal.

Is He not the One who made the earth a stable abode and created rivers flowing through it, created immovable mountains therein and created a barrier between the two seas. Is there, then, another god with Allah? Yet, most of them do not know.

It is He who answers the one in trouble when he calls upon Him and lifts the adversity and appoints you as successors on earth. Is there then another god with Allah? Little do you recollect.

He who guides you through the dark shadows of land and sea, and sends forth the wind as good news ahead of His mercy. Is there then another god with Allah? No, He is exalted above what they associate!

He who originates the creation, then brings it back, and who provides for you from the heavens and the earth. Is there, then, another god with Allah. Say: "Produce your proof, if you are truthful."

65 Say: "No one in the heavens or on earth knows the Unseen, except Allah; and they will have no inkling when they shall be resuscitated.

Has their knowledge of the Hereafter continued? No, they are in doubt regarding it, or rather, they are blind to it.

The unbelievers say: "What then, will we and our fathers be raised up, once we have turned into dust?

"We have been promised that, we and our fathers, before. These are only the legends of the ancients."

Say: "Travel in the land and see what was the end of the criminals."

70   Do not grieve for them and do not be distressed on account of what they contrive.

And they say: "When is this promise to be fulfilled, if you are truthful?"

Say: "Perhaps some of what you seek to hasten is drawing near."

Your Lord, indeed, is bountiful to mankind, but most of them do not give thanks.

And your Lord knows what their breasts conceal and what they reveal.

75   There is no hidden secret in heaven or on earth, but is in a manifest book.

This Qur'an relates to the Children of Israel most of what they differ on.

And it is, indeed, a guidance and mercy to the believers.

Your Lord will decide between them according to His judgement. He is the All-Mighty, the All-Knowing.

So put your trust in Allah; you are on the manifest and true [path].

80   You will certainly not cause the dead to hear or the deaf to hear the call, if they turn away in flight.

And you will not deflect the blind from their error. You will only cause those who believe in Our signs to hear; for they have submitted.

And when the Word[668] is fulfilled against them, We shall bring out of the earth for them a beast which shall address them thus: "Mankind has not believed with certainty in Our signs."

On the day when We shall muster from each nation a throng of those who denied Our signs; then they will be held in check.

Until they come forward and He says: "Have you denied My signs, and did not comprehend them? Otherwise, what were you doing?"

85   And the Word shall come down upon them for their wrongdoing and so they will not speak.

Do they not see that We made the night, so that they might rest in it, and the day so that they might see? Surely in that are signs for a believing people.

And on the day the trumpet is blown, those in the heavens and on earth are terrified, except for whomever Allah wills; and everyone will come to Him humbly.

And you will see the mountains and suppose them immobile, whereas

668. Divine Decree.

they are passing quickly like clouds – the handiwork of Allah who perfected everything. He is truly conversant with what you do.

Whoever performs a good deed will receive a reward better than it, and they are secure on that day against terror.

90   And those who perpetrate an evil deed, their faces will be cast into the Fire. Will you be rewarded except for what you used to do?

I was only ordered to worship the Lord of this city[669] which He has sanctified. His is everything, and I was ordered to be one of those who submit [to Allah];[670]

And to recite the Qur'an. He who is well-guided is only well-guided to his own advantage, and to him who goes astray, say: "I am only one of the warners."

And say: "Praise be to Allah. He will show you His signs and then you will recognize them. Your Lord is not heedless of what you do."

669. That is, Mecca.
670. i.e. Al-Muslimin.

SURA 28

Al-Qasas, Storytelling

In the Name of Allah, the Compassionate, the Merciful

Tah, Sin, Mim.[671]

1 Those are the verses of the Manifest Book,
We recite to you part of the news of Moses and Pharaoh truthfully, for a people who believe.
Pharaoh waxed proud in the land and reduced its inhabitants into factions, subduing a group of them, slaughtering their sons and sparing their women. He was truly a corruption-worker.
We wish to favour the downtrodden in the land and make them leaders and make them the inheritors;

5 And establish them firmly in the land and show Pharaoh and Haman and their troops what they used to fear.
We revealed to Moses' mother: "Suckle him; but if you fear for him, cast him into the water and do not fear or grieve. We shall return him to you and make him one of the messengers."
Then the folk of Pharaoh picked him up, to become an enemy and a source of sorrow for them. Pharaoh, Haman,[672] and their troops were surely sinful.
Pharaoh's wife said: "He is a comfort to you and me. Do not kill him; perhaps he will profit us or we will take him for a son." Yet they were not well aware.
The heart of Moses' mother became vacant; she almost exposed him, but for Our fortifying her heart, so that she might be one of the believers.

10 She said to his sister: "Follow his tracks", and so she observed him from a distance, while they were unaware.
And We forbade him earlier from being nursed by foster-mothers; so she[673] said: "Shall I lead you to a household who will take charge of him for you and will take good care of him?"
Then We returned him to his mother, so that she might be comforted and not grieve, and that she might know that Allah's promise is true; but most of them do not know.

---

671. The same letters occur at the beginning of Suras 26 and 27; the significance of this is not clear.
672. The minister of Pharaoh.
673. Moses' sister.

When he was fully grown, and became an adult, We conferred on him judgement and knowledge. That is how We reward the beneficent.

And he entered the city at a time when its inhabitants were unheeding; and so he found in it two men fighting, one of his own sect, the other from his enemies. Whereupon the one of his sect solicited his assistance against the one from his enemies; so Moses struck him and killed him. He said: "This is the work of Satan; he is a manifestly misleading enemy."

15 He said: "Lord, I have wronged myself, so forgive me." Then He forgave him. He is indeed the All-Forgiving, the Merciful.

He said: "Lord, in as much as you have favoured me, I will not be a supporter of the criminals."

The next morning, He became fearful and vigilant; and lo and behold, the man who had sought his assistance on the previous day was calling out to him. Moses said to him: "You are clearly in error."

So, when he[674] was about to kill the one who was their enemy, he said: "O Moses, do you wish to kill me, as you killed another living soul yesterday? Do you only wish to become a tyrant in the land and do not wish to be one of the righteous?"

And a man came from the farthest part of the city running. He said: "O Moses, the dignitaries are conspiring to kill you. Depart then, I am one of your sincere advisors."

20 So, he departed from it fearful and vigilant. He said: "Lord, deliver me from the wrongdoing people."

And when he headed towards Midian, he said: "Perhaps, my Lord will guide me unto the right path."

And when he arrived at the water of Midian, he found there a company of men watering their cattle, and he found, apart from them, two women holding back. He said: "What is the matter with you both?" They said: "We will not water our flock until the cattle-herders leave off, and our father is a very old man."

So, he watered their flock for them, and then moved towards the shade and said: "Lord, I am in dire need of whatever good you might send down to me."

Then, one of the two women came to him walking coyly. She said: "My father is calling you in order to reward you for watering our flock." So, when he came to him and told him the story, he said: "Do not fear, you have escaped from the wrongdoing people."

25 One of the two women said: "Father, hire him. Surely, the best one you can hire is the strong and faithful one."

---

674. Moses.

He said: "I want to marry you to one of these two daughters of mine, provided you serve me for eight years. If you complete ten years, that will be of your own accord; and I do not wish to make things hard for you. You will find me, if Allah wishes, one of the righteous."

He said: "This is a compact between you and me; whichever term I complete, my action will not be impugned, and Allah shall vouchsafe what we are saying."

So, when Moses completed the term and set out with his family, he observed a fire on the side of the Tur Mountain.[675] He said to his family: "Stay here, I have observed a fire. Perhaps, I can bring you some news of it or a brand of fire that you might warm yourselves."

When he approached it, he was summoned from the right side of the valley, on the sacred spot by the tree: "O Moses, it is I, Allah, the Lord of the Worlds;

30   "Cast your staff", but when he saw it shaking like a snake, he turned away running, not looking back. "O Moses, come forward and do not fear; you are certainly safe.

"Slip your hand into your bosom and it will come out white, without blemish; then press [your arm] to your side so as not to fear. Those, then, are two proofs to Pharaoh and his dignitaries from your Lord. Indeed, they have been a sinful people."

He said: "Lord, I have killed from them a living soul, and I fear that they might kill me.

"My brother Aaron is more eloquent than I; so send him with me as a supporter to vouch for me. I fear that they will denounce me as a liar."

He[676] said: "We will strengthen your arm with your brother and We will give you authority; so that they will not touch you. By Our signs, you and those who follow you will be the victors."

35   But when Moses came to them with Our clear signs, they said: "This is only faked sorcery and we never heard of this among our forefathers."

Moses then said: "My Lord knows better him who brings the guidance from Him, and him who will have the reward of the ultimate abode. The wrongdoers shall never prosper."

Pharaoh then said: "O my dignitaries, I did not know that you had any god but me. So kindle for me, O Haman, a fire upon the clay and build me a tower that I might behold the god of Moses. I really think he is a liar."

And he and his troops waxed proud in the land unjustly, and thought that they will not be returned to Us.

675. Sinai Mountain.
676. Allah.

Then We seized him and his troops and cast them into the sea; so behold what was the end of the wrongdoers!

40 And We made them leaders calling to the Fire; and on the Day of Resurrection, they will not be supported.

And We pursued them in this world with a curse, and on the Day of Resurrection they will be among the despised.

We have given Moses the Book, after We had destroyed the former generations, to serve as examples to mankind and as guidance and mercy, in order that they may remember well.

You were not on the western side [of the Mountain], when We decreed the commandment to Moses, and you were not one of the witnesses.

But We created other generations whose ages lasted for too long, and you were not dwelling among the inhabitants of Midian reciting Our verses to them, but We were sending other messengers.

45 You were not by the side of the Mountain when We called, but [We are sending you]⁶⁷⁷ as a mercy from your Lord, to warn a people who had no warner prior to you, that perchance they might remember.

And lest an adversity befall them, on account of what their hands have perpetrated, so that they could say: "Our Lord, if only You had sent us a messenger, that we might follow Your signs and be among the believers."

But, when the Truth came to them from Us, they said: "If only he⁶⁷⁸ had been given the like of what Moses had received?" Had they not disbelieved in what Moses received formerly? They said: "Two sorceries backing each other up", and they said: "We are disbelieving in both."

Say: "Bring, then, a Book from Allah giving better guidance than both,⁶⁷⁹ and I will follow it, if you are truthful."

If, however, they do not answer you, then know that they only follow their fancies; and who is more in error than he who follows his own fancy without guidance from Allah. Allah, surely, does not guide the wrongdoing people.

50 And now, We have communicated the Word to them, that perchance they may remember.

Those, whom we have given the Book before it,⁶⁸⁰ do believe in it.

When it is recited to them, they say: "We believe in it; it is the truth from our Lord. We were, even prior to it, submissive [to Allah]."⁶⁸¹

Those shall be given their wages twice, because they stood fast, and will

677. Muhammad.
678. Muhammad.
679. The Qur'an and the Torah.
680. The Qur'an.
681. That is, Muslims.

ward off the evil deed with the good one, and out of what We provided them with will spend freely.

And when they hear idle talk, they turn away from it and say: "We have our works and you have your works. Peace upon you; we do not desire the company of the ignorant."

55   You do not guide whom you wish, but Allah guides whom He wishes, and He knows better the well-guided.

And they said: "If we follow the guidance with you, we will be snatched from our land. Have We not established a safe sanctuary for them, to which are brought all kinds of fruit, as provision, from Ourselves?" However, most of them do not know.

And how many a city We have destroyed that had grown prodigal in its living. There are its dwellings, left uninhabited after they were gone, except for a few. We became the inheritors.

Your Lord, however, never destroys the cities, unless He first sends to their mother-city a messenger, to recite to them Our revelations. And We never destroy any cities, unless their inhabitants are wrongdoers.

Whatever you have been given is merely the pleasure of this life and its finery; but what Allah has in His possession is better and more lasting. Do you not understand?

60   Is he, then, to whom We have promised a fair promise then bestowed it, like one to whom We granted enjoyment in the present life and shall summon on the Day of Resurrection?

On the day that He shall call them saying: "Where are My associates that you used to allege?"

Those upon whom the sentence will be passed shall say: "Lord, those whom we induced into error, we induced into error just as we were induced. We proclaim our innocence to You. It was not us they were worshipping."

And it will be said to them: "Call your associates"; and so they call them, but the associates will not answer. They saw the punishment and they wished they had been well-guided.

On the day He will call them, saying: "What did you answer the messengers?"

65   On that day, the tidings will be obscured for them, and so they will not question each other.

But he who repents, believes and does the righteous deed, perchance he will be among the prosperous.

Your Lord creates and chooses whatever He wills; they have no choice. Glory be to Allah and may He be exalted above what they associate!

And Your Lord knows what their breasts conceal and what they reveal.

He is Allah; there is no god but He. His is the praise in the herebelow and the Hereafter and his is the judgement, and unto Him you will be returned.

70   Say: "Have you considered, what if Allah had made the night to last for you continuously till the Day of Resurrection? What other god than Allah will bring you light? Do you not hear?"

Say: "Have you considered, what if Allah had made the day to last for you continuously till the Day of Resurrection? What other god than Allah will bring you the night to rest in? Do you not see?"

It was out of His mercy, that He created the day and the night, so that you may rest in it and to seek some of His bounty, that perchance you may give thanks.

On the day He will call them saying: "Where are My associates which you used to allege?"

And We picked from every nation a witness and said: "Produce your proof." Then they knew that the truth is Allah's and those they used to invent[682] strayed away from them.

75   Now Karoon[683] belonged to the clan of Moses, then he lorded it over them. We had given him treasures, the keys of which would weigh down the mighty band. When his people said to him: "Do not exult; Allah does not like the exultant;

"But seek, thanks to what Allah gave you, the Hereafter, and do not forget your portion of the herebelow. Be charitable, as Allah has been charitable to you, and do not seek corruption in the land; for Allah does not like the seekers of corruption."

He said: "What I have been given is due to knowledge I possess." Did he not know that Allah has destroyed, before him, generations of men stronger than he and richer? However, the criminals shall not be questioned regarding their sins.

And so he went out unto his people in his finery. Those who desire the present life said: "Would that we possessed the like of what Karoon has been given. He is indeed a very fortunate man."

But those possessed of knowledge said: "Woe betide you; the reward of Allah is better for him who believes and acts righteously, and that is not accorded except to the steadfast."

80   Then, We caused the earth to cave in on him and his household; and so he had no company to support him against Allah; and he was not one of the winners.

And those who had wished they were in his place yesterday were saying:

682. Their idols.
683. That is, Korah, son of Izhar, who rebelled against Moses and Aaron and challenged their authority. *Numbers* 16, 1–35.

"No wonder that Allah increases the provision to whomever He wishes of His servants and restricts it. Had Allah not been gracious to us, He would have caused the earth to cave in on us. No wonder that the unbelievers will never prosper."

That is the Last Abode; We assign it to those who do not desire exaltation on earth or corruption; and the happy outcome belongs to the God-fearing.

Whoever comes up with a good deed will receive a reward better than it, but whoever comes up with an evil deed [should know] that the evildoers will not be rewarded except for what they have done.

He who imparted the Qur'an to you will surely return you to a safe resort. Say: "My Lord knows best who has brought the guidance and who is in manifest error."

85   You did not expect that the Book will be transmitted to you, except as a mercy from your Lord. So, do not be a partisan of the unbelievers.

And let them not divert you from the revelations of Allah after they have been sent down to you. Call upon your Lord, and do not be one of the idolaters.

Do not call, besides Allah, upon any other god. There is no god but He. Everything will perish save His Face. His is the judgement, and unto Him you shall all be returned.

SURA 29

Al-'Ankabut, The Spider

In the Name of Allah, the Compassionate, the Merciful

Alif, Lam, Mim.[684]

1   Have the people supposed that they will be left alone to say: "We believe", and then they will not be tested?

We have indeed tested those who preceded them; and Allah shall certainly know those who speak the truth and shall know those who lie.

Or have those who do the evil deeds supposed that they will outstrip Us? Wretched is what they judge!

He who expects to encounter Allah, surely Allah's term shall come; and He is the All-Hearing, the All-Knowing.

5   He who strives only strives for himself. Allah is All-Sufficient, in need of no being.

And those who believe and do the righteous deeds, We shall remit their sins, and We shall reward them with the best of what they used to do.

We have commanded man to be kind to his parents; but if they strive with you to associate with Me that of which you have no knowledge, then do not obey them. Unto Me is your return and I will tell you what you used to do.

Those who believe and do the righteous deeds, We shall admit them into the company of the righteous.

There are some people who say: "We believe in Allah", but if one of them is injured on account of Allah, he reckons the persecution of men similar to Allah's punishment. If, however, victory comes from your Lord, they[685] will say: "We were with you." Does not Allah know better what is in the breasts of the whole of mankind?

10   And Allah certainly knows the believers and He knows the hypocrites.

The unbelievers said to the believers: "Follow our path and let us bear your sins"; but they will not bear any of their sins. Indeed they are liars.

They shall bear their own burdens, plus burdens upon burdens, and they will be questioned on the Day of Resurrection concerning what they used to fabricate.

We sent Noah to his own people and he tarried among them a thousand

---

684. The same letters occur at the beginning of Sura 28; the significance of this is not clear.
685. The idolaters.

years minus fifty years. Then the Deluge overtook them; for they were wrongdoers.

Yet We delivered him, together with the companions of the Ark, and We made it a sign unto mankind.

15 And Abraham, when he said to his people: "Worship Allah and fear Him; that is far better for you, if only you knew.

"Indeed, you only worship, apart from Allah, mere idols, and you invent falsehood. Surely, those you worship, apart from Allah, have no power to provide for you. So, seek provision from Allah, worship Him and give Him thanks. You shall be returned unto Him.

"And if you denounce [the prophets], other nations before you have denounced. It is only incumbent on the Apostle to deliver the message plainly."

Have they not seen how Allah originates creation, then brings it back into being? That for Allah is an easy matter.

Say: "Travel in the land and see how Allah originated the creation; then Allah produces the other generation.[686] Allah truly has power over everything."

20 He punishes whom He pleases and has mercy on whom He pleases, and to Him you will be turned over.

You cannot thwart Him on earth or in heaven, and you have, apart from Allah, no friend or supporter.

Those who disbelieved in Allah's signs and His encounter are those who despaired of My mercy. To those is reserved a very painful punishment.

His own people's only reply was their saying: "Kill him and burn him", but Allah delivered him from fire. Surely, in that are signs for a people who believe.

He said: "You only took, apart from Allah, idols, as a bond between you in the present life. Then on the Day of Resurrection you will disbelieve in each other and curse each other. Your refuge shall be the Fire and you will have no supporters."

25 Then Lot believed in him[687] and said: "I will emigrate to my Lord; He is indeed the All-Mighty, the Wise."

And We granted him Isaac and Jacob and conferred on his progeny the prophethood and the Book, and gave him his reward in this life; and in the Hereafter he shall be among the righteous.

And [remember] Lot, when he said to his people: "You are committing the foul act[688] which no one in the whole world ever committed before you."

686. That is, Resurrection.
687. Abraham.
688. That is, sodomy.

"You approach men and waylay the traveller and commit in your gatherings reprehensible acts." To which the only reply of his people was: "Bring upon us Allah's punishment, if you are truthful."

He said: "Lord, support me against the workers of corruption."

30   When Our emissaries[689] brought Abraham the good news, they said: "We are going to destroy the inhabitants of this city. Its inhabitants have indeed been wrongdoers."

He said: "Lot is in it"; they said: "We know better who is in it. We shall deliver him and his household, except for his wife; for she is one of those who will stay behind."

Then, when Our emissaries came to Lot, he was troubled and distressed on their account, and they said: "Do not fear and do not grieve; we shall deliver you and your household, except for your wife; she is one of those who will stay behind."

We are sending down upon the inhabitants of this city a scourge from heaven, because of their sins.

And we have left as a vestige of it a clear sign to a people who understand.

35   And to Midian We sent their brother, Shu'ayb, who said: "O my people, worship Allah and hope for the Last Day, and do not spread corruption in the land."

They denounced him as a liar and so the tremor[690] overtook them, and they were left in their home prostrate.

And [remember] 'Ad and Thamud. It has become clear to you from their dwellings [what their fate was]. Satan embellished for them their deeds, barring them from the path, while they were clear-sighted.

And [remember] Karoon, Pharaoh and Haman. Moses came to them with the clear proofs, but they waxed proud in the land and they did not outstrip Us.

Each, We seized for his sin. Upon some We loosed a squall of pebbles, some were overwhelmed with the Cry, some We caused the ground to cave in under and some We drowned. Allah did not wrong them, but they wronged themselves.

40   The case of those who took up other protectors, apart from Allah, is like that of the spider who built a house. Truly, the most brittle of houses is the house of the spider, if only they knew.

Allah knows what they call upon, apart from Him, and He is the All-Mighty, the Wise.

Those are the parables We devise for mankind, and only the learned will grasp them.

689. The angels.
690. Of punishment (*Tabari*).

Allah created the heavens and the earth in truth. Surely there is in that a sign for those who believe.

Recite what has been revealed to you of the Book and perform the prayer. Prayer surely forbids the foul act and abomination. Allah's remembrance is greater and Allah knows what you do.

45   Do not dispute with the people of the Book save in the fairest way; except for those of them who are evildoers. And say: "We believe in what has been sent down to us and what has been sent down to you. Our God and your God are one and to Him we are submissive."

And thus We have sent down to you the Book. Those to whom We gave the Book[691] believe in it, and of these[692] some believe in it. Our signs are only denied by the unbelievers.

You did not recite before it any book or write it down with your right hand. Then the negators would have been in doubt.

It is rather clear signs in the breasts of those who have been granted knowledge. Only the wrongdoers will deny Our signs.

They said: "If only signs from his Lord were sent down on him."[693] Say: "Signs are only with Allah, and I am only a manifest warner."

50   Does it not suffice them that We have sent down on you the Book which is recited to them? There is, indeed, in that a mercy and a reminder to a believing people.

Say: "Allah suffices as a witness between you and me. He knows what is in the heavens and on the earth; and those who have believed in falsehood and disbelieved in Allah – those are the losers."

And they urge you to hasten the punishment; but had it not been for an appointed term, the punishment would have certainly smitten them. In fact, it will smite them suddenly, while they are unaware.

They urge you to hasten the punishment. Hell shall surely encompass the unbelievers.

Upon the day the punishment shall overwhelm them from above them and from under their feet and He says: "Taste now what you used to do."

55   O My servants who believe and do the righteous deeds, My earth is vast, so worship Me alone.

Every living soul shall taste death; then unto Us you shall be returned.

Those who have believed and done the righteous deeds, We shall install them in chambers in Paradise, beneath which rivers flow, dwelling therein forever. Blessed is the wage of those who labour!

Those who stood fast and in their Lord they trust.

---

691. The People of the Book, Jews and Christians.
692. Muhammad's contemporaries, or the Meccans.
693. Muhammad.

How many a beast does not bear its provision, yet Allah provides for it and for you. He is All-Hearing, All-Knowing.

60 And if you ask them: "Who created the heavens and the earth and subdued the sun and the moon?", they will say: "Allah." Why then do they vacillate?

Allah expands the provision for whomever He wishes of His servants or restricts it. Surely, Allah has knowledge of all things.

And if you ask them: "Who sends from heaven water [with which] He revives the earth after it was dead?", they will say: "Allah." Say: "Praise be to Allah." Yet most of them do not understand.

This present life is nothing but amusement and sport, but the Hereafter is real life, if only they knew.

When they embark in the ships, they will call on Allah, professing religion sincerely to Him. Yet when He delivers them safely to land, behold they associate.[694]

65 To disbelieve in what We have imparted to them and enjoy themselves. They will surely come to know.

Do they not see that We have set up a safe sanctuary for them, while all around them people are being snatched away? Do they, then, believe in falsehood and repudiate Allah's bounty?

Who, then, is more unjust than one who imputes falsehood to Allah or denies the truth when it comes to him. Is there not in Hell a dwelling for the unbelievers?

And those who strive in Our cause We shall guide in our ways, and Allah is with the beneficent.

694. Other gods with Him.

SURA 30

Al-Rum, The Greeks
[or Byzantines]

In the Name of Allah, the Compassionate, the Merciful

Alif, Lam, Mim.

1   The Greeks have been vanquished in the nearest part of the land; but after being vanquished, they shall vanquish,

In a few years. Allah's is the command before and after; and on that day the believers shall rejoice,

In Allah's support. He supports whom He will; and He is the All-Mighty, the Merciful.

It is Allah's promise. Allah does not break His promise, although most people do not know.

5   They know the outward aspect of the present life, but they are heedless of the Hereafter.

Have they not considered within themselves that Allah did not create the heavens and the earth and what is between them except in truth and at an appointed time? Yet many people disbelieve in the encounter of their Lord.

Have they not travelled in the land to see what was the fate of those who preceded them? They were stauncher than them in strength, and they ploughed the earth and built it up better than they themselves built it up, and their messengers came to them with the clear proofs. Allah would never wrong them, but they wronged themselves.

Then, the fate of those who committed the gravest sin was to denounce Allah's signs as lies and to mock them.

Allah originates creation and then brings it back into being. Then unto Him you shall be returned.

10   And on the day that the Hour comes, the criminals will be confounded.

And they will have no intercessors among their associates and they will repudiate their associates.

And on the day that the Hour comes, they shall be divided.

As for those who have believed and done the righteous deeds, they will be in a garden, fully joyful.

But as for those who have disbelieved and denounced Our signs and the encounter of the Hereafter as lies, those shall be summoned to suffer the punishment.

15   So, glorify Allah in the evening and in the morning.

His is the praise in the heavens and on earth at sunset and at noontide.
He brings the living out of the dead and He brings the dead out of the living. He brings the earth to life after it was dead, and you shall be brought out likewise.

And of His signs is that He created you from dust; and behold, you are mortals scattered all round.

And of His signs is that He created for you, from yourselves, spouses to settle down with and He established friendship and mercy between you. There are in all that signs for a people who reflect.

20 And of His signs is the creation of the heavens and the earth and the diversity of your tongues and colours. Indeed, there are in that signs for those who know.

And of His signs is your sleeping by night and day and your seeking some of His bounty. There are in that signs for a people who hear.

And of His signs is showing you the lightning, to fear and to hope; and He brings down from the sky water with which He revives the earth after it was dead. There are in that signs for people who understand.

And of His signs is that the heavens and the earth shall arise at His command. Then, if He summons you once, behold, you shall be brought out of the earth.

And to Him belongs whoever is in the heavens or on earth. They are all submitting to Him.

25 It is He who originates the creation, then brings it back again; and that is easier for Him. His is the loftiest exemplar in the heavens and on earth, and He is the All-Mighty, the Merciful.

He gave you a parable from your own selves. Do you have among what your hands own[695] partners in what We provided for you, so that you are equal therein? Do you fear them as you fear each other? Thus We expound the revelations to a people who understand.

Yet, the wrongdoers have followed their fancies without knowledge. Who, then, will guide those whom Allah has led astray and who have no supporters?

So, set your face towards religion uprightly. It is the original nature according to which Allah fashioned mankind. There is no altering Allah's creation. That is the true religion; but most men do not know.

Returning unto Him. Fear Him, perform the prayer and do not be like the idolaters;

30 Those who have rent their religion asunder and split into factions, each party rejoicing in what they had.

When people are visited by some adversity, they call upon their Lord,

---

695. Your slaves.

turning to Him; but when He lets them taste a mercy from Him, behold, a group of them associate [other gods] with their Lord;

So as to be ungrateful for what We have given them. Indulge yourselves, then. For you shall certainly know!

Or have We sent down to them an authority, and he speaks about that which they were associating with Him?

If We let people taste a certain mercy, they rejoice at it; but if a misfortune befalls them, on account of what their hands have perpetrated, behold, they are in despair.

35   Have they not seen that Allah expands and restricts the provision for whomever He wishes? Surely, there are in that signs for a people who believe.

So, give the kinsman his due, as well as the destitute and the wayfarer. That is better for those who desire the Face of Allah. Those are the prosperous.

And what you give in usury, so as to multiply people's wealth, will not multiply in Allah's sight; but what you give in alms, desiring thereby Allah's Face. Such are the real multipliers.[696]

It is Allah who created you, then provided for you and who will cause you to die, then bring you back to life. Is there among your associates any one who does any of all this? Glory be to Him and may He be exalted above what they associate with Him!

Corruption has appeared in the land and the sea, on account of what men's hands have earned; so that He may let them taste the reward of some of their deeds, that perchance they may return.

40   Say: "Travel in the land and behold what was the fate of those who came before; most of them were idolaters."

So, set your face towards the true religion, before a day from Allah comes, which cannot be turned back. On that day they will be rent asunder.

Whoever disbelieves, upon him shall recoil his unbelief and whoever does a righteous deed, it is for themselves that they will be preparing a comfortable abode.

That He may reward those who have believed and done the righteous deeds out of His bounty. Indeed, He does not love the unbelievers.

And of His signs is sending forth the winds bearing good news and to let you taste part of His mercy, and that the ships may sail at His command, and that you might seek part of His bounty; that perchance you may give thanks.

45   We have, indeed, sent messengers to their own people, before you, and

696. Of their wealth.

they brought them clear proofs. Then We revenged upon those who sinned, and it was incumbent on Us to give the believers support.

It is Allah who sends forth the winds, which stir up clouds. Then He spreads them out in the sky, as He pleases, and causes them to break up into pieces; and you see the rain issuing from their midst. Then, when He allows the rain to reach whomever He wishes of His servants, behold, they rejoice.

Whereas they were, before that, despondent.

Behold, then, the marks of Allah's mercy, how He revives the earth after it was dead. He, indeed, is the One who revives the dead and He has power over everything.

And were We to send forth a wind and they saw it turning yellow, they would continue thereafter to disbelieve.

50   For you cannot make the dead hear and you cannot make the deaf hear the call, if they flee turning their back.

And you shall not lead the blind away from their error. You will only make those who believe in Our signs hear. For they are submitting.

It is Allah who created you from a weak substance, then gave you strength after weakness, then after strength weakness and grey hair. He creates what He pleases and He is the All-Knowing, All-Powerful.

And the day the Hour comes, the criminals shall swear that they did not linger more than an hour. Thus they had been perverted.

But those who have been given knowledge and faith will say: "You have lingered in Allah's Book till the Day of Resurrection. This is the Day of Resurrection, but you did not know."

55   On that day, the excuses of the wrongdoers will not avail them and they will not be allowed to plead for pardon.

We have cited in this Qur'an every manner of parable; indeed were you to bring the unbelievers a sign, they would only say: "You are purveyors of falsehood."

Thus Allah places a seal upon the hearts of those who do not know.

Be patient then, for Allah's promise is true; and do not be disheartened by those who lack the certitude of faith.

SURA 31

Luqman, The Wise

In the Name of Allah, the Compassionate, the Merciful

Alif, Lam, Mim.

1   Those are the signs of the wise Book;
     A guidance and mercy to the beneficent,
     Those who perform the prayer, give the alms and are certain of the Hereafter.
     Those are accorded guidance from their Lord and those are the prosperous.

5   There are some people who purchase idle talk in order to lead away from Allah's path without any knowledge; and take it in jest. Those will have a demeaning punishment.

And if Our revelations are recited to him, he turns away arrogantly, as though he did not hear them, or as though there is a heaviness in his ears. Announce to him, then, the news of a very painful punishment.

Those who have believed and do the righteous deeds will inherit the Gardens of Bliss.

Dwelling therein forever, having been given Allah's true promise. He is the All-Mighty, All-Wise.

He created the heavens without pillars that you can see and laid down in the earth immovable mountains, lest it shake with you, and scattered throughout it every variety of beast. And We have sent down water from heaven, thereby causing to grow in it every noble kind [of plant].

10   This is Allah's creation; so show Me what those apart from Him have created. Indeed, the wrongdoers are in manifest error.

We have, indeed, imparted wisdom to Luqman:[697] "Give thanks to Allah." Whoever gives thanks, gives thanks only for his own good and whoever disbelieves will find Allah All-Sufficient, Praiseworthy."

And when Luqman said to his son, exhorting him: "My son, do not associate others with Allah; associating others [with Allah] is a mighty evil."

We have admonished man regarding his parents; as his mother bore him in weakness upon weakness, weaning him in two years: "Give thanks to Me and to your parents. Unto Me is the ultimate return.

"If they strive with you so as to associate with Me that of which you have no knowledge, do not obey them; but keep them company in the present

697 Luqman is a legendary figure in Islamic lore, regarded as a paragon of wisdom.

257

world honourably. Follow the path of those who turn to Me. Then unto Me is your return, whereupon I will tell you what you used to do.

15 "O my son, if there be the weight of a mustard seed, whether in a rock, in the heavens or in the earth, Allah will bring it forth. Surely, Allah is Subtle, Well-Informed.

"O my son, perform the prayer, command the honourable and forbid the dishonourable and bear patiently what has befallen you. That is an instance of constancy in one's affairs.

"Do not turn your face away from people and do not walk in the land haughtily. Allah does not love any arrogant or boastful person.

"Be modest in your stride and lower your voice; for the most hideous voice is that of asses."

Have you not seen how Allah has subjected to you whatever is in the heavens and on earth and granted you His blessings, both outward and inward? Some people, however, continue to dispute regarding Allah, without any knowledge or guidance or an illuminating Book.

20 If it is said to them: "Follow what Allah has sent down", they say: "Rather, we will follow what we found our fathers doing." It is as though Satan was summoning them to the punishment of Hell.

Whoever surrenders his will to Allah, while doing the right, has surely grasped the firmest handle. Unto Allah is the ultimate issue of all affairs.

Whoever disbelieves, let not his disbelief sadden you. Unto Us is their return and then We will tell them what they did. Allah knows well the secrets of the breasts.

We allow them to indulge themselves a little, then We will compel them to taste a harsh punishment.

And if you ask them: "Who created the heavens and the earth", they will certainly say: "Allah." Say: "Praise be to Allah." However, most of them do not know.

25 To Allah belongs what is in the heavens and the earth. Allah is, indeed, the All-Sufficient, the Praiseworthy.

Were all trees on earth so many pens and the sea, coupled by seven other seas, supplying them with ink, Allah's words would not be exhausted. Allah is, indeed, All-Mighty and Wise.

He did not create you or resuscitate you but as a single soul. Indeed, Allah is All-Hearing, All-Seeing.

Have you not seen how Allah causes the night to phase into the day, and the day to phase into the night; and He has subjected the sun and the moon, each of them running to an appointed term, and that Allah is well-aware of what you do?

That is because Allah is the Truth and what they call upon, apart from Him, is the falsehood and that Allah is the All-High, the Great.

30   Have you not seen that ships cruise upon the sea by Allah's grace, to show
you some of His signs. There are in that signs for every steadfast, thankful
one.

And if waves cover them like a canopy, they call upon Allah, professing
religion sincerely to Him; but when He delivers them to the dry land, some
of them are lukewarm. Yet none repudiate Our signs except every ungrateful
traitor.

O people, fear your Lord and beware of a day when no father shall stand
for his child and no infant shall stand for his father in the least. Allah's
promise is true, so let not the present life delude you or let any deceiver
delude you regarding Allah.

Allah surely has the knowledge of the Hour and He sends down the rain.
He knows what is in the wombs, whereas no soul knows what it shall earn
tomorrow; nor does any living soul know in what land it shall die. Allah is
All-Knowing, Well-Informed.

SURA 32

Al-Sajda, The Prostration

In the Name of Allah, the Compassionate, the Merciful

Alif, Lam, Mim.

1   The revelation of the Book from the Lord of the Worlds, wherein there is no doubt.

Or do they say: "He invented it?" Say: "Rather, it is the truth from your Lord, so as to warn a people to whom no warner came before you, that perchance they might be well-guided."

Allah, who created the heavens and the earth in six days, sat upon the Throne. You have no guardian or intercessor, apart from Him. Do you not recollect?

He manages the affair from the heaven to the earth; then, it ascends to Him in one day whose measure is a thousand years of what you reckon.

5   That is the Knower of the Unseen and the Seen, the All-Mighty, the Merciful.

Who fashioned well everything He created, and originated the creation of man from clay.

Then He fashioned his progeny from an extract of fluid.

Then He shaped him well and breathed into him of His spirit. He gave you hearing, sight and hearts. How little do you give thanks!

They say: "What, if we stray aimlessly in the land, shall we be created anew?" Indeed, they disbelieve in the encounter of their Lord.

10   Say: "The angel of death, who was charged with you, will carry you off; then you will be returned to your Lord."

If only you could see how the criminals are hanging their heads down before their Lord, saying: "Our Lord, we have seen and heard; so send us back that we might do the righteous deed. Now we believe with certainty."

Had We wished, We would have granted every soul its guidance, but My word is now fulfilled: "I shall fill Gehenna[698] with *jinn* and men, all together."

So, taste, for forgetting the encounter of this day – We have forgotten you too, and taste the punishment of eternity, for what you used to do.

Yet those believe in Our signs who, when reminded of them, fall down prostrate and celebrate the praise of their Lord, and they are not overbearing.

---

698. Another word for Hell.

15   Their sides shun their couches as they call on their Lord in fear and hope, and of what We have provided [them with, they give in charity].

No soul knows what was laid up for them secretly of joyful relief, as a reward for what they used to do.

Is he who believes, then, like he who is a sinner? No, they are not equal.

As for those who believe and do the righteous deeds, they will have gardens of refuge to receive them, for what they used to do.

But, as for the sinners, their refuge is the Fire. Every time they want to get out of it, they are brought back and it will be said to them: "Taste the punishment of the Fire which you used to deny."

20   We shall surely let them taste the nearer punishment, prior to the greater punishment, that perchance they might repent.

Who is more unjust than he who is reminded of Our signs, then he turns away from them? We will certainly wreak vengeance upon the criminals.

We have, indeed, given Moses the Book; so do not be in doubt concerning his encounter, and We made it a guidance to the Children of Israel.

And We appointed some of them as leaders, guiding by Our command, when they stood fast and believed firmly in Our signs.

It is your Lord who will judge between them on the Day of Resurrection, regarding that whereof they used to differ.

25   Was it not shown to them how many generations We have destroyed before them, while they were strolling in their dwellings? Surely, there are signs in that; do they not hear?

Do they not see that we conduct the water onto the barren land, bringing forth thereby vegetation, from which their cattle and their own folk eat? Do they not see, then?

And they say: "When will this victory come, if you are truthful?"

Say: "On the day of victory, their profession of faith will not avail the unbelievers and they will not be given respite."

So turn away from them and wait; they too shall be waiting.

SURA 33

Al-Ahzab, The Confederates

In the Name of Allah, the Compassionate, the Merciful

1 O Prophet, fear Allah and do not obey the unbelievers and the hypocrites. Allah is All-Knowing, All-Wise.

And follow what is revealed to you from your Lord. Indeed, Allah is well-informed about what you do.

And trust in Allah; Allah suffices as a guardian.

Allah did not create two hearts within the breast of any man; and He did not make your wives, whom you compare to your mothers' backs;[699] and He did not make your [adopted] sons your sons in fact. That is your own claim, by your words of mouth. Allah speaks the truth and He guides to the right path.

5 Assign them to their own fathers. That is more equitable in the sight of Allah; but if you do not know their real fathers, then they are your brothers in religion, your adopted fellow-Muslims. You are not at fault if you err therein; but only in what your hearts intend. Allah is ever All-Forgiving, All-Merciful.

The Prophet is closer to the believers than their own selves and his wives are like their mothers. The kinsmen are closer to each other, in Allah's Book, than the believers or the Emigrants; unless you are doing your friends an honourable deed, that has already been inscribed in the Book.

And [remember] when We took from the prophets their covenant and from you and from Noah, Abraham, Moses and Jesus, son of Mary, too; and We took from them a solemn covenant;

So as to question the truthful about their truthfulness, and He has prepared for the unbelievers a very painful punishment.

O believers, remember Allah's grace on you when enemy hosts[700] came upon you; then We sent against them a wind and hosts you did not actually see. Allah perceives well what you do.

10 When they came upon you from above you and from below you, and your eyes looked askew and your hearts reached your throats, while you entertained false thoughts about Allah.

There and then, the believers were sorely tried and shaken very violently.

---

699. That is, you divorce them saying: "You are as our mothers' backs."
700. Of confederates allied against Muslims in the Battle of the Ditch (Khandaq) during the siege of Medina or Yathrib 5 AH.

And when the hypocrites and those in whose hearts is a sickness were saying: "Allah and His Apostle have only promised us vanity."

And when a group of them said: "O people of Yathrib,[701] there is no place for you to abide in, so turn back"; while another group of them were seeking the Prophet's permission, saying: "Our homes are exposed", whereas they were not exposed. They only wanted to flee.

And were it[702] entered from its different quarters, and then they were asked to apostatise, they would certainly have done so, without lingering but a short while.

15   Although they had made a pledge to Allah, before, that they will not turn their backs. Allah's pledges are always accountable.

Say: "Flight will not profit you, if you flee from death or murder; for then you will not partake of enjoying life except briefly."

Say: "Who will defend you against Allah, if He wishes you ill or if He wishes you well." They will find for themselves, apart from Allah, no protectors or supporters.

Allah would surely know those of you who hinder the others and those who say to their brothers: "Come over to us"; and they do not partake of fighting, except a little.

They are ever niggardly towards you, but if fear overtakes them, you will see them look at you, with their eyes rolling like one who is in the throes of death. But when fear subsides, they cut you with sharp tongues. They are niggardly in times of prosperity;[703] those are no believers. Thus Allah has frustrated their actions, that being for Allah an easy matter.

20   They think the Confederates have not departed, but were the Confederates to show up, they would wish that they were desert-dwellers with the Bedouins asking about your news. However, were they in your midst, they would fight but little.

You have had a good example in Allah's Apostle; surely for him who hopes for Allah and the Last Day and remembers Allah often.

When the believers saw the Confederates, they said: "This is what Allah and His Apostle have promised us, and Allah and His Apostle are truthful." And it only increased them in faith and submission.

Of the believers, there are men who fulfilled what they pledged to Allah; some of them have died, some are still waiting, without changing in the least.

So that Allah might reward the truthful for their truthfulness and punish

---

701. The old name of Medina, the Prophet's City.
702. The city of Yathrib.
703. As a result of the spoils of war.

the hypocrites, if He wishes, or forgive them. Surely Allah is All-Forgiving, All-Merciful.

25   Allah turned back the unbelievers in a state of rage, having not won any good,[704] and Allah spared the believers battle. Allah is, indeed, Strong and Mighty.

And He brought those of the People of the Book who supported them from their fortresses and cast terror into their hearts, some of them you slew and some you took captive.

And He bequeathed to you their lands, their homes and their possessions, together with land you have never trodden. Allah has power over everything.

O Prophet, say to your wives: "If you desire the present life and its finery, so come along that I might provide for you and set you free kindly.

"But if you desire Allah, His Apostle and the life to come, surely Allah has prepared for the beneficent among you a great wage.

30   "O wives of the Prophet, whomever of you commits a flagrant foul act, her punishment will be doubled; and that for Allah is an easy matter."

Whoever of you obeys Allah and His Apostle and does the righteous deed, We shall pay her wage twice over, and We have prepared for her a generous provision.

O wives of the Prophet, you are not like any other women. If you are God-fearing, do not be abject in speech, so that he in whose heart is a sickness may covet you, but speak in an honourable way.

Stay in your homes and do not display your finery as the pagans of old did; perform the prayer, give the alms and obey Allah and His Apostle. Allah only wishes to turn away abomination from you and purify you fully, O People of the House.

And remember what is recited in your homes of Allah's signs and of wisdom. Indeed, Allah is Subtle, Well-Informed.

35   Men and women who have submitted, believed, obeyed, are truthful, steadfast, reverent, giving in charity, fasting, guarding their private parts and remembering Allah often, Allah has prepared for them forgiveness and a great reward.

It is not up to any believer, man or woman, when Allah and His Apostle have passed a judgement, to have any choice in their affairs. Whoever disobeys Allah and His Apostle have gone astray in a manifest manner.

And [remember] when you said to him whom Allah favoured and you favoured:[705] "Hold on to your wife and fear Allah", while you concealed

704. In the form of spoils.
705. This is addressed to Zayd Ibn Harithah regarding his wife, Zaynab Bint Jahsh, whom the Prophet married upon her release from Zayd.

within yourself what Allah would reveal and feared other men, whereas Allah had a better right to be feared by you. Then, when Zayd had satisfied his desire for her, We gave her to you in marriage; so that the believers should not be at fault, regarding the wives of their adopted sons, once they have satisfied their desire for them. For Allah's command must be accomplished.

The Prophet was not at fault regarding what Allah prescribed for him as was His way with those who were gone before. And Allah's command is a pre-ordained decree.

Those who were delivering Allah's messages and feared Him, fearing none other than Allah. Allah suffices as a reckoner.

40 Muhammad is not the father of any of your men, but is the Apostle of Allah and the seal of the prophets. Allah is cognizant of everything.

O believers, remember Allah often;

And glorify Him morning and evening.

It is He Who blesses you, with His angels, that He may bring you out of the shadows of darkness into the light; and He is ever merciful towards the believers.

Their greeting, when they encounter Him is: "Peace", and He has prepared for them a generous reward.

45 O Prophet, We have sent you as a witness, a bearer of good news and a warner,

Calling to Allah by His leave, and an illuminating beacon.

Announce to the believers that they will have a generous bounty from Allah.

And do not obey the unbelievers and the hypocrites, overlook their injury and trust in Allah. For Allah suffices as a guardian.

O believers, if you marry believing women then divorce them, before touching them, you owe them no fixed term to reckon. So make provision for them and set them free in an honourable way.

50 O Prophet, We have made lawful, for you, your wives, whose dowry you have paid, what your right hand owns[706] out of the spoils of war that Allah gave you, the daughters of your paternal uncles, the daughters of your paternal aunts, the daughters of your maternal uncles, the daughters of your maternal aunts who emigrated with you, and any believing woman who gives herself freely to the Prophet, if the Prophet desires to marry her, granted exclusively to you, but not the believers. We know what We have prescribed for them, regarding their wives and what their right hands own, so that you may not be at fault. Allah is All-Forgiving, Merciful.

706. Slave-girls.

You may defer any of them you wish, and take in any of them that you wish, or any that you may have cut off. So you are not liable to reproach. For thus it is more likely that they will be delighted and will not grieve, but be content with what you have given each one of them. Allah knows what is within your hearts; and Allah is All-Knowing, Clement.

Thereafter, other women are not lawful to you, nor is substituting other wives for them, even if you admire their beauty, except for what your right hand owns. Allah is Watchful over everything.

O believers, do not enter the houses of the Prophet, unless you are invited to a meal, without awaiting the hour; but if you are invited, then enter; but when you have eaten, disperse, without lingering for idle talk. That is vexing to the Prophet who might be wary of you, but Allah is not wary of the truth. If you ask them[707] for an object, ask them from behind a curtain. That is purer for your hearts and theirs. You should never hurt the Apostle of Allah, nor take his wives in marriage after him. That is truly abominable in the sight of Allah.

Whether you reveal a thing or conceal it, Allah has knowledge of everything.

55 They[708] are not at fault, regarding their fathers, their sons, their brothers, their brothers' sons, their sisters' sons or their wives and what their right hands possess; so fear Allah. Surely, Allah is witness of everything.

Allah and His angels bless the Prophet. O believers, bless him and greet him graciously, too.

Those who cause Allah and His Apostle any injury, Allah has cursed them in this life and the life to come and has prepared for them a demeaning punishment.

And those who injure the believers, men and women, except for what they have incurred, have borne the burden of falsehood and manifest sin.

O Prophet, tell your wives and daughters and the wives of the believers, to draw their outer garments closer. That is more conducive to their being known, and not being injured. Allah is All-Forgiving, Merciful.

60 If the hypocrites, those in whose hearts is a sickness and those who spread lies in the city, do not desist, We will certainly urge you against them and then they will not dwell with you therein as neighbours but for a short time.

Accursed, wherever they are encountered they will be seized and slaughtered –

That is Allah's way of dealing with those who have gone before, and you will never find any alteration of Allah's way.

707. The wives of the Prophet.
708. The wives of the Prophet, if they appear unveiled.

People will ask you about the Hour. Say: "The knowledge thereof is with Allah." And what do you know? The Hour may be close at hand.

Allah has cursed the unbelievers and prepared for them a blazing fire;

65   Dwelling therein forever, not finding a protector or supporter.

The day their faces are turned around in the Fire, they will say: "If only we had obeyed Allah and the Apostle."

They will say: "Lord, we have obeyed our masters and our chiefs and so they have led us astray.

"Lord, give them the punishment twofold and curse them mightily."

O believers, do not be like those who injured Moses, but Allah exonerated him from what they said, and he was highly regarded in Allah's sight.

70   O believers, fear Allah and speak in a straightforward way.

He will set right your deeds and forgive you your sins. Whoever obeys Allah and His Apostle has won a great victory.

We offered the Trust to the heavens, the earth, and the mountains, but they refused to carry it and were afraid of it, but man carried it. He has indeed been unjust and ignorant.

That Allah might punish the hypocrites, men and women, the idolaters, men and women; and that Allah might pardon the believers, men and women.

SURA 34

Saba', The City of Sheba

In the Name of Allah, the Compassionate, the Merciful

1 Praise be to Allah, to Whom belongs whatever is in the heavens and whatever is on earth, and praise be to Him in the Hereafter. He is the All-Wise, the All-Informed.

He knows what penetrates into the earth and what goes out of it, what descends from heaven and what ascends to it. He is the All-Merciful, the All-Forgiving.

The unbelievers say: "The Hour will not come for us." Say: "Yes, indeed, it will come, by my Lord, Knower of the Unseen, from Whom not the weight of a speck of dust will escape in the heavens or on earth; nor is anything smaller or bigger than that but is in a Manifest Book."

Those who have believed and did the righteous deeds – those shall receive forgiveness and a generous provision.

5 But those who go around striving to rebut Our signs – those shall have the punishment of a very painful scourge.

And those who were given the knowledge,[709] which was sent down from your Lord, will see that it is the Truth and it guides onto the path of the All-Mighty, the All-Praiseworthy.

The unbelievers say: "Shall we show you a man who will tell you that, once you have been torn to pieces, you shall become again a new creation?

"Does he impute falsehood to Allah or is he possessed?" No, those who do not believe in the Hereafter will undergo the punishment and are in grave error.

Have they not looked at what is in front of them and behind them of the heavens and the earth? Had we wished, we would have caused the earth to cave in under them, or dropped fragments from heaven upon them. Surely, in that is a sign to every repenting servant.

10 We have given David a bounty from Us: "O mountains, proclaim the praise with him, and you birds", and We softened the iron for him.

"Fashion ample coats of arms and measure well the links; and do you all the righteous deeds. I am fully observant of what you do."

And We subjected the wind to Solomon, blowing in the morning the space of a month and in the evening the space of a month; and We smelted

---

709. The People of the Book, or Jews and Christians.

for him the fount of brass. Of the *jinn* some worked before him, by the leave of his Lord, and whoever of them swerved from Our command, We shall make him taste the punishment of the blazing Fire.

To fashion for him whatever he wished of palaces, statues, basins like water-troughs and immovable cooking pots. "Work thankfully, O David's House; for few of My servants are truly thankful."

When We decreed his death, nothing indicated to them that he was dead except an earth-worm gnawing away at his staff. Then, when he fell down, the *jinn* realized that, had they known the Unseen, they would not have continued in the demeaning punishment.

15   For Sheba there also was a sign in their dwelling – two gardens, to the right and the left: "Eat of your Lord's provision and give thanks to Him: a good land and an All-Forgiving Lord."

But they turned away; and so We loosed upon them the Overwhelming Flood,[710] and We substituted for their two gardens another two gardens bearing bitter fruit and having fir trees and a few lotus trees.

Thus We penalized them for their disbelief; and do We ever penalize any but the unbeliever?

We established between them and between the cities, which We blessed, other visible cities, and We determined the measure of travel therein: "Travel therein for nights and days in perfect security."

Then they said: "Lord, prolong the stages between our travels." They wronged themselves, so We reduced them to mere tales and tore them up utterly. Surely, there are in that signs for every steadfast and thankful man.

20   And Iblis definitely proved right his opinion of them, and so they followed him, except for a group of believers.

Yet he had no authority over them; but that We might distinguish him who believed in the Hereafter, from him who was in doubt regarding it. Your Lord is Watchful over everything.

Say: "Call upon those you allege, apart from Allah. They do not possess the weight of a speck of dust in the heavens or on earth, and they have no partnership in either of them; nor is any of them[711] a helper to Him."

Intercession will not avail with Him except for him whom He gave permission; until fear is lifted from their hearts, then they will say: "What has your Lord said?", they will say: "The truth, and He is the All-High, the Great One."

Say: "Who provides for you out of the heavens and the earth?", say: "Allah, and you or we are either rightly guided or in manifest error."

710. *Sadd al-'Arim* (following the break of the Ma'rib Dam in Yemen).
711. The associates of the idolaters.

25 Say: "You will not be questioned about our misdeeds and we will not be questioned about what you do."

Say: "Our Lord shall bring us together and judge between us rightly. He is the All-Knowing Judge."

Say: "Show me those you have attached to Him as associates. Allah is rather the All-Mighty, the All-Wise."

We have not sent you but to the whole of mankind, as a warner. Yet most people do not know.

They say: "When will this promise be fulfilled, if you are truthful?"

30 Say: "You have the appointment of a day from which you shall not be delayed nor advanced a single hour."

The unbelievers say: "We will never believe in this Qur'an, nor in what came before it." If you could only see when the wrongdoers are arrayed before their Lord, each one reproaching the other, the downtrodden saying to the arrogant: "But for you, we would have been believers."

The arrogant will say to the downtrodden: "Did we really bar you from the guidance after it came to you? No, you were rather ungodly."

Then the downtrodden will say to the arrogant: "It was rather your cunning night and day, when you commanded us to disbelieve in Allah and assign equals to Him." They will be secretly remorseful, when they see the punishment. We will put shackles round the necks of the unbelievers; will they be rewarded but for what they used to do?

We never sent forth a warner to a city but the extravagant in it said: "We disbelieve in the message you have been sent with."

35 They say: "We have more abundant wealth and children and we will not be punished."

Say: "Indeed, my Lord expands the provision to whomever He wishes and restricts it; but most people do not know."

It is not your wealth or your children that bring you closer to Us, but it is he who believes and does the righteous deed. To those will be meted out the double reward and in the lofty chambers they shall be secure.

But those who go around challenging Our signs – those will be summoned to the punishment.

Say: "It is my Lord who expands the provision to whomever of His Servants He wishes and restricts it. Anything you spend, He will replace it. He is the best Provider."

40 On the day that He will muster them, then say to the angels: "Are those the ones who used to worship you?"

They will say: "Glory be to You; You are our Protector, apart from them." No, rather, they used to worship the *jinn*, most of them believing in them.

Today, none of them has the power to profit or harm the other, and We will say to the wrongdoer: "Taste the punishment of the Fire which you used to question."

And when Our signs are recited to them clearly, they say: "This is only a man who wishes to bar you from what your fathers used to worship." They also say: "This is nothing but a fabricated falsehood"; and the unbelievers say of the Truth when it comes to them: "This is nothing but manifest sorcery."

We did not bring them heretofore any Books to study and we did not send them before you[712] any warner.

45　Those who preceded them denounced the messengers, although they had not attained the tenth of what we gave them; yet they denounced My messengers as liars. How, then, was My wrath?

Say: "I only give you one exhortation, that you arise for Allah in couples and singly, then to reflect that there is no madness in your companion.[713] He is merely a warner on the eve of a terrible punishment."

Say: "Whatever wage I asked you for is yours [to give]. My wage is with Allah and He is a witness of everything."

Say: "My Lord hurls down the truth. He is the knower of the Unseen."

Say: "The Truth has come. Falsehood neither originates nor brings back anything."

50　Say: "If I go astray, I only go astray to my loss; but if I am guided, it is merely by reason of what my Lord reveals to me. He is All-Hearing, All-Nigh."

If you could see how they were terrified. There was no escape, and they were seized from afar.

And they say: "We believe in it", but whence can they attain it[714] from afar?

They have already disbelieved in Him and they speculate about the Unseen from a far-off place.

And they were barred from what they desired, as was done with their ilk before. Indeed, they were in disturbing doubt.

712. Muhammad.
713. The Prophet.
714. The belief.

SURA 35

Fatir, The Originator of Creation

In the Name of Allah, the Compassionate, the Merciful

1 Praise be to Allah, Originator of the heavens and the earth, Who appointed the angels as messengers, having wings twofold, threefold and fourfold. He increases the creation, as He wills. Allah, indeed, has power over everything.

Whatever mercy Allah accords to mankind, none will be able to withhold; and whatever He withholds, none will be able to release thereafter. He is the All-Mighty, the All-Wise.

O people, remember Allah's grace upon you. Is there a creator other than Allah, providing for you from heaven and earth? There is no god but He; how then will you be diverted?

If they denounce you as a liar, surely they have denounced other messengers before you; and unto Allah all matters shall be returned.

5 O people, Allah's promise is true, so do not let the present life delude you and do not let the Deceiver[715] delude you concerning Allah.

Satan is an enemy of yours, so regard him as an enemy. He only calls upon his partisans that they may be companions of the Blazing Fire.

Those who disbelieve will incur a terrible punishment and those who believe and do the righteous deeds will earn forgiveness and a great wage.

What of him whose evil work was made attractive to him and so he regarded it as fair? Allah surely leads astray [whomever] He wishes and guides [whomever] He wishes; so do not let your soul waste away in regrets for them. Allah is fully aware of what they do.

It is Allah who looses the wind, so as to stir up clouds; then We drive them towards a dead land, reviving the earth therewith after it was dead. Such is the Resurrection!

10 Whoever wishes glory, it is to Allah that the glory utterly belongs. Unto Him good words ascend and the righteous deed uplifts it. Those who contrive evil deeds will incur terrible punishment and the contriving of these will come to grief.

Allah created you from dust, then from a sperm, then made you into couples. No female bears or gives birth, save with His knowledge, and no man advances in years or his life-span is diminished, except as ordained in a Book. That indeed is an easy matter for Allah.

---

715. Satan.

The two seas are not the same; one is sweet, clear and delectable to drink and the other is salty and bitter. Yet from both you eat tender flesh and extract ornaments which you wear, and you see the ships cruising therein, that you may seek His bounty, and that perchance you may be thankful.

He causes the night to phase into the day and the day to phase into the night and He has subjected the sun and the moon, each running for an appointed term. That is Allah, your Lord to Whom belongs the dominion, whereas those you call upon, apart from Him, do not possess a date's crust.

If you call upon them, they do not hear your call; and were they to hear they will not answer you. On the Day of Resurrection they will repudiate your idolatry. None will inform you like the well-informed One.

5   O people, it is you who have need of Allah, whereas Allah is the All-Sufficient, Praiseworthy One.

If He wishes, He will annihilate you and bring forth a new creation.

That for Allah is not a grave matter.

No laden soul shall bear the burden of another; and if a heavy-burdened soul calls for its burden to be borne, not a whit of it will be borne, not even by one who is a kinsman. You[716] only warn those who fear their Lord although He is unseen, and who perform the prayer. He who purifies himself purifies himself for his own good, and unto Allah is the ultimate return.

The blind and seeing man are not alike.

0   Nor dark shadows or light;

Nor shade and torrid heat.

Nor are the living and the dead alike. Allah makes whomever He wishes to hear, but you will not make those in their graves hear.

You are only a warner.

We have sent you forth in truth as a bearer of good news and a warner. There is no nation to whom a warner has not come and gone.

5   If they denounce you as a liar, those before them have also denounced; their messenger came to them with clear proofs, with scriptures and the illuminating Book.

Then I seized the unbelievers; how then was My wrath!

Have you not seen how Allah sends water down from the sky, and then We bring forth thereby fruits of diverse hues. And of the mountains there are lanes, white and red, of diverse hues, and some pitch dark.

And of people, beasts and cattle, some are of diverse hues also.

Indeed, of His servants, only the learned fear Allah. Allah is All-Mighty, All-Forgiving.

716. The reference is to the Prophet.

30 Surely, those who recite the Book of Allah, perform the prayer and spend of what we provided for them, secretly and publicly, may hope for a trade which does not slacken.

That He might pay them their wages and increase them from His bounty; He is indeed All-Forgiving, All-Thankful.

What We have revealed to you of the Book is the truth, confirming what preceded it. Allah is Well-Informed about His servants, All-Seeing.

Then We bequeathed the Book upon those servants We chose; but some of them wrong themselves, some are lukewarm and some are forerunners in good deeds, by Allah's leave. That truly is the great distinction.

Into Gardens of Eden they enter, wherein they are adorned with gold bracelets and pearls and their clothing therein will be silk.

35 They say: "Praise be to Allah Who lifted off our sorrow. Our Lord is indeed All-Forgiving, All-Thankful.

"He who out of His bounty has made us dwell in the Abode of Everlasting Life, where no fatigue will touch us, nor any weariness."

But the unbelievers shall have the Fire of Hell, wherein they will not be finished off and die, nor will its punishment be lightened for them. Thus We will reward every thankless person.

Therein they will cry out: "Our Lord, bring us out and we will do the righteous deed, differently from what we used to do." Did we not prolong your life sufficiently for him to remember who is apt to remember? The warner came to you, so taste now. The wrongdoers shall have no supporter.

Surely, Allah knows the unseen of the heavens and the earth. He knows fully the secrets within the breasts.

40 It is He who made you successors in the lands. Then he who disbelieves, his unbelief will recoil upon him; and their unbelief will only increase the unbelievers in contempt in the sight of their Lord. No, their unbelief will only increase the unbelievers in perdition.

Say: "Have you seen your associates upon whom you call, apart from Allah? Show me what they have created on earth? Do they have any share in the heavens, or have We given them a Book, so that they are in possession of a clear proof therein? In fact, the wrongdoers only promise each other vanity."

Allah holds the heavens and the earth firmly lest they become displaced; were they displaced, none will hold them together after Him. He is indeed Clement, All-Forgiving.

They swore their most earnest oaths that if a warner came to them they would surely be more rightly guided than a certain nation.[717] But when a warner came to them, that only increased their aversion.

717. The Jewish or Christian nation.

Out of arrogance in the land and evil cunning. Yet the evil cunning will only recoil upon its perpetrators. Do they then look to anything other than the way of the ancients? For you will never find any alteration of Allah's way, and you will never find any deflecting of Allah's way.

45 Have they not travelled in the land to see what was the fate of those who came before them and were even mightier than they? Nothing in the heavens or the earth can thwart Allah; He is indeed All-Knowing, All-Powerful.

Were Allah to take men to task for what they have earned, He would not have left upon the face of the earth a single creature that crawls; but He defers them unto an appointed term. Then, when their term arrives, Allah is surely fully conversant with His servants.

SURA 36

Ya Sin

In the Name of Allah, the Compassionate, the Merciful

Ya, Sin.[718]

1   By the wise Qur'an.
You are truly one of the messengers.
Upon a straight path.
It is the revelation of the All-Mighty, the Merciful.

5   To warn a people, whose fathers were not warned and so they are heedless.
The sentence has been passed against most of them, for they do not believe.
We have placed shackles upon their necks down to their chins; and so their heads are held high.
And We placed in front of them a barrier and behind them a barrier, and We have covered their eyes so they do not see.
It is the same whether you warn them or do not warn them, they will not believe.

10   You only warn him who follows the Reminder and fears the All-Compassionate secretly. Announce to him, then, the good news of forgiveness and a generous wage.
It is We who bring the dead back to life and write down what they have advanced and their vestiges too. Everything we have enumerated in a clear Master Register.[719]
And relate to them the case of the people of the city, when the messengers came thereto.
When We sent them two men, but they denounced them as liars, and so We reinforced them with a third. Then they said: "We are indeed messengers unto you."
They said: "You are only mortals like ourselves and the All-Compassionate has not sent down anything. You are only lying."

15   They said: "Our Lord knows that We are indeed messengers unto you.
"And it is up to us to deliver the Manifest Message."
They said: "We augur ill of you. If you will not desist, we will stone you and a very painful punishment from us will afflict you."

718. Ya, Sin came to be one of the Prophet's names.
719. The reference is to *Umm al-Kitab* or *al-Lawh al-Mahfuz*, the original and eternal codex of the Qur'an in heaven.

They said: "Your bird of omen is with you, if you are reminded, but, you are an extravagant people."

Then a man came from the farthest point of the city. He said: "My people, follow the messengers.

20 "Follow those who do not ask you for a wage and are rightly guided.

"And why should I not worship Him who created me and unto Him you shall be returned?

"Shall I take, apart from Him, gods whose intercession, should the All-Compassionate wish me ill, will not avail me anything and they will not deliver me?

"Then, I am truly in manifest error.

"I have believed in your Lord, so listen to me."

25 It was said: "Enter Paradise." He said: "I wished my own people knew;

"About my Lord's forgiving me and making me one of the favoured."

After him, We sent down no troops from heaven; nor would We ever send any down.

It was only one cry; and behold they were silenced.

Woe betide the servants; no messenger comes to them but they mock him.

30 Have they not seen how many generations before them We destroyed and that unto them they will not return?

And all of them will be brought before Us?

A sign unto them is the dead land, that We revived and brought out of it grain, from which they eat.

And We caused to grow in it gardens of palms and vines, and caused springs to gush forth therein.

That they might eat from its fruit, although their hands brought it not out. Will they not, then, give thanks?

35 Glory be to Him Who created all the pairs of what the earth brings forth, of their own kinds and of what they know not.

And a sign unto them is the night, from which We strip off the day; and lo, they are in darkness.

And the sun runs unto its fixed station. That is the decree of the All-Mighty, the All-Knowing.

And the moon, We have determined its phases, until it became like an old twig.

The sun ought not to overtake the moon, nor the night outstrip the day; and each in its orbit is floating.

40 And a sign unto them is that We carried their progeny in the laden Ark.

And We created for them the like of it that which they could board.

And if We wish, We would drown them; then there is none to deliver them, nor will they be rescued.

Except for a mercy from Us and enjoyment for a while.

If it is said to them: "Beware what came before you and what is behind you, that perchance you might receive mercy."

45   Yet, no sign of their Lord's signs comes to them but they turn away from it.

And if it is said to them: "Spend freely from what Allah provided for you, the unbelievers say to the believers: 'Shall we feed him whom Allah would have fed, if He wished. You are only in manifest error?' "

And they say: "When is this promise coming, if you are truthful?"

They are only awaiting a single cry to seize them, while they are feuding.

So they cannot make a testament nor return to their own people.

50   And the Trumpet is blown, then behold how from their graves, unto their Lord, they slink away.

They will say: "Woe betide us; whoever has roused us from our sleep? This is what the All-Compassionate has promised, and the messengers have spoken the truth."

It was only a single cry, and behold they were all brought before Us.

So, today no soul shall be wronged a whit, and you will only be rewarded for what you used to do.

Today, the Companions of Paradise are busy enjoying themselves;

55   Together with their spouses they are reclining on couches in the shade.

Wherein they have fruit, and have all they call for.

"Peace", uttered by a merciful Lord.

"Be singled out today, O criminals.

"Did I not exhort you, O Children of Adam, not to worship Satan? For he is a manifest enemy of yours.

60   "And worship Me; for this is a straight path.

"He has surely led astray numerous generations of you. Did you not understand, then?

"This, then, is Hell which you were promised.

"Burn in it today for what you used to disbelieve."

Today, We set a seal upon their mouths, and their hands will speak to Us and their feet will bear witness, regarding what they used to earn.

65   And had We wished, We would have blotted out their eyes. Then they would race upon the pathway but how will they see?

And had We wished, We would have deformed them upon their own seats, so that they could not take off or turn back.

Whoever We grant old age, We would cause to shrink in form. Do they not understand, then?

We did not teach him[720] poetry, nor did it become him. It is only a Reminder and a Manifest Qur'an;

So as to warn those who are alive and the word may be fulfilled against the unbelievers.

0 Have they not seen that We have created for them, of Our handiwork, cattle whereof they are now the owners?

And We subdued them to them, so that of some are their mounts and of some they eat.

And from them they have many benefits and beverages. Will they not, then, give thanks?

Yet, they have taken, apart from Allah, other gods that they might receive support.

But they cannot support them, although they are arrayed as troops for them.

5 Do not let their words cause you grief; We know what they reveal and what they conceal.

Does not man see that We created him from a sperm; and behold he is a manifest trouble-maker?

And he produced an equal for us, forgetting Our creating him. He said: "Who brings the bones back to life, once they are withered?"

Say: "He who originated them the first time will bring them back to life and He has knowledge of every creation."

It is He who produces fire from green trees for you; and behold you are kindling flames from it.

0 Is not He who created the heavens and the earth able, then, to create the like of them? Yes, indeed, and He is the All-Knowing Creator.

His command is indeed such that if He wills a thing, He says to it: "Be", and it comes to be.

Glory, then, to Him in Whose hands is the dominion of everything and unto Whom you will be returned.

---

720. The Prophet.

Al-Saffat, The Rangers

In the Name of Allah, the Compassionate, the Merciful

1 By the rangers ranged in rows;
By the reprovers reproving;
By the reciters of a Reminder;
Your God is surely One,
5 The Lord of the heavens and the earth and what lies between them, Lord of the Orients.
We have adorned the lower sky with the ornament of the planets,
To guard against every rebellious devil.
They do not listen to the Higher Assembly and are pelted from every side;
Expelled; and theirs is a lasting punishment.
10 Except for him who eavesdropped once; and so a shooting star followed him.
So ask them: "Are they mightier in constitution than those We have created?" We have actually created them from sticky clay.
You rather wonder, while they mock.
If they are reminded, they will not remember.
And if they see a sign, they simply scoff.
15 And they say: "This is only manifest sorcery.
"What! Once we are dead and turn into dust and bones, shall we be raised from the dead?
"Or our forefathers?"
Say: "Yes, and you will be totally subdued."
It is only one shout, and behold, they are watching.
20 And they say: "Woe betide us, this is the Day of Judgement.
"This is the Day of Decision which we used to question."
Gather together those who were wrongdoers, their spouses and what they used to worship;
Apart from Allah, and lead them to the path of Hell.
And arrest them for they are accountable.
25 Why is it you do not support each other?
Instead, today they have surrendered.
And some of them turned to one another asking.
They said: "You used to come to us from the right."

They said: "No, you were no believers.

30 "And we had no authority over you; for you were an aggressive people.

"And thus the punishment of our Lord was meted out to us; therefore we are surely tasting it.

"So, We misled you, being misled ourselves."

Therefore, they are on that day partners in punishment.

This is how We treat the criminals.

35 For when it used to be said to them: "There is no god but Allah", they would wax proud.

And they would say: "Are we going to forsake our gods for the sake of a poet possessed?"

Indeed, he brought the truth and confirmed the other messengers.

You shall indeed taste the painful punishment.

And you shall only be rewarded for what you used to do.

40 Except for Allah's sincere servants.

To those is assigned a fixed provision,

Of fruits; and they shall be honoured;

In the Gardens of Bliss;

Upon couches, facing each other.

45 A cup of pure spring water shall be passed around them;

Snow-white, a delight to drinkers.

Wherein there is no gall and they are not intoxicated by it.

And they also shall have wide-eyed maidens averting their gaze.

They resemble hidden pearls.

50 Then, they will advance one towards the other asking each other.

One of them will say: "I had a comrade;

"Who used to say: 'Are you then one of the confirmed believers?'

"Will we, once we are dead and have become dust and bones, be really judged?"

He said:[721] "Are you looking down?"

55 He looked and saw him in the centre of Hell.

He said: "By Allah, you almost caused my perdition.

"But for my Lord's grace, I would have been one of those brought forward.

"Are we not then going to die,

"Except for our first death? And will we not be punished?"

60 Surely, this is the great triumph.

For the like of this, let the workers work.

Is that a better outcome or the Tree of Bitterness?

---

721. To his companions.

We have made it a temptation for the wrongdoers.
It is a tree that grows out of the bottom of Hell;
65   Its shoots are like the heads of devils.
They shall eat from it till they fill their bellies.
In addition, they have with it a mixture of boiling water.
Then, their return is unto Hell.
Indeed, they found their fathers steeped in error.
70   And so they are fast following in their footsteps.
And before them, most of the ancients were in error.
We had sent forth from them some warners.
But behold what was the fate of those who were warned.
Except for Allah's sincere servants.
75   Noah called Us in times past; blessed then are the Answerers.
We delivered him and his people from the great calamity.
And made his progeny the survivors.
And We bequeathed to him, among those who succeeded:
"Peace upon Noah among all the nations."
80   Indeed, this is how We reward the beneficent.
He was truly one of Our believing servants.
Then, We drowned the others.
And of his partisans was Abraham.
When he came to his Lord with a sound heart.
85   He said to his father and his own people: "What are you worshipping?
"Do you desire, falsely, other gods, apart from Allah?
"What do you think, then, of the Lord of the Worlds?"
Then he cast a glance at the stars.
And said: "I am really sick."
90   Whereupon, they turned away from him in flight.
And he turned towards their gods, saying: "Will you not eat?
"Why do you not speak?"
Then, he proceeded to hit them with his right hand.
Then, [his people] came towards him in haste.
95   He said: "Do you worship what you hew?
"When Allah created you and what you do?"
They said: "Build him a pyre"; and so they cast him into the furnace.
They wished him ill, but We reduced them to the lowest rung.
And he said: "I am going to my Lord; He will guide me.
100   "Lord, grant me a righteous child."
So, We announced to him the good news of a prudent boy.
Then, when he attained the age of consorting with him, he said: "My
son, I have seen in sleep that I am slaughtering you. See what you think."

He said: "My father, do what you are commanded; you will find me, Allah willing, one of the steadfast."

Then, when they both submitted and he flung him down upon his brow;
And We called out to him: "O Abraham,
105 "You have believed the vision. Thus We rewarded the beneficent.
"This, indeed, is the manifest calamity."
And We ransomed him with a large sacrifice.
And We left with him for later generations:
"Peace be upon Abraham."
110 Thus, We reward the beneficent.
He is indeed one of Our believing servants.
And we announced to him the good news of Isaac as a prophet, one of the righteous.
And We blessed him and blessed Isaac; and of their progeny some are beneficent and some are wronging themselves manifestly.
And We have favoured Moses and Aaron;
115 And delivered them and their people from the great calamity.
And We supported them, and so they were the victors.
And We gave them both the clarifying Book.
And We guided them unto the straight path.
And We left with them both for later generations:
120 "Peace upon Moses and Aaron."
Thus We reward the beneficent.
They are indeed among Our believing servants.
And Elias[722] too was one of the messengers.
When he said to his people: "Do you not fear God?
125 "Do you call upon Baal,[723] forsaking the Best of Creators,
"Allah, your Lord and the Lord of your forefathers?"
But they denounced him as a liar; and behold, they shall be brought forward.
Except for Our sincere servants.
And We left with him for the later generations:
130 "Peace be upon the family of Elias."
Thus, We reward the beneficent.
He is one of Our believing servants.
And Lot was one of the messengers.
When We delivered him and his whole family,
135 Except for an old woman who was among the lost.
Then We destroyed the others.

722. The biblical prophet Elijah.
723. The Phoenician god of fertility.

And you pass by them in the morning,
And at night. Do you not understand, then?
And Jonas was one of the messengers.
140   When he fled towards the laden Ark.
He cast lots, but was one of the losers.
Then the whale swallowed him, and he was to blame.
Had he not been one of those who glorified [Allah];
He would have stayed in its belly until the day they will be resuscitated.
145   Then We cast him out in the wilderness while he was sick.
And made to grow over him a gourd tree.
And We sent him forth to a hundred thousand or more.
They believed, and so We accorded them enjoyment for a while.
Ask them: "Are the daughters your Lord's, and theirs the sons?
150   "Or have We created the angels as females, while they were witnesses?"
It is out of their perversion that they will say:
"Allah has begotten", but they are liars.
Has He preferred the daughters over the sons?
What is the matter with you; how do you judge?
155   Do you not remember?
Or do you have manifest authority?
Produce your Book, if you are truthful.
And they alleged between Him and the *jinn* a kinship, whereas the *jinn*
know very well that they will be summoned.
May Allah be exalted above their allegation.
160   Except for Allah's sincere servants.
Surely, neither you nor what you worship,
Against Him can ever turn anyone;
Except he who will be roasting in Hell.
No one of us has a well-known station.
165   And we are indeed the rangers.[724]
And we are those who glorify.
Even though they might say:
"If we had been given a Reminder from the ancients,
"We would have been among Allah's sincere servants."
170   Then, they disbelieved in it.[725] Surely, they will learn.
Our Word unto Our messengers has already gone out.
"They will surely be supported.
"And Our hosts are the true victors.
"So, turn away from them for a while.

724. The reference in verses 163 and 164 is to the angels.
725. The Qur'an.

75 "And look at them; they shall soon be able to see."

Are they seeking to hasten Our punishment?

When it descends upon their backyard, wretched is the morning of those forewarned!

And turn away from them for a while.

And look, for they shall soon be able to see.

80 Exulted be your Lord, the Lord of Glory, above their allegation.

And peace be upon the messengers.

And praise to Allah, the Lord of the Worlds.

SURA 38

Saad

In the Name of Allah, the Compassionate, the Merciful

Saad.[726]

1 By the Qur'an which contains the Reminder.

But the unbelievers are steeped in arrogance and strife.

How many a generation We have destroyed before them? They called out, but time was past escaping.

They marvelled that a warner has come to them from their own, and the unbelievers said: "This is a lying sorcerer.

5 "What, has he made the gods one single God? This, indeed is a very strange thing."

And the dignitaries among them went forth saying: "Go on and be steadfast regarding your gods. This indeed is a matter premeditated.

"We have not heard about this in the latest religion.[727] This is only a mere invention.

"Has the Reminder been sent down upon him alone, apart from us all?" Indeed, they are in doubt regarding My Reminder. But, they have not yet tasted My punishment.

Or, do they possess the treasuries of your Lord's mercy, the All-Mighty, the All-Giving.

10 Or do they have the dominion of the heavens and the earth? Let them, then, ascend its rungs.

A host of the Confederates will be defeated there.

Before them, the people of Noah, 'Ad, Pharaoh of the Pegs;[728]

And Thamud; as well as the Companions of the Thicket,[729] all those factions denounced.

None of them but denounced the messengers, and so My retribution struck them.

15 These are only awaiting a single cry which will not cease.

They say: "Our Lord, hasten for us our share before the Day of Reckoning."

Bear patiently with what they say and remember Our servant, David, the mighty one; he was a true penitent.

---

726. One of three Suras which open with one symbolic letter only.
727. Christianity.
728. A metaphor for power or grandeur.
729. Mentioned four times in the Qur'an, they are probably the people of Madyan.

We have subjected the mountains together with him, to glorify in the evening and at daybreak;

And the birds were mustered; everything returning unto Him.

20   And We strengthened his kingdom and gave him wisdom and the decisive speech.

Have you heard the news of the enemy when they scaled the sanctuary?

When they entered upon David and he was afraid of them. They said: "Do not fear. We are two adversaries, one of us encroached on the other unjustly; so judge between us with justice and do not transgress, and guide us to the straight path.

"This is my brother, who has ninety-nine ewes and I have only one. So he said: 'Let me take charge of it,' and he overcame me in the argument."

He[730] said: "He has wronged you by asking for your ewe on top of his ewes. Indeed, many partners have encroached one on the other, except for those who believe and do the righteous deeds; and how few they are?" David thought that We had tried him, so he asked forgiveness from his Lord and fell down on his knees and repented.

25   So, We forgave him that. Indeed, he has a close relationship with Us and a fair recourse.

O David, We have appointed you a vicegerent on earth; so judge justly among men and do not follow your fancy, lest it lead you away from the path of Allah. Indeed those who lead others away from the path of Allah will have a terrible punishment, because they have forgotten the Day of Reckoning.

We have not created the heaven and the earth and what is between them in vain. That is the presumption of the unbelievers; so woe betide the unbelievers because of the Fire.

Or shall We regard those who believe and do the righteous deeds like those who work corruption in the land, or shall We regard the God-fearing like the transgressors?

It is a Blessed Book that We have sent down to you, that they may ponder its verses, and that those possessed of understanding may remember.

30   And We granted David, Solomon, a blessed servant. Indeed, he was penitent.

When the light-footed horses were presented to him in the evening,

He said: "I have preferred the love of earthly good to the mention of My Lord, till the sun disappeared behind the veil."

730. David. A possible reference to Nathan's report of a dispute he submitted to David. cf II *Samuel*, 12.

"Bring them back to me." Then he proceeded to wipe their shanks and necks.

And We tried Solomon and cast upon his throne a dead body; then he repented.

35 He said: "Lord, forgive me and grant me a kingdom that no one after me will deserve; you are indeed the All-Giver."

So, We subjected the wind unto him, to blow at his command softly, wherever he wished;

And of the demons every builder and diver;

And others shackled in fetters.

"This is Our bounty; so give or withhold without account."

40 And he has to Us a close relationship and a fair recourse.

And remember Our servant Job when he called out to his Lord: "Satan has visited me with weariness and torture."

"Stamp with your foot, and behold, here is a cool washing-place, and water to drink."

And We granted to him his family and the like of them also, as a mercy from Us and a reminder to people of understanding.

"And take with your hand a bundle of twigs and strike with it, and do not break your oath." We have indeed found him steadfast, a blessed servant. He was truly penitent.

45 And remember Our servants, Abraham, Isaac and Jacob, men of might and perception.

We have favoured them with the pure trait of remembering the Abode.[731]

They are surely for Us among the well-chosen, the pious.

And remember Isma'il, Elias and Dhu'l-Kifl; each was one of the pious.

This is a Reminder and the God-fearing will surely have a fair resort.

50 Gardens of Eden whereof the gates are wide-open for them.

Reclining therein and calling for abundant fruit and beverage.

And they have mates of equal age, averting their gaze.

"This is what you are promised for the Day of Reckoning.

"This is Our provision which will not end.

55 "That is that, but the aggressors shall have the worst resort.

"Hell, in which they roast. Wretched is their couch!

"That, let them taste it, as boiling water and pus.

"And another, of the same kind, manifold.

"This is another throng marching with you; no welcome to them, they will roast in the Fire."

60 They say: "No welcome to you; you have offered it to us in advance, and what a wretched resting-place!"

---

731. Paradise.

They say: "Our Lord, whoever has offered this to us, multiply his punishment in the Fire."

And they say: "What is it with us that we do not see men here we used to reckon among the wicked?

"We took them for a laughing-stock, or have our eyes been diverted away from them?"

This is perfectly true, the feuding of the people of the Fire.

65 Say: "I am only a warner and there is no god but Allah, the One, the Conqueror.

"The Lord of the heavens and the earth and what is between them, the All-Mighty, the All-Forgiving."

Say: "It is great news,

"From which you are turning away.

"I had no knowledge of the Higher Host, when they were disputing among themselves.

70 "It is only revealed to me that I am a manifest warner.

"When your Lord said to the angels: 'I am going to create a mortal out of clay.

"'When I have fashioned him and breathed into him of My spirit, fall prostrate before him.'"

Then all the angels prostrated themselves entirely;

Except for Iblis; he waxed proud and was one of the unbelievers.

75 He said: "O Iblis, what prevented you from prostrating yourself before what I created with My own hands? Have you waxed proud or were you one of the exalted?"

He said: "I am better than he; you created me from fire and you created him from clay."

He said: "Get out of here;[732] you are truly accursed.

"And My curse shall pursue you till the Day of Judgement."

He said: "Lord, give me respite till the day they shall be resuscitated."

80 He said: "You are one of those respited,

"Till the day of the well-known time."

He said: "By Your glory, I will seduce them all,

"Except for your sincere servants among them."

He said: "Truly, and I say the truth;

85 "I will fill Hell with you and those of them who follow you all together."

Say: "I ask you no wage for it and I am not one of those who pretend.

"It is only a Reminder to mankind.

"And you will learn its message after a while."

732. Paradise.

Al-Zumar, The Throngs

In the Name of Allah, the Compassionate, the Merciful

1 The sending down of the Book is from Allah, the All-Mighty, the Wise.
We have, indeed, sent down the Book to you in truth; so worship Allah professing the religion sincerely to Him.

Sincere religion truly belongs to Allah. Those who took other protectors, apart from Him, say: "We only worship them so as to bring us closer to Allah in rank. Allah surely judges between them with respect to what they differ upon. Allah surely does not guide him who is a thankless liar.

Had Allah wanted to take to Himself a child, He would have chosen from what He has created whomever He pleases. Glory be to Him; He is Allah, the One, the Conqueror.

5 He created the heavens and the earth in truth. He wraps up the night around the day and He wraps up the day around the night. He has subjected the sun and the moon, each running for an appointed term. He is indeed the All-Mighty, the All-Forgiving.

He created You from a single soul; then, out of it, He made its mate, and brought down for you of the cattle eight pairs. He creates you in your mothers' bellies, one creation after another, in three shadows of darkness. That indeed is Allah, your Lord. His is the dominion; there is no god but He. How, then, are you diverted?

If you disbelieve, Allah does not need you, although He does not approve disbelief in His servants. However, if you give thanks, He will approve that in you. No sinning soul shall bear the burden of another. Then unto your Lord is your return and He will tell you what you used to do. He knows the secrets within the breasts.

If some adversity touches man, He will call upon his Lord, repenting unto Him; then, if He confers on him a grace of His, he forgets what he was calling for before that and assigns equals to Allah, so as to lead others astray from His path. Say: "Enjoy your disbelief a little; for you are truly one of the Companions of the Fire."

Is he who worships devoutly in the watches of the night, prostrating himself and standing up, fears the Hereafter and hopes for the mercy of his Lord [like unto the other]? Say: "Are those who know and those who do not know alike?" Only those possessed of understanding will remember.

10   Say: "O My servants who have believed, fear your Lord. Those who have been bounteous in this world will have a bounty, and Allah's earth is vast. The steadfast will be paid their wages in full, without reckoning."

Say: "I have been commanded to worship Allah, professing to Him the religion sincerely.

"And I have been commanded to be the first of those who submit."

Say: "I fear; if I disobey my Lord, the punishment of a great day."

Say: "Allah alone I worship professing to Him my religion sincerely.

15   "Worship, then, what you wish, apart from Him." Say: "Indeed, those who have lost themselves and their families on the Day of Resurrection are the real losers. That is truly the manifest loss."

They shall have over them awnings of fire and under them other awnings. That is what Allah frightens His servants with: "O My servants fear Me, then."

Those who shunned the worship of idols and turned in repentance unto Allah, theirs is the good news. "Announce, then, the good news to My servants."

Those who hear the Word and follow the fairest of it; those are the ones whom Allah has guided and those are the people of understanding!

He upon whom the word of punishment has been uttered, are you able to deliver from the Fire?

20   But those who fear their Lord will have chambers over which other chambers are built and beneath which the rivers flow. That is Allah's promise. Allah does not break His promise.

Have you not seen that Allah has sent down water from heaven, then threaded it as springs in the ground. Then He brings out vegetation of various hues through it. Then it withers, and you see it looking yellow; then He turns it into scraps. In that, there surely is a reminder to people of understanding.

Now, what of one whose breast Allah has dilated unto Islam, so that he basks in light from his Lord? Woe betide then the hard-hearted, upon Allah's mention. Those are in manifest error.

Allah has sent down the fairest discourse as a Book, both insistent and corroboratory, from which the skins of those who fear their Lord shiver. Then their skins and hearts mellow at the mention of Allah. That is the guidance of Allah whereby He guides whomever He wishes; and he whom Allah leads astray will have no other guide.

Is he who wards off with his face the evil punishment on the Day of Resurrection? And it is said then to the wrongdoers: "Taste what you used to earn."

25   Those who preceded them denounced as liars [the messengers], whereupon punishment afflicted them from whence they did not know.

And so Allah made them taste disgrace in the present life; but the punishment of the Hereafter is surely greater, if only they knew.

We have given mankind every kind of parable in this Qur'an, that perchance they might remember.

We made it an Arabic Qur'an without any defect that perchance they might be God-fearing.

Allah has given as a parable a man owned by partners who are at odds and a man owned exclusively by one man. Are they equal in status? Praise be to Allah, but most of them do not know.

30   You are mortal and they are mortal too.

Then on the Day of Resurrection, you shall appear before your Lord defending yourself.

Who, then, is more unjust than one who imputes lies to Allah and denounces the Truth as a lie when he hears it? Is not in Hell an abode for the unbelievers?

But he who brings the Truth and believes in it – those are the true God-fearing people.

They shall have what they wish from their Lord. That is the reward of the beneficent.

35   That Allah might remit their worst deeds and reward them their due according to the fairest deeds they used to do.

Does not Allah suffice His servant? Yet they frighten you with those apart from Him.[733] Whomever Allah leads astray will have no other guide.

And whomever Allah guides none will lead astray. Is not Allah All-Mighty, Vengeful?

If you ask them: "Who has created the heavens and the earth?", they will reply: "Allah." Say: "Do you see, then? What you call upon, apart from Allah, should Allah wish me ill, will they lift His ill? Or should Allah will a mercy for me, will they withhold His mercy?" Say: "Allah suffices for me. In Him those who trust should put their trust."

Say: "My people, act according to your ability. I am acting; then you will know.

40   "Whoever is visited by punishment will be degraded by it and a lasting punishment will befall him."

We have sent the Book upon you for all mankind in truth. He who is well-guided is guided to his own gain, and he who goes astray, will go astray to his loss. You are not their overseer.

Allah carries off the souls of men upon their death and the souls of those who are not dead in their sleep. He then holds back those whose death He

---

733. That is, idols.

has decreed and releases the others till an appointed term. Surely, there are in that signs for a people who reflect.

Or have they taken intercessors, apart from Allah? Say: "Even if they have no power whatever and no understanding."

Say: "To Allah belongs all intercession. His is the dominion of the heavens and the earth. Then unto Him you will be returned."

45 If Allah alone is mentioned, the hearts of those who do not believe in the Hereafter shudder; but if those apart from Him are mentioned, behold, they rejoice.

Say: "O Allah, Creator of the heavens and the earth, Knower of the Unseen and the Seen, You shall judge between your servants regarding that whereon they used to differ."

Had the wrongdoers possessed all that is on earth and the like of it too, they would have redeemed therewith themselves from the terrible punishment on the Day of Resurrection, and there would have appeared to them from Allah that which they did not count on.

And there would have appeared to them the evils of what they have earned, and what they scoffed at would have afflicted them.

When an injury touches a man, He calls upon Us. Then if We accord him a bounty from Us, he says: "I have been granted it on account of some knowledge." However, it is a mere trial, but most of them do not know.

50 Thus those who preceded them have said it, but what they had earned did not avail them.

And so the evils of what they had earned smote them, and the evil-doers among these[734] will be smitten by the evils of what they earned; and they will not frustrate Us.

Did they not know that Allah expands the provision to whomever He wishes and constricts it? Surely, there are in that signs to a people who believe.

Say: "O My servants, who have been excessive against themselves: 'Do not despair of Allah's mercy; Allah remits all sins. He is indeed the All-Forgiving, the All-Clement.'

"Return to your Lord and submit to Him before punishment visits you for then you will have no support.

55 "And follow the fairest of what has been sent down to you from your Lord, before punishment visits you suddenly while you are unaware.

"Lest any soul should say: 'Woe betide me for what I have neglected of my duty to Allah and for having been one of the scoffers.'

"Or it should say: 'Had Allah guided me, I would have been one of the God-fearing.'

734. Muhammad's contemporaries.

"Or it should say, when it sees the punishment: 'If only I had a second chance, then I would be one of the beneficent'."

Yes indeed! My signs came to you, but you denounced them as lies and waxed proud and were one of the unbelievers.

60   On the Day of Resurrection, you will see those who told lies against Allah with their faces blackened. Is not there in Hell a resting-place for the arrogant?

And Allah will save the God-fearing on account of their felicitous deeds. No evil will touch them and they will not grieve.

Allah is the Creator of everything and He is the Guardian of everything.

His are the keys of the heavens and the earth; and those who have disbelieved in Allah's signs are the losers.

Say: "Do you, then, command me to worship anyone other than Allah, O ignorant ones?"

65   He has in fact revealed to you[735] and those who preceded you: "If you associate any others with Allah, He will frustrate your work and you will certainly be one of the losers."

Instead, worship Allah and be one of the thankful.

They have not recognized Allah's true measure. The whole earth shall be in His grasp and the heavens shall be rolled up in His right hand on the Day of the Resurrection. Glory be to Him, and may He be exalted above what they associate with Him.

And the Trumpet shall be blown, so that whoever is in the heavens or on earth shall be made to expire, save him whom Allah wishes. Then it shall be blown another time, and behold, they shall arise, looking out.

And the earth shall shine with the light of its Lord and the Book shall be laid down. Then, the prophets and the witnesses shall be brought forward, and judgement shall be passed justly between them, and they shall not be wronged.

70   Every soul shall be paid in full for what it has done, and He knows best what they do.

And the unbelievers shall be driven to Hell in throngs; so that when they have reached it, its gates will be opened and its keepers will say to them: "Have not messengers from your own people come to you reciting to you the revelations of your Lord and warning you against the encounter of this your day?" They will say: "Yes, indeed"; but the word of punishment has come to pass against the unbelievers.

It will be said: "Enter the gates of Hell, dwelling therein forever. Wretched is the dwelling of the arrogant."

And those who feared their Lord will be led into Paradise in throngs.

---

735. Muhammad.

Then, when they have reached it and its gates are opened, [they will enter it] and its keepers will say: "Peace be upon you; you have fared well, so enter it to dwell therein forever."

And they will say: "Praise be to Allah who has been truthful in His promise to us and has bequeathed upon us the land, wherein we are able to settle in Paradise whenever we wish. Blessed is the wage of the labourers!"

75 And you will see the angels circling around the Throne proclaiming the praise of their Lord. And it will be justly decided between them and it will be said: "Praise be to Allah, the Lord of the Worlds."

SURA 40

'Ghafir, The Forgiver

In the Name of Allah, the Compassionate, the Merciful

Ha, Mim.

1   The sending down of the Book is from Allah, the All-Mighty, the All-Knowing.

The Forgiver of sins, Receiver of repentance, Terrible in retribution, the Bountiful. There is no god but He. Unto Him is the ultimate return.

No one disputes concerning the signs of Allah, except the unbelievers; so do not be deceived by their wandering in the lands.

Before them, the people of Noah and the Confederates after them have denounced, and each nation sallied forth against their messenger to seize him, and they disputed falsely to repudiate therewith the truth. Then I seized them. How, then, was My retribution?

5   And thus your Lord's Word against the unbelievers was fulfilled, that they are, indeed, the companions of the Fire.

Those who carry the Throne and those around it proclaim the praise of their Lord, believe in Him and ask forgiveness for the believers: "Lord, You have encompassed everything in mercy and knowledge; so forgive those who have repented and followed Your path, and guard them against the punishment of Hell.

"Lord, and admit them into the Gardens of Eden which you have promised them and those who have been righteous, of their fathers, their spouses and their progeny. You are indeed the All-Mighty, the All-Wise.

"And guard them against evil deeds. He whom you guard against evil deeds on that day, you have surely been merciful to; and that is the great triumph."

To the unbelievers it shall be announced: "Allah's contempt is greater than your self-contempt, when you were summoned to believe, but you disbelieved."

10   They will say: "Our Lord, you have caused us to be dead twice and brought us to life twice, and so we have confessed our sins. Is there now a way out?"

That is because if Allah is called upon alone, you disbelieve; but if others are associated with Him, you believe. Judgement is Allah's, the All-High, the All-Great.

It is He who shows you His signs and sends down from heaven provision for you; but only He who repents will remember.

So, call on Allah professing religion sincerely unto Him, even if the unbelievers should resent it.

Exalted in rank, Owner of the Throne, He casts the spirit by His command upon whomever of His servants He wishes, to warn of the Day of the Encounter.

15 The day on which they will emerge, nothing of theirs being concealed from Allah. "Whose is the sovereignty today?" "It is Allah's, the One, the Conqueror."

Today, every soul will be rewarded for what it has earned. There is no injustice today. Allah is surely quick in reckoning.

Warn them of the Day of Imminence, when the hearts shall come up to the throats. The wrongdoers will have then no intimate friend and no intercessor who will be heeded.

He knows what the eyes betray and what the breasts conceal.

Allah judges rightly, but those upon whom they call, apart from Him, judge of naught. Allah is the All-Hearing, the All-Seeing.

20 Have they not journeyed in the land and seen what was the ultimate fate of those who came before them? [They were mightier than they in powers and vestiges they left in the land.] Then Allah seized them because of their sins, and against Allah they had no protector.

That is because their messengers used to come to them with the clear proofs, but they disbelieved. So Allah seized them; He is indeed strong, Terrible in retribution.

We have indeed sent Moses forth with Our signs and a manifest authority,

Unto Moses, Haman and Korah[736] but they said: "A lying sorcerer."

When he brought them the Truth from Us, they said: "Slay the sons of those who have believed with him, but spare their women." However, the cunning of the unbeliever is in error.

25 And Pharaoh said: "Let me kill Moses, and let him call upon his Lord. I fear that he may change your religion and cause corruption to spread in the land."

Moses said: "I seek refuge with my Lord and your Lord from every arrogant one who does not believe in the Day of Reckoning."

Then a believing man of Pharaoh's folk, who kept hidden his belief, said: "Will you kill a man for saying: 'My Lord is Allah', and he has brought you the clear proofs from your Lord? If he is a liar, his lying will recoil upon him, but if he is truthful, you will be smitten with some of what he is promising you. Allah will not guide one who is an extravagant imposter.

"O my people, yours is the dominion today, supreme in the land; but

736. See Sura 28: 76, 79.

who will protect us against Allah's might, if it should smite us?" Pharaoh said: "I do not show you except what I see, and I do not guide except in the path of rectitude."

Then the one who had believed said: "O my people, I fear for you the like of the Day of the Confederates.

30   "Like the wont of the people of Noah, 'Ad, Thamud and those who came after them. Allah does not intend wronging the servants.

"O my people, I fear for you the Day of Altercation.

"The day you will turn away in flight, having no defender against Allah. Whomever Allah leads astray will have no one to guide him.

"Joseph brought you the clear proofs before, but you continued to doubt what he brought you. Then, when he perished you said: 'Allah will never send forth a messenger after him.' This is how Allah leads astray whoever is extravagant and suspicious.

"Those who dispute concerning Allah's signs without any authority given to them – how hateful is that in the sight of Allah and the believers. That is how Allah places a seal on the heart of every arrogant bully."

35   And Pharaoh said: "O Haman, build me a tower that I may perchance reach the pathways,

"The pathways of heaven; and then look upon the God of Moses. For I think he is a liar." That is how embellished for Pharaoh was his evil deed and how he was barred from the path. Pharaoh's guile was only destined to fail.

Then he who had believed said: "O my people, follow me and I will guide you to the path of rectitude.

"O my people, this present life is a fleeting pleasure, but the world to come is the abode of permanence.

"Whoever does an evil deed will only be rewarded its like; but whoever does a righteous deed, whether male or female, being a believer – those shall enter Paradise receiving therein provision without measure.

40   "O my people, do I call you unto salvation, while you call me unto the Fire?

"You call me to disbelieve in Allah and associate with Him that whereof I have no knowledge, while I call you unto the All-Mighty, the All-Pardoner.

"No wonder that what you call me unto has no callers in this world, nor in the Hereafter; and that our ultimate return is unto Allah; and that the extravagant are the true companions of the Fire.

"You will remember what I am saying to you. I entrust my fate to Allah. Allah is surely well aware of the servants."

Then, Allah guarded him against the evils of their scheming; and the evil punishment encompassed Pharaoh's folk;

45   The Fire to which they shall be exposed morning and evening. And the day the Hour shall come to pass, it will be said:[737] "Admit Pharaoh's folk to the worst punishment."

And while they dispute in the Fire, the weak will say to those who waxed proud: "We were followers of Yours. Will you, then, withhold from us a part of the Fire?"

Those who waxed proud will say: "We are truly all in it. Allah has judged between the servants."

Those in the Fire will say to the keepers of Hell: "Call on your Lord that He may remit a day of punishment for us."

They will reply: "Did not your messengers bring you clear proofs?" They will say: "Yes indeed." They will reply: "Call then, although the call of the unbelievers is in vain."

50   "We shall support Our messengers and the believers in the present life and on the day the witnesses shall arise;

"The day when their excuses will not profit the wrongdoers, and the curse will be upon them and they will have the worst dwelling."

We have indeed given Moses the guidance and bequeathed to the Children of Israel the Book,

As a guidance and a reminder to people of understanding.

So stand fast; Allah's promise is true. Seek the forgiveness of your sin and proclaim the praise of your Lord evenings and mornings.

55   As for those who dispute regarding Allah's signs without any authority given to them, there is nothing in their breasts but the desire for grandeur, which they will never attain. So, seek refuge with Allah; for He is surely the All-Hearing, the All-Seeing.

Surely, the creation of the heavens and the earth is greater than the creation of mankind, but most people do not know.

The blind and the seeing man are not equal; nor are those who believe and do the righteous deeds and the evil-doer. Little do you remember!

The Hour is indeed coming, no doubt about it; but most people do not believe.

Your Lord has said: "Call on Me and I will answer you. Those who are too proud to worship Me shall enter Hell totally abased."

60   It is Allah who made the night for you, to rest in it, and the day to see your way. Allah is truly bountiful to mankind, but most people do not give thanks.

That for you is Allah your Lord, Creator of everything. There is no god but He. How then are you perverted?

Thus as those who used to repudiate Allah's signs were perverted too.

737. To the angels.

It is Allah who made the earth a fixed station for you and the sky a high edifice. He fashioned you in a shapely manner and provided you with the good things. That for you is Allah, your Lord; so blessed be Allah, the Lord of the Worlds.

He is the Living One; there is no god but He. So call on Him professing sincerely the religion unto Him. Praise be to Allah, the Lord of the Worlds.

65   Say: "I have been forbidden to worship those you call upon, apart from Allah; since the clear proofs have come to me from my Lord and I have been commanded to submit to the Lord of the Worlds."

It is He who created you from dust, then from a sperm, then from a clot. Then He brings you out as infants; then allows you to come of age, then become old men. Some of you will pass away before that, but you will attain a fixed term, that perchance you might understand.

It is He who brings to life and causes to die. Then, if He decrees a certain matter, He only says to it: "Be", and it comes to be.

Have you not observed those who dispute regarding Allah's signs, how they are perverted?

Those who disbelieved in this Book and in what We sent Our messengers with; they shall surely know.

70   When the fetters and chains shall be upon their necks and they shall be dragged along.

In the boiling water; then, in the Fire they will be consumed.

Then it will be said to them: "Where are those you used to set up as associates,

"Apart from Allah?" They will say: "They strayed away from us. Indeed, we did not call upon anything formerly." Thus Allah leads the unbelievers astray.

That is because you used to rejoice on earth in what is other than the truth and because you used to frolic.

75   Enter then the gates of Hell, dwelling therein forever. Evil is the dwelling of the arrogant.

So, bear up patiently; Allah's promise is true. We will either show you[738] what We are promising them, or We will call you unto Us. Then unto Us they will be brought back.

Indeed, We have sent messengers before you. Of some We have told you the tale and of some We did not tell. It is not in any messenger's power to bring a sign, save by Allah's leave. Then, when Allah's decree comes, the issue shall be decided justly; and there and then the seekers of vanity shall perish.

---

738. Muhammad.

It is Allah who created for you the cattle, so that some you may ride and some you may eat.

And in them, you have other benefits as well; and upon them you may attain any need within your breasts. And upon them and upon the ships you may be borne along.

80   And He shows you His signs. Which signs of Allah will you then deny?

Have they not travelled in the land, then, to see what was the fate of those who preceded them? They were more numerous than they and had greater power and influence in the land. Yet what they used to earn availed them nothing.

Then, when their messengers came to them with the clear proofs, they rejoiced in the knowledge they had and were afflicted with that which they used to mock at.

But when they saw Our might, they said: "We believe in Allah alone and disbelieve in that which we used to associate with Him."

Yet, their belief, upon seeing Our might, did not profit them. It is Allah's way of old regarding His servant; and the unbelievers shall be lost there and then.

SURA 41

Fussilat, Well-expounded

In the Name of Allah, the Compassionate, the Merciful

Ha, Mim.

1   This is a revelation from the Compassionate, the Merciful;
A Book whose verses have been well-expounded, an Arabic Qur'an
addressed to a people who know;
Bearing good news and warning. Yet most of them have turned away and
are unheeding.
They say: "Our hearts are shielded against what you call us unto, in our
ears is a heaviness and between us and yourself is a veil. So act, we are acting
too."

5   Say: "I am only a mortal like you, to whom it is revealed that your God is
One God; so head straight towards Him and seek His forgiveness, and woe
betide the idolaters;
"Those who do not pay the alms, and in the Hereafter they disbelieve."
Surely, those who believe and do the righteous deeds shall have an
unstinted wage.
Say: "Do you really disbelieve in Him who created the earth in [two days]
and assign equals to Him? That is the Lord of the Worlds."
And He set up immovable mountains upon it and blessed it, and
ordained therein their varied provisions in four days equally to all those who
ask.

10   Then He arose to heaven while it was smoke, and He said to it and to the
earth: "Come over, willingly or unwillingly." They said: "We come
willingly."
Then He completed them as seven heavens in two days and assigned to
each heaven its proper order. And We adorned the lower heaven with lamps
as protection.[739] That is the determination of the All-Mighty, the
All-Knowing.
If they turn away, then say: "I warn you against a thunderbolt like the
thunderbolt of 'Ad and Thamud."
When the messengers came to them from their front and their rear
saying: "Do not worship any one but Allah", they said: "Had our Lord

---

739. From the demons.

302

wished, He would certainly have sent down angels. Therefore, we disbelieve in the Message you have been sent with."

As for 'Ad, they waxed proud in the land unjustly and said: "Who is superior to us in strength?" Did they not see that Allah who created them is superior to them in strength? And they used to repudiate Our signs.

15 So, We loosed upon them a roaring wind on inauspicious days, so as to make them taste the punishment of disgrace in the present life. However, the punishment of the Hereafter is more disgraceful and they shall not receive support.

But as for Thamud, We extended guidance to them; yet they preferred blindness to guidance, and so the thunderbolt of humiliating punishment seized them on account of what they used to earn.

And We delivered those who believed and were God-fearing.

And when the enemies of Allah are mustered unto the Fire, they shall be held in check.

When they reach it, their hearing, sights and skins shall bear witness against them regarding what they used to do.

20 And they will say to their skins: "Why did you bear witness against us?" They will say: "Allah who gave everything speech gave us speech, and He is the One who created you the first time and unto Him you shall be returned.

"You did not try to hide from the witness that your hearing, sights or skins would bear against you; but you thought that Allah does not know much of what you do.

"And that thought you entertained regarding your Lord led to your destruction, and so you were numbered among the losers."

Now if they bear up, then the Fire is their dwelling; and if they seek restoration to favour they will not be among those restored.

And We have ordained for them companions, who embellished what is in front of them and is behind them. The sentence then was pronounced against them, along with nations which had gone before them, of *jinn* and men. Truly, they were the losers.

25 The unbelievers said: "Do not listen to this Qur'an, but babble in reading it, that perchance you might win."

Truly, We shall make the unbelievers taste a terrible punishment, and We shall reward them for the worst of what they used to do.

That is the reward of Allah's enemies, the Fire wherein they shall have an eternal abode, as a reward for that they used to repudiate Our signs.

The unbelievers shall say: "Lord, show us both those who led us astray of *jinn* and men, that we might trample them under our feet and that they may be reckoned among the lowliest of creatures."

Those who say: "Our Lord is Allah", then are upright, the angels shall descend upon them saying: "Do not fear or grieve, but rejoice in the Paradise which you were promised.

30   "We are your protectors in the present life and in the Hereafter, wherein you shall have whatever your hearts desire and you shall have therein whatever you call for;

"As hospitality from an All-Forgiving, Merciful One."

Who is fairer in speech than one who calls unto Allah and performs the righteous deed and says: "I am one of those who submit."

The fair and evil deeds are not equal. Respond with that which is fairer, so that he against whom you have a grudge shall be like an intimate friend.

None shall be accorded this rank except those who have stood fast, and none shall be accorded it except one blessed with great good fortune.

35   And if a temptation of Satan should visit you, then seek refuge with Allah. He is indeed All-Hearing, All-Knowing.

Of His signs are the night and the day, the sun and the moon. Do not prostrate yourselves to the sun or to the moon, but prostrate yourselves to Allah Who created them, if it is He you truly worship.

Should they wax proud, then those with your Lord do glorify Him by night and day, without growing weary.

And of His signs is that you see the earth desolate but when We send down water upon it, it quivers and swells. Indeed, He Who revised it shall revive the dead. Truly He has power over everything.

Those who turn away from Our signs are not hidden from Us. Is he, then, who is cast in the Fire better than he who comes forward safely on the Day of Resurrection? Do what you please; He is fully aware of what you do.

40   Nor are those who have disbelieved the Reminder when it came to them [hidden from Us]. It is surely a noble Book,

To which falsehood does not come from its front nor from behind it – a revelation sent down from the Wise, Praiseworthy.

You are not told except what was told to the messengers before you. Surely, your Lord is a Master of forgiveness and a Master of painful retribution.

Had We made it a foreign Qur'an, they would have said: "If only its verses were well expounded!" What, whether foreign or Arabic, say: "It is for the believers a guidance and a healing; but for those who do not believe, it is a heaviness in their ears, and for them it is a blindness. It is as if, those[740] were called from a distant place."

We have given Moses the Book, but it was the subject of controversy.

740. The unbelievers.

Had it not been for a word that preceded from your Lord, a decision between them would have been made. Yet they are, with respect to it, in disquieting doubt.

45 He who performs a righteous deed performs it to his own advantage, and he who perpetrates evil perpetrates it to his loss. Your Lord is not unjust to His servants.

Upon Him devolves the knowledge of the Hour. No fruit comes out of its bud and no female bears or delivers but with His knowledge. And on the day He shall call out to them: "Where are My associates?", they will say: "We proclaim unto You: 'None of us is a witness.'"

And what they used to allege formerly will stray away from them and they will realize that they have no escape.

Man does not tire of praying for good, but when evil touches him he becomes downcast and despondent.

And if We let him taste a mercy from Us after some adversity that has visited him, he will say: "This is mine and I do not believe the Hour is coming. If I am returned to my Lord, I will surely have the fairest reward." We shall, then, inform the unbelievers about the things they did and will make them taste an awful punishment.

50 If we are gracious to man, he slinks away and turns aside; and if an evil touches him, he is given to constant prayer.

Say: "What do you think? If it[741] is from Allah and then you disbelieve in it, who is more astray than one who is given to profound contention?"

We shall show them Our signs in the distant regions and in their own souls, until it becomes clear to them that it is the Truth. Does it not suffice your Lord that He is a witness of everything?

Lo and behold, they are in doubt regarding the encounter of their Lord. Lo, He truly encompasses everything.

741. The Qur'an.

SURA 42

Al-Shura, The Counsel

In the Name of Allah, the Compassionate, the Merciful

Ha, Mim, 'Ain, Sin, Qaf.[742]

1 Thus Allah, the All-Mighty, the All-Wise reveals to you and to those who preceded you.

To Him belongs what is in the heavens or on earth, and He is the All-High, the Great.

The heavens are almost rent asunder above them; while the angels proclaim the praise of their Lord and ask forgiveness for those on earth. Lo, Allah is truly the All-Forgiving, the Merciful!

Those who have taken other protectors, apart from Him, Allah oversees them and you are not their guardian.

5 And so, We revealed to you an Arabic Qur'an in order to warn the Mother of the Cities[743] and those around it and to warn of the Day of Forgathering which is undoubted, whereon a group shall be in Paradise and a group shall be in Hell.

Had Allah wished, He would have made them a single nation, but He admits whom He wishes into His mercy. Yet, the wrongdoers have no protector or supporter.

Or have they taken, apart from Him, other protectors? Surely Allah is the Protector and He revives the dead and has power over everything.

Whatever you disagree upon, unto Allah is the decision thereof. That, then, is Allah, my Lord. In Him I have put my trust, and unto Him I repent.

Creator of the heavens and the earth. Of yourselves He has made couples and of the cattle pairs, multiplying you thereby. Nothing is like unto Him; He is the All-Hearing, the All-Seeing.

10 To Him belong the keys of the heavens and the earth. He expands the provision to whom He wishes or constricts it. Indeed, He has knowledge of everything.

He has enacted for you as a religion that which He charged Noah with and that which We revealed to you, and what We charged Abraham, Moses and Jesus with: "Perform the religion and do not diverge therein."

---

742. This Sura has two sets of symbols, which is unusual.
743. Mecca.

Outrageous in the sight of the idolaters is what you call them to. Allah elects unto Himself whomever He pleases and guides to Himself whoever repents.

They did not split up except after the Knowledge came to them out of contention among themselves. Yet, but for a Word which preceded from your Lord deferring them until an appointed term, judgement would have been pronounced upon them. Indeed, those to whom the Book was bequeathed, after them, are in disquieting doubt concerning it.

Therefore, summon and be upright as you were commanded, and do not follow their fancies, but say: "I believe in whatever Book Allah has sent down. I have been commanded to judge justly between you. Allah is our Lord and your Lord; we have our deeds and you have your deeds. There is no dispute between us and you; Allah will gather us together and unto Him is the ultimate return."

Those who argue concerning Allah, after His call was answered, their argument is null and void in the sight of their Lord, and upon them is a scourge, and a terrible punishment awaits them.

15 It is Allah who sent down the Book in truth, and the Balance[744] too. What do you know? Perhaps the Hour is near.

Those who do not believe in it ask you to hasten it, whereas the believers are in awe of it and know that it is the Truth. Indeed, those who are in doubt concerning the Hour are in profound error.

Allah is kind to His servants, providing for whomever He wishes; and He is the All-Powerful, the All-Mighty.

He who wishes the tillage of the Hereafter, We will increase his tillage, and he who wishes the tillage of the present life, We will give him thereof; but in the Hereafter, he will have no share.

Or do they have associates who enacted for them as a religion that for which Allah did not give leave? But for the Word of Decision, judgement would have been pronounced upon them. Surely, the wrongdoers will suffer a painful punishment.

20 You see the wrongdoers in awe of what they have earned, although it is bound to catch up with them; but those who believe and do the righteous deeds shall be consigned to the greenest gardens, wherein they have whatever they desire from their Lord. That is the great bounty.

That is the good news which Allah announces to His servants who believe, and do the good deeds. Say: "I ask you no reward for it except friendship towards kinsmen." Whoever performs a good deed, We shall increase its goodness. Allah is truly All-Forgiving, Thankful.

Or will they say: "He has imputed falsehood to Allah"? Had Allah willed,

744. The Balance of right and wrong.

He would have put a seal upon your heart. He obliterates falsehood and confirms the Truth by His words. Surely, He knows the secrets hidden in the breasts.

It is He who accepts the repentance of His servants, pardons the evil deeds and knows what you do.

And He answers those who believe and do the righteous deeds and increases them of His bounty; but the unbelievers will suffer a terrible punishment.

25   Had Allah expanded provision for His servants, they would have exceeded the bounds of injustice in the land; but He sends down in measure whatever He wishes. He is truly Well-Informed about His servants, All-Seeing.

It is He who sends the rain down, after they have despaired, and spreads out His mercy. He is the Protector, the Praiseworthy.

And of His signs is the creation of the heavens and the earth and the beasts He has scattered abroad in them; and He is able to gather them together, whenever He wishes.

Whatever calamity might hit you is due to what your hands have earned; yet He pardons much.

You are not able to thwart Him on earth and you do not have, apart from Allah, any protector or supporter.

30   And of His signs are ships sailing in the sea like high mountains.

If He wishes, He will calm the wind, and then they will remain motionless upon its surface. In that are signs to every steadfast and thankful person;

Or destroy them for what they[745] have earned, while pardoning many;

That those who dispute concerning Our signs might know that they have no escape.

For whatever you have been given is only the enjoyment of the present life, but what Allah has is better and more enduring for those who believe and put their trust in their Lord;

35   And those who avoid the grave sins and foul acts, and, if angered, will forgive;

And those who answer their Lord, perform the prayer – their affair being a counsel among themselves, and of what We provided them with, they spend;

And those who, if they are oppressed, will overcome.

The reward of evil is an evil like it, but he who pardons and makes amends, his wage is with Allah. Indeed, He does not like the wrongdoers.

---

745. The passengers.

He who overcomes after being wronged – upon those there is no reproach.

40   The reproach is surely upon those who wrong mankind and transgress in the land unjustly. To those a painful punishment is in store.

But he who bears patiently and forgives – that is a sign of real resolve.

Whoever Allah leads astray will have no protector apart from Him; and you will see the wrongdoers when they see the punishment saying: "Is there a way of going back?"

You will see them being exposed to it,[746] abject in their humiliation, looking askew. The believers will say: "The losers are truly those who have lost themselves and their families on the Day of Resurrection. Surely, the wrongdoers will suffer lasting punishment."

They have no protectors to support them, apart from Allah. Whoever Allah leads astray has no way out.

45   Answer your Lord's call before a day comes from Allah that cannot be turned back. Upon that day you will have no shelter, no disclaimer.

Should they turn away, We have not sent you as a guardian to watch over them; incumbent on you is delivering the Message only. Indeed, when We make man taste a mercy from Us, he rejoices in it; but when they are afflicted with a misfortune, on account of what their hands had previously perpetrated, then man is truly thankless.

To Allah belongs the dominion of the heavens and the earth. He creates whatever He pleases, and grants whomever He wishes females, and whomever He wishes males.

Or He marries them, males and females, and makes whomever He wishes sterile. Indeed, He is All-Knowing, All-Powerful.

It is not given to any mortal that Allah should speak to him, except by revelation or from behind a veil. Otherwise, He sends forth a messenger who reveals by His permission whatever He wishes. He is, indeed, All-High, All-Wise.

50   That is how We revealed to you a spirit by Our command. You did not know what the Book is nor what is belief; but We made it a light, by which We guide whomever We wish of Our servants. You will surely guide unto a straight path;

The path of Allah, to whom belongs whatever is in the heavens or on earth. Lo, unto Allah will all matters ultimately revert.

746. The Fire.

SURA 43

Al-Zukhruf, Adornment

Ha, Mim.

1   By the Manifest Book.

We have made it an Arabic Qur'an that perchance you may understand.

And, indeed, it is in the Mother of the Book, with Us, lofty and wise.

Shall We then divert the Reminder from you mercifully, because you are an extravagant people?

5   How many a prophet have We sent unto the ancients?

But not a prophet came to them whom they did not mock.

So We destroyed a people mightier than they in valour; and the example of the ancients was gone.

If you ask them: "Who created the heavens and the earth?", they will certainly say: "The All-Mighty, the All-Knowing created them."

He who made the earth level ground for you and made for you pathways therein, that perchance you may be well-guided;

10   And Who sent down water from heaven in set measure; and so We revived therewith a dead town. Thus you shall be brought forth;

And Who created all the pairs and made for you such ships and cattle as you can mount.

That you might sit upon their backs, then remember the grace of your Lord when you are seated thereon and say: "Glory be to Him who subjected this to us, whereas we were not equal to it.

"And, surely, unto our Lord we shall return."

They have attributed to Him part of His servants. Man is indeed manifestly thankless.

15   Or has He taken for Himself daughters from what He creates, and favoured you with sons?

And when one of them is given the news of what he attributes the like thereof,[747] to the All-Compassionate, his face becomes darkened and he is filled with gloom.

What, one who is brought up in luxury but in the art of disputation is not well-versed?[748]

---

747. That is, daughters. Thus are daughters distinguished from boys.
748. To be assigned to God?

And they have made the angels, who are servants of the All-Compassionate, females. What, have they witnessed their creation? Surely, their testimony will be written down and they will be questioned.

They say: "If the All-Compassionate had willed it, we would not have worshipped them." They have no knowledge of that at all; they are only lying.

20   Or have We given them a Book prior to this one,[749] so that they are clinging to it?

No, they say: "We found our fathers upon this course,[750] and we are actually following in their footsteps."

Likewise, We never sent forth a warner to any city before you, but its affluent chiefs have said: "We have found our fathers upon a certain course, and we are actually following in their footsteps."

He said: "What if I were to bring you a more certain guidance than what you found your fathers upon?" They said: "We are definitely disbelievers in what you were sent forth with."

So, We wreaked vengeance upon them. Behold, then, what was the fate of those who deny.

25   When Abraham said to his father and his people: "I am certainly quit of what you worship;

"Except for Him who created me. He will certainly guide me well."

And he made it an enduring word in his progeny, that perchance they might repent.

Yet, I gave these and their fathers some enjoyment, till the Truth and a manifest messenger came to them.

But when the Truth came to them, they said: "That is sorcery, and we are definitely disbelieving therein."

30   They also said: "If only this Qur'an had been sent down upon some outstanding man from the two cities."[751]

Do they apportion the mercy of your Lord? Is it We who have apportioned their livelihood among them in the present life and raised some of them in rank above others; so that some would be subservient to the others. Your Lord's mercy is better than what they amass.

And were it not for fear that mankind would be a single nation, We would have assigned to those who disbelieve in the All-Compassionate, roofs of silver for their houses and stairways upon which they ascend;

And portals for their houses and couches upon which they recline;

749. The Qur'an.
750. *Ummah*, path or creed.
751. Mecca and Ta'if.

And adornment of gold; but all that is nothing but wordly enjoyment. Yet the Hereafter with your Lord is reserved for the God-fearing.

35 And he who is blind to the remembrance of the All-Compassionate, We shall assign to him a demon, who will be his constant companion.

They[752] will certainly bar them from the path, while they think that they are well-guided.

But when he comes to Us, he will say: "Would that between me and you is the distance between East and West." What a wretched companion!

Today, it will not avail you, being wrongdoers, that you are partners in punishment.

Are you able, then, to make the deaf hear or guide the blind and him who is in manifest error?

40 Were We to carry you off, We would then wreak vengeance upon them;

Or show you that which We have promised. For We certainly have power over them.

Cling then to what was revealed to you; you are certainly upon a straight path.

And it[753] is surely a Reminder to you and to your people; and you shall be questioned.

Ask those of Our messengers We sent before you: "Have We ever set up, apart from the All-Compassionate, any other gods to be worshipped?"

45 We have in fact sent Moses with Our signs to Pharaoh and his dignitaries. He said: "I am the messenger of the Lord of the Worlds."

But when he brought them Our signs, lo, they laughed at them.

Yet, We did not show them a sign but it was greater than its counterpart. Then We seized them with punishment, that perchance they might retract.

And they said: "O Sorcerer, call upon your Lord for us, by the pledge He made with you. We shall, then, be well-guided."

But when We lifted the punishment from them, behold, they broke their pledge.

50 And Pharaoh called out to his people: "O my people, do I not have the kingdom of Egypt, and these rivers flow beneath me? Do you not see, then?

"Or, am I not better than this weakling who cannot speak clearly?

"Why, then, no bracelets of gold were cast down upon him or angels came with him in company?"

Thus, he incited his people and so they obeyed him. They were, indeed, a sinful people.

752. The demons.
753. The Qur'an.

Then when they roused Our anger, We wreaked a vengeance upon them and drowned them all.

55 And so, We made them a people gone by, and an example to the others.

And when the son of Mary was held up as an example, behold, your people turned away from him.

They said: "Are our deities better or he?" They only cited it to you disputatiously. Indeed, they are a contentious people.

He was merely a servant whom We favoured and set up as an example to the Children of Israel.

Had We wished, We would have made of you angels to be successors on earth.

60 And it is surely the knowledge of the Hour; so do not doubt it and follow Me. This is a straight path.

And let not Satan bar you. He is, indeed, a manifest enemy of yours.

When Jesus brought the clear proofs, he said: "I have come to you with the Wisdom and to make clear to you part of that whereon you are differing. So fear Allah and obey me."

"Allah is, indeed, my Lord and your Lord; so worship Him. This is a straight path."

Then the factions among them fell apart. Woe unto the wrongdoers, from the punishment of a painful day.

65 Are they only waiting for the Hour to come upon them suddenly, while they are unaware?

Friends on that day shall be enemies of one another; except for the God-fearing.

O My servants, today you have no cause to fear nor to grieve.

Those who believe in Our signs and are submissive.

"Enter Paradise, you and your spouses joyfully.

70 "Platters and cups of gold shall be passed around them, and therein shall be whatever souls desire and eyes delight in, and in it you shall dwell forever."

That is the Paradise which you were given as an inheritance for what you used to do.

Therein you have abundant fruit from which you will eat.

Indeed, the criminals shall suffer the punishment of Hell forever.

They will not be relieved and they are in it completely confounded.

75 We did not wrong them, but they were the wrongdoers themselves.

They call out: "O Malik,[754] let your Lord be done with us." He will say: "You are surely staying on.

---

754. The keeper of Hell.

"We brought you the Truth, but most of you were averse to the Truth."
Or had they contrived some scheme. We are certainly contriving too.

Or, do they think that We do not hear their secret and their private
counsels. Yes, indeed, and Our messengers[755] are in their midst writing
down.

80   Say: "If the All-Compassionate has a child, I would be the first
worshipper."

Exalted be the Lord of the heavens and the earth, the Lord of the Throne,
above what they describe.

So leave them to romp and frolic till they encounter their day which they
have been promised.

It is He who in heaven is God, and on earth is God; and He is the
All-Wise, the All-Knowing.

Blessed is He Who has the dominion of the heavens and the earth and
what is between them, and Who has the knowledge of the Hour, and unto
Him you shall be returned.

85   Those upon whom they call, apart from Him, do not have the power of
intercession, except he who bears witness to the Truth knowingly.

If you ask them: "Who creates them?", they will say: "Allah." Why, then,
are they perverted?

And his[756] petition is: "Lord, these are surely a people who do not
believe.

"Pardon them, then, and say: 'Peace.' For they will certainly come to
know."

755. The angels.
756. Muhammad.

314

SURA 44

Al-Dukhan, The Smoke

In the Name of Allah, the Compassionate, the Merciful

Ha, Mim.

1   By the Manifest Book.

We have sent it down on a blessed night. We were then admonishing.

Therein, every wise matter is determined,

As a command from Us. We have been sending forth revelations,

5   As a mercy from your Lord. He is indeed the All-Hearing, the All-Knowing.

The Lord of the heavens and the earth and what is between them; if you only believe with certainty.

There is no other god but He. He gives life and causes to die; your Lord and the Lord of your forefathers.

Yet, in doubt, they frolic.

Await, then, the day when heaven shall bring forth visible smoke;

10   Enveloping the people. This is a painful punishment,

"Our Lord, lift the punishment from us, for we are true believers."

How will they have a Reminder, when a manifest messenger has come to them?

But they turned away from him saying: "He is a tutored madman."

We will lift the punishment a little. Surely, you are reverting.

15   On the day when We shall strike the mightiest blow, then We shall take Our revenge.

In fact, We have tried the people of Pharaoh before them, and a noble messenger came to them [saying]:

"Deliver to me Allah's servants,⁷⁵⁷ for I am unto you a faithful messenger.

"Do not rise arrogantly against Allah; for I come to you with a manifest authority.

"I seek refuge with my Lord and your Lord, lest you stone me.

20   "And if you do not believe me, then leave me alone."

Then he called out to his Lord: "These are indeed a criminal people.

"Therefore set out with My servants at night; for you are being followed.

"Leave the sea behind as still as ever; for they are a drowning host."

How many gardens and well-springs did they leave behind?

---

757. The Children of Israel.

25 And plantations and a noble station;
And prosperity which they thoroughly enjoyed.
So it was, and We bequeathed them to another people.
Neither the heavens nor the earth cried for them and they were given no respite.
And thus We saved the Children of Israel from the demeaning punishment;
30 From Pharaoh; for he was haughty and extravagant.
We have indeed chosen them knowingly, above all other peoples;
And given them many signs wherein there was a manifest trial.
Truly, these people[758] will say:
"It is only our first death and we will not be raised from the dead.
35 "Bring then back our fathers if you are truthful."
Are they any better than the people of Tubba'[759] and those who preceded them? We destroyed them all; for they were criminals.
We did not create the heavens and the earth and what is between them in jest.
We only created them in truth, but most of them do not know.
The Day of Decision is truly their appointed time all together.
40 The day when no master shall profit a client a whit, and they will not be supported;
Except for him upon whom Allah has mercy. He is indeed the All-Mighty, the Merciful.
The Tree of Zaqqum[760] will certainly be
The food of the sinner.
Like molten lead, which boils in the bellies;
45 Like boiling water.
"Take him and thrust him into the pit of Hell.
"Then pour over his head the agony of the boiling water;
"Saying: 'Taste, you are truly the mighty and noble one.'
"That is the punishment which you used to doubt."
50 However, the God-fearing are in a secure place;
In gardens and well-springs.
They wear silk and brocade facing each other.
Thus it will be; and We gave them wide-eyed houris in marriage.
They call therein for every fruit in perfect security.
55 They do not taste death therein, except for the first death; and He guards them against the punishment of Hell;

758. Quraysh and their ilk, who questioned Muhammad's prophetic call.
759 Tubba' refers originally to the kings of southern Arabia, in pre-Islamic times.
760. The Tree of Bitterness.

As a bounty from your Lord. That is the great triumph.
We have made it[761] easy in your own tongue, so that they may remember.
So wait and watch; they are waiting and watching.

761. The Qur'an.

SURA 45

Al-Jathiyah, The Kneeling One

In the Name of Allah, the Compassionate, the Merciful

Ha, Mim.

1   This is the revelation of the Book from Allah, the All-Mighty, All-Wise. Surely, in the heavens and the earth there are signs for the believers.

And in your creation and the beasts scattered abroad, there are signs for people who are of certain faith.

And in the alternation of the night and the day and in what Allah has sent down from heaven as provision, reviving thereby the earth after it was dead and in the disposition of the wind – there are signs for a people who understand.

5   Those are the signs of Allah which We recite to you in truth. In what discourse other than Allah's and His signs, then, will they believe?

Woe unto every sinful liar;

He hears Allah's signs recited to him, then perseveres in his arrogance as though he did not hear them. Announce to him, then, the good news of a painful punishment.

And if he learns about any of Our signs, he takes them in jest. Such people shall have a demeaning punishment.

Behind them is Hell and what they earned will not profit them a whit, nor what they have taken, apart from Allah, as protectors; and they will have a terrible punishment.

10   This is true guidance, and those who have disbelieved in the signs of their Lord will have the punishment of a painful scourge.

It is Allah who subjected the sea to you, so that ships might sail in it at His command, and that you might seek some of His bounty, and that perchance you might give thanks.

And He subjected to you what is in the heavens and the earth all together, [as a grace] from Him. There are in that signs to a people who reflect.

Tell the believers to forgive those who do not hope for Allah's Days, that He may reward a people for what they used to earn.

He who does a righteous deed, it is to his own advantage, and he who perpetrates evil, it is to his own loss. Then, unto your Lord you shall be returned.

15   In fact, We gave the Children of Israel the Book, the Judgement and the

Prophecy. We provided them with the good things, and preferred them to all the other peoples.

And We gave them clear proofs of the Decree, but they did not diverge except when the knowledge came to them, out of spite among themselves. Surely your Lord shall judge between them on the Day of Resurrection, regarding that over which they used to diverge.

Then, We set you upon a right course[762] of the Decree; so follow it and do not follow the fancies of those who do not know.

They will avail you nothing against Allah; and indeed the wrongdoers are friends of each other, but Allah is the friend of the God-fearing.

This[763] is an illumination for mankind, a guidance and mercy unto a people who believe with certainty.

20   What, do those who have perpetrated the evil deeds believe that We shall regard them as equal to those who have believed and done the righteous deeds, whether in their life or death? Evil is their judgement!

Allah created the heavens and the earth in truth, so that every soul may be rewarded for what it has earned; and they shall not be wronged.

Have you seen him who has taken his fancy as his god and Allah has led him astray knowingly, and set a seal upon his hearing and his heart, and placed a veil upon his sight. Who, then, will guide him besides Allah? Do you not remember?

They say: "There is nothing but this our present life. We die and we live and we are only destroyed by time." However, they have no certain knowledge of this; they are only conjecturing.

And when Our signs are clearly recited to them, their only argument is to say: "Bring our fathers back, if you are truthful."

25   Say: "Allah gives you life, then causes you to die, then musters you unto the Day of Resurrection, which is undoubted. Yet most people do not know."

To Allah belongs the dominion of the heavens and the earth, and when the Hour shall come, on that day the negators shall lose.

And you will see every nation kneeling; each nation being called unto its Book: "Today, you shall be rewarded for what you used to do."

"This is Our book which speaks against you truly. In fact, We used to record what you were doing."

As to those who believed and did the righteous deeds, their Lord will admit them into His mercy. That is the manifest triumph.

30   But as for those who disbelieved [they will be asked]: "Were not My signs recited to you, but you waxed proud and were a criminal people?"

762. *Shari'ah.*
763. The Qur'an.

And when it was said: "Allah's promise is true and the Hour is undoubted", you said: "We do not know what the Hour is. We only conjecture and are by no means certain."

Then the evil of their deeds shall appear to them and they will be smitten by that which they used to mock.

And it will be said: "Today We forget you, as you forgot the encounter of this your day, and your abode is the Fire and you will have no supporters.

"That is because you took Allah's signs in jest and the earthly life lured you." So today they will not be brought out of it and they will not be allowed to repent.

35   Praise, then, be to Allah, the Lord of the heavens and the Lord of the earth, the Lord of the Worlds.

Unto Him is the grandeur in the heavens and on the earth, and He is the All-Mighty, the All-Wise.

SURA 46

Al-Ahqaf, The Sand-Dunes

In the Name of Allah, the Compassionate, the Merciful

Ha, Mim.

1   This is the revelation of the Book from Allah, the All-Mighty, the All-Wise.

We have not created the heavens and the earth and what is between them except in truth and for an appointed term. Yet the unbelievers do not heed what they were warned against.

Say: "Have you considered what you call upon,[764] apart from Allah? Show me what they have created of the earth, or whether they have a share of the heavens? Bring me a book before this one or some vestige of knowledge, if you are truthful?"

Who is farther astray than he who calls, apart from Allah, upon him who does not answer his call till the Day of Resurrection? They are even heedless of their calling.

5   And when people are mustered, they will be their enemies, and even their worship they will disclaim.

And when Our clear signs are recited to them, those who have disbelieved will say to the Truth when it comes to them: "This is manifest sorcery."

Or do they say: "He invented it"? Say: "If I have invented it, you have no means of helping me against Allah. He knows best what you are expatiating upon. Let Him suffice as a witness between me and you. He is the All-Forgiving, the All-Merciful."

Say: "I am not the first of the messengers and I do not know what will be done with me or with you. I only follow what is revealed to me and I am only a manifest warner."

Say: "Have you considered? What if it be from Allah and you disbelieve in it, while a witness from the Children of Israel bears witness to the like of it and believes, whereas you wax proud? Surely, Allah does not guide the wrongdoing people rightly."

10   The unbelievers say to the believers: "Had it been any good, they would not have beaten us to it", and since they have not been guided by it, they will certainly say: "This is an old fabrication."

And before it, there came the Book of Moses, as a guidance and a mercy;

764. The idols.

and this is a corroborating Book in Arabic tongue to warn the wrongdoers and serve as good news to the beneficent.

Indeed, those who say: "Our Lord is Allah", and then are upright, have no cause to fear and they shall not grieve.

Those are the Companions of Paradise dwelling in it forever, as a reward for what they used to do.

We have commanded man to be kind to his parents; his mother bore him painfully and delivered him painfully, his gestation and weaning totalling thirty months. When he is fully grown and turns forty years, he will say: "Lord, inspire me to be thankful for the favour, with which you have favoured me and favoured my parents; and to do a righteous deed, well-pleasing to You. Grant me righteousness in my progeny; I have truly repented to You and am one of those who submit."

15   Those from whom We accept the best of what they do and overlook their evil deeds shall be reckoned among the Companions of Paradise, this being the promise of the truth which they were promised.

But as for him who says to his parents: "Fie upon you. Do you promise me to be raised up,[765] while generations have already gone before me?" They both call upon Allah to help them: "Woe unto you, have faith. Allah's promise is true." But he will say: "These are merely legends of the ancients."

Those against whom the Decree was pronounced, from among nations which passed away before them, both of *jinn* and mankind, were truly the losers.

To each will be allotted ranks according to what they did, and He will certainly pay them in full for their works, and they shall not be wronged.

On the day that the unbelievers shall be exposed to the Fire: "You have squandered your goods in your worldly life and enjoyed them. Today, then, you will be rewarded with the punishment of humiliation, because you used to wax proud on earth, without any right, and because you used to sin."

20   And remember the brother of 'Ad, when he warned his people upon the sand-dunes, warners having gone before him and after him, saying: "Do not worship any one but Allah. I fear for you the punishment of a great day."

They said: "Did you come to divert us from our deities? Bring us then what you are promising us if you are truthful."

He said: "Knowledge is only with Allah and I am conveying to you the message I was charged with, but I see that you are an ignorant people."

Then, when they saw it[766] as a cloud-burst coming towards their valley, they said: "This is a cloud-burst raining upon us." No, it is what you sought to hasten, a wind wherein is a painful punishment;

---

765. That is, raised from the dead.
766. The punishment.

Destroying everything at the behest of its Lord. Then when they woke up, there was nothing to be seen except their dwellings. Thus do we reward the criminal people.

25 We had established them firmly in a manner We did not establish you, and We gave them hearing, eye-sight and hearts; but their hearing, eye-sight and hearts availed them nothing, as they repudiated the signs of Allah; and so they were overwhelmed by that which they used to mock.

We have also destroyed the cities surrounding you and expounded the signs, that perchance they might return.

Why, then, were they not supported by those whom they took, apart from Allah, as favourite deities? No, they abandoned them. That was their fabrication and what they used to allege.

And when We dispatched towards you a group of *jinn* to listen to the Qur'an, and they attended to it, they said: "Listen", but when it was finished they returned to their own people to warn them.

They said: "O our people, we have heard a Book sent down after Moses, confirming what came before it and guiding to the truth and to a straight path.

30 "O our people, respond to the caller[767] unto Allah and believe in Him, and He will forgive you some of your sins and save you from a painful punishment."

He who does not answer the caller unto Allah will not thwart Him on earth and he will not have any protectors apart from Him. Such people are in manifest error.

Have they not seen that Allah, who has created the heavens and the earth and has not been wearied by creating them, is able to raise the dead? Yes indeed, He has power over everything.

And on the day that the unbelievers shall be exposed to the Fire [they will be asked]: "Is this not just?" They will say: "Yes indeed, by our Lord." He will then say: "Taste now the punishment for your disbelief."

So bear up patiently, as the Constant Messengers[768] bore up, and do not seek to hasten it[769] for them. On that day they shall see what they were promised, as if they had not lingered except for a single hour of the day. This is a proclamation. Shall any but the sinful people be destroyed?

767. Muhammad.
768. Noah, Abraham, Moses and Jesus.
769. Punishment.

SURA 47

Muhammad (the Prophet)

In the Name of Allah, the Compassionate, the Merciful

1 Those who have disbelieved and barred others from the path of Allah, He will render their works perverse;

But those who have believed and done the righteous deeds and believed in what was sent down upon Muhammad, which is the Truth from their Lord, He will remit their sins and set their minds aright.

That is because those who have disbelieved have followed falsehood, but those who have believed have followed the truth from their Lord. Thus does Allah frame their parables for mankind.

So, when you meet the unbelievers, strike their necks till you have bloodied them, then fasten the shackles. Thereupon, release them freely or for a ransom, till the war is over. So be it. Yet had Allah wished, He would have taken vengeance upon them, but He wanted to test you by one another. Those who die in the cause of Allah, He will not render their works perverse.

5 He shall guide them and set their minds aright;

And shall admit them into Paradise which He has made known to them.

O believers, if you support Allah, He will support you and steady your footsteps.

But as to the unbelievers, wretched are they and perverse are their works.

That is because they despised what Allah has sent down; so He foiled their actions.

10 Did they not travel in the land and see what was the fate of those who preceded them? Allah brought utter destruction on them; and the like of this awaits the unbelievers.

That is because Allah is the Protector of the believers, but the unbelievers shall have no protector.

Allah shall admit those who believe and do the righteous deeds into gardens beneath which rivers flow; but the unbelievers shall take their pleasure and eat like cattle, and the Fire shall be their abode.

How many a city that was mightier than your city,[770] which cast you out, have We destroyed, and they had no supporter?

---

770. Mecca.

Is he who relies on a clear proof from his Lord like one whose evil action has been embellished for him? They have simply followed their fancies.

15 The likeness of the Garden which the God-fearing have been promised is this: rivers of water not stagnant, rivers of milk whose taste has not changed, rivers of wine delighting its drinkers and rivers of distilled honey. Therein they have every variety of fruit and forgiveness from their Lord too. Are they to be compared with those who dwell in the Fire forever and are given to drink boiling water which will rip up their bowels?

There are some of them who listen to you, but as soon as they leave you, they say to those who have been given the Knowledge: "What did he say just now?" Such are those upon whose hearts Allah has set a seal and who have followed their fancies.

But those who are rightly guided, He increases them in guidance and accords them their piety.

Do they, then, only expect that the Hour should come upon them suddenly? In fact, its signs have already come. How then, when it comes, will they regain their recollection?

So, know that there is no god but Allah, and ask forgiveness for your sins and for the believers, men and women. Allah knows your goings and comings, and your settling down.

20 The believers say: "If only a sura is sent down", but when a sound sura is sent down and fighting is mentioned therein, you will see those in whose hearts is a sickness look at you like one who has fainted in the throes of death. Far better for them,

Would have been obedience and a fair word! So when the matter is resolved, it would have been better for them to be true to Allah.

Would you, perhaps, if you were to rule, spread corruption in the land and sever the bonds of your kin?

Such are those whom Allah has cursed, and has made them deaf and blotted out their eyesight.

Will they not ponder the Qur'an, or are there locks upon their hearts?

25 Surely, those who have turned upon their heels after the Guidance was manifested to them, it was Satan who insinuated to them and deluded them.

That is because they said to those who disliked what Allah has sent down: "We shall obey you in part of the matter", but Allah knows their secretiveness.

How, then, will it be when the angels shall carry them off, beating their faces and their buttocks?

That is because they have followed what has angered Allah and were averse to His good pleasure. So He has foiled their works.

Or do those in whose hearts is a sickness think that Allah will not bring their rancours to light?

30   Had We wished, We would have shown them to you, so that you might know them by their mark. And you shall surely know them by their distorted speech. Allah knows your works.

And We shall test you so as to know who are the fighters among you and who are the steadfast; and We shall test your news.

Indeed, those who have disbelieved and barred from Allah's path and were at odds with the Apostle, after the Guidance became manifest to them, will not cause Allah any harm, and He will foil their works.

O believers, obey Allah and obey the Apostle and do not render your actions vain.

Indeed, those who have disbelieved and barred from Allah's path, then died as unbelievers, Allah will not forgive them.

35   So do not weaken and call for peace, while you have the upper hand and Allah is with you. He will not stint you your actions.

Indeed, this present life is but sport and amusement; and if you believe and are God-fearing, He will give you your wages and will not ask you for your possessions.

Were He to ask you for them and press you, you will surely be niggardly, and He will bring your rancours to light.

There you are; you are called upon to spend freely in Allah's cause, but some of you are niggardly. Yet he who is niggardly is only niggardly unto himself. Allah is the All-Sufficient and you are the destitute. If you turn back, He will replace you by a people other than you, and they will not be like you at all.

SURA 48

Al-Fath, The Victory

In the Name of Allah, the Compassionate, the Merciful

1   We have indeed given you a manifest victory,

That Allah may forgive you your former and your latter sins, and complete His blessing upon you and lead you unto a straight path;

And that Allah may give you a mighty victory.

It is He who has sent down the Serenity upon the hearts of the believers that they may increase in faith upon their faith. To Allah belong the hosts of the heavens and the earth; and Allah is All-Knowing and Wise.

5   That He may admit the believers, men and women, into gardens beneath which rivers flow, dwelling therein forever, and that He might remit their sins. That, in Allah's sight, is a great triumph.

And that He may punish the hypocrites, men and women, and the unbelievers, men and women, who think evil thoughts of Allah. Upon them is the evil turn of fortune. Allah is wrathful at them, curses them and has prepared Hell for them; and what a wretched fate!

To Allah belong the hosts of the heavens and the earth, and Allah is All-Mighty and Wise.

Indeed, We have sent you forth as a witness, a bearer of good news and a warner;

That you[771] may believe in Allah and His Apostle, to honour, revere and glorify Him, morning and evening.

10   Those who pay you[772] homage are actually paying Allah homage. Allah's hand is above their hands; so he who breaks his oath only breaks it to his loss, and he who fulfils what he had pledged unto Allah, He will grant him a great wage.

The Bedouins who stayed behind[773] will say to you: "Our possessions and our families preoccupied us; so ask forgiveness for us." They say with their tongues what is not in their hearts. Say: "Who can avail you anything against Allah, if He wishes to harm you or He wishes to profit you? No, Allah is fully aware of what you do.

"Rather, you thought that the Apostle and the believers will never return

---

771. People of Medina.
772. The Prophet.
773. During the siege [of Mecca] in the year eight of the Hijrah.

to their families; and that was embellished in your hearts and you entertained evil thoughts and were a useless people."

He who does not believe in Allah and His Apostle, We have, indeed, prepared for the unbelievers a Blazing Fire.

To Allah belongs the dominion of the heavens and the earth; He forgives whomever He wishes and punishes whomever He wishes. Allah is All-Forgiving and Merciful.

15   Those who stayed behind will say, when you set out after certain spoils to seize them: "Let us follow you"; intending to change Allah's words. Say: "You shall not follow us; thus has Allah said already." They will then say: "No, you are jealous of us." Rather, they understand but a little.

Say to those who stayed behind: "You shall be called up against a people of great might; you shall fight them or they shall submit. If, then, you obey, He will grant you a fair wage; but if you turn away as you turned away before, He will inflict a painful punishment upon you."

The blind are not to blame, nor the cripple is to blame, nor the sick are to blame. Whoever obeys Allah and His Apostle, He will admit him into gardens beneath which rivers flow; but he who turns away, He will inflict upon him a painful punishment.

Allah was well pleased with the believers, when they paid you homage under the tree; so He knew what was in their hearts and sent down the Serenity upon them and rewarded them with a victory near at hand,

And with many spoils for them to seize. Allah is All-Mighty, All-Wise.

20   Allah has promised you many spoils, for you to take, and He has hastened this one[774] and held the hands of people back off you, that it may be a sign to the believers and that He might guide you to a straight path.

And another one[775] which you could not take; Allah had besieged it already. Allah has power over everything.

Had the unbelievers fought you, they would certainly have turned their backs in flight; then they would have found no friend or supporter.

It is Allah's way which has gone before; and you will never find any alteration of Allah's way.

It is He who held their hands back from you, and your hands from them in the valley of Mecca, after He gave you victory over them. Allah observed whatever you do.

25   It is they who disbelieved and barred you from the Sacred Mosque, and the offering was prevented from reaching its sacrificial site. Had it not been for some believing men and some believing women, whom you did not know, lest you should trample them and earn thereby the guilt unwittingly,

774. The spoils of Khaybar.
775. Mecca.

that Allah might thereby admit into His mercy whomever He wishes. Had they stood apart, We would have inflicted on those of them who disbelieved a painful punishment.

When the unbelievers instilled in their hearts fierceness, the fierceness of paganism, Allah then sent down His Serenity upon His Apostle and upon the believers, and imposed on them the word of piety, they being more deserving thereof and worthier. Allah has knowledge of everything.

Allah has fulfilled His Apostle's vision in truth: "You shall enter the Sacred Mosque, if Allah wishes, in security, your heads shaved and your hair cut short, without fear." For He knew what you did not know and gave you, prior to that, a victory near at hand.[776]

It is He who sent forth His Apostle with the guidance and the religion of truth, that He may exalt it above every other religion. Allah suffices as witness.

Muhammad is the Apostle of Allah and those who are with him are hard on the unbelievers, merciful towards each other. You will see them kneeling and prostrating themselves, seeking bounty and good pleasure from Allah; their mark is upon their faces, as a trace of their prostration. That is their likeness in the Torah and their likeness in the Gospels; just as a seed which puts forth its shoot, strengthens it and grows stout, then rises straight upon its stalks, delighting the sower, to vex thereby the unbelievers. Allah has promised those who believe and do the righteous deeds forgiveness and a great wage.

776. By signing the peace of Hudaibiyah and capturing the settlement of Khaybar.

SURA 49

Al-Hujurat, The Chambers

In the Name of Allah, the Compassionate, the Merciful

1   O believers, do not advance hastily before Allah and His Apostle, and fear Allah. Allah is indeed All-Hearing, All-Knowing.

O believers, do not raise your voices above the Prophet's voice and do not be loud in speaking to him, as you speak loudly to one another, lest your works come to grief while you are unaware.

Surely, those who lower their voices in the presence of Allah's Apostle are those whose hearts Allah had tested for piety. They will have forgiveness and a great wage.

Those who call you from behind the Chambers, most of them do not understand.

5   Had they waited for you to come out to meet them, it would have been better for them. Allah is All-Forgiving and Merciful.

O believers, if a sinner brings you a piece of news, make sure you do not cause some people distress unwittingly, and so regret subsequently what you have done.

Know that Allah's Apostle is in your midst. Were he to obey you in much of your affairs, you would suffer hardship; but Allah has endeared belief to you and embellished it in your hearts, and He has made you to hate unbelief, sin and disobedience. Such are the rightly guided.

As a bounty from Allah and a favour. Allah is All-Knowing and Wise.

If two parties of the believers should fight one another, bring them peacefully together; but if one of them seeks to oppress the other, then fight the oppressor until it reverts to Allah's command. If it reverts, then bring them together in justice and be equitable; for Allah loves the equitable.

10   Surely, the believers are brothers; so bring your two brothers together and fear Allah, so that you may receive mercy.

O believers, let not one people scoff at another people, lest they be better than they; nor women at other women, lest they be better than they. Do not slander yourselves and do not revile each other with false names. Wretched is the name of ungodliness, after belief! He who does not repent, such are the wrongdoers, indeed.

O believers, avoid much suspicion; for some suspicion is a sin. Do not spy and do not backbite one another. Does any of you wish to eat his brother's flesh dead? You would surely hate it. Fear Allah, for Allah is truly Absolving, Merciful.

O mankind, We have created you male and female and made you nations and tribes, so that you might come to know one another. Surely the noblest of you in Allah's sight is the most pious. Allah indeed is All-Knowing, All-Informed.

The Bedouins say: "We believe." Say: "You do not believe, but say: 'We submit'; for belief has not yet entered your hearts. If you obey Allah and His Apostle, He will not stint you any of your works. Allah is surely All-Forgiving and Merciful."

15   Indeed, the believers are those who have believed in Allah and His Apostle, then were not in doubt, but struggled with their possessions and themselves in the cause of Allah. Those are the truthful ones.

Say: "Will you inform Allah about your religion, while Allah knows what is in the heavens and in the earth? Allah has knowledge of everything."

They regard it a favour to you that they have submitted. Say: "Do not regard your submission a favour to me; rather Allah has favoured you when He guided you to belief, if you are really truthful.

"Allah knows the secrets of the heavens and the earth, and Allah sees well the things you do."

SURA 50

Qaf

Qaf.

1 By the glorious Qur'an.

Yet, then marvel that a warner has come to them from among them, and so the unbelievers say: "This is a strange thing!"

"What, when we are dead and have become dust – that is a far-off return!"

We know well what the earth shall swallow up of them; for We have a recording book.

5 Yet, they have denounced the Truth when it came to them, and so they are in a confused state.

Have they not beheld the heaven above them, how We erected it and adorned it, and it has no cracks?

And the earth We have spread out and set in it immovable mountains; and We cause to grow in it every delightful variety;

As a guidance and reminder to every penitent servant.

And We brought down from heaven blessed water and caused thereby gardens to grow and harvest-grain;

10 And tall palm trees with clusters well-knit,

As provision for the servants; and We have revived thereby a dead town. Thus will the Resurrection[777] be.

Prior to them, the people of Noah, the Companions of al-Riss and Thamud denounced [the Prophets].

'Ad, Pharaoh and the brethren of Lot, too;

And the Companions of the Thicket and the people of Tubba', they all denounced the messengers and so My warning was fulfilled.

15 Were We wearied by the first creation? No, they are in doubt regarding a new creation.

We have indeed created man, and We know what his soul insinuates to him. We are to him closer than the jugular vein.

When the two angels receive, one sitting on the right, the other on the left;

He does not utter a word but is observed by a vigilant observer by his side.

---

777. Or Exodus.

The death pang has come in truth. "That is what you were turning away from."

20 The Trumpet will be blown: "That is the Day of Warning."

Every soul will come forward with a driver and a witness:

"You were oblivious of this; so We lifted your cover from you and your vision today is keen."

His companion[778] will say: "This is what I have; it is ready.

"Cast into Hell every obdurate unbeliever;

25 "Hinderer of the good, transgressor and doubter;

"Who has set up, together with Allah, another god. Cast him, then, into the terrible punishment."

His companion will say: "Our Lord, I did not mislead him; but he was already in profound error."

He[779] will say: "Do not dispute before Me; for I had warned you in advance.

"No word can be changed before Me, and I am no oppressor of servants.

30 "On the day We shall say to Hell: 'Are you full?', and it shall respond: 'Is there more to come?' "

Paradise will be brought closer to the God-fearing, not a far distance.

"This is what you were promised; to every penitent keeper,[780]

"He who fears the Compassionate in the Unseen and comes forward with a penitent heart.

"Enter it in peace; that is the Day of Immortality."

35 They will have whatever they desire therein, and We have yet much more.

How many a generation mightier than they have We destroyed before them? Search the land, then, is there any escape?

In that is a reminder to whoever has a heart or lends an ear, while he witnesses.

Indeed, We have created the heavens and the earth and what is between them in six days, and We were not touched by weariness.

Bear up with what they say and proclaim the praise of your Lord before sunrise and before sunset.

40 And in the night and in the wake of the prostrations, glorify Him.

And listen on the day the caller shall call out from a nearby place;

The day they shall hear the Cry of Truth: "That is the day of rising again."

It is We who give life and cause to die and unto Us is the ultimate return;

778. His demon.
779. Allah.
780. Of Allah's ordinances.

The day that the earth shall be rent asunder around them, as they hasten forth. That, indeed, is an easy mustering for Us.

45   We know better what they say and you are not a tyrant terrorizing them. So, remind, by the Qur'an, him who fears My Warning.

SURA 51

Al-Dhariyat, The Scattering Winds

In the Name of Allah, the Compassionate, the Merciful

1 By the scattering winds, as they scatter:
And the clouds, bearing their burden;
And the smoothly cruising ships;
And the angels which apportion the Command.
5 Surely, what you are promised is true;
And the judgement shall come to pass.
By the heaven with its many tracks,
You are at variance in what you say.
From it[781] are diverted those who would be diverted.
10 May the imposters perish!
Those who are bemused in their perplexity.
They ask: "When is the Day of Judgement coming?"
The day they shall be exposed to the Fire.
"Taste your ordeal; this is what you were trying to hasten."
15 The God-fearing shall be amidst gardens and springs;
Availing themselves of what their Lord has given them. Before that time,
they were beneficent.
They used to sleep but a short watch of the night;
And at daybreak, they used to ask for forgiveness,
And of their possessions, the beggar and the destitute had a share.
20 In the earth are signs for those of certain faith;
And in your souls too. Do you not see?
In heaven is your provision and what you are promised.
By the Lord of the heaven and earth; it is certainly true, just as your own
speaking is true.
Has the tale of Abraham's honoured guests reached you?
25 When they entered upon him and said: "Peace", he replied: "Peace; you
are an unknown people to me."
Then, he went back to his own family and brought a fattened calf.
He offered it to them, saying: "Will you not eat?"
So, he conceived a fear of them. They said: "Do not fear", and they
announced to him the good news of a clever boy.

781. The Qur'an.

Then his wife came shouting and she smote her face and said: "I am a barren old woman."

30 They said: "That is what your Lord has said. He is indeed the Wise, the All-Knowing."

He[782] said: "And what is your business, O envoys?"

They said: "We have been sent forth to a criminal people;

"To unleash on them stones of clay,

"Marked by your Lord for the extravagant.

35 "So, we brought out such believers as were therein.

"But did not find in it except one house of those who have submitted.

"And we left therein a sign for those who fear the painful punishment."

And in Moses,[783] when We sent him forth to Pharaoh with manifest authority.

He[784] turned away with his retinue and said: "A sorcerer or a madman."

40 So, We seized him and his hosts and cast them into the sea; for he was blameworthy.

And in 'Ad, when We loosed upon them the barren wind;

It left nothing it came upon, but reduced it to rubble.

And in Thamud, when it was said to them: "Enjoy yourselves for a while."

Then, they disdained arrogantly the command of their Lord, and so the thunderbolt struck them, while they looked on.

45 They were unable to stand upright, and they were not victorious.

And We destroyed the people of Noah before that. They were indeed a sinful people.

And heaven, We have built it mightily, and We shall surely expand it.

And the earth, We have spread it out; and how excellently we smoothed it down!

And of everything, We have created a pair, that perchance you might remember.

50 Therefore, flee unto Allah. I am to you a manifest warner from Him.

And do not set up with Allah another god. I am to you a manifest warner from Him.

Likewise, no messenger came to those who preceded them but they said: "A sorcerer or a madman."

Have they attested to each other concerning him?[785] No, they are an unjust people.

782. Abraham.
783. Is a sign.
784. Pharaoh.
785. Muhammad.

So, turn away from them; you are not to blame.

55 And remind; for the reminder will benefit the believers.

I have not created the *jinn* and mankind except to worship Me.

I do not desire provision from them, and I do not want them to feed Me.

Surely, Allah is the All-Provider, the Mighty One, the Strong.

The wrongdoers will have a portion like the portions of their fellows; so let them not rush Me.

60 Woe unto the unbelievers on that day which they have been promised.

Al-Tur, The Mount

In the Name of Allah, the Compassionate, the Merciful

1   By the Mount,
    And a Book inscribed,
    In a rolled-out parchment.
    And by the inhabited House,
5   And the upraised roof,
    And the roaring sea,
    The punishment of your Lord is surely coming.
    No one will be able to avert it.
    On the day when heaven shall turn round and round;
10   And the mountains shall be set in motion.
    Woe, on that day, unto those who denounce;
    Those who are stumbling about in confusion.
    On the day they will be driven into the Fire of Hell by force.
    "This is the Fire which you used to deny.
15   "Is this magic or do you not see?
    "Burn in it. Bear up or do not bear up; it is the same for you. You are
only rewarded for what you used to do."
    The God-fearing are indeed in gardens and bliss,
    Rejoicing in what their Lord has given them; and their Lord shall guard
them against the punishment of Hell, [saying]:
    "Eat and drink merrily, for what you used to do."
20   Reclining on ranged couches, and We shall wed them to wide-eyed houris.
    And those who have believed and their progeny, followed them in belief,
We shall join their progeny to them. We shall not deprive them of any of
their work; every man shall be bound by what he has earned.
    And We shall supply them with fruit and meat, such as they desire.
    They will exchange therein a cup wherein there is no idle talk or vilifica-
tion.
    And boys of their own will go round them, as if they were hidden pearls.
25   They turn one to another asking each other questions;
    They say: "We were formerly in the midst of our families living in awe;
    "Then Allah was gracious to us and guarded us against the torment of the
scorching wind.

"We used formerly to call on Him; He is the All-Gracious, the Merciful."

So remind [them]; for you[786] are not, by the grace of your Lord, a soothsayer or a madman.

30 Or do they say: "A poet for whom we await an uncertain fate."

Say: "Await, I am indeed with you awaiting."

Or do their minds bid them do this; or are they, rather, an aggressive people?

Or do they say: "He fabricated it"? No, they believe not.

Let them bring, then, a discourse like it, if they are truthful.

35 Were they created out of nothing, or are they like creators?

Or did they create the heavens and the earth? No, they do not believe with certainty.

Or do they possess the treasuries of your Lord; or are they the domineering ones?

Or, do they have a ladder whereon they listen? Let their listener, then, bring a manifest authority.

Or, does He have the daughters and you have the sons?

40 Or, are you asking them a wage; therefore they are weighed down with debt?

Or, do they have the knowledge of the Unseen, and so they are writing it down?

Or, do they desire to scheme? The unbelievers are truly the objects of scheming.

Or, do they have a god other than Allah? Allah be exalted above what they associate!

If they see a lump falling down from the sky, they say: "A mass of clouds."

45 Leave them, then, till they encounter the day on which they will be thunderstruck;

The day when their cunning will avail them nothing, and they will not be supported.

And the wrongdoers shall suffer a punishment beyond that; but most of them do not know.

Bear with your Lord's judgement, for you are in Our thoughts; and proclaim the praise of your Lord when you arise;

And in the night, glorify Him, and at the receding of the stars.

786. That is, Muhammad.

SURA 53

Al-Najm, The Star

1   By the star when it goes down,
    Your Companion[787] has not gone astray or erred,
    And he does not talk capriciously.
    It[788] is only a revelation being revealed,
5   Taught him by a mighty one,[789]
    Possessed of steadfastness. And so he arose,
    While he was on the highest horizon;
    Then, he came closer and hovered around;
    Coming thus within two bows' length or closer.
10 Then he revealed to His servant what he revealed.
    The heart did not deny what it saw.
    Do you, then, dispute with him concerning what he saw?
    He has indeed seen him a second time;
    By the Lotus Tree of the outermost limit.
15 Close by it is the Garden of Refuge.
    As the Lotus Tree was covered by that which covers it;
    His gaze did not shift nor did he exceed the bound.
    He saw some of the great signs of his Lord.
    Have you, then, seen al-Lat and al-'Uzza?
20 And Manat, the third one, the other?
    Do you have the male and He has the female?
    That indeed is an unjust division.
    These are mere names you and your fathers have named, for which Allah
    did not send down any authority. They only follow conjecture and what the
    souls desire; yet guidance has come to them from their Lord.
    Or will man have whatever he wishes?
25 For to Allah belongs the last and the first life.
    How many an angel is there in the heavens whose intercession avails
    nothing, except after Allah gives leave to whoever He wishes and is well-
    pleased with.

787. Muhammad.
788. The Qur'an.
789. The angel Gabriel (Jibril).

Those who do not believe in the Hereafter will surely give the angels the names of females.

Yet, they have no knowledge thereof. They only follow conjecture, but conjecture avails nothing regarding truth.

So turn away from him who has given up Our mention and only desires the present life.

30   That is their attainment in knowledge. Your Lord indeed knows better those who have strayed from His path, and He knows better those who are well-guided.

And to Allah belongs whatever is in the heavens and on the earth, that He may reward the evildoers for what they did, and reward the righteous with the fairest reward;

Those who avoid grave sins and foul acts, except for venial ones. Your Lord's forgiveness is indeed ample. He knows you very well since He produced you from earth, and while you were still embryos in your mothers' wombs. Do not commend yourselves, He knows very well who is God-fearing.

Have you considered him who turned away;

Gave a little then held back?[790]

35   Does he have the knowledge of the Unseen and is therefore a seer?

Has he not been told about what the scrolls of Moses contain?

And Abraham who fulfilled his pledge;

That no sinning soul shall bear the burden of another soul;

And that man will only earn what he strives for;

40   And that his striving shall be witnessed;

Then he will be rewarded for it the fullest reward;

And that unto your Lord is the ultimate return;

And that He causes people to laugh and to cry;

And that He causes some to die and to live;

45   And that He has created the pairs, both male and female;

From a sperm when it is emitted;

And that upon Him devolves the second creation;

And that He gives riches and possessions;

And that He is the Lord of Sirius;

50   And that He destroyed the first 'Ad;

And Thamud, as well, leaving nothing behind;

And the people of Noah before that; for they were more unjust and more domineering;

And brought down the subverted city;[791]

---

790. The reference is to al-Wahid Ibn al-Mughirah, who wanted to bargain his sins away for money; so he made a down payment and withheld the rest of the money.

791. That is Sodom, city of Lot.

So, He covered it with what He covered.
55 Which of your Lord's bounties, then, do you doubt?
This is one of the first warnings.
The Last Day is imminent;
It has, apart from Allah, no discloser.
Do you then marvel at this discourse?
60 You laugh and do not cry;
While you are fully distracted.
Prostrate yourselves before Allah, then, and worship Him.

SURA 54

Al-Qamar, The Moon

In the Name of Allah, the Compassionate, the Merciful

1   The Hour is drawing near and the moon is split asunder.
If they see a sign, they turn away and say: "Continued sorcery."
They denounced and followed their fancies, while every matter had been settled.
And they have received such news as would deter,

5   An outstanding wisdom; so what good are warnings?
Turn away from them. On the day the caller shall call out unto an abominable thing;
They will come out of their graves, with their eyes downcast, as if they were swarming locusts,
Scrambling towards the caller. The unbelievers will say: "This is a very hard day."
The people of Noah denounced before them; they denounced Our servant as a liar and said: "A madman", and he was rebuffed.

10   So, he called upon his Lord: "I am beaten; so give me support."
Thereupon, We opened up the gates of heaven with torrential water;
And caused the earth to gush with springs, and so the waters converged in accordance with a foreordained decree.
And We carried him along upon a ship made of boards and iron plates;
Sailing before Our very eyes, as a reward to him who was disbelieved.

15   We have indeed left it as a sign. Is there, then, any one who will remember?
How, then, were My punishment and My warnings?
And We have made the Qur'an easy to remember. Is there, then, any one who will remember?
'Ad denounced; how, then, were My punishment and My warnings?
We have loosed upon them a mighty wind, on a day of constant misfortune;

20   Uprooting people, as though they were the stumps of fallen palm trees.
How, then, were My punishment and My warnings?
We have made the Qur'an easy to remember. Is there, then, any one who will remember?
Thamud denounced the warnings as lies.

So they said: "Shall we follow a lone mortal from among us? We are indeed in error and folly.

25   "Has the Reminder been sent down upon him alone from among us? No, he is an arrogant liar."

They will surely know tomorrow who is the arrogant liar.

We shall send the she-camel as a test for them; so watch them and be patient.

And tell them that the water is to be divided between them, each drinking in turn.

They called their companion, and so he took charge and hamstrung [her].

30   How then were My punishment and My warnings?

We released upon them a single cry and they became like the stubble of a corral-builder.

We have, indeed, made the Qur'an easy to remember. Is there, then, any one who will remember?

The people of Lot denounced the warnings as lies.

We loosed upon them a squall of pebbles, except for the family of Lot whom We saved at dawn,

35   As a grace from Us. Thus do We reward those who give thanks.

He had warned them of Our onslaught, but they doubted the warnings.

And they even solicited of him his guests; so We blotted out their eyesight: "Taste, then, My punishment and My warnings."

Early in the morning, they were visited with implacable punishment.

"Taste, then, My punishment and My warnings."

40   We have, indeed, made the Qur'an easy to remember. Is there, then, any one who will remember?

The warnings also came to Pharaoh's folk.

They denounced all Our signs as lies; so We seized them in the manner of One who is mighty and strong.

Are your unbelievers better than all those; or have you been exonerated in the Scriptures?

Or do they say: "We are a band which will conquer."

45   The host will certainly be routed and turn their backs in flight.

No, the Hour shall be their appointment; and the Hour is very grievous and bitter.

The criminals are indeed in error and blazes;

The day they will be dragged upon their faces into the Fire: "Taste now the touch of Saqar."[792]

---

792. Another name for Hell.

Indeed, We have created everything in measure.
50   Our command is but one word, like the twinkling of an eye.
We have destroyed your likes; is there anyone who will remember?
Everything they have done is recorded in the Scriptures.
Everything, small or big, is written down.
The God-fearing are, indeed, amid gardens and rivers;
55   Upon a seat of truth in the presence of an Omnipotent King.

SURA 55

Al-Rahman, The All-Compassionate

In the Name of Allah, the Compassionate, the Merciful

1   The Compassionate,
     Has taught the Qur'an.
     He created man;
     And taught him elocution.
5   The sun and the moon move according to a plan.
     The shrubs[793] and the trees prostrate themselves.
     And the sky, He raised and He set up the balance;
     That you may not transgress in the balance.
     Conduct your weighing with equity and do not stint the balance.
10   And the earth, He set up for all mankind.
     In it, are fruit and palm trees in buds;
     And grain in blades and fragrant plants.
     So, which of your Lord's bounties do you, both,[794] deny?
     He created man from hard clay, like bricks.
15   And He created the *jinn* from tongues of fire.
     So, which of your Lord's bounties do you, both, deny?
     The Lord of the two Easts and the two Wests.
     So, which of your Lord's bounties do you, both, deny?
     He unleashed the two seas so as to merge together.
20   Between them is a barrier which they do not overstep.
     So, which of your Lord's bounties do you, both, deny?
     From them both come out pearls and coral.
     So, which of your Lord's bounties do you, both, deny?
     To Him belong the seagoing ships towering upon the sea like mountains.
25   So, which of your Lord's bounties do you, both, deny?
     Everyone upon it[795] is perishing;
     But the Face of your Lord, full of majesty and nobility, shall abide.
     So, which of your Lord's bounties do you, both, deny?
     Whatever is in the heavens or on the earth petitions Him, and every day
     He is attending to some new matter.
30   So, which of your Lord's bounties, do you, both, deny?

793. Or stars (*al-najm*).
794. *Jinn* and humans.
795. The earth.

We shall attend to you, O two races?[796]

So, which of your Lord's bounties do you, both, deny?

O *jinn* and human folk, if you can pass through the bounds of the heavens and the earth, pass through them. You will not pass through without some authority.

So, which of your Lord's bounties do you, both, deny?

35 A flame of fire and brass will be loosed upon you, so that you will not receive any support.

So, which of your Lord's bounties do you, both, deny?

When the heaven shall be rent asunder and turned red like pigment.

So, which of your Lord's bounties do you, both, deny?

On that day, none shall be questioned about his sin, whether a man or a *jinn*.

40 So, which of your Lord's bounties do you, both, deny?

The criminals shall be known by their marks; then they shall be seized by their forelocks and their feet.

So, which of your Lord's bounties do you, both, deny?

This is Hell, which the criminals deny.

They circle between it and between a hot-water cauldron.

45 So, which of your Lord's bounties do you, both, deny?

But, for him who fears his Lord two gardens [are reserved].

So, which of your Lord's bounties do you, both, deny?

They have numerous branches.

So, which of your Lord's bounties do you, both, deny?

50 And there are therein two flowing springs.

So, which of your Lord's bounties do you, both, deny?

Therein is a pair of every fruit.

So, which of your Lord's bounties do you, both, deny?

Reclining upon couches whose linings are of brocade and the fruits of the two gardens are near at hand.

55 So, which of your Lord's bounties do you, both, deny?

Therein are maidens lowering their glances and they have not been touched, before them by any man or *jinn*.

So, which of your Lord's bounties do you, both, deny?

They are like rubies and coral.

So, which of your Lord's bounties do you, both, deny?

60 Shall the reward of beneficence be other than beneficence?

So, which of your Lord's bounties do you, both, deny?

And beneath them[797] are two other gardens.

796. Of men and *jinn*.
797. The two gardens.

So, which of your Lord's bounties do you, both, deny?
Of dark green colour.
65 So, which of your Lord's bounties do you, both, deny?
Therein are two gushing springs.
So, which of your Lord's bounties do you, both, deny?
Therein are fruits, palm trees and pomegranates.
So, which of your Lord's bounties do you, both, deny?
70 Therein are beautiful, virtuous maidens.
So, which of your Lord's bounties do you, both, deny?
Wide-eyed, cloistered in pavilions.
So, which of your Lord's bounties do you, both, deny?
No man or *jinn* touched them before.
75 So, which of your Lord's bounties do you, both, deny?
Reclining upon green cushions and superb rugs.
So, which of your Lord's bounties do you, both, deny?
Blessed be the name of your Lord, full of majesty and splendour.

SURA 56

Al-Waqiʿa, The Happening

In the Name of Allah, the Compassionate, the Merciful

1 When the Happening comes to pass.
Of its occurrence there is no denial;
Abasing some, exalting others.
When the earth shall be shaken violently,
5 And the mountains shall be reduced to rubble,
So that they become scattered dust.
And you shall be three categories:
The Companions of the Right – behold the Companions of the Right?
And the Companions of the Left – behold the Companions of the Left?
10 And the outstrippers,[798] the outstrippers;
Those are the favoured ones,
In the Gardens of Bliss;
A throng of the ancients,
And a small band of the latecomers.
15 Upon beds interwoven with gold;
Reclining upon them, facing each other.
While immortal youths go round them,
With goblets, pitchers and a cup of limpid drink.
Their heads do not ache from it and they do not become intoxicated.
20 And with such fruits as they care to choose;
And such flesh of fowl as they desire;
And wide-eyed houris,
Like hidden pearls;
As a reward for what they used to do.
25 They do not hear therein idle talk or vilification;
Only the greeting: "Peace, peace!"
As for the Companions of the Right; and behold the Companions of the
Right?
They are in the midst of thornless Lotus Trees,
And braided acacias,
30 And extended shade,

798. The Companions of the Right are the blessed; the Companions of the Left, the damned. The outstrippers are the privileged few.

And overflowing water;
And abundant fruit,
Neither withheld nor forbidden,
And uplifted mattresses.
35   We have formed them originally;
And made them pure virgins,
Tender and unageing,
For the Companions of the Right;
A throng of the ancients,
40   And a throng of the latecomers.
As for the Companions of the Left; and what are the Companions of the Left?
Amid searing wind and boiling water;
And a shadow of thick smoke,
Which is neither cool nor bounteous.
45   They lived before that in luxury;
And they used to insist upon the Great Blasphemy.
They used to say: "What? When we are dead and turn into dust and bones, shall we be raised from the dead?
"And our forefathers, too?"
Say: "The first and the last,
50   "Shall be gathered upon an appointed, pre-assigned day.
"Then you, erring ones and denouncers,
"Shall eat from the Tree of Bitterness,
"Filling your bellies therefrom,
"And drinking on top of it boiling water,
55   "Lapping it like thirsty camels."
That shall be their meal on the Day of Judgement.
We have created you, if only you would believe!
Have you seen the semen you emit?
Do you create it, or are We the Creators?
60   We have decreed death upon you and We would not be outstripped;
Had We wanted to change the like of you and form you afresh in a fashion you do not know.
You have already known the first fashioning; if only you would remember.
Have you seen what you till?
Do you sow it yourselves, or are We the sowers?
65   Had We wished, We would have reduced it to rubble, and so you would have remained wondering:
"We are penalized, indeed;
"No, we are being deprived."

Or have you seen the water that you drink?

Have you brought it down from the clouds or did We send it down?

70 Had We wished, We would have made it bitter; if only you would give thanks.

Or did you see the fire which you kindle?

Did you make its timber to grow or were We the growers?

We have made it a reminder and a boon to the desert-dwellers.

Glorify, then, the name of your Great Lord.

75 No! I swear by the falling of the stars;

It is indeed a mighty oath, if only you knew.

It is, indeed, a noble Qur'an.

In a hidden Book,

That only the purified shall touch.

80 A revelation from the Lord of the Worlds.

Are you, then, regarding this discourse, dissimulating?

And do you make it your livelihood to denounce it as lies?

Would that, when the soul leaps to the throat,

And you are, then, waiting;

85 While We are closer to him[799] than you, but you do not see.

And would that, not being subject to judgement,

You are able to bring them[800] back, if you are truthful!

However, if he[801] is one of those who are favoured;

Then ease and delight, and Gardens of Bliss are his.

90 But if he is one of the Companions of the Right;

Then "Peace upon you", from the Companions of the Right.

However, if he is one of those who denounce and err;

Then he will be served boiling water,

And will be scorched by the Fire.

95 That indeed is the certain truth.

So, glorify the name of your Lord, the Great One.

---

799. The dead man.
800. The souls.
801. The dead man.

SURA 57

Al-Hadid, Iron

In the Name of Allah, the Compassionate, the Merciful

1 Whatever is in the heavens and the earth glorifies Allah. He is the
All-Mighty, the Wise.

To Him belongs the dominion of the heavens and the earth. He brings to
life and causes to die, and He has power over everything.

He is the First and the Last, the Outer and the Inner, and He has
knowledge of everything.

It is He who created the heavens and the earth in six days; then He sat
upon the Throne. He knows what penetrates into the earth and what comes
out of it; what comes down from heaven and ascends to it. He is with you,
wherever you are: Allah perceives whatever you do.

5 To Him belongs the dominion of the heavens and the earth, and unto
Allah all matters are ultimately referred.

He causes the night to phase into the day and the day to phase into the
night, and He knows the secrets within the breasts.

Believe in Allah and His Apostle and spend freely from what He has
bequeathed to you. For those of you who believe and spend freely will have
a great wage.

What is the matter with you? You do not believe in Allah, although the
Apostle calls upon you to believe in your Lord, and He has already taken
your covenant, if you are true believers?

It is He who sends down upon His servant manifest signs, so as to bring
you out from the dark shadows into the light. Allah is indeed All-Clement
and Merciful towards you.

10 And why is it that you do not spend freely in the cause of Allah, when to
Allah belongs the heritage of the heavens and the earth? Not all those of you
who spend freely before the Conquest[802] and have fought are equal.
However they are higher in rank than those who spent freely and fought
afterwards; and unto each Allah has promised the fairest reward. Allah is
fully aware of what you do.

Who is he that will lend Allah a fair loan, that He might double it for
him; and he will have a generous wage.

On the day that you will see the believers, men and women, with their

---

802. The Conquest of Mecca, 8 AH.

light beaming in front of them, and in their right hands [the sign]: "Your good news today is gardens beneath which rivers flow, dwelling therein forever. That indeed is the great triumph."

On the day the hypocrites, men and women, will say to the believers: "Wait for us, so that we may borrow from your light." It will be said: "Go back and seek for yourselves a light." Then a wall will be raised between them both, which has a door. On the inner part thereof is mercy, and on the opposite side the outer part thereof is punishment.

They will call out to them: "Were we not with you?" They will say: "Yes indeed; but you deluded yourselves, you waited long, doubted and were deceived by false hopes, until Allah's decree came and the Deceiver[803] deceived you regarding Allah."

15   Therefore, today no ransom will be taken from you, nor from the unbelievers. The Fire will be your refuge; it will be your master; and what an evil fate!

Is it not time that the believers' hearts should bow down at the mention of Allah and the Truth which was sent down, and not to be like those who were given the Book previously, but as time went by, their hearts hardened, and many of them are sinners now?

Know that Allah revives the earth after it is dead. We have expounded the signs clearly for you, that perchance you might understand.

Surely, the men and women who give in charity and who have lent Allah a fair loan will receive its double and they will have a generous wage.

And those who believe in Allah and His messengers are truly the pious and the martyrs in their Lord's sight. They shall have their wage and their light; but those who disbelieve and deny Our signs, are truly the Companions of Hell.

20   Know that the present life is but sport and diversion, adornment, boasting among you and rivalry in amassing wealth and children. It is like a rain whose vegetation delighted the unbelievers, then it withered and you see it turning yellow and then it becomes stubble. In the Hereafter there is terrible punishment, forgiveness from Allah and good pleasure. The present life is but the enjoyment of vanity.

Vie with one another unto forgiveness from your Lord and a garden the breadth whereof is like the breadth of the heavens and the earth; it has been prepared for those who believe in Allah and His messengers. That is Allah's bounty which He confers upon whoever He pleases. And Allah's is the great bounty.

Not a disaster befalls in the earth or in yourselves but is in a Book, before We created it. That for Allah is an easy matter.

803. Satan.

So that you may not grieve for what you missed, and rejoice at what came your way. Allah does not like the conceited and the boastful;

Those who are niggardly and bid people to be niggardly. He who turns away, Allah is All-Sufficient, Praiseworthy.

25   We have sent forth Our messengers with clear proofs and sent down with them the Book and the Balance, so that people might act equitably. We have also sent down iron, which has mighty power and benefits for mankind, and that Allah might know who supports Him and His messengers invisibly. Allah is indeed Strong and Mighty.

We have also sent forth Noah and Abraham and assigned prophethood and the Book to their progeny. Some of them are well-guided and many of them are sinners.

Then, We sent forth in their wake Our messengers and followed up with Jesus, son of Mary, and We gave him the Gospel and We instilled in the hearts of those who followed him compassion to them except as a means of seeking Allah's good pleasure. However, they did not observe it properly; so We gave those of them who believed their wage, but many of them are sinful.

O believers, fear Allah and believe in His Apostle, so that He might show you His mercy twofold, give you a light by which you might walk about and forgive you. Allah is All-Forgiving, Merciful;

That the People of the Book may know that they have no power over anything of Allah's bounty, and that bounty is in Allah's power; He gives it to whoever He pleases. Allah's is the great bounty.

Al-Mujadilah, The Pleading Woman

In the Name of Allah, the Compassionate, the Merciful

1 Allah has heard the words of that woman who disputes with you, concerning her husband, and complains to Allah, while Allah hears you both conversing. Allah is truly All-Hearing, All-Seeing.

Those of you, who ignore their wives saying: "You are like our mother's back", should know that they are not really their mothers. Their mothers are only those women who gave them birth, and they are certainly making a reprehensible statement and a lie. But Allah is indeed All-Pardoning, All-Forgiving.

And those who say of their wives: "You are like our mother's back", then retract what they said, have to free a slave before touching each other. That is what you are admonished, and Allah is fully aware of what you do.

As for him who does not have the means, he should fast two consecutive months, before they can touch each other; and he who cannot should feed sixty poor persons. That is prescribed that you may believe in Allah and His Apostle and these are the bounds of Allah. The unbelievers shall have a very painful punishment.

5 Those who antagonize Allah and His Apostle shall be abased by Allah, as He abased those who preceded them. We have, indeed, sent down very clear signs; and the unbelievers shall have a demeaning punishment.

On the day when Allah shall raise them all from the dead, then inform them of what they did. Allah has kept count of it, but they have forgotten it. Allah is a witness of everything.

Have you not considered that Allah knows what is in the heavens and on the earth. No three conspire in secret, but He is the fourth of them; nor five, but He is the sixth of them; nor even less than that or more, but He is with them wherever they are. Then He shall inform them of what they did on the Day of Resurrection. Allah, indeed, has knowledge of everything.

Have you not considered those who were forbidden to converse secretly, then they return to what they were forbidden from and converse secretly in sin and aggression and the disobedience of the Apostle? Then, when they come to you, they greet you with a greeting that Allah never greeted you with. They say within themselves: "If only Allah were to punish us for what we say!" May Hell suffice them; and what a wretched fate!

O believers, if you converse secretly among yourselves, do not converse in sin, aggression and disobedience of the Apostle; but converse in righteousness and piety, and fear Allah unto Whom you shall be mustered.

10   Conversing in secret is an act of Satan, so as to sadden the believers; but that will not harm them in the least, except with Allah's leave. Let the believers put their trust in Allah.

O believers, if you are told: "Make room in assemblies", then make room that Allah may make room for you; and if you are told: "Sally forth", then sally forth, that Allah may elevate those of you who have believed and those who have been given knowledge many steps. Allah is fully aware of what you do.

O believers, if you converse privately with the Apostle, then tender a free offering before your secret conversing. That is better for you and purer; but if you do not have the means, then Allah is All-Forgiving, Merciful.

Do you dread to make free offerings before your private converse? If you do not do so and Allah pardons you, then perform the prayer, give the alms and obey Allah and His Apostle. Allah is aware of what you do.

Have you not considered those who befriended a people who incurred Allah's wrath? They are not of you nor of them; and they swear in falsehood knowingly.

15   Allah has prepared for them a terrible punishment. Evil indeed is what they used to do.

They took their oaths as a smoke-screen, and so they debarred access to Allah's path. Theirs, then, is a demeaning punishment.

Neither their possessions nor their children shall avail them anything against Allah. Those are the Companions of the Fire, dwelling therein forever.

On the day Allah shall resurrect all and they will swear to Him as they swear to you, thinking that they have something to gain. Indeed, they are the liars.

Satan has taken hold of them, and so caused them to forget the mention of Allah. Those are the party of Satan; indeed the party of Satan are the losers.

20   Those who antagonize Allah and His Apostle are surely among the lowliest.

Allah has written: "I shall certainly vanquish, I and My messengers." Surely Allah is Strong, All-Mighty.

You will not find a people who believe in Allah and the Last Day befriending those who antagonize Allah and His Apostle, even if they are their fathers, their sons, their brothers or their clansmen. Those, Allah has inscribed faith upon their hearts and strengthened them with a spirit from Himself, and He will admit them into gardens, beneath which rivers flow, dwelling therein forever. Allah is well-pleased with them and they are well-pleased with Him. Those are Allah's party; surely Allah's party shall be the prosperous.

Al-Hashr, The Mustering

In the Name of Allah, the Compassionate, the Merciful

1 Everything in the heavens and the earth glorifies Allah. He is the All-Mighty, the All-Wise.

It is He who drove out the unbelievers among the People of the Book from their homes at the first mustering. You did not think that they would be driven out, and they thought that their forts would protect them from Allah. Then, Allah seized them from an unexpected quarter and cast terror into their hearts, so that they destroyed their homes with their own hands, as well as the hands of the believers. Reflect, then, O people of perception!

Had not Allah decreed dispersion upon them, He would certainly have punished them in the present life, and in the Hereafter, the punishment of the Fire shall be theirs.

That is because they have opposed Allah and His Apostle, and he who opposes Allah will find Allah terrible in retribution.

5 Whatever palm trees you cut off or leave standing upon their roots is only by Allah's leave, and that he might disgrace the sinners.

Whatever spoils Allah has bestowed on His Apostle from them, you did not send against them any horses or other mounts; but Allah confers on His messengers authority over whoever He pleases. Allah has power over everything.

And whatever spoils Allah bestows on His Apostle from the inhabitants of the cities belongs to Allah, His Apostle, the kinsmen, the orphan, the destitute and the wayfarers; so that it might not circulate among the rich of you. Whatever the Apostle gives you, take; but whatever he forbids, refrain from. Fear Allah, for Allah is terrible in retribution.

Give to the poor Emigrants who were driven out of their homes and their possessions, seeking bounty from Allah and good pleasure and assisting Allah and His Apostle. Those indeed are the truthful ones.

And those who had already established themselves and embraced their Faith before them[804] love those who emigrated to them; and they do not find in their hearts any need for what had been bestowed upon them and prefer them to themselves, even if they are in dire need. He is indeed prosperous who is guarded against the avarice of his soul.

804. That is, the people of Medina, known as *al-Ansar*, or supporters, as against the Meccans known as *al-Muhajirun*, or emigrants.

10   Those who came after them say: "Our Lord, forgive us and our brothers who preceded us in belief and do not instil in our hearts any rancour towards those who believe. Lord, you are indeed Clement and Merciful."

Have you not considered the hypocrites? They say to their brethren who have disbelieved from the People of the Book: "If you are driven out, we will go out with you and we will never obey anyone against you; and should anyone fight you, we will certainly support you." Allah bears witness that they are liars, indeed.

If they are driven out, they will not go out with them; and if anyone fights them, they will not support them. Even if they support them, they will turn their backs in flight; then they will not receive any support.

You are indeed more terrifying in their hearts than Allah. That is because they are a people who do not understand.

They do not fight you all together except in fortified cities or from behind walls. Their prowess is great among themselves. You think they are united, yet their hearts are at variance. That is because they are a people who do not understand.

15   Like those who, shortly before them, tasted the futility of their action. They shall have a painful punishment.

Like Satan, when he said to man: "Disbelieve"; then when he disbelieved, he said: "I am quit of you. Indeed, I fear Allah, the Lord of the Worlds."

Thereupon, their end together was to be in the Fire, dwelling therein forever. That is the reward of the wrongdoers.

O believers, fear Allah and let each soul consider what it has forwarded for the morrow. Fear Allah; He is aware of what you do.

Do not be like those who forgot Allah, and so He made them forget themselves. Those are indeed the sinners.

20   The Companions of the Fire and the Companions of Paradise are not equal. The Companions of Paradise are indeed the winners.

Had we sent down this Qur'an upon a mountain, you would have seen it bowing down and rent asunder out of the fear of Allah. Those are the parables which We recite to mankind, that perchance you might reflect.

He is Allah; there is no god but He, the Knower of the Unseen and the Seen. He is the Compassionate, the Merciful.

He is Allah. There is no god but He, the King, the Holy, the Peace-Giver, the Faith-Giver, the Overseer, the All-Mighty, the Overlord, the Haughty. May Allah be exalted above what they associate.

He is Allah, the Creator, the Maker, the Fashioner. His are the Beautiful Names; whatever is in the heavens and on the earth glorifies Him. He is the All-Mighty, the Wise.

SURA 60

Al-Mumtahana, The Woman Tested

In the Name of Allah, the Compassionate, the Merciful

1 O believers, do not take My enemy and your enemy for supporters, showing them friendship, when they have disbelieved what has come to you of the Truth. They expel the Apostle and expel you because you have believed in Allah, your Lord. If you have gone out to struggle in My cause and to seek My good pleasure secretly showing them friendship, while I know very well what you conceal and what you reveal. He who does that among you has surely strayed from the right path.

If they come upon you, they will be enemies of yours and will stretch out their hands and tongues against you with malice, and they wish that you would disbelieve.

Your kinsmen or your children will not profit you on the Day of Resurrection. He shall separate you one from the other; and Allah perceives well what you do.

You have had a good example in Abraham and those with him, when they said to their people: "We are quit of you and what you worship apart from Allah. We disbelieve in you. Enmity and hatred have arisen between you and us forever, till you believe in Allah alone; except for Abraham's words to his father: 'I will ask forgiveness for you, although I have no power from Allah to do anything for you.' Lord, in You We trust, to You We turn and unto You is the ultimate resort.

5 "Lord, do not cause us to be a temptation for those who have disbelieved, and forgive us, Our Lord, you are indeed the All-Mighty, the All-Wise."

You had indeed in them a good example; that is for whoever hopes for Allah and the Last Day. Whoever repents, surely Allah is the All-Mighty, All-Praiseworthy.

It may be that Allah will establish friendship between you and those of them who were your enemies. Allah is All-Powerful, and Allah is All-Forgiving, All-Merciful.

Allah does not forbid you, regarding those who did not fight you and did not drive you out of your homes, to be generous to them and deal with them justly. Allah surely loves the just.

Allah only forbids you, regarding those who fought you in religion and drove you out of your homes and assisted in driving you out, to take them for friends. Those who take them for friends are, indeed, the wrongdoers.

10   O believers, if believing women come to you as Emigrants, then test them; Allah knows better their faith. If you find them to be believers, do not send them back to the unbelievers. They are neither lawful to the unbelieving men, nor are those men lawful to them. Give them what they[805] had paid in dowry; and you are not at fault if you marry them, provided you pay them their dowries. Do not hold fast to unbelieving women; demand what you have spent and let them demand what they spent. That is Allah's judgement. He judges between you, and Allah is All-Knowing and Wise.

If any of your wives deserts you to the unbelievers, and you decide to penalize them, then give those [husbands] whose wives have gone away the like of what they had spent, and fear Allah in Whom you believe.

O Prophet, if believing women come to you to pay you homage, pledging not to associate anything with Allah, steal, commit adultery, kill their children, come up with a lie they invent between their hands and feet[806] or disobey you in any honourable matter, then accept their homage and ask Allah's forgiveness for them. Allah indeed is All-Forgiving, All-Merciful.

O believers, do not befriend a people against whom Allah is wrathful and who have despaired of the Hereafter, just as the unbelievers have despaired of the dwellers of the tombs.

805. The unbelieving husbands.
806. That is, allege that an illegitimate child is their husband's.

SURA 61

Al-Saff, The Battle Array

In the Name of Allah, the Compassionate, the Merciful

1 Everything in the heavens and on the earth glorifies Allah. He is the All-Mighty, the Wise.

O believers, why do you profess what you do not practise?

It is very hateful in Allah's sight that you profess what you do not practise.

Allah loves those who fight in His cause arrayed in battle, as though they were a compact structure.

5 When Moses said to his people: "O my people, why do you injure me, although you know that I am Allah's messenger to you?" When they swerved, Allah caused their hearts to swerve. Allah does not guide the sinful people.

And when Jesus, son of Mary, said: "O Children of Israel, I am Allah's messenger to you, confirming what came before me of the Torah, and announcing the news of a messenger who will come after me, whose name is Ahmad." Then when he brought them the clear proofs, they said: "This is manifest sorcery."

And who is a greater wrongdoer than he who imputes falsehood to Allah, when he is summoned to submission (to Allah)?[807] Allah does not guide the wrongdoing people.

They wish to extinguish Allah's lights with their mouths, but Allah will perfect His light, even though the unbelievers might be averse.

It is He who sent His Apostle forth with the guidance and the religion of truth, to make it triumph over every religion, even though the idolaters may be averse.

10 O believers, shall I show you a trade which will deliver you from a very painful punishment?

Believe in Allah and His Apostle and struggle in the cause of Allah with your possessions and yourselves. That is far better for you, if only you knew.

He will then forgive you your sins and admit you into gardens, beneath which rivers flow, and into fine dwellings in the Gardens of Eden. That is the great triumph.

---

807. The Arabic word is *al-Islam*, which means submission to the Will of God.

And another thing you love: support from Allah and an imminent victory. So announce the good news to the believers.

O believers, be supporters of Allah, as Jesus, son of Mary, said to the disciples: "Who are my supporters unto Allah?" The disciples replied: "We are Allah's supporters"; and so a group of the Children of Israel believed, while another group disbelieved. Then, We supported those who believed against their foe; and so they were triumphant.

SURA 62

Al-Jum'ah, The Congregation

In the Name of Allah, the Compassionate, the Merciful

1 Everything in the heavens and on the earth glorifies Allah, the King, the Holy One, the All-Mighty, the All-Wise.

It is He who has raised up from the common nations[808] a messenger of their own, reciting to them His signs, purifying them and teaching them the Book and the wisdom, although they had been in manifest error before that;

And others from them, who had not joined them yet. He is the All-Mighty, the Wise.

That is Allah's bounty which He imparts to whomever He pleases; and to Allah belongs the great bounty.

5 The case of those who were loaded with the Torah, then failed to carry it, is similar to an ass which carries learned books. Wretched is the case of the people who have denounced Allah's signs. Allah does not guide the wrongdoing people.

Say: "O you who have adopted Judaism; if you claim to be Allah's friends, apart from other people, then do wish for death, if you are truthful."

Yet, they will never wish it, due to what their hands have advanced. Allah knows well the wrongdoers.

Say: "The death from which you flee will surely overtake you. Then you will be turned over to Him who knows the Unseen and the Seen, and He will inform you about what you used to do."

O believers, when the call for prayer on the Day of Congregation[809] is sounded, then hasten to the mention of Allah and leave off trading. That is far better for you, if only you knew.

10 Then, when prayer is over, spread out throughout the land and seek some of Allah's bounty, and remember Allah often, that perchance you might prosper.

However, when they see trading or sport, they scramble towards it and leave you standing up. Say: "What Allah has in store is far better than sport or trading; and Allah is the best Provider."

---

808. Arabic *al-Ummiyyun*, which could also mean the illiterates, or the people with no revealed scripture, as against the People of the Book, or Jews and Christians.

809. Or Friday.

SURA 63

Al-Munafiqun, The Hypocrites

In the Name of Allah, the Compassionate, the Merciful

1   When the hypocrites come to you, they say: "We bear witness that you are indeed Allah's Apostle." Allah knows that you are indeed His Apostle and Allah bears witness that the hypocrites are liars.

They take their oaths as a shield and so they bar other people from the path of Allah. Evil is what they used to do.

That is because they believed, then disbelieved; and so a seal was set upon their hearts. Therefore, they do not understand at all.

If you see them, their bodies please you; and if they speak, you listen to their words, as though they were propped-up wooden logs. They think every cry is aimed at them; they are the enemy, so beware of them. May Allah discomfit them, how they are perverted!

5   If it is said to them: "Come, that the Apostle of Allah may seek forgiveness for you"; they bend their heads and you see them walking away, waxing proud.

It is the same for them whether you seek forgiveness for them or you do not seek forgiveness. Allah will not forgive them. Surely, Allah will not guide the sinful people.

It is they who say: "Do not spend any money on those[810] who side with Allah's Apostle until they disperse." To Allah belong the treasuries of the heavens and the earth, but the hypocrites do not understand.

They say: "If we return to the City,[811] the mightiest will drive out the lowliest therefrom." Might belongs to Allah, His Apostle and the believers, but the hypocrites do not know.

O believers, let not your possessions or children distract you from the remembrance of Allah. Whoever does that – those are the real losers.

10   Spend freely from what We have provided for you, before death overtakes each one of you. Then he will say: "Lord, if only you would reprieve me for a short period, so that I may give in charity and be one of the righteous."

Allah will not reprieve a single soul when its term comes. Allah is fully aware of what you do.

---

810. The Meccan Emigrants.
811. Yathrib, Medina.

SURA 64

Al-Taghabun, Mutual Fraud

In the Name of Allah, the Compassionate, the Merciful

1 Everything in the heavens and on the earth glorifies Allah. His is the sovereignty and His is the praise, and He has power over everything.

It is He who created you. Some of you are unbelievers, and some believers; and Allah perceives what you do.

He created the heavens and the earth in truth, and He fashioned you and shaped well your forms. Unto Him is the ultimate resort.

He knows what is in the heavens and on the earth, and He knows what you conceal and what you reveal. Allah knows well the thoughts hidden in the breasts.

5 Has not the news of those who disbelieved formerly come to you, and so they tasted the evil plight of their condition? A painful punishment awaits them.

That is because their messengers used to bring them the clear proofs, but they would say: "Will mortals guide us rightly?" So, they disbelieved and turned their backs and Allah was well content. Allah is All-Sufficient, All-Worthy.

The unbelievers claimed that they will not be raised from the dead. Say: "Yes indeed by my Lord, you shall be raised, then you will be informed about what you did. That for Allah is an easy matter."

Therefore, believe in Allah, His Apostle and the Light which We sent down. Allah is aware of what you do.

On the day when He shall gather you for the Day of Forgathering. That is the Day of Mutual Fraud.[812] He who believes in Allah and acts righteously, He will acquit him of his evil actions and admit him into gardens beneath which rivers flow, dwelling therein forever. That is the great triumph.

10 And those who disbelieved and denounced Our signs, those are the Companions of the Fire, dwelling therein forever; and what a miserable fate!

No disaster befalls but by Allah's leave. Whoever believes in Allah, He will guide his heart rightly. Allah has knowledge of everything.

Obey Allah and obey the Apostle. If you turn away, it is only incumbent on Our Apostle to deliver the manifest message.

---

812. When the inhabitants of Paradise would have defrauded the inhabitants of Hell, according to al-Tabari.

Allah, there is no god but He; and in Allah let the believers put their trust.

O believers, in the midst of your wives and children, there is an enemy of yours, so beware of them. Yet, if you pardon, overlook and forgive, surely Allah is All-Forgiving, All-Merciful.

15   Your possessions and children are surely a temptation, and with Allah is a great reward.

So, fear Allah as much as you can, listen, obey and spend freely. That is best for you. He who is guarded against the avarice of his soul – those are the prosperous.

If you lend Allah a fair loan, He will multiply it for you and forgive you. Allah is All-Grateful, All-Clement;

Knower of the Unseen and the Seen, the All-Mighty, the Wise.

SURA 65

Al-Talaq, The Divorce

In the Name of Allah, the Compassionate, the Merciful

1 O Prophet, if you divorce your women, divorce them when they have completed their menstrual period. Calculate the period and fear Allah, your Lord. Do not drive them out of their homes, and let them not go out, unless they have committed a manifest foul act. Those are the bounds of Allah. He who transgresses the bounds of Allah has surely wronged himself. You do not know, Allah may perhaps bring about something new after that.

Then, when they have reached their term, retain them honourably or part with them honourably, calling two just witnesses from among yourselves. Administer the witnessing to Allah Himself. By that is exhorted whoever believes in Allah and the Last Day. He who fears Allah, He will grant him a way out;

And He will provide for him from sources he could never conceive. He who puts his trust in Allah, Allah will be sufficient unto him. Allah shall attain His goal. Allah has meted out a measure for everything.

As for those of your women who have despaired of menstruation, if you are in doubt, then their term shall be three months; and those too who have not menstruated yet. As to those women with child, their term shall be upon delivering their burden. He who fears Allah, Allah will grant him relief in his affair.

5 That is Allah's command, which He has sent down to you; and he who fears Allah, He will acquit him of his sins and amplify his reward.

Put them up where you are lodged, according to your means, and do not badger them so as to make life difficult for them. If they are with child, support them until they deliver their burden; and if they suckle for you, then pay them their wages. Confer with each other honourably; but if you are at odds, let another woman suckle him.

Let the man of means spend out of his means, and he whose provision has been constricted, spend out of what Allah gave him. Allah does not charge any soul except with what He gave it. Allah will cause relief to follow every hardship.

How many a city transgressed arrogantly the command of its Lord and His messengers; and so We brought it to account severely and punished it with an abominable punishment.

And so it tasted the bane of its deed and the outcome of its deed was perdition.

10 Allah has prepared for them a terrible punishment. So fear Allah, O people of understanding who have believed. Allah has sent down to you, as a reminder,

An Apostle, reciting to you the signs of Allah fully clarified; so as to bring those who have believed and done the righteous deeds from the shadows of darkness to light. He who believes in Allah and does the righteous deed, Allah will admit him into gardens, beneath which rivers flow, dwelling therein forever. Allah has assigned to him a fair provision.

It is Allah who created seven heavens and of the earths their like. The Decree descends among them all, that you might know that Allah has power over everything and that Allah has encompassed everything in knowledge.

SURA 66

Al-Tahrim, The Prohibition

In the Name of Allah, the Compassionate, the Merciful

1   O Prophet, why do you prohibit what Allah has made lawful to you, seeking thereby the good pleasure of your wives? Allah is All-Forgiving, Merciful.

Allah has prescribed to you the absolution of your oaths. Allah is your Master and He is the All-Knowing and Wise.

And when the Prophet confided to one of his wives a certain matter;[813] and she divulged it, and Allah disclosed it to him too, he made known part of it, but withheld the other part. Then, when he told her about it, she said: "Who told you this?" He said: "The All-Knowing, All-Informed told me."

If you two[814] repent unto Allah, then your hearts will have certainly inclined; but if you band together against him, then Allah is his Master. Gabriel, the righteous among the believers and the angels thereupon are his supporters, too.

5   Perhaps, his Lord will, if he divorces you, give him in exchange wives better than you, submissive, believing, obedient, penitent, devout, fasting, either previously married or virgins.

O believers, guard yourselves and your families against a Fire whose fuel is people and stones; its overseers are harsh, terrible angels who do not disobey what Allah commands, but will do what they are commanded.

O believers, do not give excuses today; for you are only rewarded for what you used to do.

O believers, turn to Allah in sincere repentance, that your Lord might perchance acquit you of your evil deeds and admit you into gardens, beneath which rivers flow, on a day when Allah will not disgrace the Prophet and those who have believed with him. Their light flickering before them and in their right hands, they will say: "Our Lord, perfect for us our light and forgive us; you have indeed power over everything."

O Prophet, struggle with the unbelievers and the hypocrites, and deal harshly with them. Their refuge shall be Hell, and what an evil resort!

10   Allah gave as an instance of the unbelievers the wife of Noah and the wife of Lot. They were under two of Our righteous servants, then they betrayed

---

813. His eating of honey.
814. The two wives of the Prophet.

them. Nothing availed them against Allah and it was said to them: "Enter you two the Fire with the other entrants."

Allah has given as an instance of believers the wife of Pharaoh, when she said: "Lord, build for me, with You, a house in Paradise and deliver me from Pharaoh and his work, and deliver me from the wrongdoing people."

And Mary, daughter of Imran, who guarded her womb, and so We breathed into it of Our Spirit; and she believed in the truth of Her Lord's words and His books and was one of the pious.

Al-Mulk, The Sovereignty

In the Name of Allah, the Compassionate, the Merciful

1 Blessed be He in Whose hands is the sovereignty and He has power over everything.

He who created death and life so as to test you as to whoever of you is fairer in action. He is the All-Mighty, the All-Forgiving.

He who has created seven stratified heavens. You do not see any discrepancy in the creation of the Compassionate. So fix your gaze, do you see any cracks?

Then, fix your gaze again and again, and your gaze will recoil back to you discomfited and weary.

5 We have adorned the lower heaven with lamps, and We turned them into missiles launched against the devils; and We have prepared for them the punishment of the Fire.

And to those who have disbelieved in their Lord, the punishment of Hell is reserved; and what an evil resort!

When they are cast into it, they hear its heavy breathing, as it boils over.

It almost bursts with rage. Every time a new throng is cast into it, its keepers ask them: "Has no warner come to you?"

They will say: "Yes indeed; a warner came to us but we disbelieved and said: 'Allah did not send down anything; you are simply in grave error.' "

10 And they will also say: "Had we listened or reasoned, we would not be among the Companions of the Fire."

So, they will confess their sin. Away, then, with the Companions of the Fire!

Indeed, those who fear their Lord secretly will be accorded forgiveness and a great reward.

Conceal your words or proclaim them, He knows very well the secrets of the breasts.

Does He not know what He has created, though He is the All-Subtle, the All-Informed?

15 It is He who made the earth level for you; so stroll through its regions and eat of His provision. Unto Him is the Resurrection.

Are you sure that He who is in heaven will not cause the earth to cave in upon you? Behold how it quakes!

Or are you sure that He who is in heaven will not let loose upon you a squall of pebbles? Then you shall know how My warning sounds.

Those who preceded you have disbelieved. How then was My abomination?

Have they not considered the birds above them spreading their wings and folding them? They are only held up by the Compassionate. He is the Perceiver of everything.

20 Or who is this who is a sentinel for you to protect you against the Compassionate? The unbelievers are simply in error.

Or who is this who will provide for you, if He withholds His provision? Rather they have persisted in arrogance and aversion.

Is he who walks prone upon his face better guided, or he who walks upon a straight path?

Say: "It is He who originated you and created for you hearing, sight, and hearts. How little do you give thanks?"

Say: "It is He who scattered you abroad in the land, and unto Him you shall be mustered."

25 They say: "When is this promise to be fulfilled, if you are truthful?"

Say: "Knowledge is with Allah; I am only a manifest warner."

When they see it[815] close at hand, the faces of the unbelievers become grim, and it will be said to them: "That is what you used to boast about."

Say: "Have you considered, what if Allah destroyed me and those with me or had mercy on us, who will protect the unbelievers from a painful punishment?"

Say: "He is the Compassionate, we believe in Him, and in Him we put our trust. You will then know who is in manifest error."

30 Have you considered who, if your water drains away, will bring you pure running water?

---

815. The punishment.

SURA 68

Al-Qalam, The Pen

In the Name of Allah, the Compassionate, the Merciful

1　By the pen and what they inscribe,
　　You are not, by the grace of your Lord, a madman.
　　You will have a wage which is unstinted;
　　And you are truly a man of noble character.
5　You shall see and they shall see,
　　Which of you is the demented one.
　　Surely, your Lord knows better who has strayed from His path and He knows better the well-guided.
　　So do not obey the unbelievers.
　　They wished that you would dissimulate, so that they might dissimulate too.
10　And do not obey every lowly swearer of oaths;
　　Backbiter, going around, bearing calumny;
　　Hinderer of good, aggressor, wicked;
　　Coarse, on top of that, and quarrelsome;
　　Because he has wealth and children.[816]
15　If Our signs are recited to him, he says: "Legends of the ancients."
　　We shall brand him upon the muzzle.
　　We have tested you, just as We tested the Companions of the Garden when they swore to pluck its fruit in the morning,
　　Without any reservations.
　　Then a night-stalker from your Lord visited them while they were asleep.
20　And so it became black like a cropped-off field.
　　Thereupon they called out to each other in the morning:
　　"Go forth to your tillage, if you would crop it off."
　　So, they set out whispering to each other:
　　"Let no destitute person enter it today with you around."
25　And they proceeded next morning angrily, fully determined.
　　When they saw it, they said: "We have surely gone astray.
　　"Rather we are dispossessed."
　　The most reasonable of them said: "Did I tell you, if only you glorify."
　　They said: "Glory to Our Lord, We were indeed wrongdoers."

---

816. The reference is to a Qurashite, al-Walid Ibn al-Mughirah, an enemy of the Prophet.

30   Then, they turned to one another, reproaching each other.

They said: "Woe betide us; we have indeed been domineering.

"Maybe our Lord will give us a better substitute for it.[817] We are truly turning to our Lord."

Such is the punishment; but the punishment of the Hereafter is greater, if only they knew.

Surely, for the God-fearing there are Gardens of Bliss with their Lord.

35   Shall We consider those who submit like those who are criminals?

What is the matter with you; how do you judge?

Or do you have a Book in which you study?

Wherein there is whatever you choose.

Or do you have solemn oaths binding upon us till the Day of Resurrection? You shall have in fact whatever you judge.

40   Ask them: "Who among them is a guarantor of that?"

Or do they have associates? Let them, then, produce their associates, if they are truthful.

On the day when nothing shall be concealed and they shall be called upon to prostrate themselves, but will not be able to.

Their eyes shall be cast down, disgrace overwhelming them, although they were called to prostrate themselves while they were in a sound condition.

So, leave Me alone with those who disbelieve this discourse. We shall draw them out whence they do not know.

45   And I will give them respite; My cunning is certain.

Or will you ask them for remuneration? They are surely burdened with debts.

Or are they in possession of the Unseen, and so they are writing it down?

Bear up with your Lord's judgement, then, and do not be like the Man of the Whale,[818] when he called out fully distressed.

Had not a grace from his Lord been meted out to him, he would have been cast out in the wilderness, fully despised.

50   But his Lord chose him and made him one of the righteous.

The unbelievers will almost strike you down with their glances, on hearing the Reminder,[819] and will say: "He is truly possessed."

It is only a Reminder to all the Worlds.

817. The Garden.
818. Jonas.
819. The Qur'an.

SURA 69

Al-Haqqah, The Certain Hour

In the Name of Allah, the Compassionate, the Merciful

1 The Certain Hour;
And what is the Certain Hour?
If only you knew what the Certain Hour is.
The people of Thamud and 'Ad have disbelieved in the Great Calamity.
5 As to the people of Thamud, they were destroyed by the overwhelming Cry;
But 'Ad were destroyed by a violent, gusty wind,
Which He unleashed upon them for seven nights and eight days in succession; so you could see the people during that time prostrate, as though they were the stumps of hollow palm trees.
Do you see now any vestige of them?
Then Pharaoh came, and those before him, and the Overturned Cities, steeped in sin.
10 They disobeyed the Messenger of their Lord and so He seized them with an overpowering grip.
Indeed, when the water rose, We carried you along in the cruising ship.
So as to make it a reminder for you and to be grasped by an attentive ear.
Then when the Trumpet shall be blown a single time;
And the earth and the mountains shall be lifted and then crushed with a single blow.
15 Then, on that day the terrible Calamity shall come to pass;
And the heavens shall be rent asunder, so that on that day it shall be tottering;
And the angels shall be ranged around its borders, eight of whom will be carrying above them, on that day, the Throne of your Lord.
On that day, you shall be paraded, not a whit of your deeds will be concealed.
As to him who has been given his book in his right hand, he shall say: "Come along, read my book."
20 "I knew I was going to meet my reckoning."
Therefore, he is in a well-pleasing condition;
Living in a lofty garden;
Whose clusters are close at hand.
"Eat and drink merrily for what you did in the days gone by."

25 But as for him who is given his book in his left hand, he shall say:
"And that I did not know what my account is;
"Would that I had never been given my book,
"And that I did not know what my account is;
"Would that it had been the final death blow.
30 "My wealth has not availed me;
"And my authority has vanished from me."
[It will be said:] "Take him and shackle him;
"Then let him roast in Hell.
"Then, in a chain whose length is seventy cubits, tie him up.
35 "He certainly did not believe in Allah, the Sublime.
"And did not urge feeding the destitute.
"Therefore, today he shall have no intimate friend, here;
"And no food except foul pus;
"Which only the sinners will eat."
40 No; I swear by what you see;
And what you do not see.
It is the speech of a noble messenger;
And it is not the speech of a poet. How little do you believe!
Nor the speech of a soothsayer; how little do you remember.
45 It is a revelation from the Lord of the Worlds.
Had he[820] imputed to Us falsely some statements;
We would have seized him by the right arm;
Then cut off his great artery.
None of you would have restrained Us from him.
50 Surely, it[821] is a reminder for the God-fearing.
And We know that some of you will denounce it as lies.
And it is surely a source of grief for the unbelievers;
And it is surely the certain truth.
So, glorify the name of your Lord, the Sublime.

820. Muhammad.
821. The Qur'an.

SURA 70

Al-Ma'arij, The Ways of Ascent

In the Name of Allah, the Compassionate, the Merciful

1   A questioner asked about an imminent punishment,
    Of the unbelievers, that none can avert;
    From Allah, Lord of the Ways of Ascent.
    Unto Him the angels and the Spirit[822] ascend on a day the duration
  thereof is fifty thousand years.
5   Bear up patiently then.
    They think it is distant;
    But We think it is close.
    On the day when heaven will be like molten brass;
    And the mountains like tufted wool.
10   And no friend shall ask an intimate friend.
    They shall be made to see each other. The criminal wishes that he would
  be redeemed from the punishment of that day by his sons;
    His spouse and his brother;
    And his clan, who gives him refuge;
    And every one on earth; then that he might save him.
15   No, it is truly a blazing fire;
    Which strips off the scalps.
    It summons him who has turned his back and fled;
    And amassed wealth and hoarded it.
    Man was truly created apprehensive.
20   When misfortune visits him, he is frightened;
    But when good fortune visits him, he is avaricious.
    Except for those who pray;
    Those who are constantly at prayer;
    And those who have set aside a fixed portion of their wealth,
25   For the beggar and the destitute.
    And those who believe firmly in the Day of Judgement;
    And those who fear the punishment of their Lord.
    The punishment of their Lord cannot be averted;
    And those who guard their private parts;

---

822. Gabriel (Jibril).

30   Except from their wives or what their right hands possess; for they are not therein blameworthy.

He who seeks [pleasure] beyond that – those are the transgressors.

And those who honour their trusts and their pledges;

And those who stand by their testimonies;

And those who observe their prayer;

35   All those shall be in Gardens, well-honoured.

What is it with the unbelievers stretching their necks towards you?

From the right and the left banding together?

Does everyone of them hope to enter the Garden of Bliss?

Not at all. We have created them from what they know.

40   No; I swear by the Lord of the East and the West that We are capable,

Of replacing them by many who are better than they; and We shall not be outstripped.

So leave them to romp and play till they meet their day, which they have been promised.

The day they will come out of the tombs hastily, as though they are hurrying towards their idols;

Their eyes cast down; overwhelmed by humiliation. That is the day which they were promised.

SURA 71

Nuh, Noah

In the Name of Allah, the Compassionate, the Merciful

1 We have indeed sent Noah forth to his people saying: "Warn your people before a painful punishment afflicts them."

He said: "O my people, I am truly a manifest warner to you;

"That you should worship Allah and fear Him, and obey me.

"Then, He will forgive you your sins and reprieve you till an appointed term. Allah's term cannot be deferred, once it comes; if only you knew."

5 He said: "Lord, I have called my people night and day;

"But my call only increased them in defection.

"In fact, every time I called them, so that You might forgive them, they put their fingers in their ears, wrapped themselves up in their clothes, persisted and waxed very proud.

"Then, I called them publicly;

"Then, I proclaimed to them and spoke to them in secret.

10 "I said to them: 'Ask forgiveness from your Lord; He is truly All-Forgiving.

"'He will then loose heavens upon you in torrents;

"'And provide you with wealth and sons, and allot for you gardens, and allot for you rivers.

"'What is the matter with you? Why do you not show reverence towards Allah?

"'Although, He created you in stages.

15 "'Do you not see how He created for you seven heavens superposed upon one another?

"'And placed the moon therein as a light and made the sun a lamp?

"'And Allah caused you to grow out of the earth;

"'Then, He will cause you to return to it and bring you out.

"'And Allah has made the earth a vast expanse for you;

20 "'So that you might follow therein broad pathways.'"

Noah said: "Lord, they have disobeyed me and followed one whose wealth and children only increased him in perdition;

"And they devised a mighty plot.

"And they said: 'Do not forsake your gods; do not forsake Wadd, Suwa', Yaghuth, Ya'uq or Nasr.'823

823. These were some of the deities of the pagan Arab tribes before Islam.

"They have led many astray. Hence, increase not the wrongdoers except in greater error."

25   Because of their sins, they were drowned, and were hurled into Fire. Then, they did not find, apart from Allah, any supporters.

And Noah said: "Do not leave a single dweller upon the earth.

"Surely, if you leave them alone, they will lead Your servants astray and will not beget any but unbelieving libertines.

"Lord, forgive me and my parents, whoever enters my house as a believer and the believers, men and women; and do not increase the wrongdoers except in greater perdition."

SURA 72

Al-Jinn, The *Jinn*

In the Name of Allah, the Compassionate, the Merciful

1 Say: "It was revealed to me that a company of *jinn* listened; then they said: 'We have indeed heard a wonderful Qur'an;

"'It guides to rectitude; so we believed in it, and we shall never associate anyone with our Lord;

"'And that He, may our Lord's majesty be exalted, has not taken a consort or a son;

"'And that our fools used to speak impertinently of Allah;

5 "'And that we thought that neither mankind nor the *jinn* will impute to Allah any falsehood;

"'And that some individual humans used to seek refuge with some men of the *jinn*, and so they increased them in perversion;

"'And that they thought, as you thought, that Allah will not raise anybody from the dead;

"'And that we reached out to heaven, but we found it filled with mighty guards and comets;

"'And that we used to sit around it eavesdropping; but whoever listens now will find a comet in wait for him;

10 "'And that we do not know whether ill was intended for whoever is on earth, or whether their Lord intended rectitude for them;

"'And that some of us are righteous and some are less than that for we were of diverse persuasions;

"'And that we knew that we will not thwart Allah on earth, and that we will not thwart Him by flight;

"'And that when we heard the Guidance, we believed in it; for he who believes in his Lord need not fear to be stinted or overburdened;

"'And that some of us are submitting and some are diverging. Those who have submitted have surely sought rectitude;

15 "'But those who have diverged, have been firewood for Hell;

"'And that had they followed the right path, We would have given them abundant water to drink;

"'So as to test them thereby. He who refrains from the mention of his Lord, He will afflict him with terrible punishment;

"'And that mosques are Allah's; so do not call, besides Allah, upon anyone else;

"'And that when the Servant of Allah[824] got up calling on Him, they almost set upon him in throngs.'"

20   Say: "I only call upon my Lord, and I do not associate with Him anyone else."

Say: "I have no power to harm or guide you rightly."

Say: "No one shall protect me from Allah, and I will not find, apart from Him, any refuge;

"Except for a proclamation from Allah and His messages. He who disobeys Allah and His Apostle, for him the Fire of Hell is in store. Therein they shall dwell forever.

"Until, when they see what they are promised, they will then know certainly who is weaker in supporters and is fewer in numbers."

25   Say: "I do not know whether what you are promised is near, or whether my Lord shall extend it for a period.

"Knower of the Unseen, He does not disclose His Unseen to anyone,

"Except for any messenger He is well-pleased with. He then will dispatch watchmen before him and behind him;

"So as to know that they have delivered the messages of their Lord. And He encompasses whatever they have and numbers everything."

---

824. Muhammad.

Al-Muzzammil, The Enwrapped

In the Name of Allah, the Compassionate, the Merciful

1   O enwrapped one,[825]
    Keep vigil throughout the night, except for a little while;
    Half of it, or a little less;
    Or add a little thereto and chant the Qur'an loudly.
5   Indeed, We shall deliver unto you a weighty discourse.
    Surely, the early hours of the night are more onerous and more amenable
to straight talk.
    You have during the day a long-drawn business.
    Remember the name of your Lord and devote yourself fully to Him.
    He is the Lord of the East and the West; there is no god but He, so take
Him as your Guardian.
10 And bear up with what they say, and forsake them graciously.
    And let Me deal with those who deny and live in luxury; and give them a
little respite.
    We have indeed shackles and a blazing Fire;
    And food upon which they choke and painful punishment.
    On the day when the earth and the mountains shall tremble, and the
mountains shall turn into heaps of sand.
15 We have sent unto you a messenger, bearing witness against you, just as
We had sent unto Pharaoh a messenger.
    Then Pharaoh disobeyed the messenger; so We seized him with terrible
force.
    So, how will you guard, if you disbelieve, against a day which will make
the children white with fear?
    The heavens shall be rent asunder thereby. His promise is a thing
accomplished.
    This is truly a reminder; so that he who wishes may follow unto his Lord
a path.
20 Your Lord knows that you keep vigil a little less than two-thirds of the
night and a half or a third thereof, together with a group of your followers.
    Allah determines the measure of the night and the day; He knows that you

825. That is, Muhammad, who used to be "wrapped up" when revelation was imparted to him by the
    Angel Gabriel.

will not keep it all, and so He has absolved you. Read, then, what you can of the Qur'an. He knows that there will be, among you, sick people and others who journey in the land, seeking part of Allah's bounty, and still others who fight for the cause of Allah. Recite, then, what you can of it, perform the prayer, give the alms and lend Allah a fair loan. Whatever good you forward for your soul's sake, you shall find it with Allah growing into a greater good and a greater wage. Seek Allah's forgiveness; Allah is indeed All-Forgiving, All Merciful.

Al-Muddaththir, The Enrobed

In the Name of Allah, the Compassionate, the Merciful

1 O Enrobed one,
   Arise and warn.
   Glorify your Lord,
   And purify your garments,
5 And abandon abomination.
   Do not give in expectation of increased return,
   And for the sake of your Lord, persevere.
   Then, when the Trumpet is sounded;
   It is then a hard day,
10 For the unbelievers, not an easy one.
   Leave Me with him whom I create alone,
   And gave him abundant wealth,
   And children as witnesses;
   And I smoothed things for him.
15 Nevertheless, he is eager that I increase him.
   He has been an obdurate disbeliever in Our signs.[826]
   I will exhaust him increasingly.
   He reflected and reckoned.
   May he perish how he reckoned!
20 Again, may he perish how he reckoned!
   Then he considered;
   Then, he frowned and turned pale.
   Then, he turned back and waxed proud,
   Saying: "This indeed is nothing but sorcery recounted;
25 "This is only the discourse of mortals."
   I will roast him in Saqar.[827]
   If only you knew what is Saqar.
   It leaves nothing or spares nothing,
   Scorching mankind.
30 Upon it stand nineteen guards.
   We have only made angels the guardians of the Fire; and We have not

---

826. The reference is to al-Walid Ibn al-Mughirah, an enemy of Islam.
827. One of the names of Hell.

fixed their number except as a temptation for those who have disbelieved; so that those who received the Book[828] might be certain and those who have believed increase in belief; and that those who received the Book and the believers together may not doubt; and that those in whose hearts there is a sickness together with the unbelievers [might say]: "What did Allah mean by this allegory?" Thus Allah leads those whom He wishes astray and guides those whom He wishes rightly. None knows the hosts of your Lord except He. It is only a reminder for mankind.

By the moon;
And the night when it recedes;
And the morning when it lights up.
35   Surely it is one of the great ordeals,
A warning to mankind;
To whoever of you wishes to advance or retreat.
Every soul is a hostage to what it has earned;
Except for the Companions of the Right;
40   In Gardens, they will ask,
Concerning the criminals:
"What drove you into Saqar?"
They will say: "We were not among those who prayed,
"And we were not among those who fed the destitute;
45   "And we used to romp with the rompers;
"And we used to deny the Day of Judgement;
"Till the Certainty came to us."
But the intercession of the intercessors will avail them nothing.
Why are they turning away from the Reminder?[829]
50   As though they were startled asses,
Fleeing from a lion?
Rather, each one of them wishes to be given scrolls unrolled.
No, they do not fear the Hereafter.
No, it is indeed a Reminder.
55   So that he who wishes might remember it
But they will only remember if Allah wishes. He is worthy to be feared and worthy to forgive.

828. The People of the Book, or Christians and Jews.
829. The Qur'an.

SURA 75

Al-Qiyama, The Resurrection

In the Name of Allah, the Compassionate, the Merciful

1   No! I swear by the Day of Resurrection;
    No! I swear by the reproachful soul.
    Does man think that We will not put his bones back together?
    Yes indeed; We are able to straighten his fingertips.
5   Rather, man wishes to continue his profligacy in front of Him.
    He asks: "When is the Day of Resurrection coming?"
    Then, when the sight is dazzled;
    And the moon is eclipsed;
    And the sun and moon are joined together;
10   Man will say on that day: "Where is the escape?"
    No, there shall be no escape;
    Unto your Lord is the ultimate resort.
    Man shall be informed on that day about what he has advanced or
deferred.
    Rather, man against himself shall be a witness;
15   Even if he makes excuses.
    Do not wag your tongue with it[830] to hurry on with it.
    It is incumbent upon Us to put it together and to recite it.
    Then, when We recite it, follow its recitation.
    Then, it is incumbent upon Us to expound it clearly.
20   No indeed, you love the present life;
    And forsake the Hereafter.
    On that day, faces shall be radiant,
    Looking upon their Lord.
    And faces, on that day, shall be scowling;
25   Thinking that a disaster shall be wreaked upon them.
    No indeed, when it reaches the breast-bones,
    And it is said: "Who shall be the charmer?"
    And he[831] thinks that that was the parting;
    And leg is intertwined with leg;
30   Unto your Lord shall be the resort.

---

830. The Qur'an.
831. Abu Jahl, an inveterate enemy of Islam who persecuted the prophet and his followers in Mecca.

For he[832] did not believe nor pray;
But rather denied and turned away.
Then, he went to his own folk in a swagger.
Woe be to you and woe;
35 Then, woe be to you and woe!
Does man think that he shall be left untended?
Was he not a drop of sperm released?
Then, he was a leech; then He created and fashioned;
Making of him a couple, male and female.
40 Is not that One able to quicken the dead?

832. Abu Jahl.

SURA 76

Al-Insan, Man

In the Name of Allah, the Compassionate, the Merciful

1 Has there come upon man a period of time when he was not a noteworthy thing?

We have indeed created man from a mixed sperm to test him; and so We made him capable of hearing and sight.

We have guided him upon the path, either as thankful or thankless.

We have prepared for the unbelievers chains and fetters and a blazing Fire.

5 The pious will surely drink from a cup whose mixture is camphor,

A spring from which the servants of Allah shall drink, making it gush abundantly.

They fulfil their vows and fear a day whose evil is rampant.

And they give food, despite their love of it, to the destitute, the orphan and the captive.

[They say:] "We only feed you for the sake of Allah; We do not want from you any reward or gratitude.

10 "We fear from our Lord a dark and dreadful day."

But Allah will guard them against the evil of that day and give them radiance and joy.

And reward them for their forbearance, with a garden and silk.

Therein, they shall recline upon couches, and they shall see therein neither [blazing] sun nor bitter cold.

And its shades shall be close to them and its fruit-bunches shall be brought down.

15 And cup-bearers shall go round them with vessels of silver and goblets of glass,

Goblets of silver which they measured exactly.

And they are given therein to drink a cup whose mixture is ginger.

A spring therein is called Salsabil.

And there go round them immortal boys; when you see them, you will think that they are scattered pearls.

20 If you look there, you will see bliss and a vast kingdom.

Upon them are green silk garments and brocade; and they have been adorned with silver bracelets, and their Lord has given them a pure potion.

"This indeed has been your reward, and your endeavour has been appreciated.

"We have indeed sent down the Qur'an upon you as a revelation;

"So bear up with your Lord's judgement and do not obey any sinful or thankless one of them.

25 "And mention the name of your Lord morning and evening.

"And for part of the night, prostrate yourself to Him and glorify Him all night long."

Those people love the present world and leave behind them a burdensome day.

We have created them and fastened their joints well; and if We wish We would change their likes completely.

This indeed is a reminder; so he who wishes will follow, unto his Lord, a path.

30 Yet, you do not wish unless Allah wishes. Allah is truly All-Knowing and Wise.

He admits into His mercy whomever He wishes; and for the wrongdoers He has prepared a painful punishment.

SURA 77

Al-Mursalat, The Dispatched Ones

In the Name of Allah, the Compassionate, the Merciful

1   By those dispatched[833] in succession;
    And by the tempestuous winds;
    And by those who spread out;
    And the dividing distinguishers;
5   And by those who deliver a reminder;
    As an excuse or a warning.
    Indeed, what you are promised shall come to pass.
    When the stars have been extinguished;
    And the heavens have been rent asunder;
10 And when the mountains are blown to pieces;
    And when the messengers have been assigned a term;
    To what day have they been deferred?
    Unto the Day of Decision,
    If only you knew what is the Day of Decision.
15 Woe betide, on that day, those who denounce.
    Have We not destroyed the ancients?
    Then, We shall send after them the latter folk.
    Thus We deal with the criminals.
    Woe betide, on that day, those who denounce.
20 Have We not created them from base water?
    That We laid in a secure place;
    Until an appointed term.
    We determined, and what excellent determiners were We!
    Woe, on that day, betide those who denounce.
25 Have We not made the earth a receptacle,
    Containing the living and the dead;
    And created in it towering mountains and given you pure water to drink.
    Woe betide, on that day, those who denounce!
    Go forth to what you used to denounce as lies.
30 Go forth to a three-pronged shade;
    Which neither shades nor avails against the flames.
    It[834] shoots forth sparks as huge as a castle;

833. The angels.
834. Hell.

Which look like golden camel-herds.
Woe betide, on that day, those who denounce.

35 This is a day on which they shall not speak;
And they will not be permitted to make excuses.
Woe betide, on that day, those who denounce.
This is the Day of Decision; We have gathered you together with the
ancients.
So, if you have any schemes, then scheme against Me.

40 Woe betide, on that day, those who denounce.
The God-fearing shall dwell amid shades and springs,
And fruits of the kind they desire.
Eat and drink merrily, for what you used to do.
That is how We reward the beneficent.

45 Woe betide, on that day, those who denounce:
"Eat and enjoy yourselves a little; you are indeed criminals."
Woe betide, on that day, those who denounce.
If they are told to bow down, they will not bow down.
Woe betide, on that day, those who denounce.

50 What discourse will they believe in after this?

SURA 78

Al-Naba', The Tiding

In the Name of Allah, the Compassionate, the Merciful

1   What are they asking each other about?
    About the great tiding,
    Concerning which they are disputing.
    Indeed; they will certainly know.
5   Then, indeed; they will certainly know.
    Have We not made the earth as a couch for you?
    And the mountains as pegs?
    And created you in pairs?
    And made your sleep a period of rest?
10 And made the night as a garment?
    And made the day a source of livelihood?
    And built above you seven mighty [heavens]?
    And created a shining lamp?
    And brought down from the rain-clouds abundant water?
15 To bring forth thereby grain and vegetation?
    And luxuriant gardens?
    The Day of Decision is a term appointed.
    The day the Trumpet is sounded and you will come in throngs.
    And the heavens are opened up and turn into wide portals.
20 And the mountains are set in motion and turn into a mirage.
    Hell is, indeed, lying in ambush;
    A refuge for the transgressors;
    Tarrying therein for ages;
    Wherein, they do not taste any coolness or fresh drinks,
25 Except for boiling water and freezing hail;
    As an appropriate reward.
    Indeed, they did not expect any reckoning;
    And denounced Our signs as lies.
    Everything We have enumerated fully in a Book.
30 So taste. We will only increase your punishment.
    The God-fearing will score a victory,
    Gardens and vineyards,
    And round-breasted mates,
    And a brim-full cup.

35   Therein, they do not hear any idle talk or denunciation.

A reward from Your Lord, a sufficient gift;

The Lord of the heavens and the earth and what lies between them; the Compassionate to whom they do not have the power to speak.

The day when the Spirit[835] and the angels shall stand in line; none shall speak except him whom the Compassionate has allowed and has spoken the truth.

That will be the true day; he who wishes will return unto his Lord penitently.

40   Indeed, We have warned you of an imminent punishment, on the day when man will see what his hands have done, and the unbeliever will say: "O, would that I have been mere dust."

835. Gabriel.

SURA 79

Al-Nazi'at, The Snatchers

In the Name of Allah, the Compassionate, the Merciful

1   By those who snatch violently,
    And those who spring up lightly,
    And those who glide smoothly,
    And those who outstrip suddenly,
5   And those who conduct an affair.
    On the day that the first blast shall reverberate.
    Followed by the succeeding blast.
    Hearts on that day shall be throbbing;
    Their sights downcast.
10 They will say: "Shall we then be restored to the original condition?
    "Shall we, after we were shrivelled bones?"
    They will say: "That indeed was a losing turn."
    Then, it will be only a single blast;
    And they will be back upon the surface of the earth.
15 Have you heard Moses' story?
    When his Lord called out to him in the sacred valley, Towa?
    "Go forth to Pharaoh; indeed, he has waxed arrogant.
    "Say: 'Do you wish to be cleansed?
    "'And that I might lead you to your Lord, so that you might fear
[Him]?'"
20 Thereupon he showed him the great sign;
    But he denounced and disobeyed.
    Then, he turned back striving.
    He summoned and proclaimed.
    He said: "I am truly your supreme lord."
25 Then Allah seized him with the punishment of the last world and the
first.
    Surely, there is in that a lesson to him who fears.
    Are you, then, stronger in constitution than the heaven He has erected?
    He raised its vault and levelled it off.
    He dimmed its night and lighted its day.
30 Then, the earth, He flattened.
    From it, He brought out its water and its pasture.
    And the mountains, He established firmly,

As a source of enjoyment for you and your cattle.
Then, when the Great Calamity shall come;
35   On the day that man will remember what he has done;
And Hell shall be exhibited to whoever can see.
Then, as to him who has transgressed,
And preferred the present life;
Hell, indeed, is the refuge.
40   But as to him who fears the station of his Lord, and forbids his soul from passion;
Then, Paradise is the refuge.
They ask you about the Hour: "When shall it come?"
How far are you from remembering it?
Unto your Lord it will come to rest.
45   You are only a warner unto him who fears it.
They are, on the day that they will see it, as though they only tarried an evening or a forenoon.

SURA 80

'Abasa, He Frowned

In the Name of Allah, the Compassionate, the Merciful

1 He[836] frowned and turned his back;
  When the blind man[837] came to him.
  How do you know? Perhaps he might cleanse himself.
  Or remember, and then remembrance might profit him.
5 As for him who has grown wealthy,
  You attend to him closely;
  And it does not bother you if he does not cleanse himself.
  Yet he who comes to you running,
  While fearful,
10 You do not take any notice of him.
  Yet, it[838] is only a reminder,
  Whoever wishes will remember it;
  In scrolls highly honoured,
  Lifted up and purified,
15 By the hands of scribes,
  Honourable and pious.
  May man perish! How thankless he is!
  Of what did He create him?
  Of a sperm, He created him and determined him.
20 Then, He smoothed his path;
  Then, He caused him to die and entombed him;
  Then, if He wishes, He will raise him from the dead.
  No indeed; he did not fulfil what He commanded him.
  Let man consider his nourishment.
25 We have poured the water abundantly;
  Then, We split the earth wide open;
  Then caused the grain to grow therein,
  Together with vines and green vegetation;
  And olives and palm trees;
30 And gardens with dense trees,

---

836. Muhammad.
837. 'Abd Allah Ibn Umm Maktum, a poor man anxious to learn the Qur'an who importuned the Prophet.
838. The Qur'an.

And fruits and grass,
For your enjoyment and that of your cattle.
Then, when the Deafening Blast shall sound;
On the day, when man shall run away from his brother,
35   His mother and his father,
His consort and his sons.
To every one of them on that day is a business sufficing him.
Some faces, on that day, will be bright,
Laughing and joyful;
40   And other faces, on that day, will be covered with dust,
Enveloped in smoke.
Those are the unbelievers, the profligate.

SURA 81

'Al-Takwir, The Coiling Up

In the Name of Allah, the Compassionate, the Merciful

1 When the sun shall be coiled up;
   And when the stars shall be scattered about;
   And when the mountains shall be set in motion;
   And when the pregnant camels shall be discarded;
5   And when the beasts shall be corralled;
   And when the seas shall rise mightily;
   And when souls shall be paired off;
   And when the buried infant shall be asked:
   "For what sin was she killed?"
10   And when the scrolls shall be unrolled;
   And when heaven shall be scraped up;
   And when Hell shall be stoked;
   And when Paradise shall be brought near;
   Then each soul shall know what it had brought forth.
15   No, I swear by the alternating stars,
   Which circle then hide;
   And the night when it recedes;
   And the morning when it breaks,
   It is truly the discourse of a noble messenger;[839]
20   Who has power, with the Lord of the Throne, and is highly placed;
   Obeyed, then trustworthy.
   Your Companion[840] is not mad;
   He saw him[841] upon the luminous horizon.
   He is not, regarding the Unseen, niggardly;
25   And it is not the discourse of a devil, accursed.
   Where, then, will you go?
   It is only a reminder to all mankind;
   To whoever of you who wishes to reform their ways.
   But you will not wish unless Allah, the Lord of the Worlds, wishes.

839. Gabriel.
840. Muhammad.
841. Gabriel.

SURA 82

Al-Infitar, The Cleaving Asunder

In the Name of Allah, the Compassionate, the Merciful

1　When the heavens are cleft asunder,
　　And when the stars are scattered [about].
　　And when the seas are blown open;
　　And when the tombs are strewn around;
5　　Then each soul shall know what it advanced and what it deferred.
　　O man, what deluded you concerning your Munificent Lord,
　　Who created you, fashioned you and made you well-wrought.
　　In whichever form He wished, He put you together.
　　No, but you deny the judgement;
10　Yet over you stand watchers,
　　Noble recorders,
　　Who know what you do.
　　The pious shall, indeed, be in bliss.
　　And the profligate shall be in Hell;
15　Burning therein on the Day of Judgement.
　　And they shall never be far away from it.
　　If only you knew what is the Day of Judgement?
　　Again, if only you knew what is the Day of Judgement?
　　A day when no soul shall avail another soul anything, and the command
on that day shall be Allah's.

SURA 83

Al-Mutaffifin, The Skimpers

In the Name of Allah, the Compassionate, the Merciful

1   Woe to the skimpers,
      Who, when they measure for themselves from others exact full measure;
      But when they measure or weigh for others actually skimp.
      Do not those people think that they will be resuscitated,
5   On a great day?
      A day when mankind will stand before the Lord of the Worlds.
      Not at all; the book of the profligate is locked up in the Underworld.
      If only you knew what is the Underworld.
      A book inscribed.
10 Woe betide, on that day, those who denounce;
      Those who deny the Day of Judgement.
      Yet, only a sinful aggressor denies it.
      When Our signs are recited to him, he says: "Mere legends of the
ancients."
      Not at all; their hearts are overwhelmed with what they were earning.
15 Not at all; surely on that day they shall be screened off from their Lord.
      Then, they shall roast in Hell.
      Then it will be said to them: "This is what you used to deny."
      No indeed; the book of the pious is in the Higher World.
      And if only you knew what is the Higher World;
20 A book inscribed,
      Witnessed by those well-favoured.
      The pious are indeed in bliss;
      Upon couches gazing round.
      You will recognize in their faces the glow of bliss.
25 They are given to drink from a sealed wine;
      Whose seal is musk. Over that, let the competitors compete;
      And its mixture is from Tasnim;[842]
      A spring from which the well-favoured drink.
      The criminals used to laugh at the believers;
30 And if they pass by them they would wink at one another.
      And if they go back to their families, they would go back jeering,

---

842. A spring in Paradise.

And if they see them, they would say: "These are indeed in error."
Yet, they were not sent to watch over them.
But, today, the believers shall laugh at the unbelievers.
35 Upon couches, they gaze round.
Have the unbelievers been rewarded for what they used to do?

SURA 84

Al-Inshiqaq, The Rending Asunder

In the Name of Allah, the Compassionate, the Merciful

1   When the heaven is rent asunder;
    And hearkens to its Lord and is judged.
    And when the earth is spread out;
    And casts out what is within it and is voided;
5   And hearkens to its Lord and is judged.
    O man, you strive unto your Lord and you shall meet Him.
    As for him who will be given his book in his right hand;
    He shall be called to an easy reckoning,
    And shall go back to his people well-pleased.
10 But as for him who is given his book behind his back;
    He shall call out: "Perdition!"
    And burn in Hell-fire.
    He was, indeed, in the midst of his people, living happily.
    He supposed that he will never go back.
15 No, indeed, his Lord was observing him.
    No, I swear by the twilight,
    And by the night and what it brings forth,
    And by the moon when it is full,
    That you will mount stage by stage.
20 What is the matter with them that they will not believe?
    And if the Qur'an is recited to them, they will not prostrate themselves?
    Yet, the unbelievers are denouncing;
    And Allah knows better what they are thinking in secret.
    So announce to them the good news of a very painful punishment;
25 Except for those who believe and do the righteous deeds. They will have
    an unstinted wage.

SURA 85

Al-Buruj, The Constellations

In the Name of Allah, the Compassionate, the Merciful

1 By the heaven of the many constellations;
  And by the promised day;
  And by every witness and what is witnessed.
  Perish the Companions of the Pit,
5 The fire well-stoked;
  While they sat around it,
  And were witnessing what they did to the believers.
  They did not begrudge them except that they believed in Allah, the
  All-Mighty, the All-Praiseworthy;
  To Whom belongs the dominion of the heavens and the earth. Allah is
  witness of everything.
10 Surely, those who have tempted the believers, men and women, then did
  not repent, will suffer the punishment of Hell; and theirs is the punishment
  of burning.
  Surely, those who have believed and done the righteous deeds shall have
  gardens beneath which rivers flow. That is the great triumph.
  The vengeance of your Lord is surely terrible.
  It is He who originates and brings back;
  And He is the All-Forgiving, the All-Friendly;
15 Lord of the glorious Throne;
  Doer of what He wills.
  Have you heard the story of the hosts?
  Of Pharaoh and Thamud.
  Yet, the unbelievers continue to denounce.
20 While Allah, from behind them, is All-Embracing.
  Yet, it is a glorious Qur'an,
  In a Well-Presented Tablet.

SURA 86

Al-Tariq, The Night-Visitor

In the Name of Allah, the Compassionate, the Merciful

1   By the heavens and the night-visitor.
     If only you knew what is the night-visitor,
     The piercing star.
     Every soul has a watcher;
5   So let man consider what he was created from. He was created from
flowing water;
     Emanating from what lies between the loins and the breast-bones.
     Surely, He has the power to bring him back,
     When the consciences of men shall be tested.
     Then, he will have no power and no supporter.
10 And by the heaven which alternates;
     And the earth which is split up.
     It is indeed a decisive discourse;
     And it is no joking matter.
     They are indeed scheming mightily,
15 And I am scheming mightily.
     So, give the unbelievers some respite. Respite them slowly.

SURA 87

Al-A'la, The Most High

In the Name of Allah, the Compassionate, the Merciful

1 Glorify the name of your Lord, the Most High;
   Who created and fashioned well;
   And Who fore-ordained and guided rightly;
   And who brought out the pasture;
5   Then turned it into greenish-black straw.
   We shall make you recite; so you will not forget;
   Except what Allah wishes. He certainly knows what is proclaimed and
what is hidden.
   And We shall ease your travel on an easy course.
   So remind, if the reminder will avail.
10   He who fears shall remember;
   And the most wretched shall refrain from it;
   He who shall roast in the Great Fire,
   Then, he will neither die therein nor live.
   He who cleanses himself shall prosper;
15   Remembering his Lord's name and praying.
   No, you prefer the present life;
   Whereas the Hereafter is better and more lasting.
   That, indeed, is in the ancient scrolls,
   The scrolls of Abraham and Moses.

SURA 88

Al-Ghashiyah, The Overwhelming Day

In the Name of Allah, the Compassionate, the Merciful

1 Have you heard the story of the Overwhelming Day?
　　Faces on that day shall be downcast,
　　Labouring and toiling;
　　Roasting in a scorching fire;
5　　Given to drink from a boiling spring.
　　They will have no nourishment except from poisonous cactus,
　　Which neither fattens nor appeases hunger.
　　Faces on that day shall be blissful,
　　Well-pleased with their endeavour;
10　　In a lofty Garden;
　　Wherein no idle talk is heard;
　　Wherein is a flowing spring;
　　Wherein are upraised couches;
　　And cups ranged round,
15　　And cushions in rows,
　　And carpets spread out.
　　Will they, then, not consider the camels, how they were created?
　　And heaven, how it was raised up?
　　And the mountains, how they were hoisted?
20　　And the earth, how it was levelled.
　　So, exhort, you are a mere exhorter;
　　You are not supposed to dominate them;
　　Except for him who turns away and disbelieves;
　　Then Allah will punish him in the most terrible way.
25　　Indeed, unto Us is their return;
　　Then, upon Us rests their reckoning.

Al-Fajr, The Dawn

In the Name of Allah, the Compassionate, the Merciful

1   By the dawn,
    And by the ten nights;
    And the even and the odd;
    And the night, when it runs its course.
5   Is there in that an oath for a man of acumen?
    Have you not seen how your Lord dealt with 'Ad?
    Iram[843] of the many pillars;
    The like of which was not created in the land?
    And Thamud, who burrowed the rock in the valley?
10 And Pharaoh of the many tent-pegs?[844]
    Who waxed arrogant in the land;
    And compounded corruption in it.
    Then your Lord unloosed upon them a scourge of punishment.
    Your Lord is, indeed, ever-observan·
15 As for man, whenever his Lord tests him, honouring him and favouring
    him with bounties, he says: "My Lord has honoured me."
    But when He tests him, straitening his provision, he says: "My Lord has
    despised me."
    Not at all; you do not actually honour the orphan;
    And do not advocate the feeding of the destitute;
    And you devour the inheritance greedily;
20 And you love wealth ardently.
    No; when the earth is demolished completely.
    And your Lord comes, together with the angels, in rows upon rows;
    And Hell is brought forth on that day. Then man will remember on that
    day; but wherefrom will remembrance come to him?
    He will say: "Would that I had advanced something for this my life!"
25 On that day, none shall punish like His punishment;
    And none shall bind with fetters like His.
    O quiescent soul,
    Return unto your Lord well-pleased and well-pleasing;

843. The ancient city of 'Ad in central Arabia.
844. A metaphor for power or grandeur.

And join the ranks of My servants;

30   And enter My Paradise.

SURA 90

Al-Balad, The City

In the Name of Allah, the Compassionate, the Merciful

1   No; I swear by this city.[845]
    And you[846] are a resident of this city.
    And by the begetter and what he begets;
    We have, indeed, created man to toil.
5   Does he think that none shall have power over him?
    He says: "I have squandered a large sum of money."
    Does he think that no one saw him?
    Have We not given him two eyes,
    A tongue and two lips,
10 And guided him onto the two highways?[847]
    Yet he did not brave the rocky pass.
    If only you knew what is the rocky pass.
    The freeing of a slave;
    Or feeding, upon a day of famine,
15 An orphan near of kin;
    Or a destitute man in dire need;
    Then, being one of those who believe, command steadfastness to each
other and command compassion.
    Those are the Companions of the Right;
    But those who disbelieve in Our signs are the Companions of the Left;
20 A fire will close in on them.

845. Mecca.
846. Muhammad.
847. Of right and wrong.

411

SURA 91

Al-Shams, The Sun

In the Name of Allah, the Compassionate, the Merciful

1 By the sun and its forenoon brightness,
    And the moon when it follows it,
    And the day when it exhibits its light,
    And the night when it obscures it;
5   And by the heaven and Him who erected it;
    And the earth and Him who spread it out,
    And the soul and Him who fashioned it well,
    Inspiring it to profligacy and piety.
    Prosperous shall be he who purifies it,
10   And ruined he who corrupts it.
    Thamud has denounced, due to their arrogance,
    When their most vicious citizen emerged.
    Then Allah's messenger said to them: "Beware of Allah's she-camel and her drinking time."
    They called him a liar and hamstrung her; whereupon their Lord destroyed them for their sins and settled the matter;
15   And He does not fear its sequel.

SURA 92

Al-Layl, The Night

In the Name of Allah, the Compassionate, the Merciful

1　By the night when it darkens,
　　And the day when it lights up,
　　And by Him who created the male and the female,
　　Your striving is manifold.
5　As for him who gives in charity and fears Allah,
　　And believes in the fairest reward;
　　We shall lead him onto the easiest course.
　　But as for him who is niggardly and has grown complacent,
　　And disbelieves in the fairest reward;
10　We shall lead him into the hardest course.
　　What will his wealth avail him, if he perishes?
　　Ours is simply to guide;
　　And Ours is the Last Day and the First.
　　So, I have warned you to beware of a blazing Fire;
15　Which none except the most vicious will roast in;
　　He who denounces and turns away.
　　But the most pious shall be spared it;
　　He who gives his wealth in self-purification;
　　And none receives a favour from him, for the sake of a reward;
20　Except seeking the Face of his Lord, the Most High.
　　And he will surely be well-pleased.

SURA 93

Al-Duha, The Forenoon

In the Name of Allah, the Compassionate, the Merciful

1   By the forenoon;
   And the night when it falls calmly;
   Your Lord did not forsake you or scorn you.
   Surely, the Last Day is better for you than the First.
5   Your Lord shall surely give you [of this bounty]; and so you shall be
well-pleased.
   Did He not find you an orphan, and then gave you refuge?
   And find you in error, and then guided you?
   And find you in need, and then enriched you?
   As for the orphan, you shall not oppress him;
10   And as for the beggar, you shall not drive him away;
   And as for your Lord's favour, you shall proclaim it.

SURA 94

Al-Sharh, The Dilation

In the Name of Allah, the Compassionate, the Merciful

1   Did We not dilate your breast;
      And lift from you your burden;
      Which had weighed down your back?
      Did We not exalt your name?
5   Surely, along with hardship is ease.
      Surely, along with hardship is ease.
      So when you have finished, toil on;
      And unto your Lord, incline.

SURA 95

Al-Tin, The Fig

In the Name of Allah, the Compassionate, the Merciful

1 By the fig and the olive,
   And by Mount Sinai,
   And by this secure City;
   We have created man in the best of shapes;
5 Then brought him to the lowest ebb;
   Except for those who have believed and done the righteous deeds; they
shall have an unstinted wage.
   What then causes you to deny the Judgement?
   Is not Allah the best of judges?

SURA 96

Al-'Alaq, The Clot

In the Name of Allah, the Compassionate, the Merciful

1 Read in the name of your Lord, Who created:
   He created man from a clot.
   Read, by your Most Generous Lord,
   Who taught by the Pen.
5 He taught man what he did not know.
   Yet, man will, indeed, wax arrogant;
   For he thinks himself self-sufficient.
   Surely, unto your Lord is the ultimate return.
   Have you considered him[848] who forbids,
10 A servant when he prays?
   Have you considered whether he was well-guided?
   Or commanded piety?
   Have you considered whether he was lying and back-tracking?
   Does he not know that Allah perceives?
15 No; if he will not desist, We shall take him by the forelock,
   A lying, erring forelock.
   Let him then call his company.
   We shall call the guards of Hell.
   No; do not obey him. Prostrate yourself and come closer.

---

848. Abu Jahl.

SURA 97

Al-Qadr, The Power

In the Name of Allah, the Compassionate, the Merciful

1   We have sent it[849] down on the Night of Power.
    If only you knew what is the Night of Power.
    The Night of Power is better than a thousand months.
    The angels and the Spirit[850] descend thereon by the leave of their Lord
with every command.
5   It is peace, till the break of dawn.

---

849. The Qur'an.
850. Gabriel.

SURA 98

Al-Bayyinah, The Clear Proof

In the Name of Allah, the Compassionate, the Merciful

1 The unbelievers, among the people of the Book and the idolaters, would not desist till the clear proof comes to them;
  A messenger from Allah reciting purified scrolls,
  Wherein are valuable books.
  Those who were given the Book did not diverge except after the clear proof came to them.

5 And they were only commanded to worship Allah, professing the religion sincerely to Him as upright believers, to perform the prayer and give the alms. That is the religion of truth.

  The unbelievers, among the People of the Book and the idolaters, shall be in the Fire of Hell, dwelling therein forever. Those are the worst of creatures.

  Those who have believed and did the righteous deeds – those are the best of creatures.

  Their reward with their Lord will be Gardens of Eden, beneath which rivers flow, dwelling therein forever. Allah is well-pleased with them and they are well-pleased with Him. That is the lot of whoever fears his Lord.

SURA 99

Al-Zilzal, The Earthquake

In the Name of Allah, the Compassionate, the Merciful

1 When the earth shall quake violently,
   And the earth shall bring forth its burdens;
   And man shall say: "What is happening to it?"
   On that day, it shall relate its tales;
5 That its Lord has inspired it.
   On that day, men shall emerge in clusters to see their works.
   Then whoever has done an atom's weight of good shall find it;
   And whoever has done an atom's weight of evil shall find it.

Al-ʿAdiyat, The Chargers

1 By the snorting chargers;
    And the strikers of fire, as they run;
    And the raiders at dawn;
    Raising thereon clouds of dust;
5   Plunging therein through a throng.
    Man is truly thankless unto his Lord;
    And He is a witness thereof.
    He is indeed a passionate lover of earthly goods.
    Does he not know that when what is in the graves is scattered around?
10   And what is within the breasts is brought out?
    Their Lord is, surely, well-informed about them on that day.

Al-Qari'ah, The Clatterer

In the Name of Allah, the Compassionate, the Merciful

1   The Clatterer![851]
    What is the Clatterer?
    If only you knew what is the Clatterer.
    The Day that men shall be like scattered butterflies;
5   And the mountains like tufted wool.
    As for him whose scales shall be weighty;
    He shall enjoy a well-pleasing life.
    But as for him whose scales are light,
    His mother shall be the Pit.
10   And if only you knew what it is.
    A blazing fire.

---

851. That is, the Day of Judgement when the clatter of milling crowds fills the air.

Al-Takathur, Covetousness

In the Name of Allah, the Compassionate, the Merciful

1 Covetousness has distracted you,
   Till you visited the graveyards.
   No; you shall surely know.
   Again, no; you shall surely know.
5 No; if only you knew with certainty,
   You would surely have perceived Hell.
   Then, you will have perceived it with visual certainty.
   Then, you will surely be questioned about the Bliss.

SURA 103

Al-'Asr, The Aeon

In the Name of Allah, the Compassionate, the Merciful

1 By the aeon,[852]

Man is, indeed, a prey to perdition,

Except for those who believe, do the righteous deeds, urge each other to seek the truth and urge each other to be steadfast.

---

852. Or time.

Al-Humazah, The Backbiter

In the Name of Allah, the Compassionate, the Merciful

1   Woe unto every backbiter and slanderer,
     Who amasses wealth and counts it diligently.
     He thinks that his wealth will make him immortal.
     Not at all; he shall be cast into the Smasher.
5   And if only you knew what is the Smasher.
     It is Allah's kindled Fire,
     Which attains even the hearts.
     Upon them it is closing in;
     On pillars stretched out.

SURA 105

Al-Fil, The Elephant

In the Name of Allah, the Compassionate, the Merciful

1   Have you not seen how your Lord dealt with the Companions of the Elephant?
    Did He not turn their cunning into perdition?
    And send upon them swarms of birds;
    Hurling upon them stones of clay;
5   And so He reduced them to munched blades of grass.

Quraysh

In the Name of Allah, the Compassionate, the Merciful

1   For Quraysh's customary journey,
      The journey of the winter and summer,
      Let them worship the Lord of this House,
      Who has fed them when they were hungry and secured them against fear.

Al-Ma'un, Benefaction

In the Name of Allah, the Compassionate, the Merciful

1   Have you seen him who denies the judgement?
    It is the one who pushes the orphan around,
    And does not urge the feeding of the destitute.
    Woe unto those who pray;
5   Those who are oblivious of their prayer;
    Those who dissimulate;
    And forbid benefaction.

SURA 108

Al-Kawthar, Abundance

In the Name of Allah, the Compassionate, the Merciful

1   We have surely given you abundance;
     So pray to your Lord and offer in sacrifice.
     Indeed, your chief hater is the real childless.[853]

853. The reference is to al-Aas Ibn Wa'il, who chided Muhammad upon the death of his son.

SURA 109

Al-Kafirun, The Unbelievers

In the Name of Allah, the Compassionate, the Merciful

1   Say: "O unbelievers,
      "I do not worship what you worship,
      "Nor do you worship what I worship;
      "Nor do I worship what you have worshipped,
5   "Nor do you worship what I worship.
      "You have your religion and I have mine."

SURA 110

Al-Nasr, The Support

In the Name of Allah, the Compassionate, the Merciful

1 When Allah's support and victory come,
   And you see people entering Allah's religion in throngs;
   Then, magnify the praise of your Lord and seek His forgiveness. He is
indeed All-Forgiving.

SURA 111

Al-Masad, The Fibre

In the Name of Allah, the Compassionate, the Merciful

1   Perish the hands of Abu Lahab,[854] and may he perish too;
    Neither his wealth nor what he has earned will avail him anything.
    He will roast in a flaming fire,
    And his wife will be a carrier of fire-wood,
5   She shall have a rope of fibre around her neck.

---

854. Uncle of the prophet and an inveterate enemy of Islam in the early days.

SURA 112

Al-Ikhlas, Sincerity

In the Name of Allah, the Compassionate, the Merciful

1 Say: "He is Allah, the only One,
   "Allah, the Everlasting.
   "He did not beget and is not begotten,
   "And none is his equal."

SURA 113

Al-Falaq, The Daybreak

In the Name of Allah, the Compassionate, the Merciful

1 Say: "I seek refuge with the Lord of the Daybreak,
   "From the evil of what He has created,
   "And the evil of the darkness when it gathers,
   "And the evil of those who blow into knotted reeds,[855]
5   "And from the evil of the envious when he envies."

---

855. Witches or sorceresses.

SURA 114

Al-Nas, The People

In the Name of Allah, the Compassionate, the Merciful

1 Say: "I seek refuge with the Lord of the People,
   "The King of the People;
   "The God of the People,
   "From the evil of the slinking whisperer,[856]
5   "Who whispers in the breasts of people,
   "Both *jinn* and men."

856. Satan.

Index

437